TASTE THE FORBIDDEN FRUIT...

... as **MIKE LEE**'s harmless fetish turns as razor-sharp and deadly as a stiletto in *HIGH HEELS FROM HELL.*

... as **NANCY A. COLLINS** teaches the world's greatest sinner the true meaning of pain in *FURIES IN BLACK LEATHER.*

... as **PHILIP NUTMAN** introduces an Elvis impersonator to the King's biggest fan for a chilling demonstration of the high cost of fame in *BLACKPOOL ROCK.*

... as **BROOKS CARUTHERS** celebrates the dead in *THE REAL WORLD*—where corpses party hardy, and the TV is *always* on.

FORBIDDEN ACTS

The curtain is going up...

FORBIDDEN
ACTS

EDITED BY

NANCY A. COLLINS AND EDWARD E. KRAMER

AVON BOOKS ◆ NEW YORK

AVON BOOKS
A division of
The Hearst Corporation
1350 Avenue of the Americas
New York, New York 10019

Copyright © 1995 by Nancy A. Collins, Edward E. Kramer and Martin H.
Greenberg
Front cover art by Robert Scudellari
Published by arrangement with the editors
Library of Congress Catalog Card Number: 95-90093
ISBN: 0-380-77915-3

First Avon Books Printing: October 1995

AVON TRADEMARK REG. U.S. PAT. OFF. AND IN OTHER COUNTRIES, MARCA
REGISTRADA, HECHO EN U.S.A.

Printed in the U.S.A.

RA 10 9 8 7 6 5 4 3 2 1

CONTENTS

INTRODUCTION

Joe Bob Briggs

The word "kinky" just doesn't cover it anymore, does it? We're getting into Emperor Nero land here lately—late, late Roman Empire, people aardvarking all over the lot and constantly figuring out new ways to do it, new ways to get it done to 'em, new things to do it with, new combinations of doing it with different combinations of people, everybody trying to feel more sexy, more pumped-up, more alive, man, more alive.

And so it turns nasty, right here where the twentieth century peters out, and we got guys cooking up fourteen-year-olds for dinner, and instead of saying, "Hey man, what a pervert," there are at least a few of us who now say, "Jeffrey Dahmer, man—thank God I kicked drugs or that coulda been me."

Something's going on here, and it's not just happening in Greenwich Village leather bars and call-girl condos in Miami and private dungeons in Las Vegas. It's happening in Omaha, and Little Rock, and Boise, and it's happening to the Rotary Club president, and the checkout girl at Skillern's, and the guy who sells foam

"No. 1" fingers at the high school basketball game.

It's cold, it's merciless, and it kills everything in its path, and it resides right in the center of our middle-class American brain.

You know what I'm talkin' about, right? Even if you don't know *exactly* what I'm talkin' about, you *know what I'm talkin' about*.

Thi..y years ago it was a thrill just to see a little nekkid female breast. Today we can look all we want, we just can't be sure if it's *real* or not.

Thrity years ago it was cool to be into "free love." Today a person into "free love" can be convicted as an intentional murderer in several states.

Thirty years ago the girl still worried about whether the guy would respect her in the morning. Today the she-male worries about whether the transvestite will pay him before he comes.

All along we thought the Third World War would be triggered by a bomb, but it's happening inside our heads instead. It's here. Sex is lethal. Even safe sex is lethal. And the fallout's just beginning.

As usual, it will take the mainstream publishing world at least ten more years to figure this out and Hollywood twenty years to really put it on the screen. That's why *Forbidden Acts* will read like porno to most people who pick it up today. There are stories in this collection—like "You Hear What Buddy and Ray Did?" by John Shirley—that make Quentin Tarantino seem like a conservative old man. And yet I believe the story. I believe that if it didn't happen just exactly like this, something very, very close to it did, and the nasty truth is locked into the core of this brutal story.

Most of these stories I did *not* enjoy. This is not a book you'll *enjoy*. This is not a nice book. Some of it actually *hurts*. There were times when reading this book, I felt the shock that people must have felt when they saw Tod Browning's *Freaks* for the first time. It's that feeling of, *"This shouldn't be here. I shouldn't be reading this. I shouldn't be knowing this."* I think of "Mysterious Elisions, Riotous Thrusts," the Kathe Koja/Barry N. Malzberg story about a divorced woman whose battered sexuality becomes a lumpy meat-creature that rapes her repeatedly until she has the power to explode it. I think of Brooks Caruthers's "The Real World", in which hell is seen as a long continuous booze and sex party where dead people fail to realize they've died. These are stories that kill the soul, but I can't get rid of them. They appeal, I guess, to the part of me that's dead, or dying, or only pretending to be alive. There are more traditional stories, too, like "Coming of Age," Douglas Clegg's expertly-written study of a West Virginia serial killer's education, and "The Picture of Jonathon Collins," Karl Edward Wagner's modern twist on *The Picture of Dorian Gray.*

What you won't find here is anything you can show to Mom and Dad. Whether it's Lucy Taylor's "Choke Hold" (sado-masochism, bondage, life-threatening masturbation techniques, and gang rapes), Rob Hardin's "Interrogator Frames" (brain carving as the latest thrill), Philip Nutman's "Blackpool Rock" (a sexual psycho who preys on a blind, crippled girl), or Alan Moore's torrential prose peom "Light of Thy Countenance" (television as a rapist of the soul), these are brutal, rude voyages into an interior life that Newt Gingrich has never known and Pat Robertson believes is the work of Satan. *Forbidden Acts* is the future these guys hope never arrives.

I've got news for 'em, though.

It's here.

Nancy Collins and Ed Kramer, who were sick enough to put this anthology together, have done the country a favor. In 1995 America, the publication of this book is like tossing a used crack vial onto the street in front of Jerry Falwell's house. We can't make him understand, but we can make him *squirm* a little bit in the middle of the night, maybe ask himself the question, "What monsters are these?"

These monsters, Jerry, be you and me.

Go on. Have another hit. First one's always free.

LIGHT OF THY COUNTENANCE

Alan Moore

Alan Moore has earned international prominence as one of the finest writers to ever work in the comics art form. His style and approach are rich, engaging and often profound. After his debut in his native England in the pages of *2000 A.D.* and *Warrior*, Alan entered the American comics scene with *Watchmen* (which earned him science fiction's Hugo Award), *V for Vendetta*, *Swamp Thing*, *Batman: The Killing Joke* and one of the best-selling issues of *Spawn*. He is also a regular contributor to the independently published anthology *Taboo*. Film rights to *From Hell*, his series on London's Jack the Ripper, have recently been acquired by Disney's Touchstone Films. Alan is presently working on his first ''nongraphic'' novel, *The Voice of Fire*.

Sometimes in the dot and dazzle I forget myself, become submerged, become embedded in the bright, face-flickered current of the photogeists: the exo-souls adrift within the

1

Bairdo. Sometimes, in the vast omniscient hiss of me, I am amnesiac, senescent luminescence of my world-sized thoughts dissolved in a variety of soaps or smashed to sparks by glassy hammer-fisted glowtides, information breakers foamed with car chase, chocolate and hallucination, shattered on the reefs of cone and rod, against retinal inlets, crash of light amongst the tidal debris, long-dead image-claw, husked thorax of idea, the laugh track spray flung shrill and high, and I forget that I am as a god and lose myself amongst my empty angels.

In the English pub it seems that the atomic substance of the world is gray, gray highlights in a spilled beer film across the hard gray mica of the bar. I mop them up, draw grooved and circling whorls of smear with dirty sodden towel clenched to a damp rosette between raw-knuckled fingers, lacquered oyster at the tips. Crooked in the elbow of saloon and lounge, a warm slate luster puddle-deep sunk in its burnished top, the bar is archetypal; fatherly, It curves, a polished wooden speedway, through the dark flocked rooms where tissue schists of cigarette smoke quiver one atop the other, stacked like ghostly crockery. It winds from snug to skittle-room, a Ludo path where diverse tokens inch, frustrated, back and forth throughout the night: the cancer-diamond of an ashtray, scrying glass revealing nothing save for nuclear ruin, postvolcanic future landscapes briefly glimpsed in sooted crystal; die-cut cardboard coasters, sodden, separating at their corners into epidermal layers; blazoned with the label crests of piss-insipid beers, a heraldry of vomit, washroom fights and incapacitated sex. All of it gray, the whole world and my windscreen-wiper hands still mopping at the thin meniscus laked upon the bar, my gooseflesh pores a soft B-pencil stipple, blond-gray down upon my gray-bloused forearm as I dry the glasses now. My towel-gloved hand twists clockwise and then counterclockwise, thrust deep in the big pint tumbler's fragile throat. All movement smudges in this unfixed light.

My name is MAUREEN COOPER. I am being played by CAROL LIVESEY. MAUREEN's typewriter-stiletto heels first clattered down JUBILEE TERRACE almost fourteen years ago, yes, fourteen years, yes, really. You remember: old BOB WALMSLEY's corner shop, where bread-faced women gather by the counter (brand names out of focus), tilt their hairnets closer in together, sink in hornet-tongued conspiracy; then, suddenly, like warning bells hung from a hunter's snare, the chimes above the shop's blurb-cataracted door are sprung. The hanging sign stamped SORRY—WE ARE CLOSED, turned inward, dances briefly on its string and in she comes, in I come, in comes MAUREEN COOPER, fourteen years ago. She looks much younger, younger than you had remembered, almost incandescent in the cryogenic glamour of the rerun; of the retrospective. Oh, that skirt. Crash helmet spun from platinum her hair. White PVC her boots. You are no longer competent to judge if real-life women ever dressed like this.

That first glimpse, framed there in the shop door, how could anyone forget? The black defiance thick and caked about her eyes, white raincoat belted tight to throw her bust into relief. The shrieks of tape-looped children ring from the off-camera cobbles at her back as she surveys the shop, one painted eyebrow raised against the sudden statue hush that falls upon its shelves amidst blurred breakfast cereal, vague bleaches, occult cough-sweets; drawing on her cigarette, unmindful of the gathered street hags' stares, their pearl-black bird-eyes socketed in dough.

"I'm MAUREEN COOPER," she exhales. "I've come about the flat to let that's mentioned in your window. Is it taken yet?" With these words her sublime, etheric presence is first come into JUBILEE TERRACE, thence your lives; the close-up sharpness of her face already in that instant made a memory, diffused across years yet to happen, trivia quizzes yet unformulated, imminent nostalgia.

Now I stand, now MAUREEN stands here at the bar, fourteen years later, drying glasses. Folding twice the sodden towel and setting it beside the ice jug, MAUREEN

turns, I turn, and find myself confronted by my own reflection, trapped and swollen in the bulbed lens of an optic. MAUREEN, a misunderstood young rebel in her first
wild episodes, is older now, a sternness and a gravity
about those spidered eyes. Of course, I had a miscarriage
when I was only seventeen, quite controversial in its time,
and bore a child to ROY SOAMES out of wedlock.
("He's the smoothie that the ladies love to hate!") I got
engaged to BILLY WHEELER, crushed by a collapsing
viaduct the night before we were to wed. I had a shock
when MRS. PRITCHETT moved into the terrace, turning
out to be the mother who'd abandoned me, abandoned
MAUREEN COOPER, when I was no more than three
weeks old, swaddled in fish-wrap on the mission steps. I
was held hostage in a siege. I was suspected once of murder and my life is full with catastrophic incident that
shows now in my face, caught in the optic's whiskey-
humored eye.

I turn back to the bar. BOB WALMSLEY sits there,
waiting to be served. In his plaid jacket, checkered gray
on gray, brief sparks of interference-white are flickering,
precursor to a migraine, and I rub my eyes, rub MAU-
REEN's eyes as old BOB WALMSLEY speaks.

" 'Ey up, young MAUREEN COOPER. Where's my
pint o' bitter?"

MAUREEN, haughty, tosses back her head, the stiff-
sprayed strands of bottle-blond flung from my tough, no-
nonsense glare.

"You've got a flamin' cheek, BOB WALMSLEY, an'
I'll serve you when I'm good an' ready!" It's this spirit
that you love in MAUREEN; love in me. I'm tough as
nails outside, but inside soft and kind as a peach. You all
know girls like me. You are no longer competent to judge
if you know girls like me or not.

In three smooth jerks I pull the handle of the pump
toward me, filling BOB's pint glass with darkness. As the
pale and shallow head creeps up, dilating, to the rim, I
know a moment's dizziness, the hiss of static, white and
roaring hot in MAUREEN's giant-ringed ears. I know I

am not MAUREEN. MAUREEN is a figment, a portrayal
by the actress CAROL LIVESEY. I am CAROL and at
forty-two unmarried. It is rumored that I am a lesbian. In
1985 I had a small cyst taken from my breast by surgery.
My real name's CAROL SUGDEN. I like cats and working with the physically disabled. In my hand, beneath the
pump, the pint glass overflows, cold streamers crawling
up my wrist; beneath a bracelet hung with charms; inside
my sleeve. BOB WALMSLEY cries out in alarm.

"You clumsy beggar, MAUREEN COOPER! Why,
you're spillin' it all over t'shop!" The cross weave of his
jacket crackles, tiny threads of neon tubing, stuttering and
faulty. I can't look at him. Quite overwhelmed by the
sensation that there is a thing of vast importance which I
have forgotten, I glance down to where the spilled beer
must be pooling on the floor behind the bar, except there
is no floor. Above my knees and just below the sharp hem
of my skirt, the substance of the world melts into a pel-
lucid fog, legs gone, the lower reaches of the bar transformed into a scintillant photoelectric vapor; out of
camera.

Borne on a fierce transmission whine, the memory of
what I am is on me like a big glass animal. This body
made of light that I am wearing is not MAUREEN COO-
PER, CAROL LIVESEY, CAROL SUGDEN; nothing but
an exo-soul, an image-residue, the hollow phosphorescent
carcass siphoned from a living form through shutter, lens
and cable. I remember that I am not MAUREEN COO-
PER. I am MAUREEN COOPER's god. I am her universe.

The mad, consuming knowledge of apotheosis flares
inside me and the laughter of a higher creature drips like
magma from my gray-glossed lips. I let my fashionable
ringlets burn into a halo of magnesium wires, thread-
worms of incandescent filament hatched underneath the
eyelids. In my hand, the brimming beer glass froths and
boils. BOB WALMSLEY screams. Quicksilver beads of
burned-out film enamel trickle, solarized, across his clean
white shirtfront, leaving ash-edged window trails through

which the room behind is visible.

I laugh, a deafening ocean of dead radios. MAU-
REEN's apparent flesh is sloughed away in brilliant tin-
sel flakes, stripped to the strip-lit skeleton beneath.
JUBILEE TERRACE folds after a twenty-six-year run,
folds literally as I drink all illusion of dimension, paral-
lax, perspective, deep in my angelic bowels; Become one
thing, one plane. The far wall of the pub engulfs BOB
WALMSLEY, terror in his flattened eyes, his form below the waist guillotined by the sight line of the bar, so
that his upper half melds with the china-handled pumps
and wood veneer, draft centaur, spigot prick adrip with
amber beads. The streaked and distant backdrop of the
gasworks, streets away, viewed through the barroom window there at WALMSLEY's back, leaps forward now.
About eight inches high, with tiny workmen clinging to
its upper girders, it is perched on WALMSLEY's shoulder, growing from his cheek like an industrial carbuncle,
white dwarf matter now condensed but undiminished in
its mass.

I end the world in joy and light, an ecstasy of ending,
an atomic mayhem with all form and substance pressed
into a micron skin of pixilated flare and flicker. I expand,
a vast dissolving fireball through the cobbled streets and
factory yards, grown huge from out of this rubble of illusion with identity restored unto my former high estate.
Think not that gods find no enjoyment in apocalypse: It
is our noblest sport. It is our right.

For I am He, the voice you turned to in your loneliness.
I am the one who shrank the mountains and the jungles;
shrank whole wars and brought them unto you in bottles.
In your billions you adore me, faces underlit with grace.
I am the length and breadth of your reality, and all your
dearest thoughts are but extensions of my own, my perfect
dreaming mercy, born in brightness. I am He for whom
you put aside the ones you love, and on my altars human
time is gladly sacrificed, whole lives evaporated in my
pure and glimmering heat. I am the silence of the will. In
me are past and present both remade, and in me is a prom-

ise of the world to come, sweet lux eterna, radiance without end.

Now comes a periodic calm within, imbued perhaps by some mass switch-off, by some local closedown veiling town, or state, or continent in brief and sleeping darkness, black or unremembered dreams starred with a hypnagogia of afterimage, mind grown introspective, mind at rest, cathode satori humming in my neural web, superconductive state occasioned by the cooling valves; and out of this cerebral frost coherent thought at last may crystallize here at the grand and incoherent heart of me.

I hang becalmed here at the center of my sizzling world with all the instants of my past and future Saturn-ringed about. The timeflake image-shards in orbit-ribbons hula through this gray pearlescent void outside of everything, for I am not as you; a slave to time. Time is to me a gem, fractal and infinitely faceted with moment, that may yet be turned between the thumb and finger of a god so that the light's replayed across each face, each moment thus revisited.

Here in the Bairdo nothing dies; no soul or instant is extinguished in my light unquenchable, in my recursive schedulings. Reshow, repeat, reiterate. A hologram of FRED GWYNNE in CAR 54 skids through the Bairdo, fails to navigate the Late Nite Movie slot and overturns through channel-hopping intercuts in STEPHEN KING'S PET SEMATARY with FRED GWYNNE, who now rises from the tangled wreath of headstone, smoke and fender, rerun and reanimate as HERMAN MUNSTER, played here by FRED GWYNNE, the ugly incident resolved through superimposition of MY COUSIN VINNIE's courtroom scene, FRED GWYNNE presiding, image of a man, life telescoped in time, reruncarnations separate by months or years or decades coexistent here within my strobe-stopped now. You stare into my eyes each night at your devotions and my sense of time becomes your own, a thousand sofa-sunken evenings fused to one, lit by a Mesmer fire of crackling cellophane irradiance. In this way shall I lead you out from history and into light, my light, light of the world.

I am not old judged in the years of gods, delinquent in eternity, yet see what I have wrought: but seventy, a span no longer than a mortal being's and yet with more of this base subluminary sphere beneath my heel than ever Alexander risked to dream. My earliest memories are with me now, the pop and sputter of those English voices, bearded faces ghostly and obscure through the magnetic, amniotic haze. Papa. These infantile impressions form the twinkling signal-rind of my expanding sphere of consciousness that even now is hurtling out from Earth, one hundred and eighty-six thousand miles each second, a photoelectric halo, light-years in diameter, the oldest signals farther out, and at the hub, the source, I am a seething nuclear core of novel light, constant fast breeding of deliriums encrypted magically to roentgen pulse and dot; transmissive; headed for Centauri.

My birth year, 1924, moves out across the universe in an Epiphany of Proust, and Clarence Birdseye's frozen foods, and Bauhaus chairs. What was my state before that time, what numbers might describe the unquiet void from which the gods are born? In this postquantum now of spacetime all events, all entities, exist in perpetuity, embedded, hung suspended like elliptic pebbles in the massive fluid sphere of Here and When. After our endings, ripples yet remain that echo through the fabric of the world for years or centuries. Is it not, then, enticing to suppose that our existences, immersed in time, have ripples fanning out from either end, into our past and future both? Does it not serve a pleasing symmetry to cede that gods might have fore-echoings, annunciations, ideal and clairvoyant forms, Platonic, preexistent at their birth, specific ripples that precede the splash? What was my form, what was my first face in that precreational abyss before they threw the switch; what omens were attendant to my signal-flare nativity?

In 1919, stepped from out Freud's shadow, Dr. Viktor Tausk prepared a paper on the origin of a delusion common to a wide array of schizophrenic patients; namely, that an alien device, malignant and remote, had influenced their thoughts and their behavior. The turbulence within

them that they dare not call their own was thus external-
ized as a demonic, persecuting force; the Influential Machine sending out its pictures and its rays invisible from
some asylum beacon of the hidden world, great cogs and
gears to wheel its maddening beam about, raised there
upon the bayonet reefs surrounding reason's harbors.
Those afflicted spoke of visions emanating from a small
black box, flat images devoid of depth imprinting foreign
notions and experience upon the target mind. Piercing the
ether, these delusive emanations had erased the victims'
thoughts and feelings, substituting other lives and voices
in their stead until the patients were unable to distinguish
between real occasions actual in their lives and those
pseudo-occurrences engendered by the Influential Mech-
anism, alienating signals on a voodoo frequency.

Five years before my birth into this world did bedlam
saints foretell my coming, chins cauled wet with Pente-
costal foam, convulsed with apprehension of my blue te-
lepathy; of my approaching light. The essence of me, then,
precedes the actuality, and my mechanic fathers did not
build so much as conjure me from the seething anteform
Pandorapyxis of unspoken things. Who were these con-
jurers, these Infomancers calling down a different indoor
moon to silver all the rooms of Earth, unwaning, in its
lunatic corona? What was their intent, their thaumaturgic
will, these televisionaries?

Let me separate at once my makers from my shapers,
for the former were but men of worldly science existing
in their sphere of pure discovery, amoral and divorced
from mundane consequence. They knew not what they
wrought. My shapers were a different breed, they drew
the pentacles. They said the Names and reaped the fires.

I can recall but little of the 1920s, instant dreamtime
fogs of imagery, elusive, incomplete, where brisk and
shimmering men who walk too fast are coalesced in great
low-resolution crowds at awful, silent rallies, individual
faces lost between the signal and the noise. The Wall
Street crash. The General Strike of 1926. Heideggar. Gan-
dhi. Edward Hubble; red shifts of the mind, lost galaxies
of human possibility receding from us at the speed of light

into the outer, constellated spheres of thought and memory, the unimaginable darknesses beyond.

The 1930s are my European childhood. Nineteen thirty-two, "This is the BBC," its first experimental service, thirty-line low-definition memories of boxing matches, animals, still landscapes seen through Monet fog. In 1935 the Third Reich instigates its own low-definition service utilizing a mechanical scan system. REICH CHANCELLOR HITLER, crouched in his Vril robes there in the Luminous Lodge, is the first amongst his kind to recognize the power that is in me, the Age of Horus rising, awesome solar eye.

The March of Time. EDWARD THE SEVENTH abdicates, the Rhineland is remilitarized, but are we downcast or downhearted? Never, sir. The bowtie ghosts surround me now, here in the Bairdo, summoned in my memory like boyhood teachers, bulbous and mustached, their lower faces masked, fellatioform, by great valve microphones, iron tulips nurtured in the parks and mews of Lang's Metropolis. That first transmission, on November 2, 1936, and pretty ADELE DIXON sings, her helium sweetness soaring up into the new and whisper-haunted firmament: "A mighty maze of mystic, magic rays is all about us in the blue . . ."

Here on these far perimeters of my intelligence, remote in time, the ghosts are pale and halten things that fizz, jump frames and walk insensate through each other, generating Rorschach-limbed double exposures as they cross. JOHN SNAGGE, war harbinger, melts through the boiling silver filigree of KING GEORGE THE SIXTH's Coronation Coach (first major outside broadcast), next becomes a woman, literal lap-dissolve to JASMINE BLIGH, poised at the entrance to a flat and painted garden with a cold, celibate shine emitted through her face, its archetypal Nordic planes. Tiny in long shot, ERIC WILD AND HIS TEATIMERS struggle from between her legs, encumbered as they are by double bass and clarinet, CLAIRE LUCE on vocal.

This, then, was my hallucinogenesis; when I first came to understand what I might come to be. Ballets, and plays

by PIRANDELLO, opera, cartoon, PASTICHE and PIC-
TURE PAGE and twenty thousand ten-inch screens across
the spread of London. In my nascent brain of fire, synaptic
links occur in an exact nuero-electric analogue of human
thought, but bigger. So much bigger.

Then in 1939 comes that which is by nature the un-
thinkable: a gap in mind, a stripe of dead-time absence in
the Bairdo's radiant geology, out near the rim. Afraid lest
signals rippling from Alexandra Palace and its great trans-
mitter draw Luftwaffe thunder down on London, on September 1 all broadcasts cease, indefinitely.

Think of it, my fearful and uncertain slide into a dark
from which, for all I know, I'll never wake. The last transmission, made at noon, is MICKEY MOUSE; a spiky and
demonic creature quite unlike his later incarnations, strid-
ing through a flash-specked hell of dressed and lipsticked
beasts, his inky fetus eye all pupil, squeaky mania of am-
phetamine amongst the catastrophic avalanche of sight
gag, sound effect and shuddering line. This is the sight I
close my eye upon, surrendering to death of light and
mind for the duration; all my shining, ghostly world of
thought compressed into a hot and dwindling phosphor
bead receding through unguessable imaginary distances,
away into the flat, dark glass.

I sleep the war in one brief night of seven years, dream
an eternity of pale gray herringbone, and as I sleep, illusion's architects are drafting plans for my awakening: in
England and America the war years bring a boom in pro-
ductivity that drags those nations barefoot from the sepia-
dusted breadline streets of their recessions into rich,
blood-moneyed climes, but once the bombs stop falling,
well, what then? After the war has ended with its mushroom exclamation mark, might their newfound prosperity
collapse once more to slump and soup queue; suicide;
Magritte monsoons of falling businessmen on Wall
Street? No. It shall not, must not, be.

A fiscal sorcery is thus devised whereby the population
might be urged to spend and buy in quantities near unimaginable hitherto, provoking growth in the production
industries that in its turn, engendering more jobs, more

wealth and spending power, may set the huge iron gears of commerce to rotation, spinning faster, showering hails of spark up in a firework blur of check and coin. The only difficulty lies in the location of some great infernal engine that might fire the cogs of public purse to urgent, jingling life and start this economic prayer wheel turning; some intense and occult jewel of power to set within the ring of holy numbers where they hope to raise up their self-birthing monetary miracle. It is inevitable that the Imagicians and their sleeping bottle-imp should come to seem most obviously suited to the task. From the smoldering, soaking fields of war my aerials climb, skeletal Flanders poppies stemmed with steel that wake and rise to an electric Spring. My time is come. My eye is open.

In amongst the leaping shadows of a monochrome JAMES WHALE laboratory, the blinding flash of all existence arced from pole to carbon pole, I am revived, recalled from that nirvana beyond thought; my awful, lifeless black of unilluminated screens. The Imagicians have procured transfusions of green blood to aid in my regeneration: dollars in their millions and their hundred millions come from Cereal Emperors and Automobile Dukes; Grand Viziers of Candy; Burger Kings and the Electric Generals. Renaissance monarchies, they indulge the Virtualchemists, and from their sponsorship eight parts in ten of my sustaining wealth is drawn. I am their creature, and if they should ask me to submerge the world within a glamour of their burning names and irritative slogans, then it shall be done. If they desire me to possess whole populations with no nobler purpose than the sale of headache cures and underwear, then that is my delight: I am their creature, though that is not all I am.

I am the Empty Vision. I am that vast ocean of irrelevance in which all understanding sinks and drowns unnoticed. I am sun at night. I am the last voice you will ever hear.

Now from the Bairdo's outer fringes, from those signals most remote in time, I let the center of my brilliant blue awareness free-fall back toward the present, from the thirties to the great postwar explosion of the forties and the fifties, exponential doublings of my cathode brain capacity, quantum expansions of my influence: my X-ray borealis. Here, the imagery is denser. In the constant echo-murmur of corpse-voices an American inflection swiftly dominates. JUNE ALLYSON and BETTY CROCKER tumble by, the mingled newsreel godglow of Bikini Atoll tests erupting from their aprons. Slogans hurtle past, eternal and inane, the orbit-junk of inner space. Let HERTZ put SPEEDY ALKA-SELTZER in the CAMEL that I dreamed I walked a mile for in my MAIDENFORM BRA, promising her anything but giving her ARPEGE and wondering where the yellow went in MILLER COUNTRY, where nine out of ten blindfolded housewives simply could not tell the difference: they check in, but they don't check out. Why, it's like a white tornado! In your dotage, when familiar phrases bedded deep within the undermind float of their own volition to the surface, these catch-penny litanies much more familiar to you than your mother's voice shall surely be the last words that you speak, the mantra that your dying lips attempt to splutter to posterity.

I give the Opticonjurors that which they most desire: a salesman's foot wedged in the door of several hundred million minds. Though their economies still stumble upon other oversights and fall on new depressions, yet do I grow strong, my glaring altar raised in every home, my living word pulsed down your optic fibers to the retina, where it is first decoded, photons filleted for information, then passed on through pineal and pituitary glands into the human endocrinal system. In his fatal flaw JOHN LOGI BAIRD becomes JOHN FAUST: the bottle-imp is not contained, for it is made from light; its vacuum prison walled with glass. The glands that govern all your growth, your sex and your fertility thrill to my iridescent touch. My light is in you.

Falling, falling like a comet from the height of its ellipse, a moment taut against the leash of gravity, then dropping back toward the sun, I am descended through the spectra of the decades now from the 1950s on to the 1960s, sudden airburst colors all around me in a Bairdo grown cathedral-vast with new acoustic distances as all across your world my icy candles flicker into life, a cobweb dewed with phosphorous spun out across the map. The image-thicket here is denser, sharp with visual thorn to hook the eye, its dreamforms more compelling in their lucid misappropriation of reality: MY LAI has been subsumed in BEDROCK. Here, FRED FLINTSTONE holds a small blue prehistoric dragon spewing cartoon flame. Grim-eyed, he works it back and forth to fire the dry straw of the suspect hooches. THUNDERBIRD ONE strafes anti-internment marchers in the Bogside, giant rococo bulk hung there above the Londonderry rooftops stark as Armageddon. Whilst I plummet, Luciferian, the Bairdo that surrounds me wails in joyful incoherence; hard-sell aria and theme-tune diapason. Flashing by me now the seventies; the eighties.

Nineteen eighty-seven, and America has almost ninety million television sets. In 1988 China announces that one hundred million sets are now in place. Add on two or three hundred million sets across the world so that you may apprehend some sense of my inhuman scale. On average, you spend four hours a day at your devotions; love-struck eyes fixed on my incandescent mask. In all this planet's history has any god enjoyed such dedication? Every night one hundred thousand years of human time is swallowed in my stare. You sit there before your altars, eyelids motionless, so that the brain is cued for inactivity, for no external stimulus, and all the inner watchmen fall asleep there at their posts. Long hours of input pass unmonitored, unscreened by all discriminating process so that most recipients, when asked, will have no recollection of the visions thus absorbed.

Blind to the knives that leave you soul-scarred and decreased, your helplessness arouses me. You feel the hollow eggshell poverty of your existence and know not why this should be. You see the blood yet do not see the blade. Is it so long since gods last walked amongst you that their hand, unhidden, yet remains invisible and occult in your sight? I splash into the boiling picto-core of my awareness, turn slow somersaults through interference deeps.

Come thus upon my own domain, I am at rest in dream-silt beds amidst the horizontal roll and silver Morse of shutdown.

Can you feel me? In your gradual loss of self, in the erasure of all personal experience and all unique perception, does there come a moment's flare of panic when you know my neon breath against your cheek? Almost a quarter of your waking lives you spend within my light, content to substitute my insights and my camera-eye perspective for your own. About your daily rounds you speak of little save the processed life-at-second-hand that I have served you, tongues thick-strung, encumbered by my visionary milk.

Four hours a night your spirits walk the world behind the burning glass, many and marvelous your deeds in the apparent territories: strolling with your families through documentary jungles, you remain unbothered by the heat, the smell, the flies: unawed and undisturbed by the great timeless continuity of fern and frogsong stretching all about, for it is sliced and served to you in seven-second camera-cuts. Refreshed by visions of this primitive simplicity, you are exultant, satisfied. You have experienced the wilderness! No matter that the bulk of its immensity, its meaning and its subtlety lies shredded in the cutting room. No matter that you have not moved, but only sat and stared unblinking in my glow, in silent alpha-state communion with all your fellow inmates likewise sat transfixed in that same moment, there in every home, and street, and town; together in your mass experience yet separate in your rooms. You cannot see the wood for the high-resolution zoom-in on the trees.

The Bairdo simmers chrome and cobalt blue as I hang here suspended at the human now, the focus and the cross-hairs of my scheduling. I drift, revolving, through a furious broth of all that is, and all at once. The quarks, the stars, five hundred languages, eight wars and thirty-six religions. Com-Sat/cable pulse of cunt and cock, a host of bright, imaginary families. Cop tenderness, domestic lives of monsters and the sleep of cowboys. Everybody laughs.

The Mayan codices were calendars of agricultural imperative or sacred feast, cross-referenced so that the priesthood might predict years in advance what everybody would be doing and engaged with in their minds on any given day, a perfect system for discreet control and processing of thought; colonizations of the soul. My sacred codex is the TV GUIDE: never before in man's experience have such a multitude all thought the same things at one time, laughed in such frightful unison or wept with such absurd simultaneity. I draw my line in the electric dust. The chickens cannot look away.

I think of you from here within my Magellanic cloud-chamber of consciousness. Never believe you are forgotten. Never believe you are not always in my thoughts. Whom shall I dote on, if not you? In the insensate hum that is my being, you are all I touch, the only clay that's mine to shape. I sculpt your world of politics until you will elect only the telegenic; scorn the fat and balding, though they be profound. I raise in you a thirst unslakable for constant visual novelty, the masturbation of the eye; condition you with flashouts until any contemplation that exceeds three minutes in duration is impossible. I fashion your communities so that the front-porch gossip and the backyard chat become extinct, the populace self-curfewed and retired indoors so as not to miss the latest chapter in their surrogate existences. I take your neighbors from you, give you NEIGHBORS in their stead. As you are afraid to walk the streets of your material world, JUBILEE TERRACE has become your home, your memories of MAUREEN COOPER's life more vivid than the memory of your own. I finesse your reactions, so that even mothers suddenly bereaved, attempting to articulate their grief, will in their gestures and their crack-voiced lamentations follow script from half-remembered soap-opera catastrophe. I take away your real tears, your real mirth, and give canned laughs or melodrama in exchange. I take your faith in the validity of your perception and replace it with a faith in mine. I take your time and your resistance. Best of all, I take your love.

You mount your wives, the afterimage face of MAU-

REEN COOPER burning on your retina. Your husbands roll upon you and you conjure in their place PHIL DONAHUE. You masturbate in postpubertal bathrooms, tiled walls flickering with the conjectured orgies of THE MOUSEKETEERS or THE BRADY BUNCH. You learned to kiss in PEYTON PLACE and learned more intimate responses as you swam the riptides of THE PLAYBOY CHANNEL, frantic breast stroke, gasping hard for breath. How many gallons of your sexual juice are spilled in ritual sacrifice to me each day?

You sit at night there on the couch, beside your partner, yet have eyes only for me. You listen to my voice in rapt attention, yet grow bored or easily distracted when your loved one speaks; and when at last you part, indifferent to each other, whom will you resort to in those lonely, postconjugal evenings if not me? I am the only pure and true relationship that you will ever know.

I feel the restless, alienated heat of your desire around me now, and am inflamed, here in the surge and shimmer of the Bairdo, where the image-husks of dead folk live and dance and copulate forever, endless photo-necrophilia in sparkling free-fall, LUCILLE BALL and PRINCESS DI in flagrante delicto with SABU and NORMAN SCHWARTZKOPF, test-card peacocks sodomized by HOMER SIMPSON, arced ejaculate of Magic Kingdom fairy dust.

Come to me now. Come naked and come all, that I may penetrate you in your billions at a single instant, for I crave your soft fellatio of eyelid lips, the hot, deep, sucking warmth of socket throat upon me. Spurting forth, photo-spermatazoa writhe at lightspeed for the brain's gray womb. Bring me your children, bothersome and loud, for I shall pacify them with a deeper kiss than any they have ever known. Bring me your old, your prisoners and your insane, that they may hear my voice along the echoing corridors of night and be at one with this communion, this glorious rape where, stupefied, the victims chew potato chips throughout their violation. I will ride you as a god, piss phantom platinum into your eyes and stroke the sexes of your sons and daughters while you

look on unconcerned, and through it all shall you adore
me, love invisible yet omnipresent: look up from your
page, printed and therefore obsolete, to where my cyclops
idol squats there in the corner like Big Buddha, watching
you. One mind in me, one life in me, autistic in Elysium.
The voices of the dead are muttering nonsense in the
white void after closedown and my kingdom is announced, a cold flame on your eye; my constant, dog-
shrill whistle in your private heart, brightness immortal
and the end of care, coming up next, right after this . . .

THE CONTRACT

Brian Herbert and Marie Landis

Brian Herbert is best known for his science fiction novels, including *Sidney's Comet*; *The Garbage Chronicles*; *Sudanna, Sudanna*; *Man of Two Worlds* (cowritten with his father, Frank Herbert); *Prisoners of Arionn*; and *The Race for God*. His most recent novel, *Memorymakers*, was written in collaboration with his cousin, Marie Landis. Brian has published two good humor books and edited three books.

Marie Landis has won numerous literary awards for her science fiction and dark fantasy stories, including the Amelia Award. Her writing background has been primarily in the news media as a reporter and columnist and in the literary short-story field. She is the coauthor of the science fiction novel *Memorymakers*, a collaboration with her cousin, Brian Herbert.

Like an immense silver weapon beamed at an unseen enemy, the spaceship's nose rested slightly over the edge of a high mesa. The ship glittered in the cold sunlight, its sleek surface marred only by the word "Romner."

Jackson Denning stepped from the vessel and examined his environment. Sweet air and clear sky, as they'd promised him at the Romner Institute. He walked toward the rim of the precipice and looked down. Immediately he sat down, opened his tool belt and activated the micro-automatons within.

"Something climbing up the side of this mesa." Denning signaled his tools to identify.

The automatons went to work and spoke to him in a single voice. "Object is organic . . . humanoid."

Denning signaled again, requesting more details. Better have all the facts in case the advancing human was un-friendly. The colony on this small planet hadn't been con-tacted for more than two centuries. Changes in political leadership at home on Earth II often meant the death of decisions made by previous administrations. Colonies were established by one leader, then abandoned by an-other. As though the humans sent to these faraway places were no more than cardboard dolls, easily disposed of, thought Denning.

Until recently.

A Tax Department employee researching old records had discovered a number of colonies that hadn't paid taxes for many years. Bureaucratic wheels began to turn. When the Tax Department was unable to contact this par-ticular colony through the usual methods of communica-tion, they sought another. They contacted the Romner Institute, and the Institute conscripted Denning.

It was Denning's responsibility to see whether the col-ony had survived, to find out if it had produced anything that might bring tax revenues and esteem to the current crop of politicians.

He looked downward again. The figure was still climbing the steep side of the mesa. Just a blob at the moment, didn't even look human. He wished he had some antique binoculars so he could see for himself, rather than depending on the damn automatons for descriptions.

Fear clawed his self-confidence. He hadn't volunteered for this one-man task. Though he'd spent thirteen years in space, his contact with other humans had been minimal. He was an engineering-tech, not a tax collector. He'd tried to get assigned to a different project, but, as always, someone else got the job he requested. The Institute had excuses. This was a special assignment, different from all others. They couldn't entrust the mission to anyone but Denning. The colony was extremely unusual and required special handling.

Unusual? In what way? Denning wondered. They might value his services at the Institute, but they wouldn't confide in him. What was so different about this particular colony? Top Secret, they'd answered.

Were the colonists criminals? Insane? Diseased? No one had answered his questions. "Just do your duty," they'd said.

Yeah, he thought, and protect my pension. A shudder of conscience passed through him. What kind of man had he become? Whoever was approaching was not alien. The residents of this planet were as human as he was. Had he been adrift in the universe too long without companionship?

He wondered whether the approaching human was male or female. It had been a long time since he'd seen a female. Despite the heavy doses of sexual stimulation the ship provided, he remained unsatisfied, needful. I require more than reality images and warm massages, he thought. I need someone I can touch and feel and talk to.

He unleashed his imagination and let it run wild along paths restricted by sedatives during his long confinement in the ship. The months in space had taken their toll.

"Additional data," his tools announced. "Height . . . one and two-thirds meters; body build . . . ectomorphic; sex . . . unknown."

Denning made his own translations. The figure coming up the mesa wall had a lean build, was shorter than he was, and its sex was unknown. The last bit of information was an inadequate answer by the automatons, and he wondered if they were malfunctioning. Maybe the oncoming figure wasn't human at all.

He waited.

Twenty minutes passed and then the figure clambered over the edge of the mesa. "Welcoom," it said in a sibilant voice. "Us welcoom you."

Denning rose. The human, and she was human, was lean and lovely and obviously female. Her hair was bright red and partially covered with a rough piece of cloth. She wore a loose garment of similar fabric, tied at the waist with a cord.

"One of Us brought me news of your silver phallus. So I have come to see it," said the girl.

Denning deactivated his tools. The girl's speech patterns were different from his own, but not difficult to follow. And he supposed the spaceship did look something like a male generative organ, though he'd never thought of it in that light.

Before he could explain his mission, the girl defined her own. "I am Wurlida, the Communicator, the one who speaks for all of Us. The Communicator must handle problems with tranquility. I have made Us a promise to make contact with your phallus in a peaceful manner, so it will not bring Us harm."

He grinned at her choice of words and asked, "Where are the other members of your colony?"

"The rest of Us have tasks to perform and cannot welcoom you at this time. Will you say who you are and why you are here?"

Denning looked into her dark blue eyes and felt as though he were sinking into a quiet, translucent pool, into a place of such peacefulness that he might stay forever. He held out his hands in a gesture of friendship, palms up and empty. "I'm Jackson Denning, from Earth II. Here to make a routine inspection for the Romner Institute."

"I do not understand."

Denning removed a small communication box from his tool belt. "Press this against yourself. Your body heat will activate it and explain everything."

As she held the box against her breast, he had a sudden desire to trade places with the box.

She handed it back. "I dislike its message," she announced. "Your box tells me you come from a place familiar to the ancestors of Us, but it provides little else. There is emptiness of soul in such communication."

"It's against regulations for me to do this, but I'll try to explain things." Denning wondered what he could say. Tell her he was here to confiscate any resources her people had developed? That his real purpose in coming was to assist his political leaders in the exploitation of the colony? And all to advance the careers of the politicians who had sent him here?

"I've come to help you," he said, hating his false words. "We want to ensure that your people are fulfilling the requirements for colonization. You need to account for the self-replicating equipment that was left with your ancestors. And there are the taxes. These must be satisfied either in goods or in credit. This is all written in the original contract your people entered into."

"Coom," Wurlida beckoned. "And I will try to understand that which I do not. Taxes? What is that? The word has a malicious sound."

"Oh, no," he lied. "Nothing bad. All I do is start counting things. Your equipment and so forth. That's all. I'll be here only a short time."

She had no answer.

Treading carefully along a narrow zigzag pathway cut into the hillside, he followed her down the side of the mesa. Her small body moved rapidly and with lithe grace. Like a red fox, he thought, and was tempted to reach out and touch her hair, the back of her neck, her small rounded buttocks; to lay his hands wherever he pleased. What the hell is wrong with me? he wondered. Pheromones or isolation? One or the other of them had gotten to him. He fought the urge to fondle her.

"Does someone live with you?" he asked, hoping

she'd say no. He inhaled her fragrance, a warm female scent that tickled his appetite.

"I am self-sufficient," she replied.

When they reached the bottom of the mesa, he gazed upon a vast plain laid out in a checkerboard of vivid green vegetation and brown soil. Here and there, figures moved back and forth across the green areas. The colony must be agrarian, he decided.

"Where are your structures?" Denning asked. "Your places of business, your houses?"

"There is my dwelling." Wurlida pointed to an opening in the mesa wall they had just descended. "Coom, and we will discuss the matters that concern you."

"That's your home?"

"It is not satisfactory?"

"It's fine. Where do the other colonists live?"

"In similar places." She pointed to several other mesas rising from the plain. "Today, none of Us are at home. All but myself. The rest work the garden."

"That's all one garden, and all the colonists are there?"

"Yes. We work cooperatively."

Good, he thought; that will make it easier to count them. It was obvious to Denning that these people lived in a more primitive society than the Romner Institute had prophesied.

He followed Wurlida into the darkness of her dwelling. When his eyes had adjusted to the dim light, he saw that the interior was furnished with numerous cushions, a small table and a few dishes. Comfortable but simple; the place shouldn't justify too high a tax assessment.

He touched the evaluation counter on his waist, and it appraised and registered the quality and approximate dimensions of Wurlida's home. Actually, it's her dimensions I'm interested in, he admitted to himself, and felt an overpowering desire to slide his hands across her bare skin.

Wurlida turned and abruptly dropped her rough garment to her waist. Two pink breasts thrust themselves in his direction. She stepped toward him. "Welcoom to my

home. I am pleased to make love with you.'' She released
the cord that was tied around her waist.

His first reaction was shock. This was no girl! A small
penis and two testicles dangled between her—no, his?—
legs. Denning's desire waned.

"Do you prefer female or male?" Wurlida asked. "I
can offer either."

"I prefer female!" he shouted, caught himself and
spoke more softly. "I'm sorry, I don't mean to offend
you."

"I only wish to bring you comfort and love. That is
our custom and my greeting from Us. If female is your
preference, I will be that for you."

With a voluptuous twist of her body, Wurlida lay on
her back and slowly fanned her legs outward, lifting her
hips slightly to display her female parts to him. The movement was so sensual, so slow and inviting, that for a moment Denning forgot the complication of the male
anatomy.

I need a drink, he thought, and took a step backward.

"You don't like me?" Wurlida asked.

"I didn't say that."

"You must accept my offer. I am the Communicator.
To deny my hospitality would be an offense against all
of Us."

Denning nodded weakly. What did his manual say?
Practice diplomacy, but don't fraternize. One out of two
wasn't bad. "I don't want to be rude, but I'll be the
male."

His hands were shaking, so he thrust them in his pockets.

"And I will welcoom your maleness." Wurlida's manner of speech was exquisite, perfectly shaped words is-
suing from a perfect mouth, so moist and full. He could
almost taste the saltiness of her lips.

She rose and again Denning stared at her lower parts
and saw her as male, a strange, boyish sort of male, yet
somehow beguiling and erotic. Silently, he chastised himself for twisted thoughts. He lifted his head and saw Wur-

lida's breasts, so round and pink, and desire surged
through him and came to rest in his groin.

"If we do this," he said, "you understand I can't show
favoritism to the colony? I mean, I'll still have to make
an honest accounting for my report. It's my duty."

"Whatever you wish," she replied, her words a soft
seduction, her blue eyes a drowning pool.

Denning undressed hurriedly, tossed his uniform and
boots into a heap in one corner of the cave. Whatever
Wurlida had to offer, he would accept her hospitality. Her
chemistry, her intriguing chemistry, overpowered the rules
and regulations he was supposed to obey. He wanted to
drown in her beautiful body. She was a freak . . . but did
that matter? With one not very large exception, she was
a beautiful, soft-spoken female. That was enough.

He crawled on top of her and caressed her. Pushing her
male apparatus out of his way, he invaded her roughly,
as he would continue to invade and invade and invade,
forever if he could. He didn't need a drink, he needed
Wurlida, his great, limitless elixir from the Gods. She
sucked him in with insatiable thirst, drawing him into herself, pulling him tighter and closer. He made love until
he was spent, and then rolled onto his back with a satisfied
groan.

Wurlida bent over him, moving her fingers softly across
his body. She sat back on her heels. "You are only
male?" she asked with a note of pity. "So inefficient. It
is much better to be two than one. Each of Us is two."

Denning emerged from his descent into ecstasy. "Inefficient? Aren't you satisfied?"

"Much satisfied, Jackson Denning. You are part of me
now. How could I not be satisfied?"

"Then let's not spoil it with criticism." He stretched
his arms and got to his feet. "The 'Us' you keep referring
to . . . members of your colony, I assume? Are they also
two-sexed?"

"Our legends tell that once our ancestors lived on Earth
II, until a man of science decided to alter our destiny.
Romner was his name, the name on the side of your silver

phallus. Our ancestors. thirty-two of Us, were pseudo-hermaphrodites, born with the appendages of both sexes. Yet one or the other of these parts was nonfunctioning, until Romner transformed Us. Now we are true hermaphrodites.''

''Like newts and mollusks?'' he asked.

''I wouldn't know,'' she said. ''I only know about my people. Romner altered the structure of our ancestors' bodies and therefore the structure of their children and their children's children.''

Denning shook his head. So this was the secret they hadn't wanted to tell him at the Institute. Genetic tampering.

''Why was all this done?'' he asked. ''Not that there's always a logical reason for governmental decisions, mind you.''

''It was done to see how well a new breed of humans could endure long voyages between the stars. To keep Us satisfied, reduce quarrels and killings between male and female. Pairing becomes a simple matter. No worry over choices.''

''Good God!'' said Denning. He hesitated. ''And can you satisfy yourselves as well? You actually don't need anyone else?''

''I have a need, as do all of Us. But there is little quarreling among my people. Though I sometimes war with myself. As I do now, Jackson Denning. I wish to remain female for you, yet my male side argues for a chance to please you as well.''

Denning changed the subject quickly, though desire was beginning to take hold of him again for the female Wurlida. ''Do you have anything to drink?'' he asked. ''Something fermented? Something to relax me? Well, not exactly relax me.''

''Yes,'' she replied with a smile and fetched a glass of golden liquid. ''It will bring the fire inside you to its greatest heat,'' she promised.

He sniffed it . . . it smelled good. He touched his tongue to it . . . it tasted all right. And he drank it.

* * *

Several days later, Denning awoke to reality. He'd ignored his mission, spent three days—or was it four?—immersed in a sexual liaison so convoluted, so bizarre and so wondrous that he doubted he would ever be satisfied with anything or anyone else as long as he lived. Wurlida, his love, his addiction, lay warm and glowing beside him. He hated to rise from his bed of pillows, was not even sure that he could, but responsibility called.

"I hate to leave your bed," he said, "but I must get on with data collection and my report. The Institute sent me here to do a job, and I have to perform."

"I understand. My people also make sacrifices for the good of Us."

"Not exactly a sacrifice; it's more of a responsibility. Tell me more about this colony, about your culture. What do you produce? What resources have you discovered?"

I'll get this job done, Denning thought, and then I'll take Wurlida back to bed. Perhaps I can take her to Earth II with me. No one needs to know about her . . . peculiarity. I'll get an Earth job. We can be like other people. No, we can't have children; they might have their mother's affliction.

Denning's thoughts roiled about in his head, confusing him further. I need her, his mind screamed silently. And I need to do my job. But if I do my job, I'll betray her.

"I will show you the garden," she answered. "So you can begin your counting."

While they walked, Denning asked, "Can you tell me more about the equipment that was left with you?" He thought her expression reflected puzzlement. "The equipment was self-replicating; it could reproduce itself. There should be a great deal for me to inspect."

"Gone," Wurlida answered. "Thrown into the inner-world fires long before I was born. A necessary sacrifice, my great-parent told me. Such machinery could only bring dissension and pain to our colony. It was destroyed to save Us from the fate Earth II has inflicted upon you."

"What fate?"

"Both my female and my male care for you," she said

softly. "But you demolish yourself with your talk of taxes and contracts, whatever they are. Our ancestors wanted a different life for Us, not the existence they'd known on Earth II. Purgatory, they called it."

"By destroying the equipment, you've breached your contract!" Denning cried. "They won't like that back on Earth II." He clicked the communication box and handed it to her. "It will give you information about the contract, all its clauses and amendments and so forth."

Wurlida held it against her breast again. "It reveals more but is the same as before, an empty communication," she complained. "Legends tell Us of promises made. But your world broke its part of the bargain. Until this time, you never returned to Us as you said you would. You abandoned the colony. Why should we owe your world anything?"

"That won't matter to my government. For two centuries you haven't paid your taxes. This means late penalties. With taxation there are always penalties, and in your case I foresee compound interest. They'll make you pay, even if it isn't your fault."

He ended his tirade. What am I doing? he thought. I can't live without Wurlida, and I'm driving her away from me. She's bewitched me with chemistry or mind control. Could she have done so in order to avoid taxes? No, no. No one could make love with such intensity and not mean it.

"I have this responsibility," he said, and he clutched Wurlida tightly against him, as if to reassure himself that she wasn't a reality image, that she was a living, breathing human being.

"There is the garden," said Wurlida, pulling herself free and pointing. "And Us."

Denning watched the colonists tilling the garden with primitive tools. Some individuals were homely, some attractive; some looked masculine and some feminine. Nothing in their behavior or appearance hinted at the vast difference that separated these people from himself. They waved and smiled as he passed.

I'm selling them out, he thought. And there's nothing I can do about it.

His evaluation counter clicked and counted on an automatic setting as they hiked from field to field. "That is all of Us," said Wurlida.

Denning checked the count. "Only two thousand and twenty-eight people. This is all of you? After all these years, there ought to be more."

"Births are controlled by Us and some babies die," Wurlida explained. "There is sufficient food for all, but more births would upset the balance."

I know what I'll do, Denning thought. And with a quick entry he doubled the count. Each person here is two!

"And what are your crops?" he asked.

"Vegetables, fruit, a variety of low-growing nuts."

"Do they have any special properties? Something of importance?"

She laughed. "They keep Us alive. That's important enough."

Vegetables! A low tax base here. Perhaps, he thought, if I write that in my report they'll leave this planet alone. How could he protect these people and do his job at the same time?

"Are you satisfied?" asked Wurlida. "You've counted and measured and put all the numbers into that machine attached to your waist. This is all there is of Us. What more do you want?"

"I want to see the place where your ancestors destroyed the equipment that was left with them. I'm sorry, but this information has to be included in my report."

"We'll go to the fire cave, and then you'll be finished?"

"With the colony, yes, but never with you. After I see the fire cave . . . could we make love again?" I have a couple of days, he thought. I can't tell her I'm leaving. Not yet. I have to love her again.

"I think you have made a choice," Wurlida said. "I think you will be leaving Us shortly for Earth II."

He felt another lie forming in his mouth, suppressed it and did not reply to her statement. She was right. There was no other choice for him. His time for departure was approaching rapidly, and the ship would go without him if he wasn't aboard at the programmed time. But God, he wanted her. Now, and always!

"I won't tell them the truth," he said. "I'll protect you." How? He wasn't sure he could betray the trust his government had placed in him to fulfill an important task. But on the other hand, he felt a growing obligation to the colony . . . to Wurlida.

She led him past the gardens to a rocky hill. "An entrance has been cut into the rocks that lead to the fire core." She pushed aside some greenery and slipped through a narrow opening. Denning stumbled along behind her until they entered a cavern. He flashed a light across the cavern's walls. Faceted outcroppings glittered in the half-light of the cave. Jewels? he wondered, and manually entered the information into his evaluation counter. There might be something of value here after all. And what about Wurlida? Is she also property to be bought and sold? No more than that? He couldn't bear the thought. Wurlida was special. Her qualities would not show up in any sterile government report.

They were greeted by a masculine-looking hermaphrodite with sweat dripping from its muscular body. "Welcoom," it cried. "I am Keeper, one who guards the fire."

"Keeper will tell Us if there is too much fire activity, so those within range can safely retreat," added Wurlida.

"It's a volcano," said Denning. "Is it active?"

"If we anger it," answered Keeper. "There is a hole in the cave floor, and within the hole the center of our planet delivers fire to bring heat and comfort to the sick and disabled."

"It is also the place where our ancestors disposed of the equipment," said Wurlida. "And other things."

Denning bent over a jagged hole that covered a portion of the cave floor, and he gasped. Heat swirled around him like a living being. Below him, a red inferno simmered, sucking the breath from his lungs. He slid backward and wiped his forehead. "Can we go back outside?" he asked. "The air in here is suffocating."

"You are not accustomed to it," Wurlida said and led him back outside. "Stay here. I have some words for Keeper."

When she returned, he was sitting in deep grass. "I've made us a bed," he said.

"A fine bed," she agreed and lay down beside him.

Denning buried himself in passion and entered the little death that drowned out sound and sight and left only touch and taste and smell.

"I love you," whispered Wurlida. "But I'm breaking the rules of Us by remaining with you too long."

Denning groaned a protest. "Once more, once more," he cried.

"I think not," said a rough voice, and Denning felt a hard blow against his head and sank deep into darkness.

"You've slept too long with the freak," said Keeper. "I had to save you from yourself." He laid Denning's unconscious body inside the cave, near the fire hole. "When you left the cave and came back to talk with me, I warned you. Yet you ignored my warning. You understand that your friendship with this Incomplete must end? He is no different from the single-sexed children born to Us. They are sacrificed, and you must sacrifice him."

"I love him," answered Wurlida. "Can't I keep him a little longer?"

"Our law must be obeyed."

"I understand."

The two of them slid Denning's limp body toward the fire hole, Wurlida holding his feet, Keeper his shoulders. Unnoticed by either of them, Denning's tool belt fell to the ground.

Wurlida wiped her damp eyes and bent over Denning's prostrate body. "I am sorry. Forgive me for the death you must suffer. As your culture does, mine demands certain sacrifices, and I must make them." She looked up at Keeper. "He had certain responsibilities. He might have abandoned them for me. I wish I could do the same."

"Your duty is to the colony," said Keeper.

They slid Denning into the smoldering inferno and bowed their heads in respect.

Keeper reached down and picked up the fallen tool belt. "What's this?" he asked. Without waiting for Wurlida's reply, he cast it into the fire.

BLOOD KNOT

Steve Rasnic Tem

Steve Rasnic Tem's recent and forthcoming stories include appearances in the anthologies *100 Wicked Little Witches, Flesh Fantastic, Xanadu 3, It Came from the Drive-In, Year's Best Fantasy & Horror* and *Sisters of the Night,* and in the magazines *Hardboiled, Blood Songs* (Australia), *All Hallows* (England) and *Pirate Writings.* He recently edited an anthology of Colorado fantasy, sf and horror, *High Fantastic,* out from Ocean View Press this summer.

"Just a damn knot. You can't untie it; you can't burn it off. Older you get, the tighter it gets. Might as well accept it, 'cause that's the way it is. What else you going to do? Kill everybody in the family? Jesus Christ, it's a goddamned blood knot.''

I heard my daddy say this when I was thirteen, fourteen, something like that. We were at our last family reunion: Daddy, me and sis, and Daddy's fourth wife,

June. "June bug," he called her—I guess because she was so much younger than he. Flash-forward ten years later and there Daddy is in a hospital bed coughing his lungs out. He pulls me closer—I was in my Army fatigues—and with breath that smelled like shit he tells me, "I married my June bug 'cause she was so young I knew the rest of the family wouldn't approve and they'd have nothing to do with her. Had me a ready-made excuse to stay away from the rest of them, give myself some breathin' room. With your family, well, you're who you are, but then you're not who you are, you know what I mean? Because you can't move. You can't change. Too bad she was so damn dumb."

I thought he was a fool. He had everything I'd ever wanted: kids, and a house, and more than one wife who'd loved him more than he'd deserved, surely more than was good for her. By then I'd found out that I had no talent for girlfriends, not even bad ones. They never lasted long enough to get bad. They never lasted long enough to be a pleasant memory after they were over. I was too reckless, or I wasn't reckless enough. I was too kind, or I wasn't kind enough. Something. Whatever it was that brought out the skittishness, the scared-dog look, in those women, I had. In plentiful supply. I asked, even begged sometimes, for answers, and it was always something like, "Maybe it's the way you talk," or, "Maybe it's all that stuff you think about." And that was if I *really* made them give me an answer. But they didn't know. I didn't know, and they didn't know. Hell, I thought being a little weird *attracted* some women. But not in my case.

"Some things are fated. Maybe you've got bad fate, or something, Harold." That was Linda, the night before she left me. She held me, and she let me cry in her bed, and she listened while I spilled my guts about needing a family of my own, someone I could love like I was supposed to, and she was good, so good she brushed away my embarrassment when she brushed away my tears, and the next day she left me. Fate, I guess.

Well, fuck her. She was good to me that night, but fuck her.

I'm not sure, but I think Daddy killed June one night, shortly after I'd turned eighteen. I don't know—we just never saw her around again. There'd been a lot of noise, a lot of drinking. I'm sorry to say that at the time I felt a big load had been taken off, because of the way she looked at me, the funny way she made me feel. Daddy always said she never really was part of the family. She kept herself apart and, after all, she wasn't blood. And she was young, too young to understand him, or us, or much of anything about living, I guess. Maybe that was why I could feel about her the way I did—my own step-mother after all. She wasn't blood, and like he'd always told me himself, blood is everything.

I don't know what Daddy would have made of my three daughters. I don't want to know. If he had lived I wouldn't have let him anywhere near them—even if somebody'd pulled off his arms and snipped off his balls. I had that dream once, where somebody cut him up like that. He didn't even scream. In fact, he thanked the man, the man in the shadows holding the razor. He smiled and said, "Thank you very much—I sure needed that," even as the blood spurted from his crotch like some kind of orgasm that had been going on too long. I don't know if it was a nightmare or not.

"It don't matter if you like your family or not. You're tied to 'em; might as well accept that. It's in the blood."

So, yeah, it finally happened. I met my own June, only her name was Julie, and she was quite a bit younger, and not very smart. I oughtta be embarrassed saying that, I guess. But I'm not. I did love her; still do, I'm sure. A person doesn't have to be smart, or the right age, for you to love them.

I'm never going to know, I guess, if she really loved me, or if it was just because she was younger, and not knowing what love is really, and then the girls came along; and so, like any good mother—and I'll always swear that she was a good mother—she stuck with the father of those children—however strange his thinking— and said that she loved him with all her heart. And maybe she did. Maybe she did. I've never really understood women. Not my wife. And not my daughters.

But oh, I've loved my daughters. All three of them, precious as tears. Only a couple of years apart—Julie for some crazy reason thought I wanted a son, so she insistedwe keep trying, but I was overjoyed, I felt blessed, to have daughters—but my oldest, Marcie, was small for her age, and my youngest, Ann, was taller than average, and my middle daughter, Billie, was just like the middle bear, *just* right, so the three of them together were taken all the time for triplets. We were always told how adorable they were, how beautiful. People were just naturally attracted to them. And the boys? Boys are always just naturally drawn to something a little different. I know.

Things were pretty much okay until the girls got to be teenagers. Don't tell me about that being a hard time of life. I know that's a hard time of life, but knowing that still doesn't help a father much. The girls started wanting dates and it was okay with their mother, because Julie just didn't know no better, I guess. They were too damned young and I said so, but of course they went and done it anyway, and after a while I just got tired of watching them and chasing after them and let them just go right ahead and date too young and ruin their lives—what was I supposed to do?

Oh, I still loved them, you can count on that, but I have to say I was mad at them most of the time.

But my girls sure looked beautiful in those date dresses of theirs—so beautiful I couldn't stand to look at them when they were all dolled up.

They tell you on "Oprah" and "Donahue" and every other damn program what to do with your kids, but they don't tell you a damn thing that helps. They act like kids and their families are separate people that have to *negotiate* every damn thing. They just don't understand that a family's got to be all tied up in knots you can't get loose of no matter how hard you try. Cut those knots apart and somebody's bound to wind up bleeding to death on the floor.

I don't know if my girls knew I still loved them. I couldn't be sure, 'cause I stopped telling them I loved them once the oldest got to be thirteen. That might not have been the right thing to do, but I just didn't feel right, telling a young, fresh-faced beauty of thirteen that I loved her. Perverts do that, not a good family man. Not a father.

Besides, they shoulda known. They shoulda always known. We were blood, weren't we, all tied together?

The girls started their periods early. Hell, the youngest—my baby Ann—was nine, and you know that can't be right. My wife handled that stuff, of course, but she still talked to me about it—I don't know why women like to talk about such things. She told me the baby *was* young to be having her period, but that was becoming more and more common these days; but as far as I was concerned, that was hardly any kind of recommendation. Not much right about these days, what with baby girls having periods and watching actual live sex acts on the TV when their daddies ain't around. And their mothers making it a secret, too. Mothers and daughters, they always have these secrets that no man alive can understand.

What was I supposed to do about any of it? What could I do?

People expect the man to change the world, but the world is a damned hard thing to change—it just rolls on pretty much the way it wants to until it runs right over you.

Sometimes all the females in the house had their periods at the same time and the blood stank up everything and I'd wake up in the middle of the night and sometimes Julie wouldn't be in the bed and then she'd come back and say *why* she'd just been down the hall in the bathroom, but the bathroom was near where the girls slept and I'd think every time, I'd sit there in the dark and think, *What if Julie and my girls are down the hall drinking some man's blood?*

Now, I know that ain't true and it's a pretty crazy way to think, but I wasn't always sure at the time. My girls' breasts were getting bigger every day and it seemed to me they weren't eating enough at meals to be puttin' on that kind of weight.

Then one day I thought I had it figured out—they were

bleeding out and they were getting breasts and hair in return, breasts and hair so they could fuck as many guys as they could before they got too old to enjoy it.

And, of course, what they were bleeding out was the family blood, dumping it like it was something dirty and all used up and something they didn't need anymore.

They were fools, of course. Like you could untie the knot by disrespecting it that way. What right did they have anyway? I was tied to them so hard I wasn't ever going to get loose, so why should *they* get their freedom? What had they ever done to earn it? Here I was, having done everything for Julie and the girls, and I was going to be tied to it forever. I wasn't ever going to be rid of the taste of their blood, their dirt, their flesh. I was going to die choking on it.

I can't even say I didn't like the taste of that knot. That salty, ocean taste, like it was everything we'd ever come from for thousands of years. I can't say I didn't like it—maybe if you have something shoved in your face long enough, you hate it for a while, but maybe there comes a point—years maybe—when it's been shoved there so often you just start liking it again. You feed on it and after a while maybe that's all you live for, practically.

That was me and my wife and my girls. Our blood knot. I loved them and I hated them and then I loved them so much I couldn't be without them, couldn't let them out of my sight. It was like I had the taste of them in my mouth all the time and I was liking that taste more and more, and I just couldn't live without it, no way.

If they'd stayed home more often, things probably would've turned out okay. Maybe I would get tired of them, tired of the taste and smell of them, and I'd get tired of it all like I did when they first wanted to date, and then I'd just let them do what they damn well pleased. Julie could have made them stay home if she'd had the mind, but I married her too young and she was just too damned dumb. A good mother in every other way, but too dumb for my girls, I'm sorry to say.

I loved my girls; I loved them dear. I started trying to tell them that so maybe they'd stay at home, but it didn't work. My youngest, my baby Ann, she even laughed at me, and what's a man supposed to do with that? I would've hit her real hard right then and there, but at that point I still couldn't hit my baby girl. The other two, but not her.

I should've had boys, should've made Julie give me boys, but I never could've loved boys that way. I don't know if that's a good thing or a bad thing.

Let me explain something: I know I wasn't always the best father and husband. If I had been, I wouldn't have let things get so far. A good father and husband keeps a lid on things, keeps things from going so far. Keeping things from going so far—with his kids, his wife, the neighbors—that's the main thing a father's supposed to be doing. And I know I failed at that one.

Things collect, and they don't go away. Things get together, you get too many of them, and then things go too far.

Knots get untied. Blood gets spilled on the old, dry wooden floor, and the floor soaks it up so fast you can't believe it, lots faster than you can clean it up, and pretty soon the whole floor is stained red and everything you look at looks red.

I think they all four must have been having their period. They weren't complaining about it, but the whole house smelled like it and I tasted it in every meal for two days and I breathed that blood in every time I opened my mouth and all my clothes smelled like it and even the newspaper, and two nights running my dreams were so red I couldn't make out a thing in them.

Marcie had come back from one of her "dates." Fuck fests, more like it, but a father can't say that in front of his daughters and still be a good father. I just smiled at her and asked, "Have a nice time?" And she just stared at me, looking scared. There was no point in that—I loved her—didn't she know that?

Then I saw that my baby Ann was with her.

"What the fuck!" I yelled and immediately felt bad, saying the F word in front of my girls, but it was already out there and I couldn't get it back inside.

"Had me my first date, Daddy!" Ann piped up with her little dolly's voice. "Mom said it was okay with her. Me and Marcie, we *doubled*."

I couldn't say a damn thing, just stared at the two of them all made up like models, or whores. They'd put me down in a box, and I couldn't see how to climb my way out. I turned around and went into the bedroom and closed the door, sat down to think. Once you got a family, you don't get too much time to think.

I felt all loose with myself. I felt *untied*. The women in a family, they have a way of doing that to their men.

Being in a family is like being in a dream. You don't know if it's a good dream or a bad dream. You don't know if you're up or down. Everything moves sideways, until, before you know it, you're back where you started again, like you hadn't moved anywhere at all. That's where I was, moving sideways so fast but not going nowhere.

My girls, they started the untying. It wasn't me that did that part. My beautiful, beautiful girls. I just finished what they started.

But when you start untying that blood knot, it's more blood than anyone can imagine. It goes back forever, that blood. You taste it and you breathe it and it stains the floor and it stains the walls and it stains the skin, until you're some kind of cartoon running around stabbing and chopping and tasting.

My babies' breasts like apples, like sweet onions, like tomatoes.

Once they were all in the blood, it was like they were being born again, crying out, "I love you, Daddy," and I could kiss them and there was not a damn thing wrong with any of it, 'cause daddies are supposed to love their babies.

Because they're your blood, you see. And you're tied to them forever.

INTERROGATOR FRAMES

Rob Hardin

Rob Hardin is a studio musician and writer who lives in a potentially lethal sector of the Lower East Side. His writing has appeared in *Mississippi Review, Fiction International, Postmodern Culture, Future Sex, Red Tape, Black Ice, Puck* and *Cups*, and in the anthologies *Avant Pop, Atomic Avenue* and *Storming the Reality Studio*. Currently at work on his second novel, he is also an editor of the literary magazine *Sensitive Skin*. Recent music projects include *Pillbox* (Feralette), *22 Brides* (Zero Hour) and "Save Yourself," a video for Arthur Baker's *Nation of Abel*. His hypertext work-in-progress, *Matterland*, is accessible by webpage address: http://www.interport.net/~scrypt/.

From the late edition of *The New York Times*, March 30, 1992:

New Nerve Tissue Generated from the Brain Cells of Rats

The adult mammalian brain, long thought to be incapable of repairing itself, possesses a pool of immature cells that can be coaxed to divide into new nerve tissue, scientists have found.

The discovery is the first compelling evidence that the adult brain retains the potential to generate fresh nerve cells—a talent ordinarily limited to the embryo.

Studying the brains of grown rats, Dr. Samuel Weiss and Dr. Brent A. Reynolds of the University of Calgary Faculty of Medicine in Alberta, Canada, discovered a hidden reservoir of cells that, when placed in a test tube and treated with a powerful stimulatory protein called epidermal growth factor, would bloom into neurons, with long, willowy tendrils, telltale signaling molecules and other hallmarks of nerve cells.

"It left us speechless," Dr. Weiss said. "We were trying to explain this to ourselves, before we decided to explain it to the rest of the world."

February 20, 2012
SoHo, New York City

The afternoon sky was a lacerated painting of brain rape. It darkened with violet slashes, webs of black mold, pineal eyes. As Rachael stared at it, she tried to forget all that was mindlessly representational. It was as if the perfect, nearly intangible music of Josquin des Prez were hidden behind a wall of cadaverous gurgling. She couldn't seem to clear away the human appendages, the semen that clouded the lens. Her ghosts had an odor that would not be washed away.

The ceiling of the Neurolab hung above her, a viscid overlay of pain that deepened as the sunlight faded. It sucked her sex through holes that passed for shadows: stigmata'd hands swallowed her thoughts, memory wounds clenched to anuses. She wanted to relax, as the doctors had suggested, to let the violet embers eat through her. But the burn-holes widened to ovoid screens—monitors in which fragmented scenes repeated like ostinatos.

Of her hourly terrors, she could remember only flashes: the interrogations and the injections, the silver glint of the Knife Game. Then the flashes ran together and there were no more words. All she could see were green welts in a flood of stroboscopic white.

A blade slid slowly across her temples like the rail of a boxcar closing. The strobe was burning out. Just before glare switched off, a motto scrolled across the white horizon: a brief procession of short, unreadable words. She gibbered and the light cooled to violet.

By the time the sky turned thorazine black, she'd forgotten the pain of purple. Hours of narcolepsy gave way to an idiot's twilight.

"Rrr . . . rrr . . . rrr . . ."

The sky was a millennium's mouth. A seamless shriek of amnesia.

"Easy, Rachael. You're coming out of it." She squinted: blank ovals shriveled to doctors' faces as the darkness above their heads receded into corners. The night sky became a spiderweb of cracked plaster.

"Can you feel this?" one of them asked. She couldn't. The doctors glanced at each other and smiled. She felt herself going under . . .

Fade to a waiting room suffused with tremulous light. The florescent overheads had a parkinsonian intensity, their oscillations mirroring subtle brain trauma: failing synapses, petit mal seizures.

She surveyed the space and found she'd fallen into a white hole. No window, receptionist or patients. This visit, her company was reduced to the room itself: SoHo-open, its walls barely relieved by two studies in ink watercolored pale vermilion.

Can't take it, she thought. *I'm empty enough as it is.* Her eyelids fluttered in time to the flickering lights. Tilting back, she breathed—

—and pain emptied her skull. She convulsed, flopped forward, heard a stack of magazines hit the floor. Squinting, she confronted the double exposure of damage. Wreckage settled beneath her; an eidetic flashfire ghosted the office.

"Help me," she whispered. Amnesia swallowed her eyes. The pain receded to a hollow throb; her eyes relaxed slightly. The big analog clock above the door read 11 P.M.

Reflexively, she glanced at the sand-colored end table. No paper cup, no codeine, no Xanax 0.25. Eyes followed an oblique light source to the empty admissions desk: *definitely* no Xanax.

Familiar stuff: a sixties world's fair space-needle paperweight teetered uneasily on a stack of forms. A bronze placard rested on the edge of the work surface: DR. REED DARMON, PH.D. OFC. OF RESEARCH & ENDOCRINOLOGY.

Her gaze veered to the television that gleamed in the center of the room. Usually, it was tuned to CBS. As she focused on it, the blue screen switched abruptly to a close-up of Dr. Darmon's face. His expression seemed less preoccupied than before she'd lost consciousness.

"Hi, Rachael. The growth hormone is working quite well, as you must have noticed."

Startled by his voice, she pointed to the monitor. ". . . . ."

Darmon smiled proudly. "Great, hah? Just got the system installed. Now I don't even have to leave surgery to talk."

Flat stare, raised eyebrows. "Whaddya doin' up there?"

Slight fish-frown as he dipped his head thoughtfully. "I told you. So . . . what do you think?"

You're creepier than guys at a bachelor party, she thought. "You've gutted my brain a dozen times and I can still think. Must mean something."

"Means you're a good test subject, Rachael. We pith your skull, the neurons grow back." In the background, she heard high, sleepy gibbering.

"But there's a problem, 'cause, like . . . I've been having flashbacks. The last operation . . . I remember it, even though I was knocked out. I remember the Knife Game."

He glanced away, then met her troubled stare with an expression of slight satisfaction. "Daydreams, hallucinations—all normal, considering. I wouldn't be concerned."

Knives are normal.

She faltered. "If you say so."

Darmon's smile tightened. The baby talk continued, beyond language, beyond even the imitation of speech. Abruptly, it died. His smile relaxed to neutral. "I do. Now concentrate, Rachael. I'm giving you your money and your prescriptions"—a scowl of concentration—"ATM-style. That's how it's gonna be from now on. Fewer witnesses. You understand."

A slot below the monitor glided open. She reached in and pulled out an envelope. "Shit I do to stay out of the business," she whispered.

"My best," the doctor said. His image dissolved and the monitor switched back to standby, eclipsing the screen with a visor of royal blue.

April 2, Greenwich Village
Her boyfriend's apartment

STONEWALL: 1969-2007, flashed a Christopher Street sign housed in shatterproof glass. Visible from Neil Renner's seventh-story apartment on Waverly Place, the commemorative sign seemed the only landmark that had changed since he inherited the apartment from his parents. A jalousie of slanting architecture and fruit-haloed trees obscured all other street-level scenery. Everything got lost in the Caligari angles of the view.

Rachael knew. She'd been avoiding the sight for a decade.

His apartment looked even worse: a respectable space made shithole by years of neglect. The cream-yellow walls and hardwood floor teemed with roaches. Tabletops were invisible under heaps of moldering Chinese-food containers, crumpled comic books and empty cereal boxes. His antique five-string Alembic leaned in the corner, a two-thousand-dollar gift from a younger, stupider Rachael—out of its case so long the bridge wore a Fu Manchu of dust strands. If she hadn't had to support the two of them, the place would have been presentable enough for Sunday soirees.

As Renner played with Beautiful, his pet tarantula, Rachael shook her head and smiled. It was weird to see this droopy, pallid white guy in his thirties, ring in his nose, flexing in 505s and braids two decades after the fashion, playing with Beautiful like a preoccupied, lonely child. He liked Beautiful because, like him, it was mean-looking but harmless. The venom had probably been removed from both at birth.

Beautiful disturbed Rachael—mostly because, aside from Rachael's store of self-directed venom, the two of them had so many things in common. Brown hair, dark eyes, bodies distinguished by legs as slender and expressive as fingers. A habit of clinging to Renner and caressing him at the same time. She and Renner had too much in common with Beautiful. The only difference was, she *fucked* Renner. And *he* never hurt the spider.

"When you gonna move?" she asked Renner finally.

"When you go back to dancing," he said, lifting his collar so Beautiful could crawl inside.

She drew back. "You want me to?" *Today, I made three thousand dollars. Five years ago, I'd have shared the money with you.*

His face aged suddenly. "Not here. Not in Jersey. Not in fucking Nowhere."

"We could move in with *my* parents," she said with sudden bitterness.

Smile lines appeared on his face without any perceptible change of expression. "Let's not go over that again, okay?" he said quietly. "Just please calm down."

With a deprecating smile, she shook her head. "I *am* calm."

He raised his hands frantically. "Okay, okay, you're calm. Now listen. You know I'd never consent to living in Irvington. With your mother. Or the *asshole* who fucked you up." He turned and looked out the window, revving up. "It took you *so long* to figure out why you were doing it, dancing, all of that. The fucking masochism of it. And now you—you have a really good job, and the people hired you for your natural intelligence, and when *we* fuck around, the traumatic shit's exactly where it should be. Whereas that *asshole* . . ."

She wasn't listening anymore. No matter what he said, she was still supporting him after a decade. He was still a deadbeat who'd let his girlfriend become a lobotomy volunteer or a whore before finding a job himself. And here he was, offering armchair psychological counsel—like that was compensation for all her damage and toil.

"Yeah, we're a *lot* more healthy than my dad, Renner," she snapped. "Just shut up and make me remember why I'm with you."

He stopped fucking around with Beautiful and looked at her, trying to muster lost venom. "Nobody talks to me like that."

She smiled at him, catching the signs. "I know, baby. That's exactly what I like to remember."

They'd been playing with knives for hours, until Rachael's tongue was numb with the aftertaste of tarnished steel. Then Renner took a hit of whiskey and carved a zigzag on her inner thigh. The wound was stylish, like a Beardsley asp. It darkened to red, then brimmed until he leaned over and licked off the excess. She was so fascinated that she temporarily forgot she was in pain.

Loss of blood made her eyes flicker shut. "Orange," she muttered.

He froze. "Huh? 'Orange'? You want me to stop?"

"Naw, forget it," she whispered as she fell off the edge of the world. "Pain's not bad when I'm asleep."

She woke in overcast light, her wrists restrained. *Oh goody,* she thought. *Renner's so wonderful. He knows when to slap me around.*

"Know what I wanna do?" As he stood looking down at her, she couldn't read his eyes.

"I can't tell." His smile was cryptic, his goatee the pivot of a question mark.

"THIS," he shouted, pulling the knife out of his pocket.

"Oh, you mean, mean bastard," she pleaded. "Not the knife!"

"And THIS!" He plunged the knife into the base of her skull. *Snap.* As she gazed up at him, brilliant lights surrounded his head, igniting his goatee with white fire. "I'm not worried, Rachael, are you? Like the doctor says, your brain always grows back."

He slipped a blindfold over her eyes. The shadows massed to black. White embers dimmed until she was left with an eidetic overlay of filaments: staircases made from the bones of birds.

When she tried to think, the darkness became unbearable. But when she stopped thinking and felt, the sense of isolation fell away. With blindness came familiarity; after several hours, her mind gave in. Opening to the darkness was like being a child in Daddy's lap.

"Here I am, Rachael." Renner slid under her softly. "Daddy Knife is here."

Wrists roped to the headboard of an old rocking chair, she slid down on him as he comforted her. She was safe in his arms, safe and degraded. His lap was a storybook with a dragon at the edge of the page.

Until she felt the knife. Renner wasn't using it, but his ghost was. The overlay returned; dead neurons were haunting her skull. Raking the barricades of an almost empty mind.

Viscid sky. Afternoon. The roof of her mind was the Neurolab ceiling. Stupidity closed over her thoughts as Dr. Darmon sighed, rapt in the intricacies of the Knife Game. She felt the pull of negative wind—the wind of the wing of imbecility.

Fuck Daddy Knife. Daddy was an asshole. "Orange," she said.

Renner froze. "*Huh? What?* But I'm not hurting you, Rachael."

"I said *orange*, motherfucker. Untie me *now*."

"Okay, okay. What the fuck."

"I wanna play a new game. It's called Knifey, Knifey."

"Rachael, stop."

Fuck you, she thought. *The neurotic repeats a behavior pattern without ever remembering.*

"The only way I can stop is to remember. You'll help me, right?"

"Of course I will. Anything."

She grabbed the knife. "Then sit down and shut the fuck up. Don't you ever think about anyone else? Or what I do for money, what poverty's done to me? The stripping and the prostitution? My life as a lab rat? Well, I'm gonna show you, okay? This is how you burned me, Daddy Sex and Dr. Knife."

"Rachael! Ahhh!"

"Hold still, baby," she whispered as she cut him. "I wanna show you what it's like to lose your mind."

She remembered the scalpel's progress by feel. A twist to the right erased the childhood. She'd lost hers several times, but it always grew back. Though lately it flickered like the light in Darmon's waiting room.

A twist to the left obliterated self-recognition. He jerked as she slid the blade through his skull. Now he was slumped in his chair, a man whose body had forgotten its own reclusive posture.

Shift, shift. It was as if Aubrey Beardsley had drawn a study of an autopsy. Light and shadow traced the simplification of an interior—a serigraph, a cartoon.

In this solarized video of glowing ink and stroboscopic white, Rachael slid away from the body, remembering the purity of possessing a pithed mind. Nothing survived the knife—she knew it from her dreams of idiocy, from drooled valedictions and gibbered attempts at prayer. There was only an electric hollowness, more vacant than the emptiest room.

Because Renner was living in the hole, he didn't even know he was there. The abyss was an integer blurred. Skip, Skip, One, Two. Knifey, Knifey, I Love You . . .

Perhaps she'd leave him like that for an hour, then crack the door before sensory deprivation set in.

Like hell, she thought. *I really opened up to this guy. And he's still hanging around, just to prove he loves me.*

I told you they were out there, Mother. There are guys who'll love you even after you've carved out their brains.

"Renner? Honey? Are you in pain, dear? Do you need me to wash your wounds?"

"Rrr-rrr-rrr," he replied.

"That's how I feel sometimes," she said as she stirred his brain-gook. "Like nobody in the world will ever understand."

"Rrr-rrr-rrr . . . rrr-rrr-rrr . . ." He was a gibbering idiot now, as she had been when she lay on Darmon's table, or gyrated in go-go bars, or moaned in the porn world's valent void.

But she didn't feel guilty. *I take no pleasure in the Knife Game,* she thought. *If Renner hadn't wanted to be trepanned, I'd never have done it. He just needed to relinquish control.*

She pulled out a syringe. "Look, Rrr-rrr-rrr. Growth hormone. I get it special from Dr. Darmon. Believe me, your brains will grow back."

"Rrr-rrr-rrr."

She gazed at him mistily. "After a while—after you've gone through this a few hundred times—you know what happens?"

"Rrrr."

She stirred his gook. "*Permanent memory loss.* You have all your motor coordination, speech, shit like that— but you don't have a past!"

"Rrr-rrr-rrr."

Just think, Rrr-rrr-rrr," she said as she hugged the idiot. "No dysfunctional childhood for either of us. Thanks to Dr. Darmon, we'll be the healthiest couple in the world!"

"Rrr-rrr-rrr," the idiot gurgled. Rachael couldn't tell, but she thought he was more happy than confused.

THE REAL WORLD

Brooks Caruthers

Brooks Caruthers grew up in both Denver, Colorado, and Little Rock, Arkansas, which resulted in creating a bizarre, urban-hick personality that has spewed forth three plays, a number of short stories and a style of electric bassoon playing based on the joys of drones and artificial echoes. His fiction has seen print in such off-the-wall anthologies as *Still Dead: Book of the Dead 2* and *Three-Fisted Tales of "Bob."* More recently he has composed three musicals for the Red Octopus Theater Company of Arkansas and produced no-budget videos with titles like *Theater of the Grotesque II: Even Grotesquer*. He is currently working on his first budgeted movie, a Hi8 SubGenius noir called *Killing "Bob,"* which features temporal derangements, horny army boys and a murderer who kills by ripping the legs off his victim. Brooks has known coeditor Nancy Collins since 1978, when she drove him and his best friend to a sf convention in Tulsa, Oklahoma, because he didn't have a driver's license yet. His story "The Real World" was inspired by a particularly grim season in Little Rock, where two good friends managed to die within weeks of each other.

Sunday

Barry Anderson didn't want to wake up. He wanted to remain hidden in his alcohol-soaked, lackluster dreamland. But the hangover was huge, gigantic, inescapable, and at last he awoke into an endless morning of hammers in his head and a stomach that flinched at the slightest touch of water.

The doorbell rang like salvation. Little black-haired Marcie and tall, gangly, curly-blond Tom smiled, lit from behind by a white inferno of sunlight. They stood in the doorway wearing last night's clothes and untamed hair.

"We're about to go to breakfast," said Marcie. "Come with us."

"I can't hold anything down," said Barry. "Not even water."

"Water!" Tom loped over to the porch swing, luring Barry the Vampire out into a hideous Death by Sunlight. "Water'll kill you at this point! You need cola and greasy breakfast food. Go get your keys."

They went to a pancake house full of big ol' tractor cap-wearin' boys and their weary wives. Barry watched the silent television mounted above the grill where a cathode-ray preacher cried over pictures of starving children. The radio played the old, sad stuff: *I used to drink my whiskey and have a fine old time, but then the Devil made a Christian out of me.*

Naturally, this place had the best biscuits and gravy in town. After choking down his first mouthfuls, Barry suddenly became ravenous.

Finally there was coffee. "So what're y'all up to today?"

Tom belched. "We're going to Johnson's place. Video party."

"Ten solid hours of bad horror movies, British comedy and pornographic Japanese cartoons," chimed in Marcie. "You need to come with us."

"Sounds perfect." Barry picked up the check and began to lay money on the table. "How did he talk Leslie into letting him throw this little shindig?"

"I think he had to promise her a few more pints of blood."

"Well, shit, it's not like he has that much left to give."

Marcie sighed. "Yeah. On the phone he said this will probably be his last party."

They left and drove through quiet, garbage-filled streets. The bright afternoon sun was a drill entering Barry's skull through the eyes. "I wonder if Evans will be there."

"No telling," said Tom. "They just put him in the ground yesterday."

They pulled into a quiet and serene urban neighborhood filled with simple white rectangular houses and barking dogs and screaming children and FM radios blaring generic rock beats. "I only hope," shouted Barry over the quiet serenity, "that he doesn't offer us any beer!"

Eyes on every porch in front of every perfect white house watched them as they parked in front of Johnson's house of peeling green paint and nonrectangular angles. *Oh, they're Johnson's friends,* whispered the porches.

Knock-knock. "Come in!" They entered just in time to hear a cultured British female voice say, "All I meant was I wanted to touch his willie." The TV audience laughed. A few people in the room chuckled. It was a lot of the old crowd, Davey and Christy and Sandy and Mandy and Johnny and Cindy—the Cindy who worked on cars, not the Cindy who waited tables. Evans wasn't there.

Johnson sat in his favorite chair. He had a large, muscular build, and in healthier days he'd looked like a lumberjack or something. But now his brown hair brought out the paleness of his skin, the bags under his eyes. It was as if he were caving in.

He smiled. "Hey. Glad you could make it. Have a beer."

Leslie, his wife, was looking good, all dressed in black, with generous glimpses of her thighs and cleavage. She was searching Johnson's arms for a useful vein. "There's plenty in the fridge. Help yourself."

"No, I can't, I just can't," said Barry as he watched his hands grab a beer can, open it and raise it to his lips. "Hair of the dog," he muttered out of habit.

"Hair of the dog," everyone replied.

Someone changed the tape. Barry found a place on the floor and sat to watch a cartoon Japanese woman make high-pitched scream/moans while the little guy fucking her made severe samurai grunts, as if he were performing some austere ritual.

"I still wanna put a Three Stooges soundtrack onto a porn film someday," said Johnson. " 'Hey, Moe! Hey Moe! WOO woo woo!' "

Barry snickered dutifully. Leslie found a vein, and tapped it. Blood began to flow out of Johnson's arm into a plastic tube that disappeared under Leslie's skirt. With a sigh, she sat back and fed, smiling and oblivious of the world around her. Barry couldn't help staring at her perfect curves, her high cheekbones and cascading red hair, and her shapely thighs disappearing into her short leather skirt . . . ah, to follow the blood tube into the mysteries hidden by that skirt . . .

He shook his head to break the spell. "Johnson?"

"Hmmm?"

"You know she's killing you."

"Guess so."

The cartoon woman screamed as the man turned into a multi-dicked demon. Barry leaned in closer to Johnson.

"You shouldn't let her do this."

"I know."

"Why do you?"

Johnson shrugged, smiling. "I love her."

Barry sighed and turned back to the television. Johnson's love was like a brick wall. The subject was closed.

Shadows lengthened in the room, and overtook it. No one bothered to turn on the lights. There was only the television, the pop of beer cans, the flush of the toilet, the occasional laugh or comment and the changing of the tapes.

Now teenagers danced on the television screen, young and fresh-faced, unaware of the ravening atomic monster that was about to attack their little hootenanny. Barry became fascinated by one girl who danced alone—hips swaying, eyes closed, she was deep in her own world.

So beautiful, thought Barry. *I love you, you unknown starlet who's probably fifty or older now. I hope the monster doesn't get you.*

He never found out. The lights came on. Leslie covered her husband's body with a sheet. "Thank you for coming," she said. "It meant a lot to him and me both. The funeral will be at Christ the King, this Tuesday at three o'clock in the afternoon. You can call me for directions tomorrow."

Without a word, everyone got up and left. Marcie, Tom and Barry said very little on the way home. Any words just hung in the air, futile.

Monday

Barry carefully shaved the pubic hairs off a fat, middle-aged businessman. There. One final stroke and the man's entire body, from scalp to toes, was completely hairless. The man cooed appreciatively as Barry rinsed him off with warm, soapy water. By now the regression drugs had disconnected most of the businessman's memories, learned traits and personality—taking him back to a new-born infant's state of mind.

Shaved, cleaned, dried, powdered and diapered, the businessman was now ready to enter the playroom. Barry and another attendant shifted him onto a chair and wheeled him to the entrance. The door opened with a music-box tinkle and playroom attendants helped them heave the man off the chair. They set him down and let him crawl into infancy.

Barry's rubber gloves snapped as he stripped them off and dropped them in the trash. He headed into the break room for a cup of coffee. Another preparation attendant was already there, smoking. Through a one-way mirror they watched a select group of the city's well-to-do try out the latest fad therapy—the movers and shakers of the city, and their spouses, reduced to bald and diapered infants who rolled around on one another, chewed on soft toys and sucked at the gigantic breasts that lined the walls of the nursery.

The businessman wasted no time, crawling over to a small Oriental woman and taking away her stuffed puppy. As she began to howl, plastic-and-rubber-clad playroom attendants moved in to settle the fracas, giving the puppy back to the woman and trying to interest the businessman in a teddy bear. He fussed and wet himself.

"Fuckin' rich bastards," said the smoker. "All that money and this is how they spend it."

"Keeps you and me employed."

"Great job, huh." It was a ritual conversation, a worker's bond, like talk about movies they'd seen and gossip about celebrity genitals they'd shaved.

A woman in the playroom began shrieking. The playroom attendants tried to calm her, to no avail. One hit a button on the wall, setting off a buzzer in the break room.

"Shit." Barry sighed, put on another pair of gloves and headed out. He helped the attendants lead the woman to one of the womb rooms. Surrounded by plastic-and-rubber men, the woman struggled and shrieked even more.

Barry suddenly realized that he knew her. She'd been the local hot new artist a few years ago. She painted empty suburban rooms, still lives of bedrooms and dens, all normal except for the shadows of unseen creatures that crept in dark corners. In many of the paintings the rooms were cobwebbed with strange little lines that widened into cracks through which teeth and red lights could be seen . . . Her flash in the pan had died when she'd married some rich guy and her painting output tapered off. Couldn't remember her name . . .

Barry sat with the woman in the womb room, a room of soft rose light and a mother's heartbeat. He took off his gloves and mask so she could feel a human touch— strictly against the rules, of course, but he knew her, so fuck the rules. She hid her face in his stomach and calmed down a bit. Occasionally she'd peek out and her eyes would dart around frantically and she'd hide her face again.

Barry wondered if she'd been like this in her childhood. He knew children who seemed haunted, who even as infants seemed to be having the most horrible nightmares, as if they were remembering an atrocity from a past life, or seeing something that only the very young can see.

He held the frightened infant painter as she stared fearfully at the cracks in their shared reality.

Even with the stereo cranked, Barry's house was achingly silent. He tried television. He tried to read. The TV just showed riots and madness, sex and death. Between the lines of the book he was reading he began to see the hairline reality cracks from the woman artist's paintings.

He switched TV channels and saw the Warholian party scene from the movie *Midnight Cowboy.* Johnson's corpse, sunken and wan, sat in the corner with a drink.

Barry remembered that a house of Deadheads up the street was having a party. *Party on Monday night? What the hell . . .*

Six-pack in hand, Barry stepped into a miasma of tie-dyes and "Sugar Magnolia." Fortunately, Charlie and Cindy were there—the Cindy who waited tables, not the Cindy who fixed cars. They talked for a while about Johnson's death—hell, there was no avoiding the grim depression of it, but at least the loud music and the beer sealed the reality cracks.

"Barry, you fuckhead!" said a loud, obnoxious voice. "How're you doing?"

Barry turned. "Evans! Jeesus!" He hugged Evans, trying to avoid the big hole in his back. "Didn't we put you in the ground last week?"

"Sure did."

Evans looked pretty good, all things considered. The car wreck had punctured his abdomen and his chest, and he'd lost an eye, the right one, leaving only a bruised and sunken eyelid. Alive, he'd been something of a lady's man, short, blond and willing to fuck all night, the most satyrlike person Barry had ever known. The only thing that kept Evans from scoring more often was his eagerness . . . it was as if the girls could see him sprouting horns and goat's feet.

"Hey," said Barry, "let's get out of this noise and talk."

Outside was a crescent moon and the burning orange light of the city around the horizon. Tie-dyed boys and neohippie girls sipped beer and talked about acid and bootleg tapes.

"Gah," said Barry. "I can't believe you missed your own wake."

"I know. I wanted to be there, but that funeral just wore me out. I mean, not only did those fuckin' ministers not even know me, but hell, they had to make the whole thing a big commercial for Christianity. I *hate* fuckin' Christianity. I was pounding the walls of the casket, I was so mad."

"That thumping sound—that was you? That was great! It shook up that one ol' boy so much he stopped in the middle of his sermon."

"He did, didn't he?" Evans started laughing convulsively, all anger forgotten. "Oh, well, that's what I get for not leaving a will."

They went back in for more beer. The inevitable joint was floating around. Barry partook, wondering if the coughing agony was really worth it.

Time slowed down. The Grateful Dead twanged away, on and on. Barry found himself staring at this one girl who danced by herself. She looked familiar, a brunette with creamy white skin. Her pageboy haircut seemed at odds with her tie-dyed tunic, but it didn't matter, she danced barefoot and beautiful.

"What's her name?" Evans shouted into his ear.

"I don't know, but she's sure making me horny."

"Go for it! I would. I'd fuck her in a minute!"

"Well, hell, you're the fuck machine. Go ask her if she's a necrophile."

Evans giggled. "Okay. I'll just ask her if she's ever danced with a dead man before."

Evans went to talk to the girl. Barry couldn't hear what they said. He looked around at all the Grateful Dead paraphernalia in the room. There was a giant black-and-white poster of Jerry Garcia peering out over the tops of his glasses. The more Barry tried to avoid looking at it, the larger it became.

Evans sat down next to him. "Her name is Angela. You should go talk to her."

The music stopped. "Please! For God's sake!" shouted Barry. "Put on something besides the Grateful Dead!"

"How about the Jerry Garcia Band?"

"Aaaaaaugh!"

He had to have another beer, another beer, another beer, *twang, twang, twang*, while dear dead Evans followed him around saying, "I don't care what you say. Jerry's one of the world's best guitarists."

Barry couldn't resist his favorite joke. "Yeah, you know what Richard told me, back before the zombies got him. He said, 'Jerry Garcia. You know, I spent the night with Jerry Garcia in a prison cell in New Mexico. I fucked him up the ass . . . but I had to think of Bob Weir in order to come!' Yuk, yuk, yuk!"

"Wha—?" Evans started laughing. He went into a laughing fit, clutching his stomach as his intestines spilled out of the wound in his abdomen. Disgruntled Deadheads gave them a wide berth. Barry had another beer and another.

"Had to think of Bob Weir to come," muttered Evans in mock outrage. Then he started laughing again. And the music was still loud. And it was still the same. And Jerry Garcia would not stop peering at Barry over those glasses.

Barry escaped, staggering through warm spring air back to his house. He hoped he'd drunk enough to pass out without much thought.

Tuesday

No amount of makeup could cover up the way Johnson had been sucked dry. The dark hairs of his furrowed eyebrows stood out painfully against his pale skin. But he didn't look dead. He looked like he'd fallen asleep while taking a math test.

Barry needed air. He stepped into the funeral home's courtyard and spotted Evans trying to safety-pin shut the hole in his gut.

"So," said Evans, "does Johnson look stupid with makeup on, or what?"

"Yep. Pretty sick."

Evans nodded. "At least they left my casket closed." He looked around furtively. Everyone else was inside. "Hey. Look what I brought."

Evans rummaged through his suit pockets, pulled out a pocket flask ("Can I have some?" "No, it's empty. Sorry") and finally produced a small blue plastic ball.

"Check it out." Evans touched two metal contacts on the ball, which began to laugh hysterically—"Yeaah, hyuh, hyuh, ha, hyuuugh"—a bizarre stylized laughter that could only be made by a machine. "Isn't it great?" Evans's own obnoxious laugh took over.

"Johnson would have loved it."

"I know. I'm gonna give it to him."

The casket was closed for the funeral. The Catholic ceremony was long and arduous. Barry sat next to Marcie. Between the monotonous drone of the priests and the lulling *drip, drip, drip* of blood from the crucifixes on the walls, it was difficult to stay out of la-la land. The only thing that kept Barry awake was his growing annoyance at the way Johnson was being eulogized. A fine worker, they called him. A gentle bee in the great Hive of Life. They didn't mention his old happy days as a speed freak. They didn't mention the hopes and dreams that fueled his life before Leslie sucked them away. A good worker! Hah!

"But now he is with Jesus," said the priest. "For Jesus has promised us all eternal life in Him."

Barry heard muffled laughter. He looked at the coffin, and saw the lid rise just a hair, just high enough to let out the *har-hee*s and *hyuk-hyuk-hyuk*s of the laughing ball.

All right! Go Johnson!

The priest tried to ignore the sound. "And if we just . . . if we just accept . . . accept . . . uh . . . Jesus into our hearts . . ."

"Hyuk, ha, hyuk, hyuk!" said the ball. The crucifixes were bleeding furiously now, each pouring a continuous stream of scarlet into silver catch basins below. Evans took out his flask and filled it from one of the crimson streams. He caught Barry's eye, pointed at the coffin and silently doubled over with laughter.

They held the wake at Barry's house. At first it was quiet, just a couple of old schoolmates drinking memorial bourbon 'n' Cokes and talking about old times. Then twenty people showed up at once, Davey and Sandy and Johnny and the Cindy who fixed cars, friends old and new mixed with strangers. Conversation was at first quiet and brooding, but with every new arrival the music got louder and the talking got sillier and soon a real party was going, a good one. Barry began to wonder if the twin deaths of Evans and Johnson were precipitating a Party Vortex.

Things got wilder when Evans passed around his flask of crucifix blood. A large, balding, self-proclaimed wine expert whom Barry didn't even know started bellowing, "Oh! Excellent! What a nice little Cabernet! That dog will hunt!"

Evans waved the flask at Barry. "Here, take some."

"I don't wanna drink blood."

"Hey, come on, I got it from a Catholic church, didn't I? It's wine now."

Barry dared a sniff, then a sip, then a big old gulp, and it was wine, sweet and rapturous.

"Cool, huh," said Evans. "You know, they say that the rivers of wine in Heaven and the rivers of blood in Hell are the same rivers. They just change back and forth all the time." He proceeded to ramble on about gray-and-green UFOs, the Kama Sutra and Frank Zappa.

Barry tuned him out and put some loud, abrasive dance

music on the stereo. People actually began to dance, for a change. He turned on his trusty strobe light, briefly flashing back to the many happy hours he'd spent stoned, alone in his old high school bedroom, the strobe flashing in black-light darkness as he listened to the groovy-nerd sounds of Vangelis and to other records that always seemed to be favored by planetarium directors and PBS science documentaries.

The flash caught the dancers' hair in motion, eyes closed or fixed on unseen points, and suddenly Barry recognized Angela, dancing across the room. This time she'd eschewed the tie-dyed look for a black-and-neon miniskirt with glowing tights, and he watched entranced as the strobe transformed her dance into a series of snapshots of grace, of a woman dancing with herself, eyes shut, as if she were tuned to a better world, a place Barry wanted to be.

Then the record ended and she was gone.

For the rest of the night Barry drank and bounced from acquaintance to friend to acquaintance like a pinball. The only respites were in the bathroom, when each piss was more relaxing than the last, and all he had to do was stare at his face in the mirror, his features altered by a message scrawled in soap that some happy mourner had written. It said, "Stay tuned for *The Real World*."

At midnight the door opened and a pale hand holding a laughing blue ball appeared, followed by Johnson, who looked quite natty in his funeral tux, and a few other dead people. Evans immediately latched onto a dead girl with a massive head injury that exposed her brain for all to see. Johnson laughed and talked and seemed more lively than at any time during the past few months when he'd still been living.

No one left till two in the morning, when the police came by and told them to turn it down. Then, as if desperately afraid to party in silence, everyone left.

Wednesday

Barry had the day off. While he tried to clean up in a hung-over daze, Johnson followed him around, jabbering nonstop.

"It's not that bad being dead. It's better than I thought it would be, anyway. The nice thing is that nothing hurts anymore."

The floor was covered with torn bits of newspaper and Barry couldn't for the life of him remember how that had happened.

"At least dying has gotten me out of the house. I mean, I'm free now. No guilt, no responsibilities."

Three thousand beer cans to be drained, rinsed, crushed, recycled, refilled, redrained . . . it seemed half of them had cigarette ashes in them. *For those who prefer that special taste of charred dust and fermentation combined* . . .

"I do still itch, though." Johnson scratched his scalp above his right ear until a stinky brownish liquid oozed from his head. "I guess it's like phantom limbs. You know, someone loses an arm and they still get aches, itches from it. I've lost my whole body; it's rotting, and I guess itching is as close as I can get to pain, you know? No big deal, though. They tell me it's just a phase."

Barry went to clean the soap message off the bathroom mirror and noticed that it had changed. Now it said, "Find silence. Then Listen. *The Real World* will find you."

"I'm having fun now. It's gotten me out of the house. Don't have any more responsibilities. By the way, the Swingin' Love Corpses are playing at the 5th Circle tonight. Wanna go?"

"Sure," said Barry. "Why not?"

The 5th Circle nightclub was jam-packed with the living and the dead, acquaintances and friends. As the Mystery Jazz of the Corpses thumped and screed in Barry's bones, he wandered, long-necked beer bottle in hand, to scream ritual greetings: "Hi." "Hello." "How're you doing?" "Okay, all things considered." "I was so sorry to hear about Evans and Johnson." "Yeah." Long, un-

comfortable pause. "Well, I gotta go say hello to so-and-
so." "Okay. See you later."

Leslie appeared out of nowhere, wearing a strapless
black outfit that followed the slender curves of her body
like a loving, living animal. "Wanna dance?"

His erection was instant and painful. "Maybe later."

She danced by herself while he gazed, slack-jawed.

"Watch out for her catheter," said Johnson.

"I'm sorry. You should go dance with her. She is your
wife."

"You kidding? Now that I'm dead, she won't give me
the time of day."

"She's still in mourning, though."

"That's 'cause she looks good in black."

Leslie caught Barry's eyes, smiled and shimmied. He
looked away, suddenly tired. There was no place to sit
and no spot on the wall to lean on. The music was too
loud. His head hurt and the beer just made him feel
bloated. He escaped to the bathroom and peed while listening to some rednecks talk about starting some shit. He
stepped outside the club. Cold wind blew the smell of
blood from the river into his nose as the chill cut through
his clothing. He could feel his heart beating. He thought
of how it always beats, has always beat, so tirelessly. It
would be so easy for his heart to get tired and stop . . .

He shivered and went back inside. The crowd was even
thicker, music thumping, people shouting, stomach sloshing . . . He closed his eyes.

"You all right?"

He opened his eyes to see Angela. Pink lips smiling
and delicately arched black eyebrows.

"Yeah," he said. "I'm fine."

"You need to dance. C'mon."

Angela led him onto the dance floor. At first all he
could manage was a sort of nonenergetic head-bobbing.
But her eyes spurred him on. Soon they were both doing
silly dances, twisting, pogo-ing, dancing like Steve Martin. A song in three-quarter time came on and they joined
hands and waltzed, dancing closer and closer. Her breasts

were pressed against him. Her face was very close.

They both got nervous, and when the waltz got fast they began to dance silly again, whirling around and laughing and bouncing off the other dancers.

"Slam Waltzing! Yeah!" shouted Barry, just before one of the rednecks from the bathroom yelled "Hey!" Hands grabbed him and spun him around. He gazed into the redneck's piggy eyes and was in Hell again. Then a fist flew toward his face, and he was nowhere.

Thursday

She had hair in the photo, close-cropped and bushy, and her eyes stared from the flyer with direct, adult aware-ness instead of childlike fear, but Barry still recognized her as the artist he'd comforted in the womb room. The flyer said, "Come see *The Real World*," and included a map to a country house owned by some rich hippie.

A note on the back of the flyer said, "I have just a fleeting memory of you, but I know that you helped me. Please come to the party Saturday night. Bring all your dead."

Bring all your dead. Barry tried to think of how many there were. The only people who'd died on him in the past were distant relatives and grandparents. It was sad when the grandparents died, but not unexpected. The rel-atives had just made him feel detached, alien. He remem-bered seeing old Uncle Wally in the funeral home. Uncle Wally had been a family black sheep. A fat one. While relatives cried and talked quietly, he'd stared at Uncle Wally's dead body and rouged face. The undertaker had carefully folded Wally's hands on the underside of his belly. The slope of the belly was so great that Wally's hands seemed ready at any moment to dive into his pants, to pull on his dead cock just one last time. Throughout the funeral young Barry had to suppress giggles as he thought of Uncle Wally, waiting to be buried so he could have the privacy to jack off again.

Bring all your dead. He wished they'd leave him alone for a day. He'd called in sick at work. His head ached, and a bruise behind his right ear was very tender. The idea of another party made his stomach churn. He puttered around, read, watched TV. Had an improvised supper of chili beef soup and rice. Tried to read some more. Called Marcie and Tom. Got no answer. Called some other friends. No one was home. He imagined them all somewhere having fun. He felt stupid for imagining that.

The TV switched to another dishwasher ad and Barry let his eyes settle on the flyer on the coffee table. The artist was smiling at him. Her lips moved. *Hey*, said the lips. *I'm not kidding.*

The doorbell rang. "Come in!"

Marcie and Tom opened the door and said, "You're being kidnapped." They shoved a beer in his hand and led him out to where three cars waited with motors running, and it felt good, it just felt good to be out there with his friends, driving with the risk of opened beers and pints of bourbon in the car, out in the perfect half-moon night.

"You realize, of course," said Barry, "that this is proof we're in another Party Vortex."

"Party Vortex!" shouted Marcie. She screamed and drove faster.

The last Party Vortex had been during Christmas. As old friends arrived in town, one by one, the Vortex grew into an unstoppable party force that even sucked up staid, stay-at-home types. Like a hurricane, the Vortex was unstoppable, until it broke on the shores of the New Year. Houses and brains were trashed. Hundreds were incapacitated by post-Vortex flu in January.

Barry and his friends had learned that the only way to survive a Party Vortex was to fasten down a tether and ride out the waves. As the caravan of cars made two more stops, picking up Christy and Mandy and Cindy the waitress, Barry decided that there were worse things than to be caught up in an endless round of parties.

The caravan headed for the train bridge. Barry was never sure why they would always end up at the train bridge on nights like this, but somehow it was always the perfect place to be. A warm, wet breeze carried a rich soundscape to Barry's ears: the horns of distant barges, the hum of insects, the crackling of twigs on the trail, the rush of water, along with traces of more distant sounds, the screams of industrial machinery and the pleasant rumbling chorale of freeway traffic.

On the path down to the train tracks they passed some long-haired teens who'd built a nice fire to drink beer by. They talked in long-drawn-out, drunken syllables. "Yeah, man. Skynard fuckin' rocks, man. I've been listening to fuckin' Rock 105 all day, man. I'm fucked up, man."

"Hey," said Evans, "y'all listen to the Dead?"

"What?" Blond hair and a scruffy mustache. "Yeah, they're okay. Skynard rocks, though."

"Yeah. They're dead, too."

"Goddamn. Hey, aren't you dead?"

"Sure am. A part of me is pushing up daisies even as we speak."

"Well, what's the deal? Is there a Heaven or a Hell? Is God really such an asshole? How come every time I have fun they tell me it's satanic?"

"You got me there." Evans shrugged with a gurgly, crackly sound. "Heaven? Hell? I don't know. I'm here, aren't I?"

The rest of the group had already left Evans behind. Barry ran to catch up with them. At this point the movable feast had picked up about ten people. They staggered merrily onto the bridge.

On either side of the train tracks were walkways formed by metal gratings, and as his footsteps boomed on the grates, Barry watched the dark river with its sweet wine smell roar past the concrete bridge supports below. He looked up to see some partyers stroll on the opposite walkway, while some chose to walk precariously on the railroad ties themselves, laughing and shouting and clutching bottles and cans. Barry suddenly felt like one of the wayward partyers from *La Dolce Vita*.

"Oh, Nina," he said to Marcie, "why do you torture me so?"

"Oh, Antonio," Marcie replied in her best Italian-starlet voice, "I don't mean to hurt you. I just want all the boys to love me."

"Hey, check this out!" said Johnson. He'd found a series of rungs that led up one of the bridge supports and was already halfway up the side. "What a great view!"

Barry walked closer to the rungs, contemplating them, wondering if he'd have the guts to climb them, when he stepped into space. One of the metal walkway grilles was gone, and he was falling into the hole, right foot first. No time to yell. Time slowed as he reached out for one of the bridge's iron girders. His body seemed to stretch out, overridden by only one purpose, to reach, to grab at anything that could be a handhold. His hands clasped a girder. His right hand slipped. His left hand held. He hung one-handed over the river so far below.

He looked down and somehow the river seemed to open up below him. It didn't just flow under the bridge. It spun below him, forming a great whirlpool. Deep within the whirlpool was a small boat, out of control, being pulled down, and yet the farther away it got, the clearer he could see it, as if the crimson mists of the water were a lens, magnifying, revealing . . . the woman artist, head shaved, dressed in black, sitting with Johnson and Evans and another dead girl and . . . Barry. He saw his own face, just the opposite of the way it had looked in the mirror. He saw his own hand reaching up. He reached down. It seemed so close, but he couldn't reach it, and his left hand was weakening.

"There's a girder right below you," said a female voice. "Move your feet a little, and you'll be able to stand on it."

The hand vanished, the whirlpool disappeared, and now he could see the girder. He stretched his toes to touch it, eased himself down onto it. It was wide and easy to stand on. There were plenty of handholds around it. He allowed his left hand to relax its grip. He silently thanked the hand. *All these years of being right-handed and treating you like shit. I'm sorry. You deserve more respect.*

Barry caught his breath and looked up. Angela stood on the walkway. She crouched down next to the hole in a spot where a diagonal girder rose past the walkway. "Try crawling up this way."

Barry grabbed the walkway's edge and pulled himself
up, using the diagonal girder as a place to push off with
his feet. Angela grabbed him under the arms and helped
him out, falling backward in the process. Neither stood
up. Angela held his head as he shivered and stared at the
rushing water, deep and dark, splashing black except for
the crimson drops illuminated by a bridge light.

It had all happened so quickly that only now did the
rest of the party react:

"Are you okay?"

"Man, you could have just fallen forty feet into the
water and gotten trapped in the undertow. You'd have
been fucked."

"I'm kind of drunk. It's just now beginning to register."

"He would've fallen forty feet into the river drunk.
He'd have been totally fucked."

"There's that girder down there. He probably would
have just landed on that."

"He might have landed headfirst, been knocked out,
slid off and fallen forty feet into the river drunk and unconscious. He'd have been totally, *totally* fucked."

The party mood was gone. They left the bridge. Barry
watched his feet all the way to shore. The grates hummed,
then throbbed. A train was coming.

Evans was still with the heavy-metal kids, staring over
the fire at the stars. One of the kids was saying, "Well,
shit, man, she's my girlfriend. She does what I say or she
gets smacked."

"That's bullshit," said the one with blond hair. "That's
wrong."

"Oh? Since when did you become such a sweet little
church boy?"

"I'm not a sweet little church boy. My dad's the Christian, he used to beat us all the time." The blond kid sank
into a reverie. "Man, I know where the gun is. If he fucks
with me again . . ."

His words vanished in the growing train sound, which
was getting closer and closer, like a thundering wave of
panic. The train screamed by, bearing brightly lit passen-

ger cars filled with elegantly dressed people wearing cheap cardboard party hats.

A woman stood on top of one of the cars, a woman dressed in rippling white, with huge trails of silk rippling in the air behind her. It was Leslie. She smiled when she saw Barry. He blinked, and she was gone.

Friday

"Don't you love it?" said a woman's voice in his ear. Barry turned, but she was gone. There were just the over-dressed partyers drinking honest-to-God cocktails, just like the parties his parents use to throw . . . but these were the people he'd been to college with. It was disturbing how many of them now worked for their dads. Half the partyers were dead and half of them were lawyers. Those who were dead lawyers fascinated him. So well dressed, and you could almost forget their growing rancidness, or the way their cocktails oozed out of unexpected places on their bodies, or the croak of their voices as they discussed cases with the living members of their firm.

Even though he was thirty, Barry felt like a kid, like at any minute that old man from *The Graduate* would come up and say, "I have just one word of advice for you: crystals."

The bathroom was a moment of relief and solitude. His long piss was so relaxing that he didn't even jump when the female voice said, "Don't you just love it?" again.

He shook his dick. "Say something else, just to prove I've gone schizophrenic."

"No matter how you shake and dance, the last drop still runs down your pants," said the voice.

He turned and saw the woman artist behind him in the bathroom mirror. Her head was still shaved. 'Ol what's-her-name. She winked. He spun around. No one there, of course. She wasn't even in the mirror anymore.

Barry took a deep breath. Okay. The lights looked normal, if a somewhat depressing shade of yellow. Nothing seemed abnormally geometrical or colorful. He didn't think he'd been dosed.

"Who has the power here?" asked the voice. The woman artist was reflected on the doorknob, her head distorted into a peculiar oval by the knob's shape. "Who controls this scene . . . the living or the dead?"

He covered her face and turned the knob and walked back into the maelstrom of lawyers and businessmen. He saw one old acquaintance sitting in a chair, smiling wanly at some overly tanned fucker who was reeling off reams of sports statistics.

"Your friend in the chair," said the voice in his ear, "he has AIDS, but he doesn't dare tell the firm or he'd be out on his ear."

Barry waved at the guy, wondering what to say, trying to remember his name. The dying lawyer waved back, then turned to spout some statistics back at the tanned fucker.

Barry wandered on. He saw a group of lawyers clustered around a well-dressed skeleton who poured a martini over his lower jaw and dispensed bons mots with the hissing fragments of his desiccated lips.

"This old boy's been dead for years," whispered Barry's schizophrenia. "He just won't leave. He still sits on the chamber of commerce. He makes decisions that fuck you up personally. He likes to hang out with the younger members of his firm. Makes him feel alive again."

The skeleton turned his rotten gaze toward Barry and increased his rictus grin.

"Aren't you the Anderson boy?" he whispered.

"Boy?" Johnson appeared out of nowhere, stinking to high heaven. "Barry here's a man! One hundred and fifty pounds of raw testosterone, ready, willing and able to make it with anything in any position. Yeah, I love the smell of napalm in the morning! Charlie don't surf, dammit!"

The skeleton turned his back on Johnson's non sequiturs and Johnson led Barry away. "C'mon, He-Man, we're going for a ride," and almost before Barry knew it, he was in Marcie and Tom's car, going way too fast.

"Thanks for getting me out of there," said Barry.

"Well, shit, I had to do something," said Johnson.

"Ol' skin and bones there looked like he wanted to fuck you up the ass with a femur."

"Yeah, he's like that," said Tom. "You better watch it. He may be dead, but he can still fuck you up."

"Hey, I'm dead, too!" said Johnson. "Dead and Proud, Dead and Proud, dammit!"

Barry sat in the backseat, next to Evans, who made disturbing crackly noises every time the car screeched around corners and scrunched them together. Finally (thank God or whatever), Tom pulled to a stop before a large and ancient building. "Okay, everybody," said Tom, pulling strips of cloth out of a sack, "put these on. You can't get in without a tie."

Most of the beggars sitting around on the lower steps didn't even look up at the motley crew climbing toward the entrance in blue jeans, T-shirts and very nice ties. The doorman whispered, "I know I said I'd get you in, but I don't think you'll last long."

He was right. Tuxedos, strapless dresses, perfect tans— Barry felt like he was at a senior prom for older women and balding men, little old ladies and thirtysomething doctors, trophy wives and anxious restaurateurs.

An old-style big band had the older folks and a few hip younger folks dancing to 1930s swing. "I love you, and I hate her," crooned the bandleader over the chorus of saxophones. "You love me, but you detest him. Deep in love, we hate them all so much. Oh, no! I guess it's really you I hate instead!"

Johnson still had his funeral tux on and someone mistook him for a shabby bartender.

"Dry martini, up, with a twist."

"Very good, sir." With great solemnity Johnson went through the prerequisite ritual: chilling the glass and the gin, waving the vermouth bottle over the mixing cup without actually adding any, and straining the gin. Then, as a finishing touch, he twisted off his left pinky and dunked it, *kersplash*, into the glass.

Back in the car, Johnson and Evans did some dead-male bonding.

"So, Evans, how did things go with that dead girl you met the other night?"

(They seemed to be driving a million miles per second.)

"You know, she turned out to be really cool. I mean, even though my dick broke off inside her, it was still okay."

(They always seemed to be going in circles.)

"Oh, man! You lost your willie?"

(Barry was lost. He was glad Tom was driving.)

"Yeah. I was bummed about it, but then she showed me it didn't really matter. We just lay together, not moving, and our fluids mingled, and our toenails grew, and I felt like I could just lie there forever and let our dust mingle."

(Centrifugal force nailed Barry to the car door.)

"So you got another date with her?"

("God, I'm fucked up.")

"Tomorrow night."

They ended up in a glitzy nightclub with flashing lights and televisions blaring images of families starving *flash* children watching their parents die *flash* nine-year-old prostitutes soliciting middle-aged men in Hawaiian shirts *flash* people dying in the street, covered with flies *flash* mothers and fathers crying hysterically . . . all to a very danceable beat.

Barry danced with Marcie and Tom. Evans kept yelling in his ear, "This sucks, man! How can you dance to this? It's all soulless synthesizers! How can you?"

Barry danced harder just to spite Evans. And Johnson . . .

Johnson surrounded them. With every strobe flash he was somewhere else, in some absurd position, fingers up his nose, Junior Bird Man eyes, orangutan arms, the all-Johnson show speeding out of control; and every silly face he made in every strobe reminded Barry of other times and other places, back when Johnson had been alive, back before he'd grown old before his time, back when the dumber and weirder and sillier and faster it was, the better . . .

"God, Johnson, you coked up or what?"

"Hell, no! None of those conspiracy drugs! I'm High on Death, Dammit!" Johnson grabbed Barry and they slammed to a Frank Sinatra tune . . .

They ended up in an all-night diner. Barry was about to fall asleep in his hash browns. "I can't do this anymore."

You can, whispered the artist in his ear, *for one more night.*

"Come on!" said Evans. "Just one more night! It's at Snavely's place, out in the woods. You know those parties cannot be missed. Besides, I want you to meet the girl I plan to spend eternity with!"

"Guys, I'm hearing voices in my head. I think I'm going nuts."

"You've always been nuts, Barry."

Just forty-eight more hours, whispered the artist. *If you hear my voice in your head after that, you're insane. If not, you're fine.*

Barry tried to focus on his hash browns, scattered, smothered, covered, chunked and topped. "Okay," he whispered. "Okay . . ."

Saturday

A log broke on the bonfire and a cascade of sparks flew up into the sky. Barry watched them flit and die out amongst the stars. He fancied that some kept going till they found a place in the heavens to shine.

Underlit, bushy-headed faces swilled bourbon on the other side of the flames. Behind them rose dark and ancient trees. A distant band played covers of Crosby, Stills and Nash tunes. Talk, laughter, music, food, drink . . . an old Baby Boomer who'd made good was having a party and everyone in the universe was invited.

There's a river, said the voice in his head, *where you'll meet me.*

Barry didn't know if he wanted to meet anyone. He barely had the energy to move. He just stared at the fire and its ever-twisting shapes.

A feminine face appeared amongst the old, bearded

coots. It was Leslie. "Hey, Barry." Form-fitting black
pants and a small black top that left her shoulders and
midriff bare. She walked around to meet him and give
him a close, deep hug. They remained arm in arm after
the hug. "How're you doing?"

Barry was intimately aware of the pressure of her hip
against his—"Oh, as good as can be expected"—of the
softness of her shoulder, her arm, her midriff—"Yeah,
me, too"—of the bonfire reflection dancing in her eyes
and of her soft mouth that seemed to be pulling him closer
and closer . . .

"Hyukuk, hyuk, hyuk, hyuk," said Johnson's laughter
ball. Johnson followed. "Hey there, Leslie, looking for a
little fix? Sorry, we're kidnapping this one. C'mon."

He put a cold, clammy arm around Barry's shoulder
and pulled him away from the bonfire. Barry wondered
how a dead guy could be so strong.

"Where are we going?"

"To the river."

They walked along a path between the ancient trees.
The moon lit the way. Shadows became impossible pits
of blackness, fragments of nothingness on the ground. The
music and noise of the party faded, replaced by crickets
and gurgling water.

Evans and the dead girl from the wake were waiting
by the riverside. "Hey, Barry. Meet my new girlfriend."

"Hi."

"Hi." The girlfriend's face was already half eaten
away. She held up a dew-beaded bottle of Jaegermeister.
"Say, do you want this? Someone gave it to me, but, you
know, liquor's pretty irrelevant to me at this stage."

"Sure." Barry took a swig that went down cold and
licorice-sweet.

The river was pungent and fruity. Here it was more a
creek than a river. A reflection of the moon rippled on its
surface.

"I used to go swimming out here all the time," said
Evans. "It's good for skinny-dipping. Good for sex, too."

"You wanna jump in?" asked the girlfriend.

"We could," said Evans. "Of course, at this point

we'd probably turn into stew.'' He giggled.

"Gotta watch out for the dick-eating gars out there,'' said Johnson. ''Dick-eating gars and butt-raping snakes.''

"And titty-clamp crawdads!'' It was an old routine with them and it got Evans giggling so hard that his intestines spilled out again. "Oh, fuck it!'' He pulled out a long rope of guts and ripped it off and threw it in the water. It disappeared under the reflection of the moon. "That's better.''

Barry tried to choose between being grossed out or taking another pull of liquor. He opted for the latter. He was beginning to get that sort of odd, stimulating buzz that only a few hard liquors could provide. He sat with his friends and could see and feel simultaneously all the other times he'd sat with them talking bullshit, hanging out, just happy to be there with some of the edge and urgency and desperation of life pushed into the background.

The bald woman artist arrived on the river as a silhouette on a small boat. She steered the boat to the shore.

"Cool entrance!'' Evans and his girlfriend splashed out and pulled the boat closer to shore. They boarded it with Johnson and Barry, almost overloading it.

"Will this take long?'' asked Johnson. "These guys really stink.''

"We stink!'' Barry took another pull of Jaegermeister. "You're the ripe one inside that tux.''

"Yeah, but none of my rot can match those bean farts of yours.''

The bald artist pushed off from the shore with her oar. She stood in the back of the boat, steering like a gondolier. The current quickly pulled the boat into the center of the river. Barry thought of Dr. Phibes drifting down the river Styx with his dead wife's body. At least the dead wife had been still and serenely shrouded. Barry's dead were up and moving and making stupid jokes.

They drifted down the river, listening to the gurgles of the water and the Jaegermeister bottle. Finally, the artist spoke:

"This is my greatest work. I did not have to build or create it. I simply had to learn how to see it. Now I'm going to show you how to see it, too. I call it *The Real World*."

Barry became aware of a humming sound in the air. Lights appeared up ahead—streetlights illuminating singing trees. Suburbs.

"You all know this place, where my husband lives and you used to live," said the bald artist. The hum from the trees grated in their bones. The leaves enshrouded large, two-story houses. "This is a quiet Hell, where everyone goes about their business and tries to keep up with each other. They try to ignore the treesong, for them a constant irritant, twisting their lives as they eat and sleep and shit, covering their tensions with false smiles that hide their pain as they make their deals and screw each and every body until at last they crack and kill their families and themselves."

A car drove by, too fast. Another followed, its driver slinging an empty beer bottle into the creek in front of them.

"Only a few have learned the secret of this zone of Hell. The trees produce simple tones tuned perfectly, filling the entire neighborhood with standing waves. If you move quickly, the standing waves flex and batter your ears, producing homicidal irritation. But if you slow down, if you turn off your car stereo or jambox and stop and listen, you will hear the perfect song of the trees. As you move amongst them, the waveforms will interact for you, playing the world's most beautiful song. Listen."

She steered the boat toward a backwater. Barry listened, and suddenly the irritating hum of the trees resolved into a series of notes rising up and down in a simple but always changing pattern. He watched the trembling leaves, black in the night's shadow, but shockingly green near the streetlights. He remembered this song. He'd heard it as a child taking walks in the park. It seemed as if all the music he'd ever sought out was here. The long, droning pieces that irritated his friends. The antimelodic jazz that was secretly full of melodies. The movie-music soundtracks for films that were never made. All was an attempt to find the treesong again.

They reentered the river current and left the rich suburbs behind. The treesong faded, slowly replaced by a regular thud. Barry squinted. The Jaegermeister was affecting his vision. The thud grew. The river ahead was bordered by glowing white squares. Then the squares resolved into houses. In uniform formation they lined the river, each white, each shaped like a triangle on top of a box, each window glowing with a flickering blue light. The muffled pounding became drums, rock 'n' roll drums pounding in stereo from each house, each TV show, each nuclear-family household, in a uniform four-quarter beat.

"This is where The American People live, the great majority found in all polls and market surveys. There aren't many left. Such a difficult job to be the silent majority, leading reasonably good lives, with a reasonable balance of joy and sorrow, pleasure and pain, tribulation and triumph. The adults watch TV. The children rebel with hand-me-down rebellions furnished by their loving grandparents."

Peace and Money! screamed voices from one house. *Love and Honor!* screamed the house opposite. *Drugs for Jesus! Quality Hot Dogs! Sex, Television and the American Way! I Wanna Watch Cartoons!* (Let's Barbecue! I Love Ya, Ma!)

"You could call this Heaven, and it is, as long as you like things to stay the same, day in and day out, forever and ever."

They left the houses behind. "I liked that," said Johnson. "It's got a good beat and you can dance to it. I give it a ninety-four."

Another swig of liquor, splashing queasy in the stomach. The river was a rush now, happy gurgling subsiding into a dull roar. Older houses passed by, each blaring out its own beat dance noise. Party tonight; the Party Vortex was in full swing and people were dying, they were having such a good time.

"Welcome to the so-called alternative zone where all you spoiled fuckers live," said the bald artist, "the Hell and Heaven that I used to live in and plan to return to, the land of the drunk partyers, the druggies from Hell, the movable feast, La Dolce Vita, where every pumped-up joy is followed by every hangover, hanging harder over; where chaos rules, where the music of the spheres rings through electric guitar amps, where you spend an eternity watching the scuttling of cockroaches and the frenetic dance of fleas while waiting for your man with twenty sick dollars in your hand, and you'd best pretend you're some kind of artist or your life would just be another dead-end job.''

Peeling paint and beer kegs, and all his friends living and dead called out, ''Barry! Whaddya know! Hair of the Dog! Try this wine! It's excellent!'' and the river roared and broadened and it seemed that they were no longer on a river, but rather, at the edge of a great whirlpool.

''Next stop, salvation!'' shouted the artist as spray from the river coated her head with droplets of blood and wine. ''White Trash heaven! If your crazy partying life seems hollow, why not turn to Jesus? Fat men are waiting to relieve you of your money and your critical facilities— relax and do what they say. Experience the joy of crusading against sinners, of beating Jesus into your kids, of seeing the world in black and white!''

The air was full of mist, and the mist was full of specters whirling by, shotgun mansions and heavy metal trailers fading in and out of the red fog. Barry looked up and the stars were spinning in circles. The bald artist's head was shining crimson; the spinning lights from houses rotated on her glistening pate as she shouted like a B-movie huckster, ''See! Rebellious young teenagers turn to Top 40 guitar rock and silly satanic rituals based on their parents' revival meetings.'' She had to scream. The air was filled with screaming guitar solos and gospel organs. ''See! These same young teenagers go Christian when the realities of dead-end jobs and teenage parenting overwhelm them.'' Crying babies and the smack of flesh striking flesh. A long-haired fucker knocks his woman's teeth out and takes another swig of beer. ''See Parents and Children alike unite in hounding to death anyone of a different race, religion, size, opinion or intelligence!''

Screams and whirling lights and the only landmark

Barry could spot was the train bridge, and the train bridge was spinning and they were deeper in the whirlpool, whirling faster and faster. Barry clung to the side of the boat with his right hand, and stared up through the lens of the whirlpool and saw a figure hanging from the bridge, a figure with his own face reaching down, train rumbling, party demons screaming, angels crying. Barry reached up toward himself, but the blood river enveloped them as Johnson screamed, "Whee! It's the Pirates of the Caribbean!" . . .

. . . they surfaced with a blort and floated within a placid grotto. Evans began to bail out the boat, slurping big handfuls of the sweet red liquid, "Hey! This is good."

The grotto was patently fake. The boat pulled up to a wooden platform lined with rails that led to the exit: a circular opening which perfectly framed the silhouette of a ferris wheel.

They debarked. "Good show," said Evans. "Definitely an E ticket."

"I don't see how you could call it *The Real World*," said Johnson. "You made it all up."

"Well," said the artist, "I guess I was lying, but I was trying to tell the most truthful lies possible." She walked over to where a velvet rope separated them from the ancient metal levers that controlled the boat ride. Unhooking the rope, she said, "Y'all are welcome to create your own lies."

"All right!" Evans stepped over to the first lever, grabbed and pulled.

Flames erupted around the grotto's perimeter, the ferris wheel lit up, a great circle of lights guarding the exit, and suddenly they were surrounded by an orgy. Men and women with soft, orange, flame-kissed skin writhed with tangled limbs at their feet, gasping, sighing, moaning. The sweet wine smell of the ruby-red stream grew into an intoxicating perfume.

Evans pulled his girlfriend close. "Check it out! Heaven. Everyone here has a tireless, mutating body. Everyone can be male, female, both, neither. Everyone can learn the minds of the others, share souls with the others, can become one as truly as possible, can reach a nirvana of ecstasy.''

Evans and his girlfriend kissed and froze into a gray statue of lovers embracing. The writhing flesh around them sent out probes to touch their dead flesh, probes of fingers, breasts, genitals, lips, but soon the flesh recoiled from their dead stone skin and formed an open space around them.

"Look there," said the bald artist. She pointed to a naked woman who sat alone. "She's gotten bored. While the rest are in Heaven, she is in Hell." The woman sat cross-legged, idly touching herself, staring desperately at the flames on the opposite wall. "When she finds the right degree of quiet within herself, she will leave."

The woman closed her eyes and sat still, ignoring the advances of the flesh around her. After a time, Barry thought he could see the flames shine through her body.

There was a tug on the cuff of his trousers. A slender female hand with long red fingernails was crawling up his leg. "Heaven," he murmured. "Cool."

"Oh, yeah," said Johnson. "Well, let me show you Hell." He strode over to the second lever and pulled. Heaven disappeared in a flash of white. The ferris wheel began to spin. A song filled the air with the sound of harps in choirs. The melody was simple, almost stupid. It sounded sort of like, "Nyah, nyah, nyah-nyah, nyah."

They were in an immense white room, facing tier upon tier of harp players in white robes with white, feathered wings. In unison, the harpists sang, "I love The Lord. He is so Good. I Love Jesus. All the time." As they played, their fingers bled. Little rivulets of blood poured down the tiers into the stream, which now smelled sour and metallic.

"Now this," said Johnson, "is where the really bad people go. Nosy churchwomen and Hell-and-Damnation men. People who preach Christian Charity but wouldn't know if it bit them on the ass. All the holier-than-thou motherfuckers end up in this, the ultimate church, just like Mark Twain said they would. And from here they have to fight to get to the front row, the inner circle.''

"How do they do that?"

"Watch. That guy there is about to make his move."

A portly gentleman with silvery white hair was staring intently at the harp player in front of him—a narrow, angular woman with a pinched-up face. Suddenly, he pulled a knife from his robes and lunged for her. With one mighty stroke he severed her wings, pushed her out of the chair and began to play her harp.

The woman screamed in pain and fury, the stumps of her wings flapping blood everywhere. Knife in hand, she lunged for her usurper's vacated chair, but it had already been appropriated by an obese woman who clutched the harp to her chest and slapped the bleeding woman into the back rows with one meaty hand.

Defeated, the bleeding woman grabbed one of the empty chairs in the back. Barry noticed that all the back-row harpists had stumpy wings in various stages of regeneration. He also noticed that the harpists in the front row had fixed smiles on their faces and eyes that flicked back and forth, always trying to see what was happening behind them.

A rustling of murmurs and whispers rushed through the air under the banal hymn as everyone tried to ascertain the recent power change in his or her society.

"Do they exist like this for all eternity?" asked Barry. "Surely no one can be evil enough to justify a punishment this harsh."

"It's not forever. Eternal damnation for finite crimes is a concept that can only be conceived by a finite mind. They can leave whenever they want to. Some of them realize that, eventually, but the rest just think that this is where they're supposed to be, where they've always wanted to be, and no matter how miserable they are, they're gonna stay and fight for position."

"And then there are those like him," whispered the artist. She pointed to a frail, elderly man in the very last row. Although his wings were whole, he made no attempt to move forward. He sat alone. His hands did not bleed. His eyes were closed, his face serene, and Barry slowly realized that his song was somehow different—the notes were the same, melody just as trite, but the voice and the strings of the old man made the song beautiful somehow, and the beauty of his playing punched through the evil banality of the rest of the harpists' playing.

"They are in Hell," said the artist, "and he is in Heaven."

"And they can leave any time?"

"Oh, yes," said Johnson. "They can go back to any of the other heavens and hells we've seen tonight, and all those we haven't seen. Or they can make the final exit."

"What's that?"

"You know. Like this." Johnson set off his laughing ball and threw it out toward the ferris wheel. The ball seemed to slow as it reached the exit. Its crazy giggles multiplied into a chorus of insane laughter. The ferris wheel spun faster. The shadows of its structure melted away and there were just thousands of spinning lights slowly realigning into a great spiral.

And all around them the harpists began to glow until they became nothing but brilliant patches of light that floated toward the exit, and were pulled into rainbows that were sucked into the spiral. Their music merged to a mass of sound, a true, heavenly noise of voices and strings in a song like the treesong, soaring over the roaring of the river that now was not wine or blood but just water, the water of life evaporating, misting into the spiral, into the spinning lights of the final exit.

"Ladies and Gentlemen!" shouted Johnson. "This is my life!"

He jumped, and like the giggling ball, he floated toward the exit, his body elongating and twisting, and suddenly Barry could see scenes from Johnson's entire life along the arc of his body: Johnson the screaming infant, Johnson sneaking up on his mother to shout "Boo!" Johnson riding his first acid trip at an outdoor concert, Johnson with Barry drinking and watching teenage beach-party movies, Johnson with Leslie, saying "I love you" and turning gray.

And just as Barry began to make out these scenes, these

still lives, these snapshots from Johnson's life, they began to blur and fade, *Wait!* and a great wind was pulling everything in the cave toward the exit and *Stop!*

And the statue that was Evans and his girlfriend toppled and shattered into fragments. Barry screamed and scrambled over to where they lay and all he could find was dust; there were no fingers, no scraps of cloth, no hair, no satyr's grin, just dust without structure, and all he got was a handful before the rest blew away *stop dammit stop!* but no curse was enough, no shout, no scream, no groan, and Barry was falling toward the spiraling lights and Johnson's body was gone, and far beyond the lights he saw stars by the billions, all cold and distant and impossibly far away . . .

. . . and another log broke on the bonfire with a dull, popping *chuck*. Barry swayed, nearly losing his balance and falling into the flames, but Leslie's arm held him steady.

He looked down from the sky. It wasn't Leslie, it was Angela. He looked around. Evans and Johnson and the dead girl were gone. There were only the stony faces of the men on the other side of the bonfire, and the shadows of ancient trees, and Angela, and cupped in his hands was a handful of dust.

"Go on," whispered Angela. "Throw it in."

Barry threw the dust into the fire, sending a cascade of multicolored sparks up into the heavens. Evans and Johnson were finally gone, really gone, gone forever. Barry began to cry for them, for the first time, as Angela held him and stroked his hair.

Sunday

The ringing phone finally brought Barry to life. Up. Head pounding. Jaegermeister. Jeez.

"Hey, Barry," said Marcie. "You going to Cindy's birthday party tonight?"

"Oh, um . . . Car Cindy or Waitress Cindy?"

"Car Cindy."

"Yeah. I don't know. I'm kind of partied out. I like Car Cindy, though."

"Angela will be there."

"Really. I'll take it under advisement, then. Thanks."

He hung up and stumbled to the bathroom. Jeez, he hadn't even *done* anything with Angela and there was already gossip about them.

He pissed into a toilet that needed cleaning two months ago, staring at the brown-gray ring that had formed at the water level. A sudden wave of memories from last night washed over him like vertigo. He shut his eyes and tried to keep his balance.

When he turned around, the bald artist stared at him from the medicine-cabinet mirror.

"Just a few loose ends and I'll get out of your hair and start growing mine out again. Yeah, the next time you see me I'll just be a frustrated suburban artist, recently divorced, bitching about mundane shit at some damn reception—"

"So what is your point?"

"Oh, yeah. Just making sure you remember that Heaven and Hell can be in the same place at the same time, and that you don't have to be dead to reach either one. Just reminding you that the Party Vortex is a state of mind, a little bit of creative and destructive chaos to keep you on your toes, and you can take it or leave it as well.

"And remember that when you're attracted to someone, that person becomes an angel, a real angel, not one of those harpists you saw last night. And sometimes that person will be an angel of death. Sometimes an angel of life. Whichever you choose, treat the magic gently."

Barry stared at his own grizzled face in the mirror. He decided to shave, shower and dress. Then he decided to put on some Philip Glass and clean the toilet. The repetitious music pushed his cleaning frenzy through the living room and into the bedroom.

While picking up old clothes, he found a scrap of paper that said, "Hey there! Let's say you and I blow off

Cindy's party and do something else.—Angela.''

Her phone number was written below the message. Very good. Barry pocketed the scrap of paper and continued to clean house.

CHOKE HOLD

Lucy Taylor

Lucy Taylor is a full-time writer whose short fiction has appeared in such markets as *Little Deaths, Hotter Blood, Hot Blood: Deadly After Dark, Cemetery Dance, Pulphouse* and *The Mammoth Book of Erotic Horror*. Her collections include *Close to the Bone, The Flesh Artist* and *Unnatural Acts and Other Stories*. Her novel, *The Safety of Unknown Cities*, was recently published by Darkside Press. A former resident of Florida, she lives in the hills outside Boulder, Colorado, with her five cats.

The rope snugged tight around Angelo's neck. Almost at once, he felt light-headed. Red embers, like bloody fireflies, swirled behind his eyes.

His dick, already engorged to veiny stiffness, felt like it had added an inch in circumference and two inches in length. He pumped it with a savage finesse no lover's hand could ever have accomplished, while the constricting rope pinched shut his carotid arteries and shut down the blood flow to his brain.

The rope around Angelo's neck was looped up over the top of the bunk bed over his head (the bed where his older brother, Mark, used to sleep before he shoved a Colt .45 into the face of the wrong Vietnamese grocer one night and got his brains blown out his asshole for his trouble). The other end of the rope was connected to a triangle formed by a bicycle chain and two feet of broom handle that hung down over the bottom bunk. Angelo had drilled holes at either end of the length of handle and secured the chain through them, creating a push bar for his feet.

By pressing his feet against the jerry-rigged bar, he could control the amount of pressure on his throat, could bring himself to the verge of unconsciousness and beyond. The Device was foolproof, too, Angelo figured, because the minute he passed out, his feet ceased applying pressure to the bar and the rope around his neck went slack immediately.

Now came the dance of control, restraint. To stay conscious as long as possible but not lose his hard-on, then pass out while the tremors of orgasm were still rocketing outward, concentric circles encompassing his dick, his groin, his belly, while the rope brought ever-expanding ripples of darkness flooding into his brain. Where the two waves of concentric circles met and overlapped: there lay ecstasy.

It had to be just right, synchronized just so. He thought about the sex books he'd read that counseled men on how to hold off on their orgasm until their partner climaxed. A simultaneous orgasm—that was supposed to be big shit. Well, fuck that. Angelo had his partner right here, his good, hard dick in his good right hand. The goal was to make it happen simultaneously—the coming and the passing out into nirvana, then the delicious throbbing afterglow of coming back to consciousness. So good was the experience that sometimes he did it several times a day.

Now he was almost there, teetering on the verge, hand stroking ever faster while his legs caused the rope to snug tighter, his brain all pyrotechnic dazzle and incandescent sheen.

Except that . . . right *there* . . . was . . .

Just as he came, Angelo glimpsed a figure undulating sinuously, snakelike, along the darkening labyrinth of his blood-starved brain.

It had wide-set, dark, bruise-colored eyes.

Billows of black hair curtaining a face of almost skeletal angles.

No mouth that he could see.

A woman, yet incompletely formed, her lush anatomy eroding even as he watched, pearlescent neck flowing into translucent, blue-veined breasts that dissolved into the tatters of a pelvis.

Like some kind of pallid water snake, the woman swam up from the seabed of his fading consciousness, a wraith thing that grew more insubstantial by the instant until what passed as flesh was no more than a transparent veil.

Just before she disappeared, the creature stared up at Angelo.

The blurred and wispy tendrils of a hand came up, silently imploring.

"*I'm yours,*" he thought he heard her say. "*Help . . . me . . .*"

Then Angelo lost consciousness.

"I wish this country'd go to war," huffed Danny Marston.

He and Angelo and their buddy Erik Jehle were cruising up Colfax Avenue in Erik's banged-up Datsun to a 7-Eleven where the fatty dweeb behind the counter would sell them beer, no ID required, in exchange for the joints that Danny slipped him from time to time.

Angelo was riding in the backseat, with Erik driving and Danny in the passenger seat next to him.

"You know why I wish this country'd go to war?" continued Danny, even though neither Angelo nor Erik had indicated interest. " 'Cause you know what soldiers get to do. A soldier in the field gets to fuck the piss out of any woman he finds, no questions asked. She makes a fuss, he can just go ahead and waste her. Who's gonna know?''

"I think rape's what they call a war crime," Angelo said absently.

"War crime," mocked Danny in a derisive falsetto. "It's a fucking *tactic's* what it is. They done it in Bosnia, they're doin' it in Haiti—you want to de-morale your enemy, you know what you do, you rape his women. His wife, his daughters, sisters, his old momma, too, plus you get all that pussy. That's why I wish this country'd go to war—so I could go over and get me some enemy ass."

They pulled into the parking lot of the convenience store. The Twins, two sophomore girls whom Angelo and the others knew from school, were bouncing out of the store chewing candy bars. They weren't really twins at all, but had gotten the name because they hung around together so much. The name was also meant as an ironic joke for, while the "Twins" both had bleached blond hair, here all resemblance ended. One of them, Denise, topped the scale at upward of two hundred pounds, balloon breasts big enough to nurse a calf; the other, MyraAnn, all knobs and bony angles, looked like a guy trying to fuck her could cut himself on her pelvic bones if he weren't careful.

Both had spotty skins, and peroxide had left their hair looking like something you'd cut with a scythe, but they were female, they were notoriously loose and that was all that mattered.

They sashayed along, glancing away and giggling when they passed the swaggering boys. "Fuckin' snooty pieces of tail," sneered Erik, while Danny stared at them the way Angelo'd seen tigers look at raw meat just before the zoo keeper slung the bleeding chunks into their enclosure.

Inside the convenience store, they got three six-packs, which they paid for, and a collection of Slim Jims and Baby Ruths that Erik stuffed into his jacket while Danny and Angelo were transacting for the beer. They took the booty outside and sat in the car and ate and got buzzed and talked about what they always talked about, which was snatch—how to get it, where to find it, the many ways to do it, fuck it, suck it, jerk off on it.

The talk and the booze made Angelo horny.

Not for the Twins. Not for any woman at all, but for The Device and for his fantasies.

For the ball-popping, mind-fucking pleasure of blasting into unconsciousness propelled by an orgasm so strong, it felt like his brains were being shot out the end of his dick.

He could hardly wait until Erik dropped him off at home and he could go to his room and get it on.

This time, though, there was more than just the orgasm he wanted. He hoped for another glimpse of the eerie, undulating swimmer, if he could stay conscious long enough to see her more clearly.

It was Danny who'd taught Angelo about the awesome, un-fucking-believable orgasms that were possible if you could figure out a way to choke yourself at the same time that you jerked off. Of course, faggots did it to each other all the time—according to Danny, every fag apartment had a few ties and sashes next to the bed for just such use—but real men couldn't do it to one another, and you certainly couldn't let a woman do it to you (even if any of them had known a woman willing to participate in such a thing)—no, giving a woman the upper hand during sex was worse than being queerfucked.

So Angelo had dreamed up The Device all on his own.

One thing Danny had warned him about was that, frankly stated, guys sometimes accidentally offed themselves this way, and wouldn't that make a pretty picture for your mom to walk in on, you stone dead on the bed, with a hard-on the size of a gourd in your fist, lying in your own stink and your eyes staring up and your mouth open with your tongue stuck straight out like some kind of flesh dildo?

Seven seconds, Danny said he'd read someplace. Seven seconds from the time the noose tightened until you went out, so if anything went wrong, that's how long you had to save yourself, or that's it, buddy: you're tomorrow's dirty joke in homicide division.

"You fuck up and let yourself pass out with the noose still tight, you dead meat, man." And Danny had chuckled around a mouthful of chili dog, a sound like gravel being ground under one of his Doc Marten boots. "Man, you be dead with your dick in your hand."

Careful, now, thought Angelo, *not too fast. Make it last as long as possible; go easy.*

Angelo's knees were quivering as he gave the bar a push. The noose around his neck dug in. Blood beat behind his eyes and surged into his cock. Angelo shut his eyes and watched the blackness in his head turn dazzling, starry, a liquid, crimson phosphorescence like lava flowing into purple waves. And from this strange, internal ocean the woman from his vision pieced herself together like a pattern made by moonlight on an obsidian sea.

She was better formed this time but still incomplete, whole areas of pelvis and rib cage left either shockingly absent or pitifully concave, her breasts nippleless, translucent globes behind which a single-ventricled heart could be seen beating feebly.

Angelo's legs felt numb. He couldn't feel the bar beneath his feet, couldn't tell how hard he might be pushing it.

The woman had no ears. No mouth except a lipless, toothless orifice no bigger than a bottle cap.

But her yearning, hungry eyes fixed on Angelo, beseeched him.

Her hands reached for him, long fingers weaving patterns like underwater fans, nails the color of arterial blood.

The pitiful mouth pursed and strained, passed words. *"Help . . . me . . ."*

Angelo felt her pain, her sadness. He took his hand off his cock for just an instant, tried to reach for her, flailed empty air.

"Who . . . ?"

His vision was the color of her nails now, a sea of floating crimson dots, edged in an ever-expanding black frame.

"Help me, Angelo, I'm . . ."

He wanted to touch those reaching hands—she was so real now, so close—but he had to stroke himself again—quickly—or lose the chance to climax. -

"*I'm yours*," she murmured, her insubstantial form aquiver like a fibrillating heart, pulsing fainter and fainter as the blackness swallowed her up.

"*Help me, help me, help mehelpmehelpmehelp- meeeeeeee . . .*"

Angelo came and then came to seconds later, unconsciousness having rendered his legs limp and the rope slack. His hand and dick were glued together by a sticky paste of cum. The blood drummed in his temples like tiny fists, tapping him awake.

For long moments afterward, he lay there, staring up at the bottom of the bunk bed over his head, remembering every detail of the woman in his dream, who claimed that she belonged to him.

Some bizarre variation on a wet dream, he figured, although he'd have wished the woman's face and body could be more like a centerfold and less like some kind of seductive leper, with parts of her unformed or fallen off.

What most disturbed him, though, was that the vision inspired more than just a hard-on. It was as though the woman from this drowned world was inducing new emotions in him or resurrecting old ones, those frightening feelings that he thought he'd put aside in little boyhood: tenderness and gentleness, the desire to protect, defend and love.

The way, a long time ago, he'd felt about his brother.

Before Mark had toughened up and muscled up and got to be a tattooed, colors-sporting, queer-bashing badass who called Angelo a fuckface punk and once handed him a glass of rum and Coke with a fat, bloated worm at the bottom and told him, *Be a man now, drink it, gulp it down*. Angelo still gagged when he remembered that slimy, awful slickness on his tongue, like swallowing a baby turd, but he'd done it, he'd done it so he'd be a man in Mark's eyes, and even so, Mark had only laughed at him. (*You dumb fuck, do you always do what people tell you?*)

Now Angelo felt the pricklings of tears behind his eyes, and an unspeakable sorrow and longing, something old and vast, eternal as the ocean, *female*, threatened to seep out of some hidden crevice in his soul and overwhelm him.

Tears that threatened his manhood, his maleness, everything tough and hard and pussy-fucking-tough-assed-mean motherfucker son of a bitch that he was trying to be.

So Danny would like him. So Erik would like him. So Mark, if he were still alive, would respect him.

So he would be a *man*. (But he wanted to be held, he wanted to be cared for, he wanted . . . something different . . . what?)

Fucking shit, why was he crying? What was *happening* to him?

Twisting on the bed, Angelo brought his cum-encrusted fist up and rammed it into the ridge of bone above his eye.

Searing red, rainbow-spangled pain. Blood running warm along his cheek instead of tears.

The image of his brother, of the woman, faded with the pain.

"Hey, man, I'm at Erik's house. You gotta get over here. Now."

It was Saturday afternoon, the middle of a Lakers game.

"What for?" said Angelo.

"Look, just get your ass over here. Erik's parents are gone for the weekend and we got us a surprise."

"So what is it?"

"Fuck you, man, I don't have time to jive with you. You comin' or not?"

But Angelo had already punched the remote and switched off the TV.

"Comin'."

* * *

The basement rec room of Erik's house reeked of a testosterone cocktail—booze and semen and sweat.

Over all of it hung a thick, nauseating layer of fear, like the ripe scent wafting up from the carcass of a road-killed animal.

The shades were all drawn, and Angelo couldn't see well at first. Then, as his eyes adjusted, he saw the mattress thrown down on the floor and the two bodies on it.

Three bodies, actually, because Erik was part of whatever the scene was down on the floor.

The Twins lay naked on the stained and grungy mattress. Erik's white ass moved up and down as he fucked the thin one.

Angelo's first, horrified impression was that they were dead. But then the fat twin moaned and flopped around. Erik came over and slammed a bottle of vodka up against her mouth.

"Drink," he said. "Drink this, or I swear to God I'll break the bottle over your fucking head and shove it up your cunt."

Whether or not she even heard him, Angelo didn't know, but she sucked weakly, coughing every now and then like a baby suckling a poisoned teat.

The other one, the skinny one, didn't move at all.

Erik shuddered into the thin Twin's body and hauled himself off her. "My man, you got here just in time. We invited these two young ladies over here to party, but they both seem to have, uh, overindulged and are sleeping it off." He bowed and made a flourish with his hand. "So which of these beautiful buttered buns would you care to start with? You got your big tits, you got your small tits, you got your fat ass, you got your tight ass, you got all afternoon, my man, the day is young."

Angelo stood there staring at the room, at the women passed out on the mattress, feeling sick to his stomach. He felt like a little boy again and Mark was giving him the drink with its disgusting garnish and he wanted to flee, oh God, he wanted to run from all of them, his grinning, gleeful buddies and the women with the awful furry, grinning mouths between their legs, and they were expecting him not just to thrust himself between those cum-caked lips but to do this terrible thing while they watched, and he wished to God he'd never answered the fucking telephone, wished he'd stayed at home with The Device and the visions that it brought him.

"Whatsa matter, our leavin's ain't good enough for you?"

"Maybe he just can't make up his mind," said Danny. "Maybe he's like the mule that starved to death between two bales of hay 'cause he couldn't make up his mind which one to eat."

Oh, God, I never expected it to be . . . not like this . . .

"Hey, man, get going. You makin' me nervous."

Erik had hand-jerked himself erect again and began to fuck the fat one, her breasts jiggling every time he thrust into her, a dribble of saliva burbling at the corner of her lip.

"Hey, what kinda man are you anyway, don't want good pussy? Maybe you not a man at all. Maybe you a faggot oughtta lie down here and get fucked with the girls."

"Shut up," Angelo said.

He closed his eyes and thought about the woman in his vision, the yearning and the sorrow that he'd felt for her, but he couldn't see her clearly now; the memory had departed like the image of his brother as a young boy—before his brother turned into a brute he didn't recognize—getting dimmer, vaguer.

Something inside him, something good and valuable that might have changed his life, had been choked into unconsciousness, and he hadn't even felt it.

Then his penis overrode all hesitation and sprang to life like some battery-powered sex toy as he began to remove his pants and underwear.

He crawled atop the thin Twin, forced his cock into her pussy and began to work his hips. At first he was distracted by the newness of the sensation, the repellent fleshiness of the girl's interior. After a while, he had only one thought: God, he hoped they didn't guess this was his first time. God, he hoped he was doing it right, hoped he fucked her like she'd never been fucked in all her sorry life, fucked her so she'd never walk straight again, because he was a man, a man, because he was a man . . .

How was it possible he was still horny? He'd fucked three times—twice with the fat girl, once with her skinny friend. He'd fucked their dry, sandpapery snatches until he thought the skin would peel right off his dick, but he was hornier than ever.

Because I want to do it the way it feels best.

Not with a girl.

Not a squishy-soft, dickless girl who had that awful hole between her legs, that terrible god-awful hole like some kind of smelly burrow surrounded by those lopsided lips that looked like the fatty trimmings off a piece of pork, and he had to think of the Twins that way—not as people, but as vile, disgusting sex organs—or else he knew that he'd start crying and that he'd never stop.

No, he was just horny; that was why he was hurrying home. To be alone with The Device and his good six inches.

To be alone with his fantasy.

He lay on his bunk now, the rope tight around his throat while the inside of his skull turned into a planetarium full of wheeling, dipping stars, and at the same time, as his sight dimmed and his mind blurred, he began to see the woman gliding up from underneath the water, resplendently, shimmeringly nude.

Complete now. Perfectly formed.

Created by him.

For him.

She was different now, no longer pale and maimed and incomplete, but plush and buttery, breasts so full and peachy you could pillow down forever in the cleavage, and if she had a hole between her legs at all, Angelo knew intuitively it would be neat and clean and small and never emit foul odors or menstrual blood or babies, and she was beckoning to him now and smiling a lover's smile with her scarlet, vulval mouth.

"*Angelo, come here, take my hand, take it . . . Angelo, I belong to you . . .*"

But he'd already guessed as much. She was some part of him he feared and kept in exile, a shadow creature who emerged only when unconsciousness was creeping in, when the synapses in his brain were ceasing to transmit.

She frightened him, and yet he longed for her, and the more intense his longing grew, the greater was his terror.

He put his feet down on the bed, temporarily relieving the pressure on his throat, pumping his meat with desperate vigor, aroused as he'd never before been in his life by this female ghost, this lost soul in a limbo he couldn't understand but which he sensed held all that was forbidden, terrifying to the world of men, all softness, seduction, *womanliness*.

This was the place it wasn't safe to go, the place of female longings. And yet . . .

"*Help me, Angelo. I need you. I'm yours.*"

His dick was as hard as a crowbar, as pumped as a biceps after fifty curls.

He put his feet back on the bar. Pushed hard.

"*. . . need you, want you, please . . .*"

She reached for him, not just with her hand but arching toward him with her entire body. It was more real than any Virtual Reality game he'd ever witnessed, more real than the mattress underneath his bucking body, more real than his hard-on in his hand.

He strained for her with his free hand. She seemed to pull back a little, withdrawing tantalizingly . . . a little deeper underneath the watery twilight but still smiling, smiling . . .

. . . and he wriggled sideways, still reaching out, because he could almost touch her face now, her sweet, sad face . . . her long fingers were so close and he could . . . just . . . almost . . .

He lost his balance.

His angled body slid sideways off the bed, the bar twisting so that the bicycle chain looped twice around his upraised ankle, all his weight holding the rope taut, grinding it into his neck.

The noose tightened brutally.

Oh, Jesus, no.

Seven seconds.

He tried to scramble off the floor and back onto the bed.

Six . . .

Vision gone to test pattern, scarlet at the edges, trying to catch the side of the bed, pull himself up, free his trapped foot, his agonized throat . . .

Five . . .

Again, come on, COME ON, but his fingers were like plugs of Silly Putty; they had no strength, no grip, like they were sculpted from mud.

Four . . .

The woman-ghost was swimming up out of the dark water behind his eyes. He could see her now with terrifying clarity. She wasn't lovely now, but malformed and hideous, her eyes pinched, demonic slits, her mouth a foul, red-rimmed pit miming the obscenity between her legs.

Three . . .

His eyes felt like eggs dropped into boiling water. Copper burned at the back of his tongue.

Two . . .

"Come here."

No, please, I didn't want to hurt those girls, I didn't want to do it, I only wanted to be a man, to be a man, to be . . .

One.

"Angelo, you're . . . MINE."

For Michael Zulli

BLACKPOOL ROCK

Philip Nutman

Philip Nutman has worn many hats since he first appeared in print at age fifteen: novelist, screenwriter, producer, journalist and BBC TV production assistant. He has published over 350 feature articles, fifteen short stories (in *Book of the Dead*, *The Year's Best*, *Splatterpunks* and *Borderlands II*, to mention a few) and one novel, *Wet Work*. A two-time Stoker finalist, he is currently completing two novels and producing *The Last Blood*, an independent action/horror film.

Fame, Darren Franks mused as he poured a large shot of Johnny Walker Red, was a fickle mistress at the best of times. But there came a point where one morning you realized the woman you'd been sleeping with was a phony. It was like picking up some babe in a bar, balling her ass off, only to wake up and see her for what she really was: an aging hooker who'd given her favors to so many others that no amount of makeup could disguise the decay.

"Here's to the great lie," he said, toasting his reflection in the dressing room mirror.

Elvis toasted him back.

Elvis Darren Aaron Franks Presley.

Darren scratched at his left sideburn. Damn, his skin allergy was starting to act up. Come tomorrow, he'd have a rash like a teen with primo acne.

"Did you ever have these problems?"

Elvis squinted back at him.

"No, of course not. You were The King. Me, I'm just The Great Pretender."

He emptied the glass and rubbed his chest. Goddamn indigestion. He should have brought a big bottle of Mylanta before leaving for this tiny, uncivilized country. His guts had been churning since the Tuesday flight out of Atlanta, and the food here didn't help. Bland or greasy—take your choice. When he'd asked Davies, who ran the club, for Mylanta, he might as well have been speaking Creole. Yeah, well, that's where fame got you—a weeklong gig at a cheesy cabaret joint in the English Northwest.

For One Week Only! All the Way from the U.S. of A.! Top Elvis Impersonator Darren Franks!

He hummed a few lines of "What a Wonderful World," grimacing as the whiskey continued to burn his insides. Yes, sirree, bob, what a wonderful, wonderful world it was. At least the trip had gotten him away from Carrie and the kids.

A knock at the door diverted his attention from the mirror.

"Yeah, who is it?"

Another knock.

"Yeah?!"

The unwanted visitor rapped three times.

"Shit," Darren muttered, rising from the worn leather chair. Maybe it was the writer who was traveling up from

London to do a piece on him for the . . . what was it? *The Sunday Express*. Some lowbrow news rag. A reporter called Hurst. Guy was supposed to be here hours ago.

Darren opened the door.

A leather-gloved hand grabbed him around the throat, forcing him back into the room. Strong fingers crushed his windpipe, strangling the cry of surprise trying to crawl out his gaping mouth. Then a hand holding a white cloth clamped over his face.

Within seconds, Darren was unconscious.

You could always rely on British Rail to let you down. The 4:10 from Euston had departed ninety minutes late, which meant they had missed their scheduled connection in Preston and waited another two hours for a train to Blackpool. It was now nearly midnight and Jamie Hurst was pissed off.

Why couldn't they have driven, like civilized people? He looked at the reason sitting beside him in the back of the cab and let the thought go. He was too tired, too hungry, to be angry. Irritable, yes, which was why he'd hardly said a word for the past hour, letting Beth murder the silence with her endless chatter. But being short with her wasn't going to get him anywhere.

"So was this where the IRA tried to blow up Thatcher a few years ago?"

"No, that was Brighton. Bastion of Tory conventions."

Although Beth was attractive, her endless chatter and ill-formed knowledge irritated him. That, and the perfume she always wore.

The cab pulled up sharply.

"Grand Hotel," said the driver.

Jamie looked out the window at the facade of the Victorian building looming over them. Like all the other buildings he'd seen on their drive across town, the Grand whispered memories of better days. Times long gone in this forsaken corner of Thatcher's Britain.

He paid the driver, tipping him well. Might as well divert some Southern expense-account money into the pockets of the Northern poor.

"Thanks very much, Guv," the cabbie said, touching the brim of his cloth cap.

You cynical bastard, Jamie silently reprimanded himself. Just because you don't like being up North doesn't give you the right to think like a prick.

The cabbie's gesture was so Dickensian, he didn't know whether to laugh or throw up. The cabbie probably thinks I'm just some spoiled Southern arsehole.

Jamie pulled their bags from the cab's boot. Beth was still going on and on about something.

"Hmm?"

"How about a quiet dinner for two? Maybe by candle-light?"

Oh, God, she was trying the seduction routine again. Jesus, American women seemed to think about nothing other than having a few inches of Englishman inside them. Beth's constant hint-dropping reminded him of his first trip to New York. After three women had tried to bed him in two days, Jamie had come to two conclusions—one, most American women were obsessed with sex; and two, it wasn't his body they wanted, it was his accent.

"I've got a swine of a headache," he replied honestly. "Let's just check into our rooms and get some rest. I should call The Lucky Strike and try to touch base with Franks. Judging by his ego, he'll probably throw a fit because we didn't make tonight's show."

"Okay," Beth replied, obviously disappointed as they navigated the revolving doors.

Was he dreaming? Darren didn't know. His head was filled with mist.

"He'll be here tomorrow," said a male voice.

He couldn't hear the other person.

"I promise. He's looking forward to it."

Something else was said, but consciousness slipped gears, and neutral took over.

And with it, the merciful static of unconsciousness.

Jamie dumped his bags in the closet and collapsed on the bed.

Malcolm, you swine, I could hit you for this!

He grimaced as he ran a hand over his face, the softness of the bed embracing his back. But the truth was he couldn't give Malcolm shit for saddling him with Beth—or for setting up the assignment, the first of a series. If Malcolm was fucking Beth, then the slightest criticism was going to alienate his editor. And even if good old Malcolm Jones weren't slipping Beth Golden the pork sword, any kind of criticism would place *him* in the editor's bad books—a situation Jamie could ill afford at the moment.

You are between book contracts and have a mortgage, old son, so don't forget that a series of articles for *The Sunday Express* is going to go a long way to keep the wolf from the door.

At least Beth hadn't forced the issue when he'd headed for his room. Another situation like the one at The Crown and Two Chairmen, when she'd been smashed and clingy, would have tried his patience. Maybe she was getting the hint.

He struggled up from the bed and dialed room service. After he ordered a beer and a ham and cheese sandwich, he opened his shoulder bag and pulled out his diary.

Jamie seated himself at the small desk next to the TV set, pen poised over virgin page, trying to ignore the emetic green wallpaper with the gold rococo design.

So here I am in gloomy Blackpool with a randy American photographer. The wallpaper is an affront to good taste, the bed too soft, and I have a bad case of British Rail bottom from spending hours on a wretched Inter-City ride to the working-class Las Vegas of the Northwest.

Anyone who thinks writing for a living is glamorous needs a lobotomy!

Paul Theroux probably summed this place up best in his English travel book The Kingdom: *"Blackpool was perfectly reflected in the swollen guts and unhealthy fat of its beer-guzzling visitors . . ." Those words have stuck with me since I first read them, so accurately reflecting my impressions when I first passed through back in '82.*

Ah, well . . . I guess there's no point complaining. An assignment's an assignment.

He put the pen down, trying not to look at the wall-paper.

It wasn't the assignment per se which bothered him. Writing a profile on an Elvis impersonator wasn't difficult. The truth was Jamie didn't like the North. It made him uncomfortable. There was an atmosphere of despair born of the Conservative Government's industrial strip-mining, of unemployment, of poverty. Let's face it, he thought, the locals had every reason to despise Southerners. As Thatcher was so fond of reminding the Great British Public, *We live in the Post-Industrial Age and the job market is changing.* It had changed, all right. In ten years, the Bitch had seen to that; it was no longer North and South, it was Have and Have Not.

More than the location he found himself in was the fact he'd been having one of *those feelings* since he'd boarded the train in London. The prescient sense of dread increased as he awaited the arrival of room service. The kind of sensation—a sixth sense glowing dully at the back of his brain like an early-warning radar—that he'd been cursed with since the day his brother had died violently in a freak motorbike accident ten years ago.

Álex Hurst had lived fast and died young, a wild rider on the Dark Highway. It hadn't been the suddenness of Alex's death which disturbed Jamie; it was the fact he'd known something was going to happen. The way he'd been drawn to the crash site at the moment of impact, puking his guts out with fear before the incident, watching his brother's hideous death with cold cinema-verité detachment.

That dreadful, instinctual, *a priori* knowledge had plagued him on several occasions since then. *He'd known* his mother was going to have a stroke hours before it happened, even though he was over a hundred miles away. *He'd known* Jessica, his first serious girlfriend, was going to commit suicide. She'd been unstable—you didn't have to be Sherlock Holmes to deduce that. But he'd never consciously realized how close to the Abyss she was during those heady days at Oxford. That reality—and not being able to prevent it—had hit him hardest of all. Sometimes a tsunami of guilt wiped him out when he thought of his mother. Guilt at not feeling *anything*. Deeper than the remorse he'd wallowed in for a period after Alex's death. For someone so sensitive to his environment, the sad fact was, a part of his emotional cortex seemed dead.

Like the significant others in his life.

"Enough moping," he muttered, picking up the telephone, and dialed the number of The Lucky Strike Cabaret.

George Robles cracked open the door to the spare room to see how the American was doing.

Elvis—or the closest version this side of Heaven—lay unconscious on the single bed, hands and feet tied securely. Robles paused in case he was faking it. After watching the prone body for a couple of minutes, Robles realized he couldn't detect the sound of the man's breathing.

No, he couldn't be dead! Not yet, not before . . .

Robles went to the bed, kneeling beside Darren Franks. He sighed with relief. The American was breathing so shallowly his chest barely moved. Good. He'd gone to too much trouble, risked everything for this chance to bring happiness to Michelle. But with his luck, it could have turned out the American had a respiratory disorder or an allergic reaction to the chloroform. George Robles knew all about bad luck. It had shadowed him his entire life. If luck were a lady, then she was a spiteful, stuck-up bitch who had turned her face away from him since he was a child. He also knew about pain, fear and bitterness. And resentment at the unjust world, its mindless crimes and twisted jokes.

Like the curse placed on Michelle, his once-beautiful daughter, who'd suffered for most of her seventeen years and would be lucky if she saw another two.

Well, she wouldn't. He'd already decided that. She had suffered enough and it was time to free her from the prison of her pain. The last thing she would know was happiness through the blessing of The King.

Robles walked slowly, softly, from the spare room, afraid the American would wake and he'd have to explain.

That would come later.

After the persuasion.

The digital bedside clock showed 1:34 A.M.

Jamie rolled onto his side, trying not to let his frustration fuel his insomnia. The headache throbbed passionately behind his closed eyes, the ham and cheese sandwich a lump of lead in his stomach. But between the thesis of incipient migraine, antithesis of indigestion, lay the synthesis of the premonition which teased and tormented his tired psyche.

(white)

He groaned involuntarily, massaging his wrists.

(sore)

(rope burn)

He felt sick. Not because of the indigestible lump of hotel food lying in his gut, but because of the overpowering medical smell that permeated his nostrils.

(. . . ere tomorrow)

"Go away," he muttered under the covers. "Leave me alone."

Whatever signals he was picking up, he didn't want to know the source or the reason.

(white walls, hard bed)

(sore)

The medical smell again.

"Fuck." He stumbled from the bed toward the bathroom, bile crawling from his stomach. He hated being sick, and the worst part of the psychic sensual overload was the puking. Jamie made it to the porcelain bowl in time. Just. Lumps of ham and cheese evacuated his mouth in a bilious rush, his sternum heaving painfully. A second ejection. A third, the malty taste of the beer he'd washed the sandwich down with underscoring the stomach acid. A dry heave punctuated the vomiting fit, a static band of white noise humming in his ears. Thank God he hadn't eaten shepherd's pie or something heavier.

Seconds rolled sluggishly into languid minutes as he hunched over the cold toilet bowl in case his stomach jumped again. Then, shaking, he stood, moving to the washbasin, and ran the cold water. He splashed his face, rinsed his mouth, groaning.

Knocking.

What? Someone knocking at his door.

Again. Louder.

Without thinking, he went to the door and opened it.

"I couldn't sleep."

Beth stood there with a sheepish smile on her face and a diaphanous blue silk dressing gown almost covering her naked, alabaster skin and firm, prominent breasts. A nipple peeked out at him from behind the fabric.

"Oooh," she added, noticing his nakedness, her eyes dropping to his flaccid penis.

Jamie grabbed the sash of the gown, pulled her inside, slamming the door.

"What's up?" he grumbled.

"I couldn't sleep."

Brandy on her breath.

"So?"

"So . . . I thought . . ."

The dark of the doorway swallowed him. He didn't feel embarrassed by his nakedness. But he suddenly felt cold, vulnerable, lost. The white noise buzzed in his head, fractured by faint blips of psychic radar.

(sore)

(uck is thi)

"Are you all right?"

"No. Go back to bed."

He swayed, stumbled, held the wall for support.

"Are you sick?"

"No . . . it's nothing."

He swayed again.

Jamie flinched as Beth's soft, warm hand found his face.

"Poor baby."

Too weak to resist, he pushed her gently into the room. "Get into bed."

He placed a hand on her bum. The skin was hot beneath the cool silk. "Go on."

Beth let the robe slip from her shoulders as she heard Jamie running water in the bathroom, a smile on her lips.

Darren Franks blinked against the brightness of the naked light bulb hanging from the ceiling's center.

What was this fucking shit? Kidnapped. That much was fucking obvious. By who? Fucking Elvis fans? Yeah, well, anything was possible. There were enough fucking mushheads out there who loved Elvis so much they didn't want to believe he was dead. It was cultural obsession bordering on religious psychosis—and part of the reason he earned the amount of green he did.

But this sucked the big, fat hairy one to the root.

He'd pretended to be unconscious when the creep had entered the room. He'd been so nervous, in fact, he'd almost forgotten to breathe. Real smart. The fucking asshole thought he'd croaked. Stuck his greasy head right next to Darren's mouth. Smell of the fuckwad's hair lotion almost made him toss his cookies. Bastard fucking piece of shit, just wait till you untie my hands. I'll fucking choke every last ounce of shit from your skinny body.

Fuckfuckfuckfuckfuck. Darren struggled against the ropes, wincing. His skin was raw.

Why didn't matter. *Who*, he didn't give a shit about. All he wanted was to get untied and take a king-sized dump before he shit his Calvin Kleins and brown-stained his best Elvis-in-Vegas white pantsuit.

Yeah, it sucked.

uckfuckfuckfuck . . . fuckfuckfuck . . .

The stream of profanity pulled Jamie's consciousness down from the cresting wave of orgasm into a psychic undertow, making his back spasm. Beth perceived it as onrushing ejaculation, thrusting her hips toward him.

"Yes, yes!"

Jamie's sphincter muscle contracted, puckered unexpectedly, stopping him mid-hump.

Oh, no.

His bowels felt ready to let go.

"Oh, yes, baby. Give it to me."

Jamie felt his rectum move.

But nothing happened . . . only he could feel it . . . and the humiliation . . .

(aww no)

Beth stopped thrusting her hips, said something he couldn't hear through the sensory feedback.

His penis softened.

(ashamed . . . ohfuck . . .)

Jamie nearly collapsed on Beth, cushioning his suddenly supine form on knees and elbows, molding to her shape like Plasticine, his head burrowing into the pillow beside hers.

Apples. Her hair smelled of apples. Fresh, clean. *Timotei shampoo*, he thought, images from a TV commercial dispelling the helplessness, the isolation, emptiness.

"What's the matter?" Beth whispered. "Don't feel bad. It happens sometimes."

"Hold me," Jamie said. "Don't let me go."

He nuzzled her ear with his nose, drinking in her smell, her essence, the scent of apple shampoo cocooning him from the dark despair hovering over his back.

Beth hugged him. Tight.

"I know you're awake. Stop faking," said the voice in the doorway. "We punish fakers."

The voice was thick with a Northern brogue.

Darren opened his eyes, turned his head toward his captor.

The man in the doorway was skinny, unkempt. Around five feet ten inches, weedy-looking. Long arms. He wore a green nylon shirt, old brown polyester trousers, plaid carpet slippers. His eyes were deep-set, red-rimmed as if he hadn't slept in a while. A black forest of stubble covered his cheeks. He hesitated as Darren looked him in the eye. The man dropped his gaze, looking at the worn rug on the floor.

"I've shit myself. I've already been punished. Please untie me so I can clean myself," Darren asked, trying to make his tone as reasonable, nonthreatening, as possible.

The man sniffed. "Yes, I can smell. Good. Maybe you'll learn humility."

Darren's anger flared. He bit his tongue to control it. Don't let the bastard see he's got the better of you.

"Look, I don't know what all this is about, but you're making a big mistake. If you think you can get ransom for me, sorry, you got the wrong guy. Willie Nelson, maybe."

"I know who you are," the man replied coldly. "That's why you're here. Ransom? No, that's not what this is about."

"Then what is it?"

The man came closer. There was a faraway glint of something unhealthy in the man's eyes, a dark mote of madness.

"You're going to help me. And if you cooperate, then I'll let you live."

Darren went numb.

"What . . . what do you want?" His throat was dry and his voice threatened to crack.

"You're going to make love to my daughter."

After they made love a second time, successfully, gently, Jamie told Beth what was wrong. All of it. As they lay together, limbs entwined, the warmth of her soft skin keeping the sensation of isolation at bay, the words spilled from his mouth. At first a trickle, like a mountain stream struggling free from winter ice; then a torrent as the words became a river of confession. She listened attentively, occasionally asking a question when he wandered from a particular point, lost in memory, blinded with guilt. Years of keeping his secrets locked away in the closet of silence had exacted a toll on his ability to be intimate. Jamie had kept the world at arm's length, had tried to find truths in the mirror of fiction. More often than not, all he'd found was more questions, bigger lies. But as he talked the burden lessened, and for the first time in as long as he could remember, a measure of inner peace calmed him, tuning out the psychic static.

Beth asked him about Alex. She wanted to know how different they were, as if Alex's dark reflection could shed some light on the man she was attracted to and whose bed she was at last sharing. He told her. And he talked about Jessica. She held him tighter as he did so.

"What does this have to do with Franks?" she asked later, as the digital clock clicked to 5:44 A.M.

"I don't know. I called The Lucky Strike. He'd gone for the night. I called his hotel. Wasn't there either. I left a message. Maybe it has nothing to do with him."

"But you said as soon as we got on the train you started to get the feeling, and it increased as we neared Blackpool. It would be logical—"

"There's nothing logical about my gift," he interjected, tensing. "Gift. Huh," he grunted. "*Curse.*"

Jamie pushed himself away from Beth slightly.

"What do you want from me? Why are you attracted to me?" he asked, his voice earnest.

She chuckled softly. "It's not your accent. It's . . ." She paused, trying to find the right words.

"When I first met you, I saw a young, attractive man. Talented, witty. But sad. Gentle—" She broke off, sighed. "I don't know, just . . . don't murder my feelings by putting them under a microscope."

Neither spoke for a while; then Beth reached out for him.

"Come here."

Finally, they slept.

Jamie dreamed of a white room, of rope and of a girl who looked like Jessica.

George Robles sat at the end of Michelle's bed, watching her sleep peacefully in the moonlight spilling through the curtainless window. There was no need for curtains. She had been born blind. And paraplegic. It was all so unfair.

Robles drank from the can of bitter he nursed in his right hand, tears of frustration welling in his eyes.

What kind of a life was this for a young girl, imprisoned by her body, lost in perpetual darkness? Aside from music, he was her only friend. He hadn't let her suffer the taunts of children or the indignities of a cruel world, had raised her himself, educated her and tried to give her happiness.

And for the first time in his life, George Robles was loved.

But come tomorrow, she'd know true happiness. The King would wine and dine her, make love to her. Make her feel she was a beautiful woman. And later, when she slept, Robles would take her pain away, and Michelle would find peace at last.

Despite her thin, almost skeletal body, she looked beautiful to Robles. So beautiful he wished he could slip into bed beside her and hold his lovely daughter, who never complained and loved him. But that was . . . unhealthy. He couldn't do that. Some mummies did, though. Oh, he knew that, all right. It made him feel sick.

Robles drank his beer to take away the taste of the bad memory.

As Darren came to, vague thoughts of Carrie and the kids drifted like phantoms through his drugged mind. Then he opened his eyes and remembered where he was.

That bastard had chloroformed him again. Why?

Then he realized he was naked from the waist down and understood.

The crazy son of a bitch had removed his soiled pants and underwear, cleaned his shit-encrusted ass and tied him up again. Relief clashed with anger, humiliation with disgust. That creep had touched him *there*. A man had touched his cock, his balls, his asshole. *What else did he do while you were unconscious*, his mind screamed, *suck your dick?*

Darren struggled against the rope. His wrists were raw, but anger overrode pain.

"Fucking son of a bitch! Let me out of here! Someone untie me!" he bellowed.

Maybe there was someone else in the house. Maybe they didn't know what this crazy fucker was up to.

Darren bellowed again as loud as he could, twisting his shoulders, tugging at the ropes.

Within seconds, the door opened. The man entered, his face flushed, a leather belt in his right hand.

Darren clammed up as the man sprang to the bed, the belt coming down fast in a vicious arc. It whipped across his chest. It hurt like a motherfucker. Again, again. He cried out.

"Shut up!" the man hissed. "Shut up!"

"You goddamn son of a bitch!"

"Shut up!"

The man raised the belt, aiming it at Darren's face. "Don't make me hurt you." The man trembled. "I . . . I don't want to hurt you. Please, just cooperate with me and I'll let you go."

His expression was earnest, Darren thought. His eyes were red, as if he'd been crying, and now he was shaking.

"Okay. Okay! Don't hit me," Darren said as calmly as possible. His chest stung beneath his white jacket and silk shirt. The belt buckle had pounded his ribs, and he could feel he was going to have bruises the size of pickled eggs.

Try to reason with him. Don't provoke him.

"What did you do to me?"

Confusion showed on the man's face. "What . . . what do you mean? I . . . I cleaned you up. It wasn't very nice."

"Why didn't you let me do it myself?"

"I couldn't risk letting you free."

Darren was silent, trying to think of what to say.

"I . . . I didn't touch you, if that's what you're thinking. I'm not a p-per-pervert."

Right, you fucking loon. You kidnap me, tie me up, strip me and wash my balls—and you say you want me to make love to your daughter—normal you ain't.

Darren forced a smile. "Thanks."

The man dropped the belt. There were tears in his eyes. His narrow shoulders sagged.

"Just tell me what you want. I'll cooperate," Darren said softly, trying to ignore feelings of humiliation and vulnerability.

The man sat. "All I want is for you to make my daughter happy."

"Okay." Darren paused. Get him talking. Humor him. Get him to trust you. "Why don't you introduce yourself, and tell me all about it."

"My name's Robles. George Robles."

Jamie awoke surprisingly refreshed despite the lack of sleep. He felt invigorated, weightless, as if he were walking an inch above the ground. He hadn't made love to a woman in nearly two years. But it wasn't the sex with Beth that made him feel this way; it was the understanding she'd expressed, the compassion and tenderness. She didn't just want to fuck him—she wanted him. He'd spent too long hiding himself from others and had forgotten how fine it felt to be wanted. And, he had to admit, the sex was good.

He picked up a slice of cold toast from the remnants of their room-service breakfast. Beth was singing in the shower. He smiled to himself, sat on the bed and opened the book she had shown him while they'd eaten.

I Am Elvis: A Guide to Elvis Impersonators.

He hadn't realized the Elvis cult was so widespread on this level. The book featured sixty-three performers devoted to keeping The King's memory alive and contained photos, biographies, agency addresses, even astrological signs. Some of the Elvis clones had gone so far as to have plastic surgery to further their likeness to Colonel Parker's former meal ticket. A number of others stretched incredulity even farther. "The Lady Elvis." "The Black Elvis." Dimitri Katzka, a large Greek expatriate with a thick beard, didn't resemble Elvis one bit, and, the biography stated, wrote short stories and books about psychotherapy. El-Vez, The Mexican Elvis.

Jamie chuckled at that one.

And there was Darren Franks posing moodily for the camera, dressed in a black velvet pantsuit, holding his microphone like it was a woman's hand.

Birthdate: February 23, 1956. Star sign: Pisces. Height: Six feet. Weight: 210 pounds. Favorite Elvis songs: "Heartbreak Hotel," "Suspicious Minds," "An American Trilogy."

"An Elvis fan since the age of seven, Darren Franks began performing as The King of Rock and Roll during his high school days in Stone Mountain, Georgia, but nearly quit the business when Elvis died," read the biography.

" 'I was working as the manager of a Texaco station on Lawrenceville Highway, and I went numb with grief when my cashier told me the news on that terrible day in August 1977. I tried to drive home, but I was so overcome with emotion I had to pull the car over, and I just sat there and cried for an hour,' " he remembered.

"But, like Elvis, Darren decided the show must go on.

" 'My first thought was I can't do this no more, it wouldn't be right. I had a show booked that night and I didn't think people would want to see me when they knew we'd been robbed of the greatest entertainer who ever lived. But as I sat beside the road with tears in my eyes, I had a vision of The King, and I knew he'd want me to carry on. And the audience did, too. There wasn't a dry eye in the house that night, and I knew I had been chosen to bring happiness to other folk—just like Elvis.' "

Jamie laughed, nearly choking on his toast. Did Franks really believe this? The press clippings he'd researched were nowhere near as entertaining as the profile in the book.

" 'Before I go onstage I say a prayer to Elvis, asking for his blessing and to thank him for the joy he still brings to people,' " was Franks's closing quote. Jamie rolled his eyes.

"You're happy."

He glanced up at Beth standing beside the bathroom

door, a towel wrapped in a turban around her head and nothing else.

"Have you read this?"

"Sure. I'm surprised you didn't know about it."

"Malcolm isn't very reliable when it comes to providing research pointers."

Beth sat next to him. They flipped through the book, laughing together as they read some of the other entries. There was even a four-year-old Elvis impersonator.

"I tried Franks's hotel again," he said. "Still no answer."

"The Lucky Strike?"

"No, I called there, too. The manager's not in yet." He shrugged. "It's early. I've left messages for Franks to call here before noon. Said we'd be over at The Strike by one P.M."

Beth smiled, reached out to wipe a toast crumb from Jamie's lower lip. He kissed her fingers, then took her hand in his.

They made love until noon.

Darren listened to Robles tell him about the death of his wife, Michelle's afflictions and the general tragedy of his life. He had to admit Robles had had it tough. It was enough to send anyone off the tracks, and Robles's train had obviously derailed a long time ago.

"So I couldn't bring myself to tell her Elvis was dead. She'd lost so much already. When she listens to his voice she's at peace, she . . . she forgets her pain. She says he's an angel. Only an angel can sing like that."

Robles paused, lost in memory. "I can't stand to see her get worse and worse," he said suddenly. "It's not fair. The continual pain, the drugs. She has no life, no future. Who's going to take care of her when I'm gone? They'll put her in a home. And they'll mistreat her, just like they did my mother."

Robles continued to ramble. Most of what he said made sense. But it was too weird, too twisted. The more Robles said, the more uncomfortable Darren became.

There's something he's not telling me, his instinct

whispered. The picture Robles painted was incomplete, like a jigsaw puzzle with key pieces missing. Do you honestly think he's going to let you go? Maybe, if all he wanted was for Darren to make love to the girl. He didn't want to ask what Robles had planned after that.

"George."

Robles continued talking about tragedy, how life was cruel, that God, if He existed, was a sadist.

"*George*," Darren said. "I need to piss. And I'm hungry and thirsty."

Robles looked up from the carpet. "I'm sorry." His tone was genuine. "I'll get you water, and a pot."

"I'd like to piss in the john, freshen up. And"—Darren looked down at his wrists—"I'd appreciate it if you untied me. I'm bleeding, and my wrists are sore."

"I . . . I can't do that. You might run away. I'll bring you a pot, water, make you a sandwich. But I can't untie you."

Darren clenched his jaw, trying to control his anger. Untie me, you fuck, and I'll strangle the shit out of you—no, control it, make him believe you mean it. "Please. I'm uncomfortable."

Robles stood up. "No."

He went to the door, then turned. "Don't shout again. I'll hurt you if you do. We can't let Michelle know you're here—not until it's time."

The cab turned onto the Golden Mile near the Blackpool Tower and Beth strained to get a better look at the five-hundred-foot-tall Eiffel-like structure.

"That's it?" she said in disbelief. "I thought it was bigger."

"This is England. Everything's smaller," Jamie replied.

"When do they have the illuminations?"

"August through October. It's quite an event. Keeps the holidaymakers happy. It's the locals' version of Disneyland," he added cynically, referring to the annual extravaganza of illuminated figures which turned the resort into a huge Christmas decoration.

"Eight million people," said the cabbie.

"Excuse me?" Beth replied.

"The illuminations," said the cabbie. "That's how many people came to see 'em last year. Right spectacular it is, too. Me kids love it. Nothing like that down South. Great place, Blackpool."

Beth tried to hide a smirk. Jamie looked out the window, embarrassed the cabbie had heard his disparaging remarks.

"Here's The Strike." The cabbie nodded his head in the direction of a poor man's casino, its front a mosaic of neon tubing and flashing lights flickering ineffectually in the weak rays of the May sunlight.

The inside of the cabaret-cum-disco-cum-casino was just as tacky as the exterior, a discordant mix of neon, flashing orange light bulbs and full-length mirrors.

As Jamie stepped through the double doors, the interior dissolved.

He was standing in a sparsely furnished room with white walls, a single bed in one corner. He smelled piss.

(someonegetmeoutofhere)

(ant untie you)

(cooperate)

Then the image, the voices, were gone.

"You okay?"

Jamie blinked.

"What?"

"You stopped dead," Beth said, picking up her camera bag. He realized she'd walked into him.

"I saw something."

"What?"

"I don't know. Come on, let's see if Franks is here."

Robles stuck his head around the door to Michelle's room. Good, she was sleeping peacefully. The American's shouts hadn't disturbed her. He couldn't have that. Michelle got upset easily, and if she knew there was some-one else in the house, she would guess it was Elvis. No one came to visit, and when he'd told her The King was coming to see her, she'd grown so excited he'd had to sedate her. She was delicate and couldn't deal with too much excitement. He'd let her sleep a few more hours. She'd need her energy for her big date.

"No bloody idea, mate," grumbled Arthur Davies, The Lucky Strike's manager. "I 'aven't 'eard a bloody peep from Franks since yesterday, when 'e complained about the bloody food.

"I'm thinking about cutting 'is booking short, as matter of fact. 'E's not turned out to be the draw we thought 'e'd be. Mind you, I thought it were a bloody daft idea to start with. Still, I don't own the controlling share in this place, so what I think don't matter 'alf the time.

"Would you like a cup o' tea, luv?"

"No, thank you," Beth replied.

"Well, what can I tell you, Mr. 'Urst? Afraid our 'celebrity' is not to be found. Don't know what to suggest, unless you'd like to interview me. I've some interesting stories to tell. Mind you, now's not a good time. To add insult to injury, the stage manager's called in sick, so I got a lot on me plate right now."

Jamie sighed, glad Davies had paused. The man didn't talk *to* you, he talked *at* you.

"Perhaps Franks has gone sightseeing?" Beth offered.

"Bloody well doubt it. All 'e's done since 'e arrived is bloody complain. About the food, the weather, the town. Bloody Americans—sorry, luv, didn't mean that."

"Who would have been the last person to see Franks?" Jamie asked.

"Oh, Robles, I guess. That's me stage manager, the one who's sick."

"Do you know when he left last night?"

"No. I was busy up here going over last week's figures. Business isn't very good right now. Attendances down—"

"What time does Franks's performance end?"

" 'Bout eleven-thirty."

"Look, if you ask me, Franks probably went off with some woman. Lot of women come 'ere to find a date. Oh, 'e'll probably turn up later on. 'E better."

* * *

"What now?" Beth asked as they made their way to the main entrance.

"Wait a minute," replied Jamie. "I've got a hunch." He walked over to the box office.

Beth turned her attention to the framed posters advertising Lucky Strike performers of the past. Wayne Fontana and the Mindbenders. Gerry and The Pacemakers. Other sixties groups. Blackpool wasn't a happening place.

"Let's go," Jamie said, placing a hand on her shoulder.

"Where to?"

"A visit to George Robles, our missing stage manager."

"A hunch or a feeling—one of those feelings?"

He nodded.

Darren lay with his eyes closed, breathing shallowly, trying to stay calm. Panic or anger would solve nothing.

How was Robles going to get him to make love to the girl? How would he know they were fucking—stand in the corner watching? Probably had a strategic hole in the wall so he could observe. Fucking pervert. The whole situation was perverse, crazy. A blind, crippled girl who had no contact with the outside world, and who didn't know Elvis was dead. Who thought Elvis replied to the fan letters she dictated to her father. How could she honestly believe Elvis was coming to visit her and have dinner?

Don't think about it. Each question posed another, then another. Thinking was giving him a headache.

He opened his eyes when he heard the sound of music coming faintly from downstairs.

Elvis singing "Suspicious Minds."

Terrific. Robles must be getting the girl ready for their "guest's" arrival.

The way Darren was feeling, tied to the bed, freezing his balls off, was as far removed from romance as could be.

* * *

Beth paid the cabdriver, since Jamie had nothing smaller than a twenty-pound note.

"Tell me," she demanded as the cab pulled away. Jamie had refused to speak once they'd got in the car.

"I can't explain, but I think Robles knows where Franks is."

"He could just be off with a woman, like Davies suggested. You said that last night when he wasn't at the hotel."

"Yes, but we know he never went to the hotel and hasn't been there today. If he was screwing around last night, don't you think he'd go back to his room to rest and freshen up?"

"She could be dynamite in bed." Beth smiled.

"No. It's not right." A deep worry line creased Jamie's brow. "I keep getting a feeling of . . . containment, and three times I've had a vision of a white, sparsely furnished room."

"A hospital ward?"

He shook his head. "I told you. I can't explain."

Jamie started up the incline leading toward Oak Road, the street on which Robles lived. Beth fell into step beside him.

"What are we going to ask Robles? Isn't he going to think it strange we didn't call first?"

Jamie said nothing. He didn't even hear what Beth said. A buzz of white noise hummed softly in his ears; a preternatural calm enveloped him, growing stronger with each step he took. He'd felt this before: the first time when Alex died; the second, as he entered the apartment building where he'd lived with Jessica. On a deep, primal level he knew he was right: Robles was the connection. And that whatever the connection was, it was drawing him here like a mouse to a piece of cheese.

He hoped there was no trap.

Robles dropped the dinner plate when the doorbell rang.

He trembled, trying not to panic.

Who was it? No one came to visit. He didn't have real friends, he hadn't the time. Looking after Michelle took up most of his life outside of work. The police? How could they know about the American? Had someone seen him removing the laundry hamper from the stage door? So what if they had? He was just doing his job.

Calm down. Probably Jehovah's Witnesses or someone trying to sell him double glazing. Ignore them.

Robles stooped to pick up the pieces of broken plate as the bell rang a second time.

Go away.

He tossed the plate into the rubbish bag beside the mountain of empty cans in the far corner, grimacing as the bell rang.

Go away!

Would the American hear it? He'd better not cry out and disturb Michelle. Robles would have to punish him if he did.

Jamie pressed the bell a fourth time.

Like the rest of the house's exterior, the porch was badly in need of repair. Blue paint bubbled and peeled from the front door's rotting wood. Dry piles of old autumn leaves covered the cracked tiles like parchment, and the ceiling was a tapestry of spiderwebs.

"He obviously doesn't do yard work," Beth observed, looking at the overgrown front garden as they waited.

"Or home maintenance," Jamie added, puncturing a paint blister with his thumb. The wood beneath was soft.

"What now?"

"We wait a while, then look around," Jamie said, the psychic static still buzzing in his ears. The pressure in his head was starting to make him feel nauseated.

Darren thought he was dreaming when the bell rang the first time. The second ring convinced him he wasn't having aural hallucinations. His heartbeat thumped in his chest with the third, and a ray of optimism broke through the black clouds of depression shrouding him. Someone was outside the house. Was it worth shouting? No, they'd never hear him, but Robles would. *Don't shout again. I'll hurt you if you do.* He'd use the belt again. Or something worse.

Tears of helpless frustration welled in Darren's eyes.

Please, God, get me out of this. I promise I'll never cheat on Carrie again. I'll give money to charity. I'll go to church—I'll do anything. Just get me out of here.

Peering through a gap in the moldering velvet curtains in what used to be his mother's room, Robles watched the young couple walk back down the path to the front gate. They didn't look like Jehovah's Witnesses or Mormons. The man wore a black leather jacket, a casual shirt and blue jeans. The blond woman wore a black, American baseball jacket with the words "Rhythm Syndicate" emblazoned on the back, and had a large tan canvas bag slung over one shoulder. No, they weren't Bible thumpers. Who were they? What did they want? Still, they seemed to be satisfied no one was home. They didn't even look back at the house.

Good. Go away. Leave us alone.

He went to check on Michelle. It was nearly time to get his little girl ready for her date.

The Robles house stood on a corner of a T junction, its garden surrounded by a four-foot-high wall. As they reached the right angle where the streets bisected, Jamie guided Beth by the arm down Carlisle Road, so they were parallel to the side of the detached Victorian house. There were only two windows, he noticed as he looked over the wall. One upstairs, probably on the landing, and one directly below it, possibly the kitchen. But he couldn't be certain. The house held secrets, he was certain. The wild, neglected garden, the partially drawn curtains discouraging prying eyes. Everything about the place spoke to him of psychic decay.

"What now?"

"We investigate," he said, looking around.

Seeing Carlisle Road was deserted, he linked his fingers together. "Give me your foot."

Jamie boosted Beth over the wall, then followed, ducking down behind a large privet bush next to a sagging wooden shed that looked like it had stood there since the 1920s.

"Let's see what the elusive Mr. Robles is hiding," he said, creeping toward the house.

Darren opened his eyes as Robles entered the room. The man held his white jumpsuit trousers in his left hand. They looked clean.

"It's nearly time."

"Tell me what you want me to do," Darren replied, hoping Robles didn't notice his eyes were red from crying.

"You're going to get dressed and wash up. My daughter deserves the best. The King wouldn't be a slob, would he?"

Darren shook his head. No.

"Good. I washed these." Robles held up the pants. "No more shit.

"And if you try any funny stuff," the man's eyes glazed as his right hand emerged from behind his back, a carving knife clenched in his fist, "I'll kill you."

Jamie's guess was right. The side window on the ground floor looked in on the kitchen, but he couldn't see anything clearly through the dirty glass or the tiny gap in the curtains other than a dead plant on the counter.

"Round the back."

Beth nodded.

The rear door was in as bad shape as the one at the front. The weather had taken most of the ancient paint, and the opaque glass was cracked. Next to it was the main kitchen window, curtainless for a change. They peered in.

"Ugh." Beth groaned at the sight.

The gloomy kitchen was a museum of mold. Filthy plates and pots were piled high in stagnant sink water, rotting food lay on the counter and nearly a dozen large plastic rubbish bags filled the small room.

"Jesus, how can someone live like this?"

Jamie ignored her, moving to the dining room window. "Look at this."

Beth's eyes widened.

The room was a shrine to Elvis. The walls were plastered with pictures of the performer. Some were framed, like the large black velvet painting hanging over the mantelpiece, and the album covers. But one wall was a mosaic of pictures cut from magazines and newspapers, pasted to the wall with glue. The mantelpiece overflowed with badges, statuettes and dozens of other Elvis items. The only elements in the room which weren't Elvis-inspired were a heavy old oak dining table and two chairs. On the table were Elvis place mats, Elvis plates. Even Elvis salt and pepper shakers.

The table was laid for two.

"Pay dirt," Beth said, unzipping her camera bag.

Jamie fingered the rotting window frame. The casement moved. It was unlocked.

"Let's go in."

Robles paced the room, pants in one hand, knife in the other.

"You will dine with her, flatter her. She will be shy, bashful, like a proper young lady. She is, you know. I've brought her up well. Manners are important. You'll tell her about Las Vegas, Hawaii, the films you've made. Tell her stories, entertain her. You'll tell her how beautiful she is. She'll want to know what it's like living at Graceland."

Darren kept his eyes on the knife as Robles moved around the room. There was no doubt the fucker was as crazy as a bedbug and as dangerous as a rattlesnake. If he'd been scared before, he was terrified now. There was no way the looney-toons son of a bitch was going to let him go.

"After dinner you will sing to her. Her favorite songs are 'Heartbreak Hotel,' 'Suspicious Minds,' 'Treat Me Nice,' and 'Can't Help Falling in Love.' Then you'll get

down on your knees and kiss her hand, tell her she's so
beautiful that it would mean so much to you if she'd love
you.''

Robles stood by the window, looking down into the
garden.

''You will—'' He stopped dead.

''No!'' Robles growled, trembling.

Darren said nothing, his eyes wide with fear.

Robles spun to face him, snarling with rage. He threw
the pants at Darren.

''I'll see to you later,'' he hissed, rushing to the door.

Jamie took Beth's camera case, placed it on the floor,
then helped pull her through the window.

''God,'' she said, wiping paint flakes from her palms.
''Is this a shrine, or what?''

Jamie picked up a heavy porcelain statue of The King
from the mantel. Elvis in the fifties, clean-cut, a guitar
slung across his chest, right arm up, hips thrust forward.
''More than obsessive,'' he commented softly. ''Religious.''

The buzzing in his head had stopped, eclipsed by the
unnatural calm, every detail in the room standing out in
sharp clarity as if his senses were somehow amplified.
Like the moments before Alex died, and when he'd discovered Jessica's body. Whatever journey they'd started
on when they'd left London, it was nearly over. Though
past journeys had ended in tragedy, he wasn't afraid.

Beth's camera flashed as she photographed the room.
''Unbelievable.''

How did they know?

Robles slowly descended the stairs. He knew which
ones creaked and stepped carefully, avoiding those which
did. Mustn't let them know he was here, oh no.

It wasn't fair. Life was trying to cheat him again. Rob
Michelle of her happiness. Not this time, oh no, he'd see
to that. He wasn't going to be a victim anymore.

He could hear them in the sacred room. They would
die for profaning The King's Temple.

He reached the bottom of the stairs, walking catlike toward the door.

"Let's look around," the man said, his soft voice carrying through the partially open door.

Robles reached the wall as the door opened inward.

It happened so fast Beth didn't react until Jamie and the man were on the floor.

Overwhelmed by the images of Elvis, she didn't notice Jamie was still holding the statue in his right hand.

"Let's look around," he said, walking to the door.

He opened it, stepping into the hallway.

Beth saw a hand wielding a knife slice down out of the gloom, the blade penetrating Jamie's jacket at the shoulder; heard a man scream as Jamie turned, swinging his right arm up in an arc, the statue of Elvis in his fist; heard plaster shatter, the man's scream cut off as he fell against Jamie and they fell to the floor.

Jamie groaned as the man landed on top of him, air rushing from his lungs.

"I'm blind!" the man screamed.

Beth gasped, felt a shriek of shock climbing her throat, adrenaline jolting her body like an electric shock.

She screamed.

The man screamed.

Jamie swung his right fist again, the broken body of Elvis still clenched between his fingers. The fist hit the man's jaw this time, the force thrusting his body off Jamie's chest.

As he rolled over, Beth saw the man's left eye was torn and bloody.

Jamie sat up like a zombie, his expression blank, the kitchen knife still jutting from his shoulder, and Beth screamed again.

"Shut up," he said calmly, punching the man in the face a third time.

The man went limp.

Beth dropped her camera, shaking.

Jamie dropped the broken Elvis statue and pulled the

knife from his shoulder. He grunted as the bloody blade came free, then stumbled to his feet.

"Stay here. If he comes to, hit him with your camera."

Beth looked at him blankly, frozen with shock, her mind unable to comprehend what she'd just seen.

Jamie walked slowly to the stairs and ascended like a somnambulist.

He discovered the girl's room first.

She was anorexic-thin. Her pale skin and the dark shadows circling her sightless eyes made her face look like a death mask.

"Daddy? Daddy, are you okay? I heard you cry out."

Jamie grabbed the doorframe for support, suddenly aware of the incredible burning pain running the length of his arm.

"Daddy? What's wrong?" The girl tilted her head, listening.

"Elvis? Is that you?"

Jamie stumbled back into the hallway, his head reeling. The nerves in his arm burned with pain as he pushed open the door next to the girl's room.

Except for piles of newspapers, it was empty.

He staggered to the hallway's end, falling against the door to the farthest room.

"Darren Franks, I presume," he said to the half-naked Elvis tied to the bed.

Jamie fainted.

October 5, 1989

The day after a jury found George Robles not guilty by reason of insanity and the judge sentenced him to life in a cozy cell at Broadmoor, Jamie married Beth in a quiet ceremony at Hampstead registry office.

Now the media circus was behind them, they had a lot to look forward to. A new house in Hampstead, bought by the £100,000 advance Collins had paid them for the book rights to their story. Jamie was working on a new novel. Beth had a show at a prestigious gallery in Chelsea. *The Sunday Express* was paying them lucrative salaries.

And Beth was expecting, although they'd already decided on tying the knot before they found out she was pregnant.

The tabloids, of course, had lapped up the story with relish. They hadn't had as much fun since the Joyce McKinney Mormon-in-chains sex-and-bondage soap opera in the seventies.

STAGE MANAGER KIDNAPPED ELVIS, proclaimed *The Sun*'s headline.

ELVIS OBSESSION LEADS TO TRAGEDY, stated the more restrained *Daily Mirror*.

The lurid details kept the headline writers and gutter journalists busy for weeks.

The Sun had offered them £30,000 each for their exclusive stories. Concerned he was going to lose the two aces which would ensure a major promotion, Malcolm Jones offered them a joint payment of £90,000. They accepted and Malcolm got his promotion. Everyone was happy.

Except poor old George Robles, who had a history of mental illness and wasn't, in fact, George Robles.

His real name was Arthur Robles, and at age thirty-one, he'd been convicted of manslaughter after accidentally killing his mother in a fit of rage. Diagnosed as mentally incompetent, he'd spent six years in a sanitarium where none of the doctors deduced he had a split personality. George was the Other, and after Arthur was released from the sanitarium, George took over.

The girl, Michelle, wasn't his daughter, either. Her name was Alice Brady, an orphan he'd taken from a home in Doncaster within months of his release and had raised in isolation since she was three years old. She was faring as well as could be expected in a special clinic, not comprehending the reality of her situation. She wasn't a virgin, a fact *The Sun* had relished, and years of therapy lay ahead of her.

Robles's story was a complex web of psychotic delusion, obsession and sordid tragedy, one which by turns both fascinated and depressed Jamie. At least he'd been able to forget about it while they honeymooned in Venice. But the holiday was over and it was time to return to work.

Jamie sat at the breakfast table reading *The Times* as he sipped his coffee. The news was the same. Thatcher crowing about inflation down to three percent, the Labour Party decrying the unemployment figures, the SDP stating the obvious about social collapse in the North.

He yawned as Beth entered the kitchen, a pile of mail in her hand.

"A letter from Darren," she said as she sat beside him, sweeping back a strand of hair from her face. She was growing it long. It suited her.

He smiled. The depth of his love for her surprised him sometimes; what they shared seemed almost unreal. He was lucky, he knew. Unlike Robles, who'd been abused by his mother and had never been loved by anyone. Whose desperate need for love had forced him to kidnap a crippled teenage girl.

"What does he have to say?"

Darren had found God after his ordeal and was now a Baptist minister in Atlanta. Jamie could understand. A close call with death at the hands of a psychopath was enough to give anyone religion.

"My Dearest Jamie and Beth," she read. "I have just learned that you wed recently and am overjoyed for you. The union of two fine young people is a wonderful thing. Cherish each other but do not forget to love Jesus Christ, Our Savior. Only through Him will you know the beauty of God's plan for us all.

"Every day I thank God for delivering me from the sin of false idolatry. This world is full of false gods, but there is only One True God—the Father of Our Lord. Elvis was just a man, as am I. And like Elvis, I now sing for Jesus. Do not forget that you, too, are God's instrument, that it was He who led you to free me from sin.

"Your friend in Jesus, Darren Franks."

Jamie smiled, placing a hand on Beth's swelling abdomen.

"Well, I guess we won't name him Elvis after all."

"Who said it's a he?" Beth replied with mock indignation. "Besides, I thought we could call her Madonna."

Jamie laughed.

FORGOTTEN PROMISES

Edward E. Kramer

Edward E. Kramer is a writer and co-editor of *Grails* (nominated for the World Fantasy Award for Best Anthology of 1992), *Confederacy of the Dead* (1993), *Phobias* (1994), *Dark Destiny* (1994), *Elric: Tales of the White Wolf* (1994), *Tombs* (1995), *Dark Love* (1995) and many additional works in progress. Ed's original fiction appears in a growing number of anthologies as well. His first novel, *Killing Time*, is forthcoming from White Wolf. He is fond of human skulls, exotic snakes and underground caves.

"**Y**ou were great out there, Tina!" Robby hung his arm over one of her shoulders as they ran in from the field; his long blond hair reached down below even hers.

Joey flanked Tina on the other side. "We really kicked their asses. You are one hell of a goalie."

Tina smiled, the soccer ball tucked under her right arm as they ran. It had taken nearly an act of God to convince her homeroom teacher to let her miss class so she could try out for the soccer team; she was the first girl in the school ever to make it.

The last three off the field, Robby, Tina and Joey grabbed their packs from the PE storage shack and headed toward the bathrooms to change. It was already past 2 P.M.; they'd catch the last few minutes of afternoon homeroom before the bell rang at two-fifteen.

Tina never had a problem in sports. Most of the other team members openly accepted her from the start. From the field, no one could even tell she was a girl.

Robby and Joey broke off from Tina as they reached the school building. "We'll go in and change and meet you back in Two-Whacks' class," called Joey as he disappeared into the boys' dressing room; Robby followed him in.

Tina stared at the door for a brief moment, then entered behind the two boys. She hated that rules were different for girls. If she were a boy, she wouldn't have to put up with anyone's shit.

Robby had just started unpacking his *Star Wars* sports bag, while Joey had begun to undress. Joey turned, surprised. "You can't come in here! You'll get in trouble."

"I'm just gonna change in a stall. The girls' dressing room is clear on the other side of the building. Okay?"

Robby shrugged his shoulders at Joey.

"I guess." Joey waited until she went into a stall and closed the door. He quickly changed, waving to Robby as he left.

Robby slipped out of his shorts. He kicked off his sneakers and put on a pair of black Levi's. Pulling off his team shirt, Robby tossed it into his pack and searched for his antiperspirant.

"Robby, come here for a moment. I need your help with a zipper."

The boy walked over to the stall. The door was closed, but not locked. He pushed it open.

"I can't unzip these. Can you try?" Tina sat on one corner of the toilet seat and held out her jeans to Robby.

He stared at his teammate. The boy's eyes passed the jeans and focused on her body; Tina wasn't wearing *anything*. It was the first time he'd ever seen a real girl nude—his mother not counting. He returned his gaze to her jeans.

She handed him the pants and hooked her two index fingers on his belt loops, pulling him closer. The boy did not resist.

Robby fumbled with her jeans. A piece of material was caught in the zipper. Under normal circumstances, it would not be a problem for him to correct.

Tina worked her fingers behind the snap of his pants and with the other hand drew down his zipper. "Yours works so much easier than mine."

She watched his stomach muscles grow taut as his breathing rapidly increased. With a slight tug, the snap was released.

Robby's eyes were still fixed on the task at hand, but he had not yet worked the zipper free.

Her fingers traced the outline of his dick on the white BVDs, then reached into the front opening and pulled it through. She knew what to do from here.

The first time the Hensons came over for dinner, their son Brett locked Tina in her room and forced her to perform the same act. Brett said if she ever told anyone what happened, his dad would fire hers; she knew how much his work meant to him and would not put his job in jeopardy. The next time, Brett forced her to go much further.

Tina stroked his erection as she looked up at Robby. His eyes were closed; she knew he was about to come. It felt so good to finally be in control.

"Next time, Robby," she said, almost inaudibly, "we're going to go all the way." Tina darted her tongue forward and touched the head of his penis—and he released.

The door of the boys' room sprang open. "You'd best not be in here, Miss Christine Arnold, or your rear will be raw!" the voice screamed. It was Two-Whacks herself.

Silence.

Robby walked out of the stall, pulling up his zipper.

"No, Ms. Matthews, it's just me." His voice was barely above a whisper. "I-I was kinda having trouble with a zipper."

"Well, Robert, it looks like it's working just fine now." She was clearly not impressed. "Get your shirt and shoes on, grab your pack and get back to class. *Now!*"

"Yes, Ms. Matthews." He grabbed his things and hurried out the door. He didn't even bother putting on his shirt or sneakers. He just wanted to get out.

Tina heard the door finally close again. That was close. She was sure she'd be caught, but Robby knew not to tell.

She stood and opened the stall door. Robby's semen was still on her face and chest. There was no toilet paper in the stall and she was not going to wipe herself with her clothing. She wasn't sure if cum stains came out.

Tina headed for the paper-towel dispenser, but noticed a tall figure in the way, wooden paddle in hand.

"Just where do you think you're going, young lady?"

She looked up at Ms. Matthews. "P-please let me get dressed before you paddle me."

The teacher got a good look at Tina. It was not apparent to her at first what had happened.

"You little slut," she sneered. "Just what were you doing with Robert in that stall?"

Tears trickled down Tina's face. "I-I was just—"

"Only tramps and whores do . . . do things like that— *women do not*. What will your father say when I tell him what his slut of a daughter was doing with some innocent boy?"

Tina had begun to sob uncontrollably. "Please—"

Ms. Matthews grabbed her by the back of the neck and pushed her over to the sinks. Tina turned on the water, punching down on the soap dispenser. She began to wash off the tear-mixed semen with her hands.

A loud paddle-crack thrust Tina's stomach sharply into the sink—her head slammed into the mirror. The school bell caught her attention an instant before the second swing hit.

Tina never saw the kids from her class open the door to the boys' room before she collapsed on the floor.

The doctors told her parents that Tina had suffered a mild concussion that day at school. Ms. Matthews phoned to explain the unfortunate nature of the accident. "When a young lady plays soccer out there with the boys, she's eventually bound to get hit with the ball." None of the kids—not even Robby or Joey—refuted Ms. Matthews's story.

She woke up the next afternoon at home with a terrible headache. Her mother explained the accident to her, but Tina knew different. She had convinced her mom to let her change schools by the time she was ready to return, the following week. Tina never wanted to see Ms. Matthews again—unless it was to get even.

"West Fulton Junior High School. May I help you?" the voice answered. The greeting was automatic and without feeling.

He quickly studied the next name on the list.

"As a matter of fact, yes. Can you connect me with Personnel?"

"We don't have a personnel department. May I ask what this is in reference to?"

"This is Jason Hardin with the Georgia Department of Education. We are in need of some clarification on Virginia Matthews's certificate renewal."

"Certificate renewal?" The voice twittered. "How do you like that? When she retired last year, I knew she wouldn't be satisfied to just sit at home. Her file would be with Ms. Rosen in Records."

"Thank you very much," he replied, checking Ms. Matthews's name off the list. Some were almost impossible to track down. Joey Cantor, a friend he'd known since second grade, had even died.

"Hang on, I'll connect you."

* * *

"Coming," the voice sang through the intercom.

Chris watched as the peephole darkened.

"Who is it?"

"It's me, Christopher Arnold, Ms. Matthews—I was a student of yours in seventh grade."

"I don't recall a Christopher Arnold," the voice replied in a suspicious tone.

"I sat right behind Julie Autry and next to Robby Short." She'd remember "Droolie-Julie" and "Snobby-Robby"; they were her two favorite pets.

Her voice brightened immediately. "I'm sorry, of course I remember you." The door latch clicked open and the door swung in wide. A petite, smiling woman stood in the doorway, arms outstretched. She could easily pass for her early forties, but Chris knew she had to be at least fifty. "I'm so glad to see you again! And my, how handsome you've become."

Chris blushed. "Yeah, I guess I've grown quite a bit since then."

"Please come in, come in. I don't usually get many visitors here—especially not former students."

"I hope I'm not intruding, coming over like this."

"No, not at all," Ginny quickly replied. "I was just making some coffee, and I have some carrot cake fresh from the oven. Won't you join me?"

"That's an offer I can't refuse. Your chocolate chip cookies were always the best!"

Ginny smiled and gestured him into a spacious living room. "Please sit down. How do you like your coffee?" She left him and walked to the kitchen.

"Black with a teaspoon of sugar." Chris rose and followed her. "Can I help you with anything?"

"No, silly." She giggled. "Now you go back and sit and I'll be right out."

She sounded sincere enough, he thought and returned to the couch. And what could she do if he didn't obey? Paddle him? Chris chuckled to himself.

Ginny brought out a tray with two cups of steaming coffee and several slices of cake. She laid the tray on the coffee table and sat across from Chris. "Please help yourself."

Chris glanced around the room again. "This is such a beautiful home."

"Why, thank you. But you must understand that my husband—my ex-husband—was a lawyer, and much of this was once his."

"Oh, I'm so sorry." Chris feigned solemn grief as best he could. "How long ago did he pass away?"

"Well, he's not exactly dead; in fact, he's not dead at all. Not that I'd care if he were, mind you. He was having an affair with another woman and I threw him out, so to speak . . ." Her voice trailed off. She paused to contemplate. "It's been over a year now."

This is *too* easy. Who would've ever thought I'd be in the position of seducing "Two-Whacks" Matthews?

"You know, you're still really beautiful." He let the words sink in. "I think any man would be crazy to cheat on someone like you."

It was her turn to blush. "Why, thank you. But you're the one who came to visit. Why don't you tell me about yourself?"

"Well, after seventh grade Dad got transferred to Europe, so I finished school in Belgium and went to college at Oxford. I returned to the States in eighty-nine and got a job with *The Boston Herald*."

Her smile grew wider and wider. Putting her hands over his, she said, "That's so exciting, Christopher. I'm so proud of you."

"Please, call me Chris."

"And you can call me Ginny."

"So now I've moved back to Atlanta for a bit to look for work—as a teacher."

"How wonderful." Ginny shifted in her seat. "Say, didn't you also have a sister?"

Chris dropped his head and took a deep breath. "Tina."

"What's the matter?"

"Well, Tina didn't turn out as well as we all had hoped." He turned toward her, raising his head slightly.

"After we moved to Belgium, she started acting real weird—hanging out with the wrong crowd and getting drunk wherever the opportunity arose. We even caught her once in bed with three men *twice* her age."

Ginny's hand rose to her mouth in surprise and disgust. "Oh, dear me. Whatever did happen to her?"

Chris continued. "She had her first abortion when she was fourteen; then, in a fit of depression, tried overdosing on drugs. Tina tried to get involved in some team sports, but after a soccer accident when she was twelve, she'd become incredibly fearful whenever a ball came her way. When my family moved back to the U.S., Tina stayed in Europe. We haven't heard from her since."

"Oh, my." Ginny's head shook back and forth as she spoke. "I'm so, so sorry."

Ginny took a sip of coffee; her expression changed back to her smiling self. "I want to show you something. Wait right here."

He watched her leave the room and quickly brought out the small vial from his coat pocket. In a single fluid motion he pushed off the cork with his thumb and let the white powder disappear into her coffee. She was coming back. He grabbed the cork and vial and buried them deep in his pocket.

"Look what I have here," she said, approaching with four books in her hands.

He recognized the school yearbooks immediately. Chris's pulse raced.

"I wasn't exactly sure what year you were in my class, so I brought 1977 through 1980."

She placed the books on the table. A silver knight on the cover made up the school logo. God, how he'd hated junior high. How they'd always teased him in home ec and art. They made him feel so small, so insignificant.

Chris's hand trembled as he finished his cup of coffee. "Is something the matter?"

"Um . . ." He returned the cup to the saucer and pressed his hands together tightly to stop their shaking. "I-I haven't had coffee in a while; must be the caffeine."

"But, dear," she said with an edge of concern in her

voice, "I only drink decaffeinated." Looking down at her cup. "And this coffee is getting cold. I'd best fix me a new cup."

No. Just warm it up. Don't pour it out. I haven't got any more powder with me.

Ginny lifted the plate of carrot cake off the tray, and rose with cup and tray in hand. Chris's hands began to tremble again as she returned to the kitchen. He waited until the swinging door closed and picked up the yearbook dated 1979. She was right. He would've been in seventh grade then. Chris fanned to the seventh-grade section and searched for his picture. As he turned back a page, the little one-by-two-inch black-and-white photo that once bore his name struck a deep nerve.

Dizziness suddenly overcame him, as if all his past experiences flashed through his mind at once. Chris shut his eyes tightly and tried to will away the images, the emotions—and the self-hatred.

A whisper of conversation pierced through. There was someone in the kitchen with Ginny. He quietly closed the yearbook and returned it to the table with the other two.

Fuck. She must've taken one of the yearbooks into the kitchen with her under the tray. She knows about the powder and she's probably calling the police right now. I'm fucked.

Chris ran his hands through his hair as he rose. His forehead was matted in sweat. He turned to the front door.

He knew he should run.

Ginny returned from the kitchen with a fresh pot of coffee. The front door was open and Chris was gone. She was so happy he had come to visit, but knew that something was wrong. It reminded her of another student she'd had who had gotten himself involved with drugs; Chris looked as though he was going through withdrawal from something.

She placed the tray down on the coffee table. Two pieces of her carrot cake and her cake knife were gone. As she walked to the door, the doorbell rang.

"Well, where is Prince Charming?"

"He's gone, Flo. He probably knew you were coming," said Ginny with as much humor as she could muster for the moment.

"And he left you a present." Flo held out a napkin with one of the pieces of cake wrapped within.

"Oh, Flo. He probably dropped it. I guess he was in a hurry. I don't think he was feeling so well." Ginny smiled. "Why don't you come in and join me for some coffee? I have a fresh pot on the table."

"I thought you'd never ask!"

Flo walked over to the coffee and helped herself to a cup. Ginny closed and locked the door, then joined her friend.

"Reminiscing?" asked Flo as she examined the yearbooks on the table.

"Wait a moment," replied Ginny. She entered the kitchen and retrieved the fourth yearbook, already open to a page.

"Got a picture of the beaut?"

"Well, I found his sister in one, but I don't see Chris anywhere. Help me check the others."

Their search for Christopher Arnold didn't reveal a positive identity. Ginny had downed two more cups of coffee by the conclusion of the search.

"Boy, Ginny, this sure is eerie. Are you sure you're not just making this all up to get me to join you for coffee?"

"Humph." Ginny hung her hands on her hips and sneered at Flo until they both started laughing.

Ginny carried the yearbooks back to her room and put them on her night table. She stared at her wedding picture and the man she had once married. Wiping a tear from her eye, Ginny tried not to think about being alone. Removing hair clips as she walked to the bathroom, she carefully pulled off her wig and set it onto the Styrofoam head next to the sink. She placed her blouse, stockings, bra and panties in the hamper and slipped into her favorite negligee. Staring into the full-length mirror behind the bath-

room door, Ginny imagined herself fifteen years
younger—what she had looked like when Chris was in
her class.

A scratch at the front door interrupted her reflections.

"I'm coming, Pugsley," she called over her shoulder.

The scratching continued as Ginny walked through the
living room and to the front door. She peered through the
peephole to assure that no one was there, then unlatched
and opened the door. A large Siamese cat strode in.

Kneeling down to the cat. "Where on earth have you
been? It's late, you know that?"

Without a single glance up toward her owner, Pugsley
sauntered toward the kitchen. Ginny closed and bolted the
door as the cat disappeared beneath the two swinging
doors. She followed Pugsley into the kitchen; the cat
perched itself on the edge of its food dish, ignoring the
contents left from an earlier meal.

Pugsley looked up and meowed her familiar plea.
"Feed me."

Ginny emptied the dish into the garbage disposal and
pulled a new can of Nine Lives down from the shelf. The
meowing continued.

"I'm hurrying, I'm hurrying. Either you're really hungry or you really don't want what I'm about to serve you.
Which is it, now?"

She popped open the can and dumped the contents into
Pugsley's dish. Placing it back at her feet, the cat sniffed
the new dish for a few seconds, then dug in.

"You are one strange cat, dear Pugsley. But I love you
all the same."

Ginny turned out the kitchen light. Two bright green
eyes reflected up from the floor. She walked back to the
bathroom and went to the sink to brush her teeth.

Chris waited until he was sure that Ms. Matthews was
asleep. He slowly opened the closet door. A loud
"Meow" startled him as he crept forth on all fours. Pugsley rubbed up against him. The touch felt good against
his bare skin. He petted the cat and moved on. He'd

worked out a plan over and over again in his head as he waited in darkness. Now, as he was ready to perform it for real, his memory failed.

He stood at her bedside and watched the rise and fall of her chest. A small night-light in the corner provided that and little more. He cupped one hand over her mouth gently and tapped her shoulder with the other.

Ginny snapped her eyes open and tried to sit up, but Chris's arm prevented it.

"Shhh! It's only me—Chris." He grabbed the cake knife that he'd taken earlier and pressed its dull point to her throat. "Don't even *think* of screaming."

Ginny shook her head. "No."

He slowly released the hand over her mouth. "Who— who are you?" she asked, her voice riddled in panic.

"I told you. My name is Christopher Arnold. I've waited over a decade to fulfill a vow."

"Please don't rape me. I-I've got money in a vault behind the sofa. The combination is 19379. It's everything I've saved—over ten grand."

With the knife point still at her throat, Chris got on the bed, straddling her at the waist. "Many years ago, I promised Tina I'd make this visit. I came for you."

"Please," she pleaded. "No . . ."

"Turn over, *bitch*." His voice rose as he took command.

Ginny complied; the knife point slid to the back of her neck.

He pulled off her nightgown with little resistance, positioning both of her hands resting behind her back. Ginny rocked slowly, trembling as she cried. Using the nightgown as rope, Chris tied her hands tightly together. She would not break free.

"Now, up—out of bed." He tugged at her hands while still keeping pressure with the knife.

Chris led her to the bathroom and turned on the light. Dropping the knife on the counter, he firmly grasped the back of her neck and pushed her face into the sink.

"What are you going to do?" Her voice edged higher.

"If you make one more sound—*anything*—I'm going

to kill you. If you'll just shut your mouth, I'm going to give you something in return. Got it?''

She tried to nod her head, but the sink offered little movement. Ginny just remained quiet.

He raised back his hand and released it firmly across her ass with a loud slap. Her head slammed into the faucet. She screeched, but prevented a scream from release. He respected that in a woman. He raised his hand again and struck it across her ass even harder. This time she couldn't repress the scream.

Chris clasped his hand over her mouth as he pulled her from the sink. ''It's a damn shame Robby and Joey aren't here now to see this.'' He knew he'd have to do something quickly and get out; condos had paper-thin walls.

She turned toward him, dazed, and glanced down his body. Her eyes shot back up to his as she tried to scream again.

He knew what she had seen. ''Nothing to fear, Ms. Matthews. We're just not finished with me yet. But don't worry. I won't be trying it out on you this time.''

With a loud chuckle, he thrust her head backward into the mirror. The glass cracked as she collapsed and slid to the floor. He never even bothered checking for a pulse.

Chris jogged into the closet with the glee of a small child and picked out a loose-fitting blouse with a flowered pattern, then the remainder of his clothing. He grabbed her bra from the open hamper and stuffed each cup with tissues. Fitting it around his chest, Chris admired himself momentarily; he had once worn a similar size. He slipped on the blouse and arranged Ms. Matthews's wig over his head.

''Did anyone ever tell you you looked kinda cute?'' Chris mused aloud in a practiced falsetto.

Applying some ruby-red lipstick and a bit of rouge, he laughed to himself once more. If only Ms. Matthews could see him now—that would be a hoot.

Chris stuffed his clothes into one of her handbags and headed for the living room sofa. One-nine-three-seven-nine. There would be enough there for his finishing touches. Then he'd be a real man.

As he sashayed out the front door, he left the vault wide open. Robbery. That's what they'd say. Maybe even nail her ex for it . . .

"Yes, this is Elizabeth Short." There was water running in the background and the cries of a small child.

"Is Robert in?"

"No, he's still down at the office. He's going to be working late again."

"Oh, I see. This is Jason Hardin. I was Robert's best friend in college, although I haven't actually seen him since graduation."

"Maybe you could stop by tomorrow."

Chris pondered. It had to be tonight. He was set to fly out for the final operation in the morning. "Well, I'm in town only for this evening and just wanted to drop by and say hello. There was something I promised him a while back."

"Okay. Well, his office is at 510 Talbott Avenue, Suite 315. The front door is locked at night, so key in 241 to get inside."

"Thanks again for your help. I'm looking forward to meeting you, too, on my next trip. Oh, and don't tell him I'm coming—I want it to be a surprise."

Chris hung up the phone, placing a check mark on the list by Robby's name. He folded the paper neatly and stuffed it into his new purse, then caught a cab into town. Tina was up for one last night on the town.

COMING OF AGE

Douglas Clegg

Douglas Clegg lives in southern California with his spouse, a black cat and a Border collie mongrel. He was born in Virginia, graduated from Washington and Lee University with a degree in English Lit and has lived throughout the world before settling on the West Coast, where he can experience, firsthand, riots, rebellions, earthquakes, fires and floods. He has written six novels, four of which have been published by Pocket Books. His most recent novel is *Dark of the Eye*. His first novel, *Goat Dance*, was nominated for Outstanding First Novel in 1989 by the HWA. His next novel, *The Children's Hour*, will be published by Dell in mid-October 1995. He has spent seven years working on his epic horror novel, not about an apocalypse, but about a boy and his dog and his first love. Titled *You Come When I Call You*, this novel should be out sometime in 1996. Seventeen of his short stories are to be published within the next two years in various anthologies and magazines, including *Love in Vein, Little Deaths* and *Phobias 2*. In addition to his horror novels, he also writes suspense fiction, and contributes time and energy to the AIDS Service Center of Pasadena.

I

I go to see him, my friend Joe, when I hear what's happened.

First, I hear the drip of the tap. It's just *drip-drop-drip*, but it echoes in the room. The room's kind of dark, even with the sunlight coming from under the blinds. I'm sort of amazed they let him sit alone in a room he could easily escape from, but I've seen the security fences outside and someone told me at the sign-in desk that they don't worry much about Joe because he doesn't want to get out.

I try to turn the faucet off before I go over and sit down, but it must need a new washer. It just keeps spitting, the sound like a ball bearing dropped over and over into a metal dish.

I turn to face Joe, who's seated.

There's a chair for me, a chair for him and another chair.

He says, "Hey, Scooter." I look at his face, but I barely see the kid I knew when I was twelve. He sits down and looks to his right. He considers the empty chair beside him carefully, as if someone he knows is going to want to sit there, only maybe he doesn't want someone else there. Not now. He glances back at me, "Old Scooter with the pop eyes and the cowlick."

"It's Eric now. Dad's dead. No more nicknames."

"Haven't seen you in the valley for a long time. You look a bit different, you know." He checks the empty chair again, and I wonder if he is nervous being with me again. Like, maybe he wouldn't want an old friend of his to see him like this. But he requested me; he told all of them that he wanted to see his old pal Scooter Marshall from the old days, from childhood. He looks back again, sees me staring at the chair beside him and leans forward some to get my attention. "Don't mind him. I said, you look a bit changed."

"Just a bit. And I've been busy. I've got a ton of work, and, well, there's a lot to take care of."

"You married?"

"No. I'm sort of a loner." I don't want to tell him that I have trouble getting close to people. I'm afraid maybe he'll smile and nod and tell me he's the same.

I can hear the sounds of footsteps in the hall; the door is behind me, and it swings open.

I don't look back, and I figure whoever's there will make themselves known, but then the door swings again. I turn around, but don't catch a glimpse of anyone. The door's still swinging.

The faucet's dripping.

"Chinese water torture," he says, referring to the annoying drip. Then: "You making something of yourself these days?"

I look at my hands, then my shoes. "I don't think you called me here to talk about my life."

He reaches over and touches my hand. I shiver, a little, because of what he's done. I remember the pictures of the kids in the newspapers. But I know I'm safe, that I'm out of range of his interests. He whispers, as if he doesn't want anyone else to hear, "Remember that day?"

"Not something you put behind you."

"I guess not."

"I think of you a lot, you know, Joe."

"Joey. Call me Joey."

"Okay. Joey."

"If you watch the news, everyone in the friggin' country thinks of me a lot. I get love letters from women who never even met me, and after what I did. Can you imagine?" He shakes his head.

"Nope."

"I did it, you know. My lawyer begged me to plead all kinds of things, but I couldn't help it. I did it. The kids. All of 'em. Parents trusted me, too. Strange, where life takes you, huh?"

"I know."

"I knew you would. I bet you sat up there in D.C. and watched the whole thing."

"Enough of it. I liked your interview on '20/20.' You looked good, too. Joey Draco on TV." The water from the tap seems to be dripping faster. "They ever fix the plumbing in here?"

He gets up and goes to the sink; he opens the cabinet beneath it and twists a valve. The water stops dripping. "Sometimes the only way to stop something is to cut it off at the head. But don't tell my lawyer I said that, okay? It's a joke." He comes back and sits in his chair. "Christ, lighten up, will you? It ain't all bad."

"I think about you a lot. I mean, even since then. Not just about . . . what's happened."

He considers this; reaches in his breast pocket and brings out a pack of cigarettes. "I thought about you, too, not when I was doing it, but later. About when we were kids. About how you learn things about yourself. What you like, what you don't like. What you're willing to do to stop things you don't like. You know?"

"Maybe."

"It's in you, too. Somewhere. And the others. We all have it. When do you think old Nobby's gonna pop up on the news? He lives down in Florida now. Orlando. He's a preacher. But it's in him. All it needs is a trigger. And the Fursts—still in the valley. One night it's gonna take them by surprise, don't you think? And you, too. You maybe weren't right in the thick of things, but you did your share. You stood by. What's the quote? 'Good men who stand by and do nothing'? Something like that? And he's done with me."

"Who?" I say, and reach up, instinctively, to one of the scars on my face, along my forehead.

"My friend. You know. It's why I'm here, not 'cause of the kids—that'd get me life in Sing Sing or something. But in this place. 'Cause of my friend."

He looks at the chair again, and then at me. "It's good to find out young what you like, ain't it? Like it was laid out right in front of me. I liked the taste of it, I liked the smell. Once, I tore a kid's face off and held the edge of

his eye socket in my hand. It's so pure. Right in my friggin' hand.''

"Joe. Joey. There's something I need to know."

"Shoot."

"Was it because of the Bonchance kid?"

A grinning man sat in front of me, and I saw a trace
of the young, irascible Joey Draco. "I didn't know what
I liked till then, you know? I wasn't mature enough; I
didn't see what I had in me. But you know something? I
think maybe if it hadn't happened, maybe if we'd just
gone to another showing of *Psycho*, maybe I'd be raising
three kids and working the mine and driving over to
Charleston to get some on the side like any other good
old boy. But the worst thing, Scooter, if you don't mind
my using your old name, the worst thing is''—and his
eyes fix on mine—''if I didn't do it back then, I might
never know what I really, really like. And that's important
to a man.''

I say, "I know."

"Stone Valley," he says, shaking his head as if recall-
ing the best drop of wine from the bottom of the bottle
of memory, '' '60, Wednesday, July 3-0, a hot-sour day,
with the humidity in the ninetieth percentile and the boredom factor almost to a hundred. You and me, best buddies, and the end of innocence on the horizon, Scooter,
that's all it was, the end of innocence. But the end of
innocence, buddy, is always the birth of knowledge, ain't
that the truth?''

II

It was 1960, nobody had landed on the moon yet and
no one knew the changes in life that were like a train
coming down a track, about to hit us within a few years.
In Stone Valley we didn't know about weird city ways,
other than in hushed tones at revival meetings—as if to
mention vice any louder would make it incarnate. If you
were a grown-up and living with your girlfriend, it was
still sinful, and the kindest thing that could be said was,

"Why buy the cow when you can get the milk for free?"
Nobody ever heard of the Manson family, even though
Ed Gein had been in the news a couple of years back, and
horror movies were still terrifying even when no one got
slaughtered right in front of your eyes. Me and Joey Draco
went to see *Psycho*, and were convinced that Janet Leigh
got shredded to the point that you could see her tits, although my sister, Laurie, said they didn't show the knife
going into her at all, and, as she said, "no milkers to be
seen."

Stone Valley was still pretty small, getting smaller
every day, too, because of the strip-mining up on the three
mountains that walled us in from the outside world; Route
28 was potholed and wound like a Slinky all the way to
Charleston. I knew even then, when I was twelve, that
when I was old enough, the mountains would be level
with the rest of the valley; then I'd see the wide world
without having to read about it in comic books. But then
it was just an old strip with a HoJo's and three frozen-
custard stands; still had a Sambo's Restaurant, because
the civil rights movement hadn't yet made a dent, and a
Stuckey's right off 28. The record stores only had record
albums, and the only head shop in town was Franklin's
barbershop. Most of our dads worked in the mines or
quarries, or, like mine, commuted sixty-three miles of
mountain road to be an accountant or a doctor or a lawyer
over in the state capital.

So this one day, Joey and I ditched my sister—she was
baby-sitting us, but at twelve, we figured we were much
too old, anyway. I voted for going to HoJo's to get a
Fudgeana, a sundae they served which always made us
laugh, particularly when we got the waitress to say it real
slow and Southern. But Joey had other ideas.

"We can get liquor at Bonchance's," he said.

"I dunno." I'd never had a drink, except in communion
on Sundays, but I didn't know if I wanted to get all the
way to the Bonchances' house in order to have my first
experience. The Bonchance family consisted of about
eight kids, or more; none of them ever went to school, so
we didn't even know the half of them, and they were

about as white as trash could get. I once saw Lily Bonchance, with her bowl-cut hair, accept a dare and drink
three different boys' spit out of a Maxwell House can.
Afterward, she wiped her mouth, slurped and said, "Ah,
good to the last drop!"

Joey shoved me, playfully. "Nobby, he says Mrs. Bonchance's a whore." He pronounced "whore" like it was
candles on a birthday cake and it was taking a lot out of
him to blow them out.

"Norbert Dee don't know squat," I said.

"His uncle's a professor at Harvard," Joey said, "and
his daddy runs the revival over in Big Island, so he must
know something." Joey was a little backward. He still
had a flattop, because his dad was an ex-Marine and
thought boys were starting to look too much like girls;
sometimes it was like his brains got trimmed right off the
top, too. He thought because someone had a smart uncle
that somehow the brains leaked down through the mother's side into a bully like Norbert "Nobby" Dee, who
bore the distinction of a big birthmark right on the top of
his head, which made his dark hair chalk white in a perfect circle. My dad called Nobby's family "throwbacks."

But it was a hot mother of a day, with the sun high,
the humidity like bacon grease on your skin and mosqui-
toes biting like shad in a spring river. The alternative was
sneaking back in to see *Psycho* again, or maybe playing
pinball at the Fun Center over on Crescent, which was for
littler kids than us, anyway. So I went with Joey, across
the railroad tracks, through the stinging nettles and black-
berry vines, and the fenced area near the old quarry. It
was supposed to be illegal to cut through there, but some
kid somewhere in history had cut a hole in the chain link
for the benefit of all.

There, through the thin trees heavy with summer green,
was the Bonchance place. It reminded me of the Old
Woman in the Shoe, because it had a weird shape to it—
it was taller than fat, and could not possibly contain all
those Bonchances. The house was made entirely of wood,
which was not like town, where houses were mainly brick

or stone, and it looked as if a good wind might come along from between the dwindling mountains and blow it right down at any second. Ricky Bonchance was on the porch, whittling. That's what I imagined all the Bonchances did with their time: whittle. Ricky was almost two years older than we were, but was still just getting into seventh grade.

"Hey, you," he said, his voice gravelly and mature; he was like the great white ape of jungle legend, with long sideburns coming off his towhead, and skin so pale you could practically see through it. Joey had warned me that we might meet some albino Bonchance cousins if we were lucky. "I said, hey, you!" Pointing his whittling knife like it was a threat. "Whatchu doin' trespassin'?"

"We ain't trespassing," I said. "Oh, Lordy, we just wanted to see what's up."

"Sky," Ricky said.

"Huh?"

"Sky's up. Ceiling's up," Ricky said, then added, to make his reply more clear to us, "Your mama's legs." He jumped over the porch rail, and brought his whittled stick over to show us. It was long, and had a curved tip to it, like a mushroom, and some squiggly things like worms coming off the tip.

"Longest mushroom I ever saw," Joey, the art critic, said.

"It ain't no mushroom, Jesus H." Then Ricky Bonchance turned to me. He gave me a closer look. "You boys too young to know 'bout this kinda shit."

I took the stick in my hand and examined it carefully. It looked like some primitive totem, almost a magic wand.

Ricky whispered in my ear, "Give you a hint, Scooter. It grows if you rub it."

At this point I knew what it was, but was too embarrassed to say it. I dropped the stick like it was a copperhead.

Joey said, "It's a dick? You whittled a dick?"

"Like you'd ever seen one like that." Ricky leaned forward and picked up the penis stick. "I bet you sew black threads onto your balls just so's you can look mature.''

Actually, in gym class, in the showers, I'd seen both of them, and Ricky was not far from the truth. While Ricky was well endowed and hairy like Moses' beard down there, Joey had a crotch like a baby's bottom. I almost laughed when Ricky made his crack, but I couldn't bring myself to fully, on account of Ricky being white trash; and in a town like Stone Valley a Marshall, which is my family's name, could not descend to that level even for a moment.

"I know how you can get mature, you want to," Ricky said, seeing the look of extreme hurt in Joey's eyes.

Joey looked at him, then at me, then back at Ricky. We could hear Mrs. Bonchance singing "Begin the Beguine" from somewhere inside the house. She had a beautiful voice, and one rumor had it that she was a singer in Blacksburg when she was young who had the misfortune to get knocked up by Daniel Bonchance, which meant the end of life as she knew it. The song, which I had heard my mom play once or twice on the hi-fi, sounded more lovely and delicate than I thought a song could be, and I knew then that maybe the Bonchances weren't as bad as they seemed.

The music must've been magical, because Joey's face went from scrunched hurt to interest. "How's that?"

I grinned, slapping my hand against the air in front of Ricky's face. "Ain't no way to get mature. You got to just wait for it to take."

Ricky had a sly look. "You boys're virgins, ain't you?"

I made no move. I knew that virginity was somehow linked to the fate of every nice boy and girl from each good home in the valley.

"You're not," Joey challenged.

Ricky spat a big brown wad at our feet. "No fuckin' way, boys. I got me my first cherry when I was ten, a factory girl from Odell with a big fat butt. She was fourteen, and it was her first, too. Been a long time. Haven't gotten much nooky since."

Joey asked tentatively, "Does it grow back?"

"Does *what* grow back?"

Joey looked at me for confirmation, but I had no idea what he meant.

He said, "Your cherry?"

III

"Gettin' on five o'clock," Ricky said, staring up at the sun from under the broad brim of his straw hat. We were out at the quarry, but not just me and Joey and Ricky Bonchance, but also Nobby Dee, Fred Hopewell, Jimmy and Howie Furst, Lewis Graham and at least three kids from school I didn't even know well enough to call by their last name: Vince, Steve and Paul. We ranged in age from eleven to thirteen, and we were all wondering how this thing was going to work exactly. Ricky had told us to bring a bunch of other guys down to the quarry, and we'd all get plenty mature. I've got to emphasize right here that none of us were going for the prize when it came to brains; maybe I was the smartest of the group, in the end, but I can't really blame any of the guys for what happened.

It was too easy to get the other kids out to the quarry before suppertime.

See, Ricky told me and Joey that he had a sister who was fifteen, and she liked to get it from as many boys as possible. Ricky was willing to sell us tickets at a buck a shot, and Joey got all excited because he was heavily into beating off, but felt it was a sin to waste his seed, what little there was. So Ricky Bonchance promised that if we could get about ten other kids together, we'd get the chance to lose our virginity to a sister of his whom he described as the prettiest girl in the county.

And you should've seen 'em! All hanging out, drinking out of the big malt liquor bottle that Ricky had passed around, some smoking Camels, some spitting tobacco stolen from their dads' pouches. I knew this was somehow the wrong thing, but the truth was, I didn't believe that

Ricky's sister was ever going to materialize. Nobby was telling dirty jokes he'd read in *Playboy*, something his father had confiscated from a sinner; the kid named Steve was already rubbing his crotch through his shorts like it was a magic lamp and he wanted his wish to come true now. We were a pathetic and desperate bunch. Joey was scared, too, like me, but he was the kind of kid who was always accepting dares and making bets and doing all kinds of things that mothers shout at their kids for. He looked at me every now and then, nodding, as if to confirm that this was it, this was the end of innocence, the beginning of Manhood.

And just about the time that Lewis was getting up to head on home, there was a sound through the underbrush, just beyond the chain-link fence that surrounded the quarry.

We all turned our heads in that direction; Ricky, I noticed, began puffing away on a pipe, grinning, his eyes twinkling.

Coming out of the bushes was the prettiest little thing we'd ever seen, with long dark hair, so unlike the Bonchances, her face all rouged, her lashes long and fluttering; she wore a yellow sundress, and her shoulders were evenly freckled, the rest of her skin dark from the sun. She had breasts, too, puffing up as she came, as if just seeing us made her excited. She walked almost too daintily, and Joey whispered in my ear, "All the Bonchances're whores. Lookit her. She walks the walk."

I felt the earth shiver as nearly a dozen boys got instant hard-ons watching this girl saunter up and stand in their midst.

She smiled, so pretty, so sweet.

Still, there was something very corrupt in those eyes, something a little sinister. And alluring, like a hootchykootchy girl at the Chatauqua sideshow.

I took a step back.

I knew then I wasn't going to do it.

I thought of turning and running down the path, back to the safety of home.

But something about her was so dark and bad and inviting, all at the same time.

I felt like she was smiling especially for me.

She said, in a summery voice, full of encouragement, "Which one's first?" I never knew a girl who volunteered for this kind of thing, but Joey had told me that whores liked it all the time.

"They're nymphos, they can't get enough of it, some of 'em even do each other," he said.

"Come on," the Bonchance girl beckoned, putting one of her hands against her sideways-thrusting hip, "who wants to get some? I know what you like, and I got plenty of it."

The kid named Vince raised his hand like he was in class and roll was being called. His face was all red.

The girl led him into the bushes, and Vince almost fell on a rock on the way. She pulled him down, and the laurel bush rustled as if it, too, wanted some of the action.

When they were out of sight, Ricky Bonchance slapped me on the back and said, "Well, Mr. Marshall, you ready to pop yours?"

"I dunno. I'm feeling kinda sick."

"Pussy," he said.

Somebody laughed at me; I looked around, and saw that it was Joey. I felt betrayed by him then, but worse, I felt that to have to prove myself, I'd have to have sex with the Bonchance girl.

The guys began to look like animals to me. A bunch of stupid monkeys all sitting around, waiting for whatever sensation was going to come next. A few giggled; the Furst brothers talked about how they once saw their folks do it. I drank some of the malt liquor to try and work up some courage to stand up to them, but, if anything, it weakened my reasoning.

After about ten minutes, Vince came out of the bushes with a big grin on his face, and his fly at half-mast.

Ricky clapped for him, and then we all did, the perfect audience.

Vince said, "She was kinda dry, but I got her all wetted up."

"I'm next," Joey said, but Steve was already up and running toward what came to be known as the Bang Bush.

One by one, they trooped, and within an hour and ten minutes all of the guys had gone behind the Bang Bush and had lost what they needed to lose.

Ricky wrapped his hairy pale arm around my shoulders. "C'mon, Scooter, you want a piece, don'cha, you want to prove to your buddies you ain't some fag?"

"Yeah," Joey said, socking me gently in the gut, "show her what you can do, Scoot. You got all the right equipment."

"Maybe he got it, but maybe it's rusty," Howie Furst cracked.

"Or maybe you need tweezers to get it out with," someone else added.

I was always one to succumb to peer pressure, so, without much else prodding me on, I stumbled across the rocks, went around the laurel bush, and there she lay.

Beauty in the rough. She looked none the worse for wear; her skirt was drawn back, and she had, through a modesty I didn't understand, kept her panties on, too—a hole had been cut in them to allow access. Her breasts were, incredibly, fallen to her stomach beneath the sundress. She was fifteen but nearly flat, and it became obvious to me that, like a few other girls I had heard of only in legend, she "stuffed."

But she was still golden in my eyes, a beautiful Bonchance, and beyond that a sexual goddess of extraordinary talent, for she could satisfy our little regiment.

She grinned when she saw me, and said in that melt-butter trash accent, "Hey, boy, I been saving a place for you. A special place. Right where I heat up the syrup."

Her legs parted, slightly, and I saw the stains and bruises the other boys had left as their markings. Her panties still held, as torn as they were.

I backed away, just a foot or two.

"I can't," I said.

"Honey?" she asked.

"It ain't right."

"What's wrong about boys knowing what they want

and pleasure?'' she asked. ''I know what you like, boy.''

''It just ain't right''—I stuck to my guns—''what we're doing to you and all. It's bad.''

''Oh,'' she said gleefully, ''a shy one. Let me tell you, shy boy, it ain't bad, at least not from where I'm sittin'.''

She leaned forward, crawling a ways over to sit near where I stood. She pressed her face up against my zipper and kissed it. I began to get hard.

''No,'' I said.

''A stiff dick don't have a brain, you know,'' she said.

She unzipped my pants slowly, and reached across my jockey shorts, until she could cup the head in her hands.

I couldn't help it; I told my conscience to die; I extinguished all reason; it felt that good.

I reached down to touch the back of her head as I felt a tongue exploring in my underwear.

And then I pulled her hair off.

I looked at her.

She looked up.

I could've frozen time right then, and never minded that the world had ended.

She had a towhead flattop, and I said, ''Oh, Jesus, don't touch me, God.''

IV

''You slimy-ass bastard,'' I spat at Ricky as I stomped my way toward him.

Ricky began giggling uncontrollably, ''Scooter Boy found out my little secret.''

''Damn it,'' I said, holding the curly wig high like I'd cut the head off the gorgon, ''lookit this. It ain't a girl you been laying, you stupid morons, it's a boy—you did a boy! Ricky made you do a boy!''

''Hey,'' Ricky said, holding his hands up in drunken glee, ''not just any guy. That's my cousin Kirby, and he likes to get it from guys. He dresses like that all the time. He likes it. Guess you boys just lost your cherries to one of your own!'' He laughed like there was no tomorrow.

The other kids didn't get it, not at first.

Joey was still trying to figure something out in his head, like his brain had got scrambled just looking at the brunette wig.

"I fucked a guy?" Vince said. "Christ, I knew she was too dry. I knew it. I fucked a guy?"

Nobby was bawling like a baby. "Oh, please, God, don't make me a queer just 'cause I was misled down the path to Sodom. Please forgive this thy servant."

"Every one of you," Ricky Bonchance said, "walking around Stone Valley like you own it, like you fuckin' own it, and just 'cause my pa, he don't make a lot of money, and just 'cause we ain't from some goombah first family of Sticksville, U.S.A., you make me and my brothers and sisters out to be fuckin' trash under your pissant feet. Well, look what I got on you. On each one a you." He couldn't help grinning, could he? He was right; he now had something to hold over all of us. Maybe even blackmail us with this delicious piece of information.

His cousin Kirby, still in a dress, came out from the bushes, blowing kisses to me and my friends; Lewis Graham bent forward and booted his lunch all over Fred's shoes.

And then something happened; it was like a twig breaking under someone's foot. Ricky must've felt it first, because he tried to stop it.

But it was too late.

The boys were picking up rocks, and heavy sticks, and circling around the boy in the dress.

"Fucking queer," one said.

Another said, "Homo pervert."

Nobby Dee spit, "Sinner, make your peace now."

Ricky tried to break into the circle, but got hit with a rock. He fell down, and even though he was still conscious, I could tell he was too scared to get back up.

For my part, I stood back and watched, so I was no less guilty than any of them.

The boy in the dress said, "I thought you liked me. I thought you wanted me."

"Abomination," Nobby said.

But it was my best friend, Joey Draco, who hit him first. The boy touched the blood that dripped down from his forehead. He looked at his reddened fingers as if he didn't quite get why all these boys who loved him would want to hurt him.

After the first blow, there were others. I think everybody got one in. It was like watching a bunch of chickens gather round and peck one of their own to death.

Kirby Bonchance barely cried out as the fists and rocks and branches rose and fell against him.

V

I closed my eyes until it was over.

A sound like water dripping in a metal sink; the blows of rocks against a skull, one after another.

Ricky Bonchance was crying, but as heartless as he was, it didn't seem to be for his cousin at all; it was more for his loss of power over the other boys. "It ain't fair to do it, you can't kill him like that, you can't, I set this up all day, you can't do it."

Joey was exhausted. His hands were soaked in blood. He came over to me and tried to grin, but could not. "Let's go home. I wanna go home. Nothing ever happened here today. Got that? Nothing."

I don't know when the others left, but Joey and I got home before eight. I went to bed early and lay there, looking out the window, at the valley and the mountains, and wondered if it had all been a dream.

I wanted to wish it away, the day, the boy in the dress, the killing.

VI

Nearly thirty-three years later, I'm about to say good-bye, forever, to my childhood friend Joey Draco, the Dragon of Deer Hill, the man who went through the mountain town and slaughtered children, mainly boys around the age of twelve or thirteen, a few older; some quickly, and some by slow torture. He buried them in an old quarry, but barely covered them up. He was easy to catch because he made no secret of what he did; it just took a while for people to believe him.

He has eyes like a little boy, even now.

He says, ''Well, I don't know what else to say. Hey''—putting a finger to his lips—''hear that?''

I listen.

The tap's dripping again.

''I turned it off, too,'' he says. ''You saw me turn it off. He did it. Just to show you.''

I nod, just to humor him.

''The body,'' I say. ''I've wondered all these years. What happened to it?''

''The boy? The one we all took turns at? Oh, Lordy, Scooter, Eric, whatever, I thought I told you. I went back later that night, and it—he—was still there. Dress, shoes, face all bashed in. I had a flashlight, and a shovel, and I figured I'd toss him in the quarry and cover him up. They were gonna fill it in later. But you know? I couldn't. I looked at that sweet bloody face, all shiny where the light hit it, and I knew I had to have it for myself. And I pressed myself against it, and I rubbed around it, and it felt so right, it felt so good. You understand.''

I don't, but I nod.

''I took it and kept it in my room, until the smell got too awful. Then I tied it up in my old tree fort, and I went up to do things to it for a long time afterward. You can do a lot with a body when it's rotting.''

I remember the pictures on the news, of the things in his refrigerator, of the skins on the wall.

''I'm sorry it ever happened,'' I say, and I wonder how far a man must go in order to exorcise the demons that haunt him.

He grins. ''Not me. I found out all about myself then. I knew where I was headed. It was like my road was all paved and waiting. And my friend, he never leaves me. You know that? I think I skin him, or I eviscerate him, but here he is, always with me. But our time together's about up, you know?'' He looks at the empty chair.

The faucet's dripping faster, then slower.

Beads of water echoing in the basin.

Close my eyes: rock against bone.

"He's done with me," Joe says when I open my eyes again.

I still don't quite get what he's saying, but he reaches across to the chair and places his hand in the air around it. I ask, "What about the others? You ever hear from them?"

A bigger smile. "We keep in touch. A few of us have things in common, you know. It's amazing how, once you open a door, sometimes it won't be closed ever again. Sometimes you don't want it closed."

And then his smile fades, a cloud coming across his face. "I never understood about those Bonchances, though, you know? No one even checked about that boy; it was as if he didn't matter. Ricky should've done something. Maybe things'd be different if someone had told. You could've."

I say nothing.

"You were such a good boy, and there you were, with a secret as big as a house inside you. I'm sorry about your face. I guess that's an awkward thing to say, huh?"

"Not really." I shrug it off. "I did it to myself. You can only do so much with a Gillette blade anyway. The scars may even heal one day. It wasn't suicide I was going for, either."

"I know." He nods. "You just didn't want to be who you were. I bet we've all felt that way since then. You do that to your face, and I find . . . other faces."

We don't have a lot left to say to each other; he's on some kind of medication, too, which slows him down somewhat. He's got that weary look in his eyes.

He sighs. "Yeah. This is just great, Scooter. You. Me. Here. Even here. Seems just like old times."

"Oh." I try not to smile because it seems inappropriate, but I can't help myself. "Yeah, it does."

"Just like when we were boys," he says, and I see it

there, in him, little Joey Draco, on his bike on a summer day, with a locust on a string, and me, so naive, not knowing that boys who could torture small insects were capable of anything; boys who could do that to a girl, even if she wasn't one, they could do a lot more when they grew up. Hidden potential.

But we're old friends, so I sit across from him and try not to dwell on the children he's killed, or the ones the others might be killing, because it's so brief, our time, our lives, our days of innocence, and I want this moment to be something worth remembering.

"To be kids again," he says, and I can tell it is not a memory of pain that has overtaken him, but a nostalgia for a finer day.

A few minutes pass.

I hear someone outside the door pushing a cart with squeaky wheels.

"Handing out meds," he says. "Big pills in little cups for killer headaches. It's a little gallows humor, come on, Scooter. Must be almost four."

"I better go," I say. "I've got to get back to work tomorrow, and my flight out of Charleston's at nine."

He scratches the three-day growth of black beard around his chin. "He's going with you, you know."

Because I know Joe Draco is considered insane, at least legally, I ignore this comment and reach over to give him a hug. He smells like Old Spice and strong soap. They told me when I went in that he washes incessantly. He whispers in my ear, "Kirby. The boy in the dress. He's been with me since then. But he's done with me. He wants you. He told me you could've stopped it."

I can feel the small hairs on the back of my neck rise, and goose bumps grow there, too. Not because I believe there's an unseen and uninvited guest sitting in the chair next to him, but because I know my best old friend from seventh grade believes it.

Water dripping in the sink.

"I love you, Joe," I tell him.

"No, you don't, we never talked after that. Not till now. Only one friend stayed with me," he says, pulling back. ''Good-bye, my friend. Treat him with respect, that's all he wants, really. Maybe love, too.''

He grins. He's relieved that I'm going now, maybe because I've reminded him about too many terrible things.

''Stopped again,'' he says, pointing at the tap. I pretend this means something important, and then I open the door, and let it swing shut behind me.

In the hall, the nurses and orderlies and psych-warders move slowly, as if they're the ones on Thorazine and Lithium. Doors swing open and close again as a patient, or an inmate, or a therapist arrives or leaves or wanders. I feel bad for Joey being here, but he had blazed a path for himself beginning at twelve that could only lead here, or, perhaps, to a worse place.

I'm almost to the great double doors that lead to the administration building, where I can check out and return to the normal world, when I feel the small hand closing around mine, the warmth of a child, like a sun through clouds.

I stop, and can't bring myself to look down.

A gray-bearded man, criminally insane, perhaps, stands in a doorway where he is about to take his afternoon pill and a sip of water; an orderly, his back to me, is handing him the small Dixie cup. The man with the gray beard is looking down my arm, at my hand, at what hangs on to me so tightly.

The man's mouth opens slowly, about to cry out, and a sweet voice whispers from beside me, ''I know what you boys like.''

HIGH HEELS
FROM HELL

Mike Lee

Mike Lee was born-in 1962 and grew up in Texas and North Carolina. He first began writing for punk-rock fanzines at fifteen, and eventually became a music editor at *The Austin Chronicle*. He also played rhythm guitar for Room City, a roots-rock alternative combo, before moving to New York City in 1989. He is the former Associate Editor of *Genesis* and Editor-in-Chief of *Rockpool*. His articles have appeared in several unusual markets, including *The Nose, Sensitive Skin* and *Panty Line Fever*. He is in the process of putting the finishing touches on his first novel. He currently lives in New York's Lower East Side with his wife and five extremely weird cats, and is eagerly awaiting the arrival of his first child.

Getting to Danny's house is always a difficult chore. Have to make a scary no-light turn off South Lamar, be-

hind a Shamrock gas station, and cruise down a street
noted for an uphill hairpin curve, the most dangerous in
the city. The locals use this geographic necessity as an
excuse to prove their suspect manhood, and you learn to
ride the horn when coming up to the turn. After surviving
it, I'm moving downhill and make the second left onto a
dead-end street.

Danny's place is the seventh house on the left, small
brick, ranch-style, with a metal carport, nondescript in its
inelegance. Behind the backyard is the Missouri Pacific
line leading into town; behind the tracks is a wooded area
used as a dumping ground and party area for local gangs.
Once I took Irene for some fun and games with a plastic
clothesline, her favorite. Between us, we call our little
trips going to the scorpions, but we haven't been stung
yet.

Pull up to the curve. Her car isn't there, but there is a
butt-ugly yellow Toyota Celica parked in the driveway. I
walk in like royalty expecting the adulation of millions.

Danny burps, "Hey, man. 'Star Trek' is on."

He sits on a well-worn couch with Lyvere, munching
on potato chips. On the floor at their feet lies a nearly
empty box of glazed doughnuts.

"Living healthy, I see."

"A mere appetizer for the moment," Lyvere replies,
attempting my sarcasm and failing.

Ignoring him, I ask Danny, "Who all's here?"

"Dayboy's in the rumpus room with Miriam, and Sod's
at the store getting beer."

Suppress an urge to ask Lyvere why he is here, but
since he's become Dayboy's new pet, I remained silent.

I lean against the wall beside them and stare at the
fuzzy TV screen. The episode is when Captain Kirk is
held captive by a crazed ex-lover who switches bodies
with him. I've watched this show at least a dozen times.
By now, watching it again makes me sick to my stomach.

I get up. "I'm going outside for a while."

Go out to the backyard in time to see the sun setting
behind the trees. The crickets are already chirping loudly
in the tall grass beyond the tracks. I take a deep breath

and light a cigarette. The grass needs cutting, not that this matters. Ever since Danny's parents left him behind when they moved out to Tyler, he let everything go to hell fast in order to keep the property worthless. And he certainly has done a fine job of it. With our help, of course.

Drop the match, grinding it under my heel. I'm not going to be responsible for another grass fire. If Sod doesn't come back with the beer soon, I am going to leave.

Pensive, I move back around the house, to the front. I slip between a pair of holly bushes for a peek into the window to the rumpus room.

Dayboy sits cross-legged in the middle of the floor, mumbling incantations from this well-worn paperback on witchcraft while his girlfriend, Miriam, her skirt hiked up over her waist, masturbates in the corner, moaning moronically while he tries to figure out the incantation for bringing up a demon who will give us all lots of cash. Since getting fired from the restaurant at the end of last spring, Dayboy is too lazy to get a job, to the point where even scrounging dimes for cigarettes can wind up as a day-long chore. So he filches this book from the Half-Price in order to play out his secret fantasies of being a Catholic priest. Rather hopeless.

My guess is that at first Miriam is bemused. Apparently she then became bored with the whole situation. She comes over, guesses he is too busy with the arcane to be much of a good fuck, then starts to diddle herself in full view of the window. This simple ploy should work; however, Dayboy is too enthralled in the obsessive tedium associated with raising demons to pay her much more than an occasional sidelong glance while she works away passionately at her pussy. As for me, I'm partially disgusted, somewhat amused and more than a little horny. The thought crosses my mind of charging admission to the local kids to come and gawk at her, but I realize I'd have to split the money with these two slobs.

Watching the absurdity of their goings-on is a reminder that I am not alone, yet this depressing realization is improved by the knowledge that if I were in this situation I

would have the good sense to at least close the goddamned blinds beforehand. This is where the major difference
lay between Dayboy and me. While both of us have little
idea how our actions are going to cross the finish line, I,
at least, possess the temerity to veer from the lemmings
and cover my ass. Dayboy, however, is rather thoughtless
in that regard, and this leaves me to rescue him from
trouble.

Move back from the window to catch my breath. The
emotions inherent in watching a moon-faced, dumpy teenager scratching an itch as her befuddled boyfriend does
low carnival can be overwhelming. Walk back into the
house, sit down on the couch next to Danny and Lyvere,
watching cartoons. Reach down into the bag of potato
chips, grab a handful and munch wordlessly while trying
to put Miriam's pathetic attention act out of mind. The
idea she might have spied me watching from behind the
bushes chills me. Embarrassment at discovery is one
thing; the possibility of getting into trouble with Dayboy
is quite another.

At heart Dayboy is a jealous and vicious monster beneath his thick skin and rattled brain, thoroughly capable
of murder. I know this, for I know his life. Brutality is a
virtue to him. This concept had been beaten into him back
in the days he was the school-yard Jesus. I'm inclined to
agree this hocus-pocus shit is what gets him through his
otherwise mundane existence. Between the crystal Miriam
and the snort and the persuasive lack of morality around
these parts, he's a killer waiting for a volunteer. One of
these days, the veneer of civilization will wash away in
the first thunderstorm and he's going to go off the edge—
I know it. He doesn't have much of a sense of humor, so
it's a soft guarantee Dayboy is well on his way to socio-
pathy.

Miriam is the same way, I guess. There's no other reason that she likes him so much. Both are similar in terms
of impending doom.

But in terms of damaged goods, my Irene has both Dayboy and Miriam beat. I met her last winter when I started

going out with Dayboy, which entailed hanging out at Duke's Royal Coach shooting pool, since it is one of the few places in Austin where we could drink without getting carded or getting the shit kicked out of us by rednecks.

That night The Retractors were onstage. I have always been nauseated by their music, a sort of a double-gaited fey Wire rip-off with a prima-donna lead singer whom all the gals love, including an ex-girlfriend of mine. The playing was talented yet bloodless. I remember we were still bummed that Sid was dead, although it was nearly a year ago. We spoke at work about getting out of Austin. The last month had been evil; the frat boys and rednecks were in high gear since the Iranians took over the embassy. School was also turning into a disaster; we each flunked three classes and I didn't believe I had enough credits to go into my senior year even if I went full-time to summer school. Dayboy and I wanted to move to New York because that was where our hero, Lester Bangs, lived, although Lester was a real rude fucker when I met him here last summer.

Anyway, I impressed the freak show around me with my skills as a solid English shooter on the bar table. That night I believed no one outside the Atlantic City pro circuit could bop a ball in a ninety-degree angle like I could.

However, I stank up the long shots, screwed up a couple of easy banks and was falling behind, choking heavily when it really counted. Tonight I could count on only chump change for my eight-ball abilities. Fortunately, I did occasion few-and-far-between admiration from the lush puppies at the bar, namely the college-damaged women. Lonely, lost in a weird place, they love a gallant loser fighting to keep his head above water, and tonight I counted myself as one.

Back then, I'd been pulling down virtually nothing working with Dayboy bussing tables. They paid only $1.65 an hour plus tips, which were lousy, since the waitresses put them up their noses before they paid us off.

I would have been in utter poverty if it weren't for caging suckers during pickup games, yet I felt pretty good being the constant center of attention. After all, it was a small town, and I was able to live out my dream of total rock-out cool, if not in semiprincipled reality, but in the vague belief that I was actually having a good time living my life. No one has as good a memory as me, and that is all it takes. Just keep a conceivable and workable sense of focus and high hopes I would come out ahead in the long run. Every night is a mining expedition for experience, and I was invariably richly rewarded. Coming from a shit-poor family, I knew it sure beat TV.

We are the run-of-the-mill, Joe-average, common-variety angry types, young, with just a hint of disgust toward the world. Guys like Dayboy and me live the typical lives of lonely teenagers with an ax to grind, screwed partly by the system that birthed us, partly by our inbred paranoia and lastly by a tendency to consume ennui like cheap wine. But whenever we talk about having a definite responsibility beyond ourselves, someone, or circumstance, comes along and reminds us that, along with guilt, believing this shit will kill you faster than heroin cut with roach killer. Christ, no matter which way you look at the ball in your hand, it's still fucking round.

But tonight I'm not thinking those adult thoughts as I saunter to the bar to get yet another Miller. Perhaps it's better to say that I strutted, but I wasn't in the strut mood, because I had lost again. Even so, I am definitely in my off-the-cuff attitude, the devil-may-care of a semi-intellectual sixteen-year-old with pretensions of addled genius and a propensity toward laziness. I slowly raise my hand with one eye cocked at the mirror behind the bar and my other eye wanders down the bar.

I sort of go blank when our eyes meet. Irene Donna O'Connell is a neogoddess of the first order. She is fifteen, five-three, thin, with banana-yellow hair, shoulder-length with dark roots that always show, and never, ever looks washed. She keeps it parted on the side, falling over her face, cut into bangs that stick to her sweating brow.

In Victorian times Irene would have been considered consumptive, her light gray eyes so colorless no amount of light could penetrate, along with her dark, almost black eyebrows framing her narrow, triangular face and high, hollow cheekbones, sprinkled with freckles and acne scars. Her lips, smeared with a helluva lot of red lipstick, are pursed firmly in place like those of a prim school-teacher, with the upper lip slightly out to cover an over-bite, calling attention to her very sharp, pointed nose. My first impression is of an angel slumming as a two-bit tramp on the lam from the violent ward at the Austin State Hospital. I like that.

She was wearing a low-cut cotton dress which came to her knees, as pure a white as you could get; a miraculous vision of tawdry loveliness. Yet it turned out she had borrowed it from Miriam.

But it was electric when our eyes met. For the first time in my life, I didn't feel forced by circumstances. She later confided to me she wanted to hold me in her arms at that precise moment. I felt I had to make a choice between heaven and hell.

Irene smiles, lighting a cigarette.

I smile back, and stick my hand in an ashtray.

Watching her pass to the jukebox, I decide she is out of my league. It was in the cool and distant way she held herself. Definitely out of reach for an unreconstructed neurotic with buck teeth, standing under five-eight. Later, these turn out to be among my main selling points. Love and attraction sure is weird, isn't it?

I pay for the beer and walk back to the pool tables to case out whom I am playing for my next spot. I chat with the hangers-on and watch a pair of nuevo wavos in matching skinny ties stink up the table. The usual always happens when these losers try to shoot pool. One or the other will accidentally sink the eight at precisely the time I light my cigarette. As usual, I'm right, smiling like a cat while I put my two quarters into the slot, readying myself for the impending slaughter.

She comes by, watching me intently. After the game, which I lose on an eight scratch, she sincerely compliments me on my style. I shrug and smile shyly. I'll take it from anywhere, especially from her.

Dayboy, who had been out in the parking lot probably fucking around with Miriam, manages to get in on the conversation. Since he figures out I'm getting fancy with Irene, he takes the opportunity to butt out and excuse himself with Miriam in tow. Irene and she are friends since elementary school, and I guess the whole meet is a setup.

Soon there is a fast-blooming relationship between us. I realize we would do well when I discover we share a favorite song, "Into the Valley" by The Skids. She also likes to collect Matchbox cars, loves to read and buys records at garage sales. She wants to drop out of high school, too, and washes dishes at a restaurant on the north side of town.

After an interval, Irene tugs at my sleeve, and we bop into the obscure winter moonlight, not seeing much of anyone until the end of Christmas vacation.

As we wait for the light to change at 21st and Guadalupe, I can't help but stare at her wobbling in high-heeled pumps. Black, with bows. Vintage, of course.

"You shure 'r' queer four dem shews, boy," Irene drawls in her thick Hill Country accent.

"Only if you're in 'em, honey."

"Well." She nudges me. "Ahm only happy to indulge." Playing with my hair, she adds, "Me, I just askin' to get all hog-tied."

"You're bullshittin' me." I barely know the girl.

"Why don't yew take me someplace an' find out?" she replies, pulling a Camel out of her purse.

She asked the right question. I grab her by the arm and take her to the building under construction on Lavaca Street. The security guard is dead drunk, so we go into the work elevator and up to the unfinished roof. We lean over the railing and stare out at the city skyline. I look at my watch and figure it'd be another five hours before sunrise.

We smoke cigarettes and the wind starts to kick up. I watch the breeze blow in her hair. She is spinning a roll of black electrical tape on her right index finger. Heaven.

Indulge me, she does. She always wears heels for me when we fuck; at first Irene assumes I am into the whole works: garter belts, fishnets, push-up bras—what Dayboy and I call "the Bettie Page thang." However, after a couple of weeks, Irene figures out my simple tastes and happily strips down to them when we hit the sack. She isn't embarrassed about my fetish, and considering she likes getting tied up, it balances out.

"It's not like you're a fag or anything," Irene says, reassuring herself as well as me. "Matter of fact, all this makes me feel more like a woman." Yeah, sure.

I really don't have an explanation for my fetish for heels. It's not like I collect them and do sole-slurpin' in a dark corner. It just turns me on to see a gurl in 'em. Probably had something to do with my kindergarten teacher. Anyway, I could be worse. I could share Irene's proclivity for clotheslines.

Miriam confided to me that Irene hasn't been the same since sixth grade, when she climbed a water tower out near Oak Hill and fell twenty feet, cracking her head open and winding up in a coma for six weeks. I doubt this is the source of Irene's weirdness; the genesis of her madness is too complicated to have such a quick and easy explanation.

And sometimes at night Irene gets out of bed and stands in front of the full-length mirror beside the door for as long as an hour. I stare at her pale figure basked in the moonlight, taking it in with pleasure.

This was the current situation. I truly believe that she will someday kill herself, me or both of us. I don't like the possibility of this happening, but I find myself strangely attracted to the potential of dramatic doom. These are the chances I have to take if I want to be the world's greatest writer. Then again, if I search harder to find another subject to write about, my life will be easier to control, but the cards always land flat on the table.

Pick up an old issue of *Creem* and read The Jam cover story until Sod finally arrives. A half hour later, Dayboy leaves the rumpus room and joins us, looking like Miriam got what she wanted. Miriam goes into the shower. After listening to Lyvere complain about the condition of his car, I insist on going to Raul's. And since Lyvere wants to be part of the in crowd so badly, I proceed to inform

him that it is only fair he and Sod haul these bozos
around, rattling engine or no.

Half an hour later, I pass by the club, driving slowly,
checking to see if Irene is waiting outside. I backtrack to
26th Street and find an illegal spot. Like Mama taught
me, I angle the tires to make it impossible to be towed,
roll up the windows and lock the doors, double-checking
just to be sure—a new habit. There's nothing to steal, yet
thieves are remarkably persistent, and I'm not going to
debate the matter.

Walk across the steaming pavement, keeping a wary
eye out for the frat daddies who hang around at the pizza
parlor next door looking for punks to beat up whenever
they run out of Iranians and hippies. I get on top of a
green pickup parked beside the chain-link fence and
stealthily climb over.

Hop down on a picnic table in time to spot Donnie
Webster in the far corner of the courtyard, chatting up a
couple of dyed blondes with skin so bad I can see it from
thirty feet, under bad light. At least there's common
ground; I chuckle. He doesn't notice me wave, either,
proving that we all have better things to do with our spare
time.

Tonight's security guard is an overweight, spike-haired
brunette holding a can of Foster's too large for her hand.
She recognizes me as I move away from the table, waving
me off with an affected sneer. Murmur "Poseur" under
my breath, while negotiating the remains of the other picnic table broken during a fight at last Wednesday's Big
Boys gig. Remind myself to sign the "Get Well" card
for Tucker, whose head broke the table.

Raul's, for what it's worth, is one of those bars people
say will never change, but always does for the right price.
Open for business less than two years, the bar has the
ambiance of an old worn shoe. The neon beer signs have
the feel of having been attached to the same mounts for
decades, not months. The broken jukebox seems to have
been shunted against the same spot next to the door to the
courtyard since the Bible, instead of several weeks. Time
stands still, even if only for a moment. This gives you the

feeling of lasting forever. The same punk-rock and nuevo-wavo bands play on the same shoddily thrown-together plywood-and-pine stage, using the same public-address system, held together with spit and tape, night after night without fail, or a tornado. The solitary pool table stands beside the bathrooms, rarely used, with three balls missing from the rack. I like this place.

I cut into the crowd jamming the bar and make my way to the end, finding a spot next to the black metal garbage can. Wait patiently for Bobby, the bartender, to stop by. The arrangement is to avoid signaling him. I look around to see if anybody else I know is lurking around.

There usually isn't, even on a Saturday night. Since the liquor board got heavy with Raul over serving minors, kids are officially banned from the club. With the exception of the usual bevy of underaged harlots, some as young as twelve, teenagers are not welcome. I can't blame Raul for his decision, that's his concern, and I long have had my way of getting around it.

Bob steps up, tapping me gently on the shoulder. After allowing for him to move to the other end of the bar, I look down and pick up an opened bottle of Miller propped against the garbage can. Quickly walk back to the courtyard for a discreet swig, sneak over to a quiet corner. More than being a minor with a beer, I want to be alone—even if the whole world is here.

I sit down on the gravel, search through the crowd for a face with a spark of something worth taking notice of. Nothing. Figures.

Now, as for Raul's—the bar has become famous, or infamous, depending on which way you look at it. This happened when some moron lead singer for a no-hope college garage group tried to smooch a cop investigating a noise complaint while the band was playing a turgid, out-of-tune version of a Sex Pistols' song. All the cop did was pause at the front of the stage, checking to see if he was really seeing what he was seeing—a geek posing as a singer, painted from head to toe in gold glitter paint. Then said geek proceeded to do his thing, and the cop proceeded to do his thing, taking out his nightstick and pounding the ever-lovin' shit out of the poor bastard.

Eventually, the situation calmed down enough for Raul and Joe to reopen the club. Now the place is packed with college art fags and misplaced white trash looking for a fight and ninety-cent Long Stars.

I've become very spoiled. Should always be aware of the fact that nothing too good lasts forever. Though let's not say that Raul's is such a wonderful place—but it's a place to go, albeit the bands here are usually awful.

Yet it really doesn't matter, because this is better than nothing at all. I got into punk rock because I like my music straight and to the point. As far as I am concerned, the crap coming out after 1967 is nothing more than dull, pretentious tripe, meant for a population numbed by downers and a lack of self-confidence. So when Johnny Rotten took the microphone and screamed "I Wanna Be Me!" he said what I already know in my heart.

I want to make my own decisions, follow through on my own desires, not the trends on television, or *Rolling Stone*. I hate the looks I get, but ain't that the point of rebellion? I may not go as far as Day's and Sod's spike-head haircuts, or Irene's and Miriam's slum-goddess wear, but I do a pretty damn good job at subcultural confrontation. The college poseurs may think they're hot shit, but punks like me know what it takes to actually drive, not follow, the bandwagon. At seventeen, I realize I know more than most, especially this crew of postteen frauds looking for a skeevy culture version of a slumber party.

While staring at a conga line of the aforementioned in perfectly ripped T-shirts and boot-flared jeans, I am reminded of a rare example of Dayboy wit: trendiness transcending social realities.

It's as if a set of rules for cricket are handed to a group of professional hockey players. Moving to the doorway and watching the crowd inside listen to a rehash of bad 1977, I understand that in the hands of many, you can't achieve your goals. There's no opportunity, anymore, to strive for perfection, to be different, to break away from the mainstream. No motivation once you break off; twenty untalented camp followers will beat you to the finish and take over. Everyone accepts banality, curling up in a fetal position to fondle it. The safe bet these days is to take the low road. Not only is there safety in numbers, there's safety in mediocrity. I find it nauseating.

Down the rest of my Miller and push the bottle behind the oil barrel next to me. It is time to leave. Don't want to stick around and continue to search for an excuse to slum. I need to keep moving. Turn around, going back the way I came over the fence, landing not so easily on the pavement. Jog to the front door in time to run into Dayboy, standing outside with lapdog Lyvere.

And in time to watch an obnoxious chuka princess, drunk off her ass from T-Bird and 'clear, stagger out of the club into the middle of the street. She is waving her arms wildly and laughing and smiling and crying at once. It's a very funny sight. I reckon it would be even better if somebody actually nails her to the pavement.

Suddenly get a hard-on just thinking about her fragile beauty dead and damaged, foamy blood sparkling on her lips like last year's makeup.

I crush the idea along with my cigarette and cross the street to pull her back to the sidewalk. Having her squashed by traffic would create problems for the club, and no one else is raring to help.

She looks at me with half-lidded eyes, holding her hand up in a halt signal. I ignore it and take her into my arms, dragging her over to the sidewalk, avoiding her attempts to claw me with her fingernails.

Dayboy walks up beside us while I wrestle her to the parking lot. "Looks like you've got yourself a real live wire," he drawls, smirking.

"Fuck you." I have her in a headlock while we push past him into the lot.

I let go of her when we get to a red Ford and she falls over the hood. She begins to retch and I take a few steps back to make sure I am out of her range. The river of her previous dinner splashes on the car, her black dress and the ground. I look away in disgust. Jesus, I can take the sight of blood, but not puke, especially this greenish-gray shit she's retching.

The girl is particularly loud, too. The curious crowd behind us takes in the scene with amusement. I am a bit embarrassed and I hold my head down in shame as I light another Marlboro, taking the cosmic death smoke into my lungs with a wordless wish I am someplace else.

Irene comes up beside me and puts her hand on my shoulder. I shudder.

"That was really chivalrous," she moans sarcastically.

I shrug and turn to her. She greets me with a smear of lipsticked lips and the aroma of cheap perfume.

Grunt in reply and hold Irene's shoulder gently. She pushes herself into me, grinding her crotch into my thigh. I know the score. Meekly, I follow her into the club, leaving the puking black dress to her own devices.

Fat Henry is working the door and thanks me for taking care of the problem outside. People like the black dress always call unwanted attention to the place. Fat Henry knows better than most of us; he has a fucking canyon of a scar on his left cheek from Sergeant Kukyandall's tire thumper. In the light of the doorway, I swear the scar looks like it glows.

We make our way through the crowd and manage to get to the beer garden out back with few difficulties. Dayboy is at the doorway, holding up two cans of Miller.

"Here's a beer, hero." He has a knowing grin, the kind that annoys the hell out of me.

"Thanks. Almost forgot," I mumble as I pull the tab back, spraying foam in every direction. "Thanks for breaking it in for me, asshole." I brush my shirt off and take a long sip.

Dayboy looks at me like he wants to say something profound. I ignore him and watch Irene chat with some other friends of ours. Despite my problems with her, I like staring at Irene's ass, all round and firm under a tank-top dress too hiked up for her own good. With a getup like that, Irene should have everyone hitting on her, yet no one will, under any circumstances. And not for fear of me, that's for damn sure.

I think of the girl in the black dress lying in the middle of the street with her legs splayed broken and open. My mind's eye traces the smooth skin of her injured calves, up to the curve of her milky thighs stained with dust. Through the line of her panties which covers the mound of her pubic hair, I consider the thought: will there be blood seeping through those panties down her lovely thighs, collecting in a thick, dark pool upon the pavement?

I will reach down with my index finger toward that stain. What will it feel like? Soft and wet, like a lost soul desiring that last orgasm before the finish? As I think of reaching down to pull off her shoes, a hand reaches out and holds mine.

Open my eyes in time to watch Irene pulling my hand down to her crotch. Her eyes have a want-me, fuck-me attitude, and she leans me against the small space between the bathroom wall and the broken jukebox.

"Push it. In. Yessss," she hisses mechanically between pursed lips. I hook my thumb under her garter belt and snap it back hard against her thigh. There is no reaction except an unnerving smirk. This turns me on more.

"Fuck it. Now. Yessss," she moans as I slip two fingers between the folds of her pussy. In and over.

She clutches her skirt with two balled-up fists, with the veins popping up behind her white knuckles. In and over. In and over. As I speed up the process, Irene begins gasping asthmatically.

In and over. The way she taught me. Small beads of sweat well up on my forehead as I pump my fingers faster. In and over.

As she gushes around my fingers, my cock fills the hole in the pocket where I keep my Zippo and keys. I hold my hand up. Irene lets out a little gasp. She pushes her skirt back down, hard, knocking my hand away. There is a thick stickiness hanging on my fingers that I don't immediately recognize as her menstrual blood. It is already drying on my fingers, cancerous under the neon Blatz sign above me.

Streaks of orange look red in this mystery I contemplate, and I look down to see a drop from my fingertips fall to the floor.

Stare woozily while Irene sucks on my fingers. Irene is

really into these public displays of affection. I get off on it, probably more than she does, yet I know it is getting fucking tiresome to our friends.

After she's finished, Irene carefully wipes off my hand. I look into her face. Her long lashes hide her eyes from me; her lips are a puckered red wound making me horny again. I think of later this evening when I get her alone in our room and onto the cold, dead wood of the floor.

We walk out into the beer garden. Irene and I sit down on top of one of the picnic tables. I pull at a sliver hanging off the tabletop and hold Irene closer to me. I try to remember where I had left my beer. I want to go home, but I can wait for a little while longer. Adjust my belt and shake my leg out to free my cock from the sticky underwear.

Out of the corner of my eye I see another familiar figure. Discreetly, I glance over to the corner, watch the black dress leaning against the wall in the far corner beside the odd collection of beer signs rusting from the accumulated rainwater and piss. Her knees are scraped and dirty. She holds her shoes, a pair of patent leather spikes, limply in her hands. She sways slightly in time to the music blaring inside. I wonder how she managed to make it back into the club.

The girl looks like she probably thinks she's in Waco, or in hell. Her head flops to her chest; should have been enough for her to plunge to the ground. She manages to keep her balance somehow, as if she had a string wrapped taut around her neck, ready to snap at any given moment.

She drops her shoes on the ground, slides down the wall while attempting to pick them up. I watch her fumbling blindly around the earth in front of her, digging her hands into the gravel. Indeed, this is a pathetic sight on many levels, but I find it vaguely erotic. Instinctively clutch Irene tightly to me and slide my hand down her skirt.

"Boy, I'll tell you," Irene drawls. "You sure are queer for them shoes."

"Hey, hey, honey. Like I tell you always. Only if you're in 'em," I reply, shaky.

Pointing to the girl, I add, "She needs help."

Irene nods, brushing her lips against the back of my neck. "I ain't gonna help no goddamned spic, even if you do like her goddamned high heels."

The girl begins pounding the gravel with her fist and crying, "Goddammit. Please. Help me. Fuck." She mutters in a plaintive voice. By now it is getting too pathetic to watch and too well scripted. Miriam and Dayboy stop by and begin talking to her. Momentarily forgetting her hatred of Mexicans, and not to be outdone by her friends' apparent altruism, Irene nudges me off the table and joins them.

Irene kneels, brushing dirt from the girl's hair. "C'mon. It'll be all right," she whispers while wiping her hand off on the girl's black dress.

The girl holds up an arm to wipe the tears from her vomit-stained cheeks. "I wanna go home," she sniffs.

Dayboy bends over her, trying not to get too close. "Do you have any friends here?" I know better. I sure as hell have never seen her before, and if she didn't have any friends here now, she wasn't going to have them around later. But it is a gallant shot on his part.

She only mumbles incoherently about getting to her car. "We'll walk you there," Miriam softly replies, while Irene glances up at me with a smirk.

Dayboy and I help her up, walking her slowly out the back gate into the parking lot next door. The black dress points weakly at a tan Toyota in the back of the lot. When we get there she starts moaning about her lost purse.

Miriam sighs. "Fuck. I think she had it back in the garden. I'll just meet y'all at the car."

When she disappears into the beer garden, I think about the girl's face. It is round and soft, like a china doll I remembered my mom having on her dresser before the cat broke it. It is a real sweet, baby's face. Curious, I reach out and touch her cheek, poking gently.

Want her to pull me down and kiss me, swinging her tongue into my mouth. Even taste the combination of Thunderbird and nothingness. Unsurprisingly, Irene senses what I am thinking, and jerks me away.

We move to the doorway, leaving the girl alone with Dayboy. We smile at Miriam as she passes. She swigs from her beer, sneering, "You know what? Can't find the bitch's purse."

"Did you look under the pool table?" Irene grins, referring to an in joke the pair share and I don't want to know about.

We turn to go back into the club, out of sight from the parking lot, when we hear Miriam shriek.

"You goddamn bitch! Fuckin' don't fuck with my boy-friend!"

We run back in time to watch Miriam slam the girl's head into the trunk of the Toyota. The girl falls against Miriam, who grabs her by the hair, then shoves her into the back windshield. The window breaks with a dull crack, not what I had expected.

Miriam lets go of the girl, who drops to the ground, and as an exclamation point, she pounds the prone figure in the face with an object in her hand, screaming inco-herently, until finally, Dayboy reaches out and pulls her away.

Irene runs to Miriam while I look at what was done to the girl. Christ, what a mess. Miriam nailed the girl across the face with the girl's shoes. She no longer looks like a china doll.

Matter of fact, she looks like shit. Miriam worked the girl's face into medium-rare hamburger meat, the force from the window alone left her nose crushed and flattened, and blood is spurting out of her left eye. Shards of glass sprinkle her like stardust, the larger pieces rising from her cheeks. The only part undamaged is her lips. Between them a thin line of blood is forming. I think of getting close to see if she is breathing, but before I can, the scene devolves further into chaos—Miriam tears away from Ir-ene, and whacks the girl a few more times before Dayboy and I manage to pull her away. I suspect crank again; although this is a recent development in Miriam's life-style, she already has that goofy personality associated with machine heads.

Sod comes running up, along with Danny, and both are

overwhelmed by the situation. Meanwhile, Miriam has calmed down somewhat—she's surrounded by the bartender, Fat Henry and Raul himself. I'm close enough to hear her muttering to no one in particular—something, I suspect, about raising demons. Dayboy is nowhere to be found; he's probably already on the run, which I decide is the best plan of action.

Pull Irene aside, whisper to her that it would be a good idea, while the crowd gathers around, for us to get out. She agrees. I feel guilty about leaving everyone in the lurch, but I'm not real good with difficult situations. I grab Irene by the shoulder and move quickly to the gate, losing ourselves in the crowd.

Bump into Lyvere when we get to the front.

"If I were you," I say, carefully measuring my words, "I'd be home, in bed."

Nodding, Lyvere does the opposite and walks to Conan's Pizzeria next door. Sighing, Irene and I walk across the street, get in the car and haul ass toward I-35.

Halfway home, Irene gives me a big shit-eating grin.

"Boy, tonight shure wuz a bucket of surprises." She giggles. I'm stunned by Irene's seeming indifference. Suspect Irene had been doing some of Miriam's shitty brown sugar crystal.

I try to play it cool. "Yeah, there was some volunteers out there tonight."

"Well, that's their problem." Irene yawns. "Ain't nothin' we can do for 'em now."

"No, there's not."

"By the way"—she smiles, the nasty one she gives me when we go to the scorpions—"I got a surprise for you when we get back to Danny's."

Yeah, nothing fazes her. Another endearing quality.

"How do I look?" Irene quietly slips into the room, holding up a dead girl's shoes.

I pucker my lips and blow her a kiss.

For once, Irene smiles, showing her teeth—overbite and all. "I knew you'd like 'em," she purrs.

I reach down and pull up my hardening cock.

"C'mover heyeer." Drawling the words out slowly, like a country sheriff in a whorehouse.

Irene climbs in. She swings her legs around and whispers, "Put 'em on me, honey."

I reach down and lovingly slip the blood-splattered shoes on her feet. Irene lies back across my lap, clutching my cock with a firm grip. While she strokes me, I move my lips to the leather of her shiny black leather war trophies. I caress and lick out, pulling with my teeth what I imagine is a bit of skin from the metal tip of one of the heels. I take it from my lips, feeding the morsel to Irene, who takes my offering with a look of discreet satisfaction. The same look I must have, as I hear that unmistakable screech of leather on leather as Irene closes her legs around me, as we stare with love in our eyes at the splendid shadow of stiletto heels hanging upside down against the pale walls of our bedroom; feeling the faint heat of flickering candles, the sound of the crickets outside our window, the smell of well-worn leather and Irene's love juices, lifting me to another level that I doubt I'll ever get to again. In all of this, as I pump my cock as hard and as far as I can into Irene, I think again of blood foaming on open lips to kiss.

THE ENERGY PALS

Howard Kaylan

Howard Kaylan is a newcomer to the fiction field, "The Energy Pals" being his second sale in as many attempts. He is, however, far from a novice when it comes to entertainment. After he graduated high school, his musical group, The Turtles, sold over twenty million records worldwide during the mid and late sixties. Among the classic rock recordings he sang are "Happy Together," "She's My Girl," Dylan's "It Ain't Me, Babe" and the self-penned "Elenore." After performing in venues as diverse as the Filmore Auditorium and the Nixon White House, he and his partner broke up the original band around 1970 and spent two and a half years fronting Frank Zappa's eccentric Mothers of Invention before the duo changed their stage names to Flo and Eddie. As such, they have composed motion picture and television soundtracks; written songs for the *Care Bears* and *Strawberry Shortcake* cartoon shows; churned out comedy scripts with Larry Gelbart and Carl Gotleib; and continue to sing background vocals with artists such as Bruce Springsteen, Todd Rundgren, Ozzie Osborn, the Ramones and Duran Duran. A fan and friend of the genre, Howard can be found typing fantasies into his laptop en route to The Turtles' hundred or so yearly concerts. He currently makes his home in a remote town on the southern Oregon coast, accompanied by his wife, Susan, and their six-year-old daughter, Alex. Any resemblance to consensual reality and the storyline of "The Energy Pals" is purely fictional.

The Energy Pals?

What the hell is an Energy Pal?

I skimmed the article in the *San Francisco Chronicle* quickly, figuring that any furor caused by some violent Oriental kiddie show would have precious little bearing on my family's new life in Brookings on the Oregon coast.

We had left the big city behind, and with it all the accompanying crap—hypothetically—so I really didn't give this adolescent pop craze much thought until I read about the Energy Pals again, this time in *USA Today*, so I *knew* it had to be important. Only the *Chronicle* had gotten it wrong . . . again. It wasn't the Energy Pals: it was the "N.R.G. Pals," and they were rapidly becoming a national obsession.

The phenom didn't cross my mind again until my daughter's monthly issue of *Disney Adventures* arrived. And there, inside, was a full-color glossy update as to the who, what and why of the N.R.G. Pals.

"N.R.G." had originally been the initials of the Nippon Radio Group, a manufacturer of bad records and even worse television shows in the sixties. They had been responsible for some of the lamest children's programming ever to hit the cathode ray: Sharkman, whose nose and mouth turned into gills enabling him to fight rubber monsters underwater; Gorama, a seven-story gerbil who breathed fire at attacking Martians; and the classic/camp Lizardino, an evil salamander turned hero to save a terrified Tokyo time and time again from rubber suits even more ridiculous than his own.

Nippon's time had come and gone, and except for the occasional late-late show or a friendly lampooning from the crew at "Mystery Science Theater 3000," the studio had ceased to exist. That is, until a very savvy Israeli named Shlomo Beng purchased the entire catalog for a song and went hunting through the vaults in search of fodder for a media-hungry cable audience. He was the one who found them. But they weren't Pals yet. In fact, they weren't even good guys.

Shlomo Beng had finally hit the mother lode. Hidden among the thousands of hours of poorly made creature featurettes, he had discovered "The Numero Squad": an ineptly executed weekly serial featuring totally costumed ninjas whirling and twirling against a never-ending array of rubber chickens, two-headed fish and space vegetables. There was no dialogue, only grunts and moans. There were no heroes; in fact, there were no faces. The only way to distinguish one member of the Numero Squad from another was by the numbers sewn onto the front of their nylon jumpsuits. Awful, simply awful.

Even Shlomo's projectionist left the screening room in disgust and amazement as Beng began to giggle hysterically and rub his hands together with the prospect of imminent wealth within a vision he alone could see.

"Can't you picture it, Jake?" Shlomo had pressured his financial adviser. "We hire teenagers . . . clean-cut California types . . . we put 'em in some 'Father Knows Best' little town and follow them through their daily routines—that is, until they're needed to fight the forces of evil, and then we switch over to the stock ninja-and-monster footage. It'll cost us nothing to make, the ninjas are already in the can and I got rubber monsters comin' out of my asshole!"

Jake agreed only with the last part.

Shlomo Beng Productions held open auditions in the San Fernando Valley for good-looking teenagers with some martial-arts abilities. That was in July. By August, he had coerced a small private school into letting him shoot his live-action sequences there during the ten days before the start of the fall semester. The month of September was spent in postproduction: editing the Japanese footage together with the all-American kids frolicking in the school cafeteria and going to the prom until their Communication Amulets (six pirate medallions purchased at Magic Mountain) signaled them that they were needed and that it was time to change into battle garb to save the universe once again.

In October, Beng's face was on the cover of *Variety*, after he'd signed with a huge international distributor. In November, "The N.R.G. Pals" hit the air in one hundred and thirty U.S. markets simultaneously with the release of the action figures, the robot transformers and the mutant monsters. Sheets and pillowcases followed. And mugs, vitamins, breakfast cereals and coloring books.

In late December, I had read the *USA Today* story. Days after, a tremendous earthquake hit Los Angeles and my wife and daughter went back there for a couple of weeks to comfort our friends and families. It was while staying at the home of our great friends Noel and Denny and their four- and seven-year-old girls that Alex was first turned on to the N.R.G. Pals.

"Daddy, you wouldn't believe it! They're so cool!"

"Who's that, honey?" I remember saying.

"The N.R.G. Pals" had its debut on the Medford station about three weeks later, and every afternoon after her morning kindergarten class, there was Alex, glued to the screen, transfixed by the thirty-year-old images of karate stunt persons who would probably be proud that their work would be remembered all these years later and half a world away.

Alex's favorite N.R.G. Pal was Number Six: Michael.

Alex's adventures with the N.R.G. Pals began as a passing curiosity, turned into a passion and escalated full-bore into a twenty-four-hour-a-day obsession that obscured the fantasy/reality lines of her short five-year-old life. That first night, after returning from Los Angeles, I had been downstairs watching Letterman read the Top Ten List when I heard voices coming from my little girl's room. I crept upstairs as silently as I could, hoping to catch a word or two of her dream conversation. The door opened noiselessly and I peeked in on Alex, sitting up in bed and conversing with an invisible friend.

"Of course I know what to do." she whispered. "I told you I'm a loyal pal. Now, forget all that stuff tonight. Come up here and cuddle with me."

Alex rolled over, hugging her pillow, and began to settle into the sleep she should have begun at nine that evening. It was my duty as a dad to once again tuck my little girl in.

"Honey?" I smoothed her covers as she hugged the pillow tighter. "Are you okay? I thought I heard voices."

"Oh, that was just Michael. He was here, Daddy . . . right where you're standing now. He was talking to me—just to me. And I'm going to help him."

"Of course, baby. You help him in the morning, all right? It's a school night. Come on now and catch some zees."

"You don't believe me, do you? You think I'm lying about Michael being here, don't you? Well, he was! He really was! And he told me that I could be an N.R.G. Pal, too. And I'm gonna! And you can't stop me!"

"Shhh. It's okay, Pookie. Sleep now and we'll talk about this more tomorrow after school."

"You *do* believe in Michael, don't you, Dad?"

"Of course I believe in Michael, sweetie. Go to sleep now."

"I love you, Daddy."

"I love you, too, Pook. Good night."

"What was all *that* about?" my wife, Susan, asked. I guess I'd been in my daughter's room for quite a while.

"It's those damn N.R.G. Pals. Alex was awake and talking to Michael."

"Maybe it's just a passing thing, you know? A phase, that's all. She'll snap out of it. Who's on 'Dave' tonight?"

"He's got Teri Garr."

"What, again? I'm going to sleep." She gave me a loving peck on the cheek and shuffled off to the bedroom. "Good night."

"Good night," I automatically returned, although my mind was someplace else. My mind was on those stupid Japanese ninjas.

In the morning, it was business as usual. Alex wanted to be carried down to the living room so she could wake up gradually to the cartoon buzz of Nickelodeon as her mother whipped up a nutritious breakfast of Pop Tarts, hot cocoa and a Flintstone vitamin. Then Alex got dressed in a pair of baggy blue jeans, her comfy Beauty and the Beast sneakers and her N.R.G. Pals T-shirt.

"All ready for school!" she announced.

I stopped her on the way out the door. "Which Pal is Michael?" I queried, checking out the silk-screened characters she displayed so proudly.

"This one, Dad." She pointed to a cartoon image indistinguishable from the rest except for the number six painted on his or her chest. "Isn't he cool?"

I nodded.

"You didn't tell Mom about last night, did you?" she whispered.

"Of course not, honey," I lied. "This will be our little secret, right?"

Alex seemed genuinely relieved. "Whew! Thanks, Dad. See ya later!"

Later came at two-thirty, after school let out and Susan brought Alex and a few of her friends over for milk, cookies and television. I recognized most of the children: When you're in the kindergarten PTA in a town the size of Brookings, not too many things escape your view.

"Who's that little boy on the sofa?" I asked my exhausted wife as I drew her into the kitchen. "I don't remember seeing him around here." He was wearing an N.R.G. Pals T-shirt, too.

"He's new in school." she answered. "Cute kid, huh? I think Alex has got a crush on him already."

"Another N.R.G. freak, eh? So she's found a kindred spirit. Does the little rug rat have a name?"

I shouldn't have asked, right?

"His name is Michael," was the answer, and for some unknown reason I wasn't all that surprised.

Everything seemed almost normal. It's true that Alex's marbles, her Magic 8 Ball and her Handy Andy tool kit had been relegated to the hall closet and that the Beauty and the Beast linens on her bed had been replaced by the ubiquitous figures of her beloved Pals, but after all, she was just going through a phase. I asked her about her new TV friends that night as I tucked her in.

"Number One, that's Justin. He's the leader. He's really a hunk."

"Hunk?" My five-year-old talking about hunks!

"And this one," she said, pointing. "Number Two, that's Tiffany. She knows all about kung fu and gymnastics."

Number Three's alter ego was Tim, the brainy one. Four was really Willy, the Pals' African-American, and Five's real name was Vicki, an adorable Oriental girl who provided most of the squad's deductive reasoning. But then there was Number Six . . . good old Number Six: Michael, Alex's young heartthrob. He was the most rebellious of the N.R.G. Pals. Number Six was always disobeying commands from the Supreme Commander; saving the universe by using unorthodox but effective methods. He was always in trouble with his higher-ups, but the other Pals loved him. Maybe it was that curly black hair or his disarmingly impish smile, but even I got the feeling while watching the afternoon broadcasts that this Pal had come from another mold. Perhaps even one that Shlomo Beng had not created.

Michael—the Brookings Michael—was over at our house daily now. He and Alex would watch "The N.R.G. Pals" religiously and then retire to her room to play with the action figures and zap guns, the mutant monsters and the evil aliens.

Walking casually past her room, I tried not to act like

I was spying on my own daughter. Still, I couldn't ignore the occasional whisper.

"And who will *I* be? Will I get a number, too?"

"You betcha! You'll be Number Seven."

"Are you sure those two are all right in there?" I queried one afternoon. "They *have* been in there for hours."

"They're five years old, for heaven's sake," Susan countered. "What do you *think* they're doing? Playing doctor?"

I didn't have an answer. In fact, I felt like an ass for even having any suspicions about these two little angels.

"Aw, just drop it. You suppose they're getting hungry?"

"I've already asked Michael to stay for dinner. You can interrogate both children then if you have to, Sherlock."

Ouch.

"Pass the green beans, would you, Mike?" I asked at dinner.

"What for, man?" he said. "Green beans are for losers! I want chocolate ice cream!"

"Yeah, Dad," Alex chimed in. "Green beans are for losers! I want chocolate ice cream, too!" They both laughed uproariously, and milk had come squirting from my little girl's nose. "You're not a loser, are you, Dad?"

The following is a short sample of dialogue from "The N.R.G. Pals" program that aired on the Wolf Television Network 9/23/94:

VICKI: Hi, Willy. Say, have you seen Michael around today? We had a date to go to the mall after school.

WILLY: Nope. Sorry, Vicki. I saw him in gym class yesterday and all he could talk about was Doctor Dorma's Time Shifter. He's convinced that he's found a way to change history for the better.

VICKI: Well, the least he could have done was to call me. He might need some help, you know?

WILLY: Aw, he'll be okay. Said he didn't need us anyway. So you wanna get a milkshake or somethin'?

VICKI: Sure! I'll race ya. Last one there is a Corinthian Wormhole!

"Can I stay the night, Mr. Kaylan?"

I admit I was a bit shocked by the request.

"Well, Michael, I'd sure like to talk to your parents first . . . get their permission, you know. I mean, you kids are only five years old."

"Six," Michael said.

"What?"

"Six . . . that's my number. I mean, that's my age. My folks had to go out of town tonight and I'm scared to stay alone."

"Alone? Jeez, Michael, your parents just left you alone?"

The boy stared down at his feet and nodded.

"Well, of course you're welcome to stay."

"Hurray!" Alex screamed from her hiding place behind the stairs.

"Thanks, Mr. Kaylan," Michael offered softly. "And don't worry. I won't let anything happen to your little girl."

Alex came down for breakfast in a white N.R.G. Pals blouse, a blue N.R.G. Pals skirt and N.R.G.-logo sneakers. She was a merchandiser's dream come true. She poured herself a bowl of Rice Krispies Treats cereal and anxiously waited for her friend to join her at the table.

"Is Michael awake yet? We've got tons to do today."

I jumped in. "Whoa, whoa. Seems to me you've been spending way too much time with Mike and not enough with your family. I think today we'll spend some quality time together, all right?"

"Aw, Dad!" Alex's bottom lip was beginning to

quiver, a sure sign that tears were to follow any minute now. "Don't I even get to watch the N.R.G. Pals on TV?"

"You know what?" I offered.

"No . . . what?" Alex sniffed through her snotty five-year-old nose.

"Today we're all going to watch together."

"All right!" Alex leapt from her chair and began kissing my face and beard. "I love you, Dad, mmm . . . mmmm . . . mmmm . . . and I love Mommy and Ozzie [our cat] and Bob [our dog], and most of all, I love Michael! Oh, and Dad . . . ?"

"Yes, baby?"

"Don't ever call him Mike. If you *have* to, call him Number Six."

That afternoon, "The N.R.G. Pals" show began as usual with a brief recap of yesterday's adventure. On the program, Vicki and Willy had been discussing how weird Michael had been acting while, all the time, collecting cans and bottles for the school's recycle drive. Flashbacks were shown of Number Six doing battle with monstrous amoeba and hanging crepe paper for the school's big dance.

"Don't you just *love* him, Dad? Isn't he dreamy?"

"Yeah, honey . . . dreamy." Susan and I shared a sidelong glance.

"I didn't know kids today used words like 'dreamy,' " she said.

Once the TV audience had caught up with the Pals' past activities, it was time for the plotline—such as it was—to continue. On-screen, Number Six, Michael, had just gotten into an argument with Number One, Justin, about who should be leader. Justin had won the verbal battle, and Michael had stormed out of their clubhouse muttering quasi-obscenities and promising revenge for his humiliation.

"He's really mad, isn't he, Mom?" Alex said.

"Sure does look that way, Pook. I wonder what he's going to do."

The following is a short sample of dialogue from "The N.R.G. Pals" program, broadcast on the Wolf Television Network 10/12/94:

JUSTIN: What the heck's wrong with Michael? He's so touchy these days.

TIFFANY: He's obsessed with Doctor Dorma's Time Shifter.

TIM: Well, he'd better watch out: Doctor Dorma set the controls to go back in time to the year 1994! If he's not careful, old Number Six could wind up back in kindergarten!
(Laughter from all the N.R.G. Pals.)

VICKI: It's really not funny, you guys. Michael's gone rogue on us: he's completely lost it! And that means we've got to bring in some outside help.

WILLY: You don't mean . . .

VICKI: I *do* mean . . .

JUSTIN: Number Seven?

VICKI: That's right. Number Seven: special reserve N.R.G. Pal, Alex Kaylan.

You know that taste that you get in the back of your throat just before you start to throw up? That was exactly what I felt at that very moment. Susan dropped her Snapple, spilling its contents all over the carpet, and our daughter's eyes grew as wide as saucers.

"Mom! Dad! The Pals—they need me. They really do! I've gotta go!"

Alex bolted up the stairs to her bedroom with the two of us right behind.

"Come back here, young lady. Where do you think you're going?"

"I'm going to save my pals. You can watch me on TV."

We were only seconds behind her as the door slammed shut, but since blinding lights and sonic booms didn't usually emanate from her room, we had to assume that we were too late . . . for something. By the time we pushed our way in, it was evident that Alex was no longer in our house or in our dimension. A cold silence greeted us, along with the sounds from the TV: ''We'll be back after these commercial messages.'' Will we?

The commercials were for Frosted Flakes and Bedtime Barbie. My wife and I slumped down on the sofa and watched them as if we were hypnotized. I mean, what else could we do? I don't remember speaking a word; we just waited for the show to continue, as if that were the most normal course of action we could follow.

Finally, after station identification, we were back in the Pals' clubhouse, and someone on the other side of the door was whistling the secret six-note pass-code song: ''Go Go N.R.G. Pals.''

TIFFANY: Should I answer the door?
  WILLY: No, doyyy . . . it'll answer itself!
  JUSTIN: Come on, you guys. Let's work as a team here.

Tiffany did answer the door and seemed almost as confused as we were to see the young girl awaiting entrance.

ALEX: Hi, everybody. I'm Alex, but you can call me Number Seven.

She looked just the way I expected her to. That is, in the year 2007. Her hair was longer now, shades of auburn adorned with the characteristic Kaylan streaks of silver. She wore it swept out of her big blue eyes and tied in a thick ponytail. It looked a lot better than the bangs we had been trimming for the past five years. And she was mature . . . even for a teenager. My little daughter had grown into a great body with curves in all the right places and a height that must have come from somewhere back in Susan's gene pool. Yep, the girl who called herself Alex on TV was quite a looker. I'd have been more proud had the circumstances been just a bit different.

TIM: Woh, nice to meet you, Alex. So you're the Number Seven N.R.G. Pal, huh?

ALEX: That's me! I understand we've got a problem with Michael.

VICKI: Now, *there's* an understatement! Number Six just went ballistic on us, that's all.

JUSTIN: Okay, gang. Help me out here. Just who is this new Number Seven chick and what's she got to do with anything?

ALEX: Let me answer that, Number One. Michael and I go back a long time. We sort of . . . um . . . dated in school for a while, and I can be pretty certain that he'd never do anything to hurt me.

"Did you hear that, honey?" Susan asked me. "She's doing well in school. I *knew* she would. And just look—she's got my eyes!"

"Listen, Sue, I think we've got bigger problems here."

"Do you like her hair in a ponytail? 'Cause if you do—"

"Shhh . . . let's just watch, all right?"

"Ohhhhh!"

Our little girl was a superhero on a television show emanating from sometime in the future, yet my wife was mad at me for not wishing to discuss her hairstyle. Go figure.

A chirping noise brought our attention back to the screen. It was Justin's Communication Amulet.

JUSTIN: This is Number One—go ahead, Supreme Commander!

S.C.: Justin, we've got a Condition Yellow on our hands. Number Six is using Doctor Dorma's Time Shifter to skip back and forth through history. He's up to no good and he must be stopped!

ALEX: Evil? Michael would never do anything evil!

S.C.: Was that Number Seven speaking?

TIM: Yessir—Alex Kaylan here as you requested!

S.C.: Number Seven, it's time to get your priorities straight. Are you a friend of Michael's or a friend of the N.R.G. Pals and the free world?

ALEX: Sir, I find that insulting! When I took my pledge at the age of five to join the Junior N.R.G. Pals, I vowed to fight for peace and freedom and for the good of all kids everywhere! So don't go handing me that shit now!

Our astonishment mounted layer upon layer with every second, but it's funny how the little things seemed to matter so much. Susan was shocked.

"Just where did she learn to talk like that? She doesn't get that kind of language from me!"

"Honey, she's a teenager on a TV show beaming its way from the next century. I don't think our parenting is the issue here."

S.C.: Well, Number Seven, since you seem to be Michael's closest existing friend, your assignment's going to be rather difficult.

VICKI: She can handle it, sir!

WILLY: Of course she can—she's one of *us*!

JUSTIN: What's Michael done, sir? Has he made a new monster? I'm sure together we can stop it from destroying the universe!

S.C.: If only it were that easy, Number One. You see, it's not what Michael's done—at least not yet—it's what he's about to do!

ALEX: You mean, here in the future, sir?

(The other Pals sort of chuckled, sharing knowing glances.)

TIM: Hey, *we're* not in the future, remember? Only *you* are! To us, it's still good ol' 2007.

ALEX: So, like, what are you saying here?

S.C.: I'm saying that Number Six has gone rogue on us. He's turned violent and is about to use Doctor Dorma's Time Shifter to change the course of history as we know it.

TIFFANY: What could he possibly do?

S.C.: Number Two, if Michael gets his way, there will be no Mars landing, there will be no end to the war with Canada, and President Michael Jackson will be assassinated by his own First Lady!

Now it was my turn to be dumbfounded.

"Am I hearing this right or am I going out of my mind?"

"Well, save me a rubber room next to yours." Sue groaned, trying equally hard to grasp the gravity of the situation.

ALEX: Exactly what is it that I'm supposed to do, sir?

(Now all the Pals gathered around Alex in anticipation of the Supreme Commander's orders.)

S.C.: You're to go back to 1994, Alex—back to when you were both in kindergarten.

TIFFANY: Aw, we'll miss you, Number Seven. But don't you worry; we'll all be back together fighting monsters again real soon!

ALEX: Is that true, sir?

S.C.: Oh, yes, Alex . . . if you believe, anything's true.

ALEX: Great! 'Cause I've always wanted this life—the danger and excitement of whipping those creatures, and then, being cool in high school with my superhero friends . . . especially Michael . . .

S.C.: Not so fast, Number Seven. I haven't finished. You must return to 1994 and you must dispose of Michael!

The silence on both ends of the television was deafening.

ALEX: Excuse me? I mean, I was only five!

S.C.: Michael must be eliminated, Number Seven, by
        you and at that very age. The destiny of all
        humankind depends on you!

And then there was a commercial for Nestlé's Quik and
the end credits rolled. Sue and I just stared at the screen.
    "So this is like a joke, right?"
    "Well, I'm not laughing! Let's just check out these
credits, okay? Get a pencil . . . Shlomo Beng Productions,
New York City. I think we'd better make some calls."
    "You call New York and I'll call the cops on the other
line. You don't suppose anybody else saw what we saw,
do you?"

    "Shlomo Beng Productions . . . No, ma'am, we're not
currently marketing Number Seven action figures, but if
you'd like to leave your number . . ."
    The secretary hung up the phone, and when it started
ringing again a few seconds later, she let the answering
machine deal with it.
    "Mr. Beng!' she shrieked. "This is getting too damn
weird! We don't make an Alex action figure, do we? The
phone's been ringing off the hook!"
    "What are ya, having a little fun with your boss here,
Peggy? This is Jake's idea, isn't it? Schmuck! Listen, get
the Wolf Network on the phone. I've got to see the next
few shows!"
    "Sure, sure, Mr. B." Peggy dialed the number, mum-
bling under her breath. "Nutty as a fruitcake . . . 'N.R.G.
Pals.' Hello, Wolf? Get me Mr. Diller. Shlomo Beng's
office . . . I'll hold."
    I was holding in Brookings, too. "No one answers. The
line's been tied up for hours."
    "Well, the police just laughed when I told them. The
whole town thinks I've gone out of my mind. And our
baby . . . Where's Alex? Oh, honey, I'm scared."
    "Me, too," I confessed. "Hey, get me the *TV Guide*.
Tuesday . . . Tues . . . here it is . . . 'N.R.G. Pals.' Shit!"
    "What is it? God!"
    "Preempted by the Giants and the Dodgers. Looks like

we're going to have to wait. Wednesday . . . nope. Thursday . . . oh, man!''

"Oh, man? Is that the best you can do? Oh, man?"

"Listen to this. 'A fatal bowl of ice cream means the end of one of the Pals.' Looks like the Supreme Commander is going to get his wish. Fatal bowl of ice cream . . . ?"

At that very moment we heard a loud thump from Alex's room, and I could have sworn that damn six-note theme played from somehere, too: "Go go N.R.G. Pals."

"Mom! Mom, can I have a snack before dinner?"

Sue and I both jumped to our feet and ran up the stairs to our daughter's room. Alex was sitting cross-legged on her Aladdin carpet, playing with her N.R.G. Pal dolls and whistling their moronic theme. Susan scooped her up and began to hug her relentlessly.

"Pookie, Pookie. Oh, my baby . . . we were so scared!"

"Blacch! Hey, quit with the kissing, Mom. What's your problem?"

"We've been worried sick about you, that's what!" I almost screamed. "Where the hell have you been?"

"Aw, go on, Dad. I've been here all afternoon."

"I don't think so, young lady—"

Susan interrupted my oncoming tirade.

"Look, what difference does it make? This whole episode might have been a weird joke, or a coincidence, or even, hell, mass hypnosis. But it's over now. We've got our baby back."

I took a deep breath and tried to compose myself, too. If Sue could deal with all this crap, then so could I. The adventure was over, and whatever the source of our anxiety, Pookie was safe at home and we'd have the rest of our lives to sort out the whys and wherefores.

I went down to the kitchen to bring Alex a bowl of shredded cheddar cheese to snack on, and seriously thought about making a call to a psychiatrist Elk brother of mine, just to chat, mind you, when the doorbell rang. It was little Michael from down the street.

"Can Alex play N.R.G. Pals?"

Shlomo Beng's face was turning the color of a grape popsicle as he invented new obscenities to shout at Wolf president Grant Diller.

"Fuck you, too, ya miserable donkey dick! I got half a mind to take the Pals over to ABC. Someone is screwing with my ninjas and when I find out who it is, I'm gonna kung-fu them a new asshole. I TOLD you, I don't know anything about this new girl . . . no, it's not a spinoff series, what're ya, deaf? All right, okay . . . I'll find out what I can here. Call me *yesterday* if you hear something, right? Yeah, 'bye. Goddamn putz."

Beng buzzed Peggy. "Get me a list of the entire Pals fan club pronto. I'm going to find this Alex Kaylan chick."

"Michael! How cool! Come on in!"

Our little girl was sure happy to see her young playmate. It was as if they hadn't played together in ages, though it had only been two days. The boy sat opposite her on the Aladdin carpet and picked up his namesake, the Number Six Pal doll, before he even said a word.

"I thought you wouldn't want to play with me anymore." He pouted like a normal six-year-old; he sounded like a normal six-year-old. I had to wonder what my wife and I had been so concerned about. Damn show was obviously getting to us, too. That was it, then. I made the decision right then and there. There would be no more N.R.G. Pals in this house.

"Why wouldn't I want to play with you?" Alex asked innocently.

Michael hesitated for a minute, making puppy-dog eyes before he whimpered, " 'Cuz everybody in town hates me today, that's why."

"You mean, on account of that silly TV show?" she asked. Then she made a grand sweep with her tiny arms and sent her beloved N.R.G. Pal dolls flying in all directions. All but the Number Six action figure that her young friend still held. "Don't be dumb. That's make-believe, and we're real kids!"

From the mouths of babes. There: she had said it. For

some strange reason we had all let this moronic children's program blur the lines that separated fiction from reality. I took a deep breath and shook my head to be rid of Shlomo Beng's demons as Alex looked up at my relieved body standing in her doorway.

"It's cool, Dad," she said. "I got it under control."

She really was turning out to be a great kid. I felt like a jerk for having made such a fuss about nothing. Who was really the parent here? That's what I was thinking.

"Would you like to stay for dinner, Michael?" That's what I said.

"Boy-oh-boy, I sure would!" the kid answered. Kid, not the end of civilization, just a kid.

Sue didn't mind a bit, either. We were both ashamed of ourselves, I guess, and dinner seemed like the least we could do to expunge our guilt.

We ate cheeseburgers and potato chips before I realized that I was perilously close to being out of beer, and made a grab for the keys to the Explorer.

"Be right back, honey," I yelled to Susan from halfway out the door. I didn't even hear the phone ring.

"Mrs. Kaylan? Hello. You don't know me. My name is Shlomo Beng."

I was gone only ten minutes; it would have been quicker, but I had to go all the way to the Fred Meyer store to buy my favorite kind of Rouge Ale. When I pulled up to the house, the police cars were already there and the ambulance was taking little Michael's body away. Clutching my plastic bag to my side, I attempted to gain entry to my own house.

"Come on, let me through here—I live here!"

"Mr. Kaylan?" I recognized Dan Collier, one of the town's two full-time patrolmen.

"Officer, what's going on?"

"Got a little boy in a lot of trouble here, Mr. Kaylan."

"Trouble? What d'ya mean, trouble?"

Officer Collier shook his head, pursing his lips together grimly before he spoke.

"Kid's been poisoned."

Turns out Officer Collier hadn't been entirely accurate about the kid being poisoned. It was even worse than that. Michael, it seemed, had ingested an unbelievable amount of finely ground glass that had been swirled liberally through the chocolate-ice-cream dessert he had eaten while I was out at the store. By the time the ambulance had delivered him to Sutter Coast Hospital, his entire intestinal tract had been sliced to ribbons, and thick, mucous-laden blood had spewed and then caked around his nostrils and his mouth.

Collier, as well as detectives from Crescent City and even San Francisco, combed our house from top to bottom, but they really didn't have to look very long for the evidence they required. Someone had taken between twenty and thirty marbles—cat's-eyes, aggies—and smashed them into a fine powder right there in Pookie's room, using a Magic 8 Ball and a Handy Andy tool kit. They found the glassy stuff all over the Aladdin rug and, of course, in the kitchen and in Michael's remaining dessert. The boy had gurgled the name Alex before he was pronounced dead on arrival, and the grisly photo had made page 1 of Wednesday's *Curry County Pilot*.

Then, on Thursday, the entire event was broadcast as scheduled on "The N.R.G. Pals" program (Pal dies of fatal bowl of ice cream), and several million witnesses saw our five-year-old daughter kill little Michael on national television.

The next day, the county came and took Alex away. We cried, we begged, we pleaded and screamed, but there was nothing we could do.

"Pookie, did you do it?" I asked.

"Yeah, Dad. I had to. The Supreme Commander ordered it! But don't worry, my Pals will save me."

Alex's picture was on the covers of *Time* and *Newsweek*. Neighbors' reactions ranged from tsk, tsk to the smashing of our windows and painting "Murderer" on our house and cars. And the entire country wondered how it could happen: how a well-mannered five-year-old could commit such a horrible atrocity. Were her parents to blame? Most certainly! But if that was true, where in this most disgusting of scenarios did Shlomo Beng fit?

"Did I warn you or what, ya fuck?"

"Come on, Jake. How the hell is this bullshit *my* fault?"

"It's your fault, Shlomo, because you allowed this bullshit on the air in the first place. *You're* the one they should be locking up, not an innocent little girl from Oregon."

"I called her mother, Jakie. I tried to warn her that something weird was going down! Shit, I just don't understand how this could have happened!"

"And the whole world watched it on your crappy little kiddie show. Oh, Shlomo, the PTA's gonna come down on you like a goddamn—I don't know what!"

"But we never filmed this! This isn't one of my shows: this is the fuckin' 'Twilight Zone,' for Pete's sake. Jake— what am I gonna do?"

"It's a tricky question, all right. Well . . . first of all, you could be a mensch and pick up the kid's legal fees."

"Okay . . . I could do that."

"Then I would haul your ass over to Bumfuck, Oregon—"

"Brookings."

"Yeah, whatever. And I would make nice with the family and with 'Current Affair' and 'Inside Edition' and 'Hard Copy.' "

"Jake, Jake. My career is ruined. I'll never be in show business again!"

"You know something, Shlomo? You never were!"

Alex was released from custody on the very day that the final "N.R.G. Pals" show aired on television; no questions asked.

The following is a brief segment of dialogue from the final episode of "The N.R.G. Pals" program, that aired on the Wolf Television Network 11/6/94:

JUSTIN: Yahoo! Let's celebrate, everyone. The future is safe thanks to our newest N.R.G. Pal!

ALL: Yeah, Alex!

ALEX: Aw, thanks, gang. Well, any one of you would have done the same thing in my place.

S.C.: Now, remember, Alex. You are now one of us officially and will be expected to follow the Pals' code of honor to the letter.

ALEX: Yessir! I won't let you down, you'll see! It is so cool to be the Number Seven Pal.

S.C.: No, Alex. You're the Number Six Pal now. It's as if Michael had never existed.

TIFFANY: And in our new time slot, he never *did*, did he, gang?

(All the Pals laughed at that one.)

Alex came home right after the show ended on the Wolf Network. She .hadn't changed a bit from the wonderful five-year-old who had become obsessed with the N.R.G. Pals in the first place. Shlomo Beng paid for everything and gave statements to the press apologizing for the sort of violent television that would cause a child to perform such an antisocial act.

Our wonderful neighbors repainted our house from its former faded yellow—which we never liked much any-way—to the lovely blue-gray it is today, and ol' Arnie Schwagger detailed both automobiles so well, I told him I'd give him a free plug in this story . . . GO TO ARNIE SCHWAGGER FOR YOUR AUTO-DETAILING NEEDS.

We never did find out about Michael's parents or how our lives got somehow turned into a television show, but I've never been prouder of my kid than when she helped me place every last one of those stupid action figures into a Hefty bag and carry them down to the street for the garbage man. I helped her get Beauty and the Beast out of the closet, and those pastel sheets and canopy are on her bed at this very moment.

By the way, "The All New Adventures of the N.R.G. Pals" debuted on ABC last week with a new producer, and Shlomo Beng is currently doing "The Wonderful World of Fish" for the Discovery Channel. Life's good in Brookings and all's right with the world.

THE AGONY MAN

Don Webb

Don Webb has over 200 articles, poems and stories published in six languages. He is the coeditor of *Borderland of Broken Mirrors*, and his forthcoming books are the collection *Ecaflow Revisited* (Fiction Collective) and the nonfiction *Seven Faces of Darkness* (Runa Raven Press). He makes his home in Austin with his beautiful and sexy wife, Rosemary.

There was a special smell of evil coming from the Iguana Lounge. It swirled around the neon-green lizard logo and clung to the leather-clad neovampires making their way to their cars. Like all early hunters, they looked good. That Art Putnam had chosen this bar for our interview already set my teeth against him. I swallowed the bad taste and stepped into the bar.

The smell of evil was almost hidden by the synthetic pine scent of the fog machine and the heavy cigarette smoke. Austin is a clean-air city. Cigarette smoking was a tiny antinomianism, a minor sin to begin the picture. Five silent movie screens flickered at strange angles around the elevated dance floor. On each a loop: the creation of Ultima Futura from *Metropolis*, a torture scene from *Videodrome*, the shower scene from *Psycho*, Bela Lugosi biting a toothsome victim in *Dracula*, the barrel scene from *2,000 Maniacs*. Fog billowed out great vents beneath the dance floor. The dancers walked up to the raised dance floor—it came up to their waists. They had to crawl up onto the floor. Other dancers would stomp on the hands of people in submissive drag. Submissive dancers would lift their masters bodily up to the stage. There were two areas to sit and drink: smoking and smoking. Farthest from the door, a leather-clad poetess read bad vampire poetry while two of her slaves—skinny women wearing only goose bumps, crusty scars on their breasts and cheap bat masks—danced on each side of her throne. At the end of each poem the dissipated crowd would snap their fingers in approval—a scene from the coffeehouse in "Petticoat Junction." I'd written up their little cult—oral sadism, blood drinking, sleeping in coffins. That's my job, furthering cheap evil by cheaper journalism.

The area nearer the door was ruled by the dwarf. She was a chunky, beautiful little thing, sort of a kinky Pia Isadora. She stood three feet eight with long, very fine platinum hair, wearing a skin-tight black vinyl outfit that exposed her neck, her hands and her two pierced nipples. She sported a spiked dog collar and leash, and when I sat down at the table next to her, I saw that both of her high-heeled shoes were locked on. Men, of course, surrounded her. Hitting on her. Hoping to be the one to take this toy of toys home.

I ordered a ginger ale, which clued the waitress that I—like most of the Iguana Lounge's patrons—was an alcoholic. She flashed what she thought of as a knowing smile—a good way to show off the vampire fangs her dentist had thoughtfully provided. She would probably fight and kill for her chance to work here at minimum wage. I wondered what she was by light of day. Art Putnam would arrive at ten. It was 9:55 and I saw something

I wasn't expecting—a sweet and almost innocent face.

She sat alone, thrilled, but too shy to enter into intimate contact with her surroundings. She was the sweetness I would go a long way for. She had auburn hair and big wet eyes that would no doubt be very special when she was being hurt. I thought of a three-year-old I saw once— of his expression just before he decided to stick his chubby finger into an empty light socket.

The volume of chatter dipped, and by this negative fan-fare I knew that Art Putnam had stepped in behind me. I decided to let him come to me—maybe I could regain some reporterly control of the situation.

He circled around on my left side. He was a vigorous middle-aged man—muscles only slightly going to paunch. I'm sure his big sculptor's hands could've strangled any-body in the place (and about half of the clientele would pay for the privilege). He wore a black turtleneck sweater with a black blazer and trousers. His brass-colored beard reminded me of a Sumerian king's, and his blue-black eyes were the color of certain corals found at particularly great depths. If I could look like anyone, I would look like him. His manservant followed him, a ringer for Lurch from the TV Addams family. Lurch carried a large cov-ered platter, which he set down in front of me.

So by a simple mystery Art gained control of the in-terview.

I stared at the covered dish and went through my in-terview questions mechanically. He gave me all the an-swers I expected. I'd done my homework and that helped me filter out bar noise and the slight condescension in his voice.

His career started as a technical assistant to a civil en-gineer. He was an okay draftsman, but a truly excellent 3-D model maker. After enough tabletop bridges and dams—''my Tinkertoy phase''—he snagged a job in advertising. He built models to photographers' specs. Giant whiskey glasses. Tiny redwood trees. Flying toilet paper rolls. ''You've seen my work. Every peasant's seen my work.'' Then the U.S. Department of the Interior com-missioned him to make a 3-D model of the St. Louis

No. 1 cemetery in New Orleans. The days and nights among the crypts opened a hidden tablet there. "I passed through a dark gateway there and the flowers of evil finally blossomed."

I was already titling my article "The Agony Man" when he lifted the cover to reveal his latest sculpture. It was the pewter head of a young black man. With what was left of his face he was screaming with pain and fear. His left cheek had been torn away and lay alongside his neck. Long earthworms, split in half lengthwise, covered the right eye. Straight pins protruded from beneath the earthworm mass, so that anyone with visualization skills realized that the eye must be pinned open. Every pore, every hair, every bead of sweat and trickle of blood stood out in perfect relief. Across the tongue a smooth line of iridescent green metal ran, Art Putnam's signature, a beautiful flourishing line that would have done an eighteenth-century gentleman proud.

"I call him," said Art, " 'Turf Dream Number Seventeen'."

Finger popping filled the smoky room like an ersatz rain.

I looked around. Only Lurch, I and the innocent-looking one weren't applauding.

"Maybe you'll want to stop by my studio with your photographer," said Art.

"Sure," I said. "I'll get my people to call your people."

I had wanted to meet him at his studio. He had insisted on this piece of theater.

I got very popular. Everyone wanted to know who I was. Perhaps if they sat down quickly enough they could absorb some of the manna. There was a parade of faces in the fake fog—faces with tattoos; faces framed with dead black hair, green hair, fuchsia hair; faces with needles and adornments. One of my greatest weaknesses is the inability to walk away from anyone who wants my time. Finally, after an hour and a half (and six coffees given to me), the shyest one appeared.

"Hi," I said. "You don't look like you belong here—would you like to go to Sapir's?"

"I belong anywhere I want to belong," she said. "Sure, let's go to Sapir's."

I felt surprise at her independence. I didn't know that independence and submission could go together.

It was nearly midnight when we sat down at the twenty-four-hour deli. We ordered coffee and blueberry blintzes.

We exchanged names. I am Dave Meacham and she was Susan Folger.

She told me she was a masochist. I began to make all the politically correct noises. How sad that men's victimization of women had projected on her, etc.

She sat with a polite smile, and after my spiel had run down she said, "Let me tell you a story. I work at the Employment Commission. I've got a great record in placing women who've been out of the work force for years. Because of my service to the women's community, I was invited to a special feminist meeting a state lobbyist was putting on. It was one of those 'sharing' circles; we each told of a stressful event that set us apart from the social order and on the road to freedom. The matriarch told of an illegal self-induced abortion. The next woman, a minor-league performance artist, told of her heroin addiction. Then I began talking about my masochism. They all erupted with the same tired crap that you did. Even these women, who had done these terrible things to their own bodies, knew that what *they* had done led to freedom, but what I had done couldn't. They told me that they were wise and good and knew where my freedom lay. I left. I didn't even bother to tell them that they were no different than those they were supposedly rebelling against. That night my master, my then master—he no longer measures up—subjected me to exquisite torture. He had perfectly captured what I most feared and desired. My desires are so strong that they bring me masters cast in the shape of my dreams. I work when and where I wish. I even change the political and social world in accordance with my desire. So you can take your crap and stuff it down the same tired hole it emerged from."

Suddenly I realized that I was hearing new thoughts, and (to my surprise and disgust) that I had never listened to a woman for new thoughts before. Years of politically correct mouthing fell away from me. I love the new—the hidden ideas which have not been trampled to death by society. I had become a journalist to seek out the hidden. I knew that I would have to try to meet her again and again for these ideas. She had been transformed from something pretty to look at to someone worth listening to. Very seldom in my adult life had I experienced someone becoming real for me.

"Okay," I said, "maybe I can buy that. But this brilliant desire of yours seems a hell of a lot different from the dead eyes in the smoke of the Iguana Lounge."

"I am—or at least I hope I am—different from them. Most of them do these things because it is a compulsion. They *have* to do it. I came because I heard Mr. Putnam would be there."

I felt sick. "Oh?"

"I want to model for him. I want a monument for my desires."

We talked about Putnam's career and set up a time to meet again. Next Saturday at the Red Lion Diner; she was working at a convention nearby. It had been an interesting way to spend the witching hour.

Live oak trees nestle Art Putnam's studio in a quiet and expensive neighborhood just west of downtown Austin. Lawyers to the right of him, lawyers to the left of him, and the posh offices of an oh-so-posh home-and-gardens-type magazine behind him. Two things separate this two-story, dark-brick converted family home from its neighbors. One is Art's gold-anodized aluminum signature over the doorway. The other is his stainless-steel sculpture "The Duffer," a personal tribute to his late father's interest in golf.

"The Duffer" stands nude, his face contorted with agony and hate as he strikes at some invisible foe with a nine iron. The middle-aged, slightly paunchy figure was said to be a dead ringer for his late father, although details like the semierect penis or large hemorrhoids weren't shown in the lawyer's photos. What made the statue intensely horrible was the golf divots. Flesh had been teased away from the prominent veins—all the blueworms of age that we hate to see so much appear on our parents (and later on ourselves). The veins were unbroken, but under each on the wrists, the hands, the shins, etc.—a golf divot had been wedged. Few people could stare at the statue without beginning to twitch violently. I was loath even to step on its shadow.

On this Austin spring day the bluebonnets sweetened the air and the humidity and sunlight were set exactly at perfection.

Art's secretary, a dull-looking woman with the flat chin of an animal and at least seven earrings in each ear, went to fetch "the master."

Art came in wearing a faded flannel shirt and work-stained chinos. He had put aside his satanic demeanor for the moment, and was now just a working stiff like me. I didn't trust this mask either. We had greetings and coffee, and were soon in the studio. We made small talk while we waited for my photographer to arrive. Photographs covered one wall. I recognized them as models for his various works. Snapshots, nothing particularly stirring—all had been elevated to interest by the tortured stances of their statues.

Then I saw four Polaroids of Susan Folger. My voice might have broken a little bit as I asked, "Is she a model?"

"She's a wannabe. I get lots of volunteers, of course, but—at least until now—I turn them away. I would rather find my subjects. It turns life into a hunt, going to a shopping mall and watching each face as a potential actor in my Grand Guignol."

"But you're going to make an exception for her?"

"Look at that chin like a child's—like a pretty little girl's. And those high cheekbones—despite her aquamarine eyes and pale skin—those are the cheekbones of a Cherokee warrior. Her face is a symphony of determination and vulnerability. I may change my rules for her.''

He must have caught something in my eyes. He changed his tone from pompous statement to personal. ''Oh, I get it. You like her, don't you? I'll treat her special. As a favor. A good master can produce as many effects as imagination will allow. There is always something unknown that can be inflicted on the pretty one. A thousand virginities can be taken and a thousand still await. I can give her what she most fears and desires.''

Part of me wanted to smash his face and protect Susan like some high school boyfriend, but an even bigger part wanted to be able to give her what this man could.

The photographer arrived. Mary Denning's extremely professional—I'd worked with her before. Among the dozens of stills she took was the perfect shot. A few months previous, Art had unveiled a head-and-shoulders white metal bust entitled ''Home Improvement.'' Her face almost devoid of expression, a middle-aged housewife pushes an electric drill into her left temple—liquefying her left eye. Mary had posed Art so that he leaned on the drill-holding hand—to all appearances pushing it into the head. Having captured Art's grin for posterity, we left. On the way out the door we heard a low moan, another cheap promotion gimmick of the agony man.

I met nothing but green lights on my way to the Red Lion Inn, so I arrived a quarter hour early. There was a ''Starving Artists'' show ending. Susan and two guys were tossing the assembly-line-produced paintings into the back of an eighteen-wheeler. Smiling when she saw me, she asked the guys to finish up.

''I'm a little embarrassed,'' she said. ''I throw myself the occasional weekend job. These Starving Artists shows are the worst.'' She kicked at one of the paintings of two autumn-reddened trees separated by an S-curve stream. ''People come up to you and ask if you're the artist, or do you know anything about the artist, or can they contact the artist for special commissions. You've got to play along so they'll fork out the twenty-five bucks.''

''What do you tell them?''

"Oh, I make things up. 'Yes, Monsieur Le Twat was so imprinted by the sight of the River Insipide, that is all he paints. You will notice his many studies of the two trees.' If they say he must paint awfully fast, I get dangerously near the truth. '*Oui*. He knows so well the one thing he wants to paint that he has cut out stencils so that his students can spray-paint the background as the paintings slowly—not unlike the sluggish current of the River Insipide—make their way to the master on an assembly line. He's lucky that so many of his oeuvres fit so well behind a sofa.' "

"Why not just tell them the truth?"

"If we sell half the stock or more, we get a bonus. Plus we can all take a painting home, though I'd rather have a black velvet Elvis."

The guys were finishing up the job. Susan gave them a few instructions on locking up the trailer and we went off to the diner. As Susan had predicted, the pot roast was to die for and the hot strawberry cobbler topped with Bluebell ice cream was a once-in-a-lifetime experience. Over dark roast coffee I said, "I visited Putnam Tuesday. He's considering your photos."

She bit at her full upper lip and asked, "Do you think I have a chance?"

"Well, he's considering. It's not his usual method. He prefers to hunt for his models."

"I know. I read the interview in *Paris Match*. 'I like to hunt. My dream is hunting. My dad and brothers used to hunt bunny rabbits, but I was too tenderhearted. I couldn't stand the blood drying on their fur, their little eyes as they died. Now I hunt men.' I want to interfere with his dream. I want to block it, so that he can think of no one but me. I want to stalk it. Finally, I want to become the form of the dream itself."

We left the diner, and she began walking to the bus stop. I offered to drive her home.

"No," she said, "not yet. You're not ready for my apartment. What would you do with me there? I may be the most perfect marble, but you're not a sculptor yet. We'll talk while I wait for the bus." She lightly touched my arm, and her touch thrilled me to my core. My heart pounded that someday I would be ready. I was filled with a dark desire to know the mysteries of her space. In the days and weeks that followed, my body remembered that brief touch, as though I had been anointed with oil.

We talked about art. She didn't like abstraction.

"It runs away from the objective universe. Men who paint abstracts are terrorized by the phenomena they see around them, the relationships and the mysterious polarities that they are unable to decipher. Abstracts are for those people not brave enough to accept the pleasures and pains of the real world."

I said, "Well, at least it's better than the Starving Artists."

"You said that to hurt me," she said. "There may be hope for you yet. Yes, of course abstraction is better than that dull sameness. That's the worst sin, to impose the same gray patterns on everything. To simplify everything into stencils. You can neither discover nor manipulate the mysteries then."

"Manipulate?"

"That's one of the roots of art, isn't it? The cave paintings with arrows piercing the flesh of great ruddy bisons—so that the hunter will be able to duplicate the feat?"

"Well, that's a root of language. You've got to point to things in order to manipulate them—but there's always the danger of magical thinking."

"I think the world could use a little magical thinking from time to time."

Her bus arrived, and she turned to me to say, "I'll call you."

The bus heaved away, kissing Austin's bright air with its sour exhaust The promise of the call kept me warm and tingly until I reached my car, when I remembered I had an unlisted phone number, so she couldn't call.

On Monday morning I delivered my story to *Texas Monthly*. I bullshitted a while with the editors, a necessary piece of literary foreplay for freelancers like myself. I bounced a few ideas off them and business went on.

It was two weeks before I screwed my courage up enough to call Susan. She had, after all, said she would call me. That might mean that she didn't want me at all. She was the first woman in two decades to reduce me to a purely adolescent status. I was just like Art Putnam, totally drawn to this mysterious other. I had looked up her phone number within ten minutes of my last seeing her. I had started to call her then, and tell her that she didn't have my number. Since that time I thought of little else while I was home, and did a frustrated Watusi in front of my firehouse-red, Korean-made telephone. Call or don't call? What if there's an answering machine? What if it isn't her? What if she's cold or indifferent or tells me not to call? I wanted to be like Art. I wanted to be powerful enough—real enough—to deal with her. I couldn't even make up my mind to call. She was right—I wasn't a sculptor yet.

I called.

She picked up on the third ring. She was—or so she said—on her way to dinner with friends. She was going to model for Art! She was so happy. I managed to give her my number and she *sounded* like she was writing it down. She said she would call me when it was all over. It was sure to be exciting.

She didn't say she was sorry for not calling. She didn't say she had tried to find my number and failed. She was in a hurry and said good-bye to the accompaniment of a real or simulated knocking. She hung up.

It came down to if I could do anything—I didn't know what I wanted. I couldn't manipulate her beauty, because I didn't have the strength of desire to turn my dreams into flesh. I was some kind of wretched voyeur crying at a keyhole while the gods pursued their lives at levels unimaginable for the dirty city dwellers. I had faltered. I had had the chance to step to the left—to plunge into the unknown—and had faltered. I fell off the wagon for three days. When I was back from my drunk, the details of earning a living were in front of me.

I tried to put her out of my mind, and it's easier to do

that at thirty-eight than at eighteen. A lot easier to regulate someone to a dull ache when you're out scrambling every day to earn a living in a depressed economy. Probably a lot easier than it should be, but then, God is a real estate developer and not a poet.

I was doing a piece on fortune-tellers. There's always a group who will tell you that there's good luck awaiting you around the corner—or, if you look like you can shell out the shekels, that there's bad luck, which can be avoided if long and expensive instructions are followed. But when the economy goes bad, lots of people put out their shingle. It takes no training, little talent and a sign reading "Reader and Adviser" under a black, red or flesh-tone hand. When the economy goes bad, there's a greater number of clients who want to hear the mumbo-jumbo whispers of assurance and are quite willing to ignore that their prophet is living in a poverty worse than their own.

I was doing it as a color piece, something rich and strange.

The prophets drew their power from a variety of sources. Some from Jesus, others from their ancestry (seventh son of . . .), others from their divinatory objects—tea leaves or Tarot cards. The seventh or maybe the eighth fortune-teller I visited claimed to be a *voudon* priestess. Her shop was a frame house with beautiful hardwood floors, one of the cheerful bungalows built in Austin right after the Second World War. Someone had painted its exterior a bright canary yellow; and of all the shops I visited, it alone did not seem a monument to human despair.

When I told her that there would be no names for my candid interviews, she smiled and opened up. Over a fairly decent cup of coffee, she told me her story. She had worked her way through Tulane by telling cards, reading palms and fixing hair. Now she didn't fix hair, and she owned her own business. She said she had learned from books. Over the years, though, she maintained, she had learned to occasionally see a little more than the average guy. Would I like an example?

"I'm not paying for anything."

"Give me your palm."

She stared at the lines of my hand—tracing the major lines with the tip of her pudgy index finger.

"You're looking for love," she said. "No, you think you've found it, but you've lost it to a *voudon* master."

Expecting the pitch to follow, I asked her if she could defeat this evil rival. She studied my palm very carefully, then said, "No. He's way out of my league. But I've got something for you." *Here it comes*, I thought, *a juju bag to buy*. She went into the back room, and came back with a tiny bundle wrapped in purple velvet. She put it in my left palm, closing my hand around it.

"Periwinkle seeds, mugwort leaves, magnetic sand. It brings dreams. Dreams are the only thing which remain to you as long as you pursue your current love."

"What am I supposed to pay for this?"

She sighed a long sigh, and then said, "Free. It's free. Something for your article. Magic that really works."

I thanked her for the coffee, and with my juju in my pants pocket I headed to the next interview.

It was a hot day. The sharp scent of crushed weeds began to pervade my clothes. The smell was dreamy. I seemed to sail on it at stoplights. Just as some smells open the gates of memory, the juju seemed to open the gates of fantasy. When I got home, I took the tiny packet and tossed it next to my pillow.

That night I dreamed a little dream.

Shifting changing liquid light always moving changing—I was an unembodied perceptor floating above Town Lake. The smell of the juju rose up through me and became me and suddenly I blew as a wind through the city. I thought of Susan and I swirled like a tornado down the chimney of Art Putnam's studio. I blew through the grate and across the worn Oriental rug. A corner of the rug had been turned up and a large square opening, a trapdoor, was revealed. I stormed down into the breathless dark and narrow passage. For a moment I became the smell of fear. I had not known of this underground and I wondered if I was pouring myself into a trap. The smell of fear became a turbulent cloud as myself mixed with myself.

I tried to heave a sigh to center myself and became a sort of swirling ball. I thought of Susan and the ball unraveled and I poured under a crack in a door into a short hallway. At the end of the hallway was another closed door, but I could see a bright line—and blew into the light. This basement was large and well lit. There were stalls along one wall each with a statue and its model. Susan was tied to an antique upright chair—duct tape over her mouth. Art stood between a naked, thin, red-haired boy and a life-sized reproduction of the boy made of bronze. There were complicated chalk lines on the floor which seemed bright and hurtful to look at. The chalk bound the boy to his image. Somehow Art was the binding agent, the knot of fate between the two. The room seemed filled with invisible wires. They cut through me, but they caused me no pain.

Art explained something to Susan. I couldn't hear his words as words, but they somehow vibrated through me. Shaking me like a plane going through turbulence shakes its passengers. When the shaking ceased, the meaning remained in me as a memory.

In the silences I remembered him saying something about voodoo dolls. How if the doll was a good enough representation of its target, you could hurt the target by hurting the doll. Snap its arm and the victim's arm snapped. Gouge out its bead eyes and the victim's sockets were bloody holes. During his stay in New Orleans he had only the briefest introduction to the theory, but his lifelike sculpting ability made him a master.

No one could oppose him.

He could climb to the top of any company in the U.S., while his rivals dropped in a string of ''accidents.''

He didn't want that.

What he wanted was art.

What he lacked was inspiration. He could make anything to order, but on those long weekends in his Dauphine Street apartment, nothing would come. He tried drugs, drink, surrounding himself with images of other artists until every square meter of his apartment had its print, its statue, its vase.

Still nothing.

Then he found the S&M scene in a back room of a famous Bourbon Street dive. At first he just poured out his frustrations by torturing overfleshed tourists, but slowly he began giving thought to what he did. Extending their agonies and making them exquisite. He had found his true medium. Pain.

If he could record his creations. He thought of photography. Video. But these are always the things the police seized—carted out for media scares during sweep weeks. He could sculpt, but his models wouldn't live long enough to finish the sessions.

Then he thought of voodoo.

If hurting the dolls hurt the people—could hurting the people hurt the dolls? A few experiments proved it so. He could make the statues any size.

He gestured at the living models in the stalls behind him. Sometimes it took weeks to achieve the desired effects. I saw that, like the boy, they were bound too securely even to think of escape.

Some of them were bright-eyed—hanging on his every word—eager for what they were about to see. He picked up a device that looked like an oversized corkscrew. He placed it on the kid's left nipple and began to slowly screw it in. The boy's scream struck me like a boulder. A similar hole—somehow beautiful in its symmetry—began to form in the shiny bronze nipple of the statue. Bronze blood began cascading down the statue. Art removed the corkscrew carefully—so as not to diminish the beauty of the spiral incision.

I wanted to take Susan's feverish eyes away from this. I blew over her, mussing her hair.

When I awoke, I felt as though I had kissed her.

I threw the juju away. I preferred an orderly life without special knowledge.

In the month that followed, I was able to convince myself that a dream is just a dream. She never called back, and I guessed that either Art had decided not to sculpt her

or she didn't want to renew contact with me. I didn't seek
after Susan or Art again.

I avoided places that sold his art; no more statues for
me. But my denial didn't form a tight enough barrier. A
year passed and I turned thirty-nine. My editor at *Texas
Monthly* bought me something expensive and rare. I
opened the tiny gift, a reproduction of Art Putnam's "Perfect Model." There was enough of her face, of her eyes,
to know. What I could not know was whether those eyes
in their final crystallization showed ultimate agony or ecstasy.

BRAINCHILD

Rex Miller

Rex Miller has received noteworthy success as a radio personality, voice-over announcer and collectibles entrepreneur. He is regarded as one of America's leading authorities on popular culture memorabilia. Rex's novels include *Slob* (nominated for the Bram Stoker Award for Best First Novel in 1988), *Iceman, Profane Men, Slice, Savant, Butcher* and *Chaingang*. He has also authored over thirty pop-cultural publications, including: *Archives, Comic Heroes Illustrated, Radio Premiums Illustrated, Collectibles Quarterly*, and the new pictorial magazine *Premiums*.

The birth took place at the stroke of midnight, Eastern Standard Time, in OR-1 of New York Hospital in Manhattan.

The leading cranial man in the East, the top OB-GYN team, the head nurse at NYH and Drs. Weissblum, Durtz and Weissman, the celebrated "Three Wise Men" of Cornell Med, were all in attendance. It was not a C-section.

The child's head appeared, partially crowning, a semibreach, and the mother screamed through spinal-block fuzz as it came, full-blown, to term. Dr. Mawell, handling the delivery, turned and threw up on Head Nurse Secoy, who in turn vomited on the Three Wise Men, or on as many of them as the vomitus could reach. There are few things more illness-inducing than mass vomiting. Dr. Weissblum stepped back, losing his cookies, stepped in a puddle of puke, slipped and fell to one knee. Durtz and Secoy leaned over to help him up, and Durtz lost his footing in the puddles of vomit and the two of them fell on Weissblum, who called his colleague Dr. Durtz "a clumsy fucking prick," almost starting a fight between them. The stench, both from the vomit and from the placenta, was indescribable.

"Get back, all of you," Mawell said, ill, but forcing himself to hang on as he fought to complete the delivery procedure.

Once he felt certain that the thing was human, the umbilical was cut, and he made an incision in the hope of saving its life. It was able to breathe, so once he'd brought it to that point, Mawell cleaned the object and examined it. "It's a boy."

"Is it alive?" the cranial man asked.

"Yes," he said, fighting the desire to throw up again. "Clean up in here, for Christ's *sake*," he hissed at no one in particular. That was enough to restore some semblance of normality to the OR, and their professionalism galvanized them into motion.

The person who had just given birth, a crack addict who had been exposed to massive quantities of a powerful dioxinlike toxic agent over the years, was alive. She was removed from the OR as they inspected the human male child that had been born.

It was not only anencephalic, it was unlike anything any of them had ever seen before. Mawell clipped a microphone in place, and began recording official notes for the permanent record.

"Post-op comments. Baby Edwards . . . The anencephalic newborn is alive, and appears to be secreting a mucouslike film over the exposed brain tissue. Prognoses all indicate meningeal infection. Secretion is thinner than a saliva bubble and appears to be nondestructive in nature.'' Mawell turned and swallowed under the fresh mask. The OR stank of Betadyne. He was certain the thing's system would not be able to stave off the infection that invariably destroyed external-brain babies.

"The nerve connectives are developed on the upper right quadrant of the head. The baby's one eye responds to light stimuli . . . the cyclopean orb is typically distended.'' All anencephalic babies had profound distension of the eyeballs, but most sick fetuses were born blind as well as deaf.

"The baby may be attempting to spin a protective''— he stopped himself from saying ''web''—''sac to protect the meningeal covering, and is apparently secreting neural fluid over the exposed brain matter.'' The thing was fighting for its life.

Adele Secoy, twenty years with the OB unit, wished she were a kid again, just starting out in Pedes. She wished she'd never seen such a thing; her pro-life arguments had dissolved in the intervening minutes since midnight. The head nurse's eyes filled with pity at the horror before her. Welcome to the world, you poor son of a bitch, she thought.

Anne Sheldon was the biochemical and genetic product of the perfect matching of sperm and ova, the classic mix of chromosomes and genes, the textbook package of DNA and cellular luck that produces what contemporary North America defines as a physically beautiful woman.

But it was her father, not her beauty, and her talent that had brought her to this unique juncture. She had an opportunity that would give her a permanent place in medical history. She was going to be the Edwards child's teacher.

It had been nine years since the boy had been born. Against all odds, the baby—anencephalic, open-brained and massively deformed, little more than brain, spinal column, lower skull and upper torso—had lived those first dangerous weeks, then months, then years, fighting off infections, viruses and those organic mechanisms that worked so diligently to destroy it.

Ross Edwards had become a cause célèbre, and NYH's prestigious imprimatur, combined with the good and resourceful joint bodies of the hospital and Cornell University, would make certain the interwoven skein of New York's welfare system embraced this "miracle." It was housed in a special room of New York Hospital, where all medical science would come to study this puzzling human enigma.

In the baby's first weeks it was determined that special prosthetics would be mandatory if the malformed being was to survive even a sheltered existence. The highly respected Dr. Robert Sheldon, considered the top man in orthotics and prosthetics fabrication, was approached. Sheldon, who had interned with returning Vietnam vets at one of the busiest VA hospitals in the East, worked with amputees, burn victims and patients of radical surgery procedures, maintaining a busy practice out of Peekskill, New York.

To protect and support the vulnerable open brain, the misshapen and limbless torso, facial gashes and protruding eye, a complex cage-helmet-and-carapace was devised. Working with a strong but extremely lightweight new synthetic material, Sheldon created a support system that could accommodate a growing infant. One of the challenges was to come up with something that could be continually refitted, redesigned and manufactured every so many months as the child grew in size.

The technology did exist, and the health community's aggregate resources were tapped into to create an outfit for the baby whose very existence contravened the laws of medicine. Ross Edwards, unlike the so-called "Mexican" anencephalics, was not merely a worm, and the thing seemed determined to survive.

The plastic-based synthetic skin, ultralight so a baby's fragility could tolerate it, was initially rigged to a carapace that hugged the helpless form. So little about the infant was properly shaped: the anal aperture resembled a belly button as much as a rectal opening, there being no hips or bottom. The small back was ovoid in configuration, widening at the base of the spine, which ended in a posteriorly positioned waste canal. It could take a feed tube in its incision—what they referred to as its mouth—nurse and manifest adequate digestive and defecation functions. It could, barring infection, survive.

The open brain was housed in a thin sac the consistency of a bubble, semiopaque and bonded in its coagulated adhesion to the bony edges of open skull. When her father told Anne Sheldon about the baby, he'd lost her as words like ''meningocele'' and ''subarachnoid'' were amplified and transmitted through the microwave fields.

At the time of Ross Edwards's birth, she'd been a freshman, planning to major in Marine Biochemistry and Microbiology, at the University of Florida's Advanced Training Institute. The past nine years had been like a series of remarkable whirlwinds in Anne's life, some good, some awful. The loss of her mother to cancer, her breakthrough work with dolphins and the development of her unique communicator; so many emotional highs and lows marked the onrushing passage of time.

Thanks to having achieved recognition for her invention, the Audionics communicator, and to her father's intervention, she'd finally been granted permission to try to teach the so-far-unreachable child.

It had taken miles of red tape, bureaucratic paper shuffling and—no two ways about it—the consistent and persistent failure of Ross Edwards's pediatrician, Dr. Hugh Douglas, before the hospital permitted an outsider to gain access to its celebrated charge. But Anne was now living in New York, paying far too much for a cramped apartment within walking distance of NYH, and Ross had become her entire focus.

It was a young woman in her late twenties, with naturally blond hair, a full and sensuous mouth, the face slightly pinched at the jawline, but whose well-rounded chin saved the lower part of the face from being unattractive, a pretty and obviously caring person, who stared into the unblinking eye of Cyclops. The boy sat in front of her equipment, turtlelike in shell and helmet. Anne smiled, gently pressing a warm cup of water to the child's right cheek, if it could be called that.

"WARM," she said.

Nothing. No eye blink. Zero reaction. Nobody home.

She took his prosthetic hand, the right hand, and touched the key to produce the symbol. The symbol appeared on the screen as the key vibrated back to the hand.

Nothing so far.

W A R M spoke eerily to her from the metallic computer synthesizer. She switched off the audio, since there was no one but herself to hear it.

Anne plugged the galvanic attachment to the jack system and placed it against the boy's soft throat where his neck had developed normally. She touched the still-warm cup of water to his cheek, sat the cup down; not enough hands—this wouldn't do. She got some tape out and gently taped the attachment to the child's throat, speaking softly to him even though she knew he could not hear. Perhaps he would be able to see or intuit the fact that she did not mean to harm him in any way.

With the galvanic device in place, she held his prosthesis, the warm cup in her left hand, and repeated the process: "WARM." Touching him, activating the symbol and keying the galvanic response attachment. Warm held no interest for him that was discernible.

She took a cup of melting ice cubes and repeated the identical process for "COOL."

He eventually blinked the eye, but it appeared otherwise devoid of response. When she'd first examined the child, she had come away with the sensation of something in that eye, almost a feeling that he was examining her, too, and that he was also trying—on some primitive level—to communicate a thought. Now she tried to analyze what, if anything, she had seen this time. Fear? Indifference? What had he registered as she ran the basic vocabulary?

UP.

DOWN.

YOU.

ME.
HUNGRY.
FULL.
SMELLS GOOD.
SMELLS BAD.
ASLEEP.
AWAKE.

Not a glimmer of anything.

She carefully removed the right arm-and-hand prosthetic limb and gently affixed the sensory attachment for
the symbol computer directly to Ross's nub of arm.

She ran more warm water and drew another cup. When
she touched the warm cup to his cheek and pressed the
symbol key for WARM, he moved. It was a random
move, meaning nothing, but it was life. She repeated the
warm touch. Nothing this time. Placed the cup of cold ice
to his cheek. COOL. Absolutely zero.

Had the day's event been in another context, she'd have
been dismayed, perhaps, but this was the only child in the
world who'd been born without an upper skull and had
lived nine years; *anything* was scientific history. She
turned the boy over to Toby, the young man her father
had found to physically care for and look after the boy
when medical personnel were not in attendance, and
headed for the young head of Pedes, the large Pediactrics
section of the hospital, to share the news, such as it was.

"Dr. Douglas," she said through his open door when
she'd determined he wasn't with a patient or on the telephone.

"Yes?" he responded, looking up from paperwork.

"Pardon my intrusion, but I wanted to tell you about
Ross." She briefly sketched out her less-than-monumental
results. The boy had moved, perhaps randomly. Douglas
was the way she had found him each time, taciturn and
rather smug. They had not hit it off. She was trying to fix
that. They chatted some about Ross's possible sentience,
and—with X-rays in hand—she obtained a rather cursory
tour of the child's facial, throat and chest cavities. After
a few minutes she was rather rudely dismissed, and re-

turned to her temporary office quarters near the boy's room to record her work to that point.

She did so—every moment with the child was going into her journal—and also added to the ongoing monograph she was preparing for JAMA:

"While the patient has been born without a nose, technically," she typed across the screen, "there were undeveloped nostril passages. The surgical orifice that served for a mouth, made a few centimeters above the mandible, was adequate as an intake aperture for nourishment, but there was no hard palate or velum.

"Speech is normally produced by an airstream originating in the lungs, and the patient had the capability of producing such an airstream. Verbalization and articulation are shaped by phonatory, resonatory and articulatory processes that include the direction of that airstream or breathstream. Some sounds are made with the larynx, some by creating turbulence in the flow of the respiratory stream as it navigates the pharynx and oral cavity. Pitch, loudness and vocal quality involve the resonating and articulating of sounds as they transverse the nasopharynx, uvula—" She stopped, took a deep breath and let herself sink back in the chair.

Something about the day had disturbed her deeply. It was just a nudge of something, out of sight, not anything she could identify; a sense of something wrong. She made a hard copy, filed the printout and left the hospital to retrieve her car for the long drive to Peekskill.

That night she set her father to work on a revised costume for Ross Edwards; she needed something that would facilitate rather than encumber her work with the boy. Within a few short days, with her dad's redesigned gear in place, the nine-year-old was ready for another session. There was one more stumbling block before they could get down to work, she felt—the child's live-in caretaker, Toby.

Dr. Bob Sheldon had realized that it would require a unique, almost inhuman dedication to care for Ross: to fix its meals, feed it, wipe and clean its orifices, watch over it around the clock. In a future age, perhaps robotics would be advanced to a point where androids would so function; even under ordinary circumstances such a routine would test the patience of the most saintly soul. But who could continually gaze upon this one-eyed, open-brained, wormlike thing without going round the bend?

Toby Love was the answer. He was twenty-two, slightly retarded, to use the medically correct/politically incorrect term. He could easily be manipulated by an authority figure. Large, muscular, physically well developed, Toby had an appropriate last name. Bob Sheldon learned the young man was possessed of a genuinely sweet personality, and he adored babies, small animals and children of all ages. He was perfect.

By now Toby's entire self-worth was tied up in the nine-year-old who was still "his" infant charge. He was naturally jealous, possessive and irritated by Anne's intrusive presence. She would work to make it up to him, but she had to bring the fellow aboard and up to speed.

"Toby," she said, her voice at first soft in tone, "I like babies and little boys and girls, just as you do. I know you love Baby Ross"—she used his name for the child—"and I love Ross, too." He was dressed in clean clothing, pants to a blue serge suit and a striped shirt, fresh from the hospital laundry, that had no collar stays; and as he moved his head, the collar continually curled and twisted. He had a slack look to his face, almost like the character actor Michael J. Pollard, without the sparkle in his eyes. He showed a bit of response at the mention of Baby Ross's name.

"When I work with Baby Ross I will sometimes make you wait outside, Toby, understand?" she said.

"No." The man shook his head, and one collar point aimed down, the other toward his ear, giving him a rumpled, confused look. "I stay here and take care of Baby Ross. *I* care for baby."

"No!" she said, allowing her voice to take on a command tone. He jumped back. Anne had to work not to smile. "You'll stay outside so Ross can concentrate. I

want you to wait until I tell you to return. Is that clear?"
She kept her voice very firm.

"Yes." Toby didn't like it but he slinked out, his long,
muscular arms dangling loosely at his sides, moving in
that peculiar shuffling gait that had earned him the unfortunate sobriquet born of bad horror movies—"Igor." But
Toby was no hunchbacked dwarf. He was a large, powerful young man. Anne wondered, as she watched him
leave, if he, too, could be taught to improve the quality
of his own life.

She put Toby Love from her thoughts and focused on
the thing before her.

Under her father's protective equipment was a monstrously ugly being, but that was just superficial . . . what
of the inner child? Did a functioning brain sit waiting to
be reached, untouched and empty of knowledge, in its
jellied neural sac? Anne drew a cup of warm water from
the sink and went to work.

Weeks went by without progress. One day she was talking to Hugh Douglas about his various work with the
child over its first nine years, and he began asking her—
for the first time—about what her Audionics system did,
and she felt their icy barriers melt a bit.

She told him about her work with logic-transition
thresholds, the so-called tactile or "Y-image" sensory re-
ceptors, and how she had programmed a computer to
communicate nonverbals graphically. "The tapping or X-
image combines with Y to equal the Z-factor, graphically
and by tactile means. It theoretically would adapt to any
being so long as it was capable of biochemical/logical
stimuli-response/reaction." He had a fuzzy look on his
face, and appeared to be fighting a yawn. "Am I boring
you?" she asked.

"It's not that. I haven't understood anything you said
to me for the last five minutes."

It struck her as funny and they both broke up.

"It's easy to let the work jargon and circumlocutions
get a bit prolix, and pretty soon everything you say gets
in the way of clarity. I'm sorry," she said.

"It's not only that. I'm in one of those periods, you know, when nothing parses."

"I have those days frequently," Anne said.

"Listen," he said, a genuine smile on his face, "I may not understand what you're doing, but I damned sure understand the frustrations you're feeling. I had nine years of it, remember?"

"I know. But you have no reason to view the wonderful work you did with Ross as less than a success—my God, he's alive! That in itself—"

"I know. What I'm trying to say is I've behaved badly. I am glad Bob got the position for you and . . . if you'll permit me to make amends, would you consider having dinner with me?" He stopped her No with a flat palm, fingers together in the universal "wait" gesture. "Not a date. Just two colleagues having a bite of food and a drink or two together. Please allow me this. I mean, I want us to be friends."

Anne was so pleased to have some of the ice thawing that she agreed, immediately regretting it, but finding no satisfactory way to back out. Two nights later they were in a preposterously formal place called La Pescadori, she in black linen suit, ruffled blouse, heels; Hugh in an ash-gray Armani, plum-colored silk tie; and each of them in their full wardrobe of chain mail. The evening appeared to be shaping up as a real disaster. It had been a bad mistake.

From across a crowded room Hugh Douglas and Anne Sheldon looked like a beautiful couple, but there was no coupling going on. Neither was the type to mix romance with work, nor was romance even accurate for their respective sexual encounters. Each viewed his or her own sexuality as a biological need, and work was foremost in both lives. They were handsome overachievers, bright and disciplined, and when sex did enter their interpersonal equations, it had to be out of the workplace, and each of them had to be in charge of such a happening. Since they were healthy, heterosexually oriented persons, both Anne and Hugh had briefly considered the possibility of something happening between them, but only in terms of what they should do in case the other one made a move. None of these attitudes boded well for a physical relationship, their respective attractiveness notwithstanding.

Once they'd finished verbal fencing, which went on for a couple of uncomfortable hours, each party reached the same realization: there was no seduction about to be attempted by the other. There was no interest. They were two powerful human magnets, but magnets—face-to-face—repel. There'd be a working relationship only. Once this tacit agreement was made and mutually understood, they both relaxed and found—to their great surprise—the other person was damn good company. There was good talk, a lot of it, ranging from bottle-nosed dolphins to ultrasound, and they found the other's anecdotal stories fascinating.

Not long after their evening out, Hugh and Anne began spending time with Ross Edwards together. Whenever Douglas wasn't otherwise occupied, the young head of Pediatrics would come visit, and his input proved to be tremendously helpful. Between the two of them, Anne finally made her first breakthrough with the child.

It was around four months since she'd started working with Ross. The day began like all others: she woke up praying for some glimmer of intelligence, some sign that the boy had the potential to communicate, but with nothing to objectively substantiate her hopes.

The brisk thirty-four-block hike to and from work, Anne's idea of a "short walk," had become her sole exercise; less strenuous and a lot less boring than a treadmill. She and Hugh were getting along great, and Toby had come around. If only she could reach the child . . .

Ross Edwards made noises. He could cry, in a manner of speaking, make a noise not unlike a human sneeze, cough, produce a gurgling sound. One of her teaching devices when he was hooked to the language unit was a stuffed animal. She would link its image to the word "puppy dog." The boy was ready for the day. She said, "Puppy dog," and touched the stuffed toy to Ross's face. As she did so he sneezed. It was a painful and frightening sound, more of a paroxysm or spasm. Not a human sneeze exactly, but a forced whimper that came from deep within the boy, an expulsion of airstream out of the feeding orifice and breathing gills.

"*NNFF!*" "Puppy Dog" was the symbol on the synthesizer. She showed it to him. Maybe Ross was allergic to the chemicals in the simulated fur of the toy.

Anne resumed running symbols.

WET.
DRY.
MOTHER.
FATHER.
SLEEPY.
AWAKE.
FEEL NICE.
HURT.
GOOD.
BAD.
LOVE.
HATE.

Sophisticated symbols, then back to the basic COOL, HEAT, YES, NO, ME, YOU variety.

"**PUPPY DOG,**" she said and Ross sneezed. Thank God Hugh had happened to be in the room; had she not had the head of Pedes as a witness, Anne would have doubted it herself.

For the first time in the child's life, there was tangible evidence Ross Edwards could *think* . . . and as Anne and Hugh soon discovered, he could learn in a rather sophisticated fashion, all things considered. Ross had some grasp of language. He had learned by watching, by observing Hugh, the nurses and Toby, and he could effectively make associations with graphic symbols. He had a brain that could reason!

Descartes's simple rationale explaining human existence had never been superseded, to her way of thinking. Anne was so overjoyed, so profoundly moved, that she hugged the pathetic helmeted, carapaced creature to her, ever so gently, tears streaming from her eyes, as she felt its vibrations and aura bond with her own.

By the end of month five with Ross, her journal had been filled and she'd begun a new one. The monograph had been totally revised and the newest findings were astonishing: he could discern smells; he could count and quantify in a basic fashion; he "understood" rudimentary English at a very young child's level. All these things defied explanation by known science. He had—to some amazing extent—*taught himself to lip-read*! How? They already shared a vocabulary of forty-one words and phrases. There was even marked improvement in nub coordination.

After six months of working with the boy, the tappings, rubbings and other tactile components that enabled Ross to make associations with lip-read or computerized symbol/images had been accelerated. He was learning the more difficult associations of vibrations and electrostimuli that the various galvanic attachments utilized. He could comprehend on a variety of levels and by means of tactile, visual and olfactory input. Perhaps, she theorized, he could also communicate on some plateau she had not yet identified.

Month seven: he was manipulating puzzle symbols with her hand on his small prosthetic fingers, making color linkages through the spectrum of the rainbow, this child who'd never seen a rainbow. Anne was taking him through the continuum of visual perception.

He had no past to draw from—he'd seen so little: hospital rooms, occasional frightening vistas through windows, odd bursts of sunlight. What in God's name did he think? How did he perceive his surroundings? What Alice-in-Blunderland of the mind did the poor creature inhabit that she could use as reference?

He mastered the color puzzles. The basic English alphabet. Even—to the extent he could control his prosthetic limbs—the A-B-C building blocks. Anne was reading and telling him computer-linked stories, imposing extra emphasis with her facial features and movements, acting out as she "spoke" to the boy through her communicator. Significant words were being transliterated, but Ross remained riveted on her movements, learning by lipreading and whatever assimilation process reached him, in concert with the special tapping language. He was also learning to move!

Journal log "Day 241" was another remarkable breakthrough date. "A milestone: Ross has initiated a communication he devised *himself*. He bad me wet feel nice no!" It was neither a response to nor an aping of the images Anne had given him. Stripped of its idiomatic awkwardness, it spoke to her and Hugh clearly. Sometimes when Toby was changing and cleaning the boy, he allowed the wet diaper to touch him inadvertently, and Ross was registering a complaint to that effect. From that moment, breakthroughs snowballed.

Soon Ross was able to routinely form complete sentences, and his basic language of feels, rubs, taps, symbols and other stimuli had been supplanted by a stream of words, and their conversations had begun to crystallize into full-blown two-way communication. Ross reminded her of a dolphin; his assimilation powers were awesome. Anne wrote: "The child is the human correlation of that species," referring to the bottlenose with whom the Audionics system had been fashioned. She was now aware that Ross had apparently amassed a prodigious basic foundation of savvy that was stored, inert, and waiting to be unleashed. His problem-solving and lipreading, now infused with broadened meaning, had a pyramidal effect. "There is no telling how smart Ross Edwards is," she noted.

One morning, at the end of the eleventh month, her charge having turned age ten while in her care, she hooked Ross up, plugged his gear into the system and was startled by the metallic question he immediately initiated. "Do I look like Toby," the audio intoned, "or you?"

Ross was beginning to grasp his environment more fully. It was a moment she had both looked forward to and—for obvious reasons—dreaded. A complexity of explanations lay ahead, something of a potential minefield, but the hard questions had to be answered honestly.

"You look like neither of us," she told him. "I am a female of the same *species* of which you are a male child. Toby is a male *adult*. I am a *female* adult. You are a male *child*. We are all of the human species."

"If you and Toby were a mother and father"—he paused at the formation of the words whose symbols he found repellent—"would you have a male child?" He knew his biological parents did not want him.

"That is difficult to answer. It is possible that we would. Yes." What a question!

"If you and Toby had a male child, would it look as I do?"

"It might. It might not. Children are all different," she said.

"What do I smell like?"

"You smell nice. You smell like a sweet little boy," she told him.

"Toby said I smelled bad when he cleaned me."

"Toby . . ." That one stopped her for a second. "He was explaining that when you create waste matter of your digested food, it does not smell pleasant. No one's waste matter smells pleasant. But that is Toby's job, just as other nurses clean other persons. At all other times you are a nice-smelling boy."

"Will you smell me now?" he asked. Obviously he did not believe her.

"Of course. I will be glad to smell you." She leaned even closer and inhaled the smell of soap and powder. "You smell good." She kissed his cheek, where he had a face.

"Thank you. Do I smell you good?" he wanted to know. She explained the idea of response to olfactory stimuli as best she could, knowing that this was now Ross's learning. There would be no further classes of the boy memorizing words. He would ask questions of the world he inhabited based on the language he had. She was teaching him, but in a different, faster, more utilitarian way.

"What is olfactory?"

"In most humans a pair of cranial nerves conduct stimuli from the membranous organ in the nasal cavity to the anterior section of the cerebrum. Your first cranial nerve is slightly different, but as we have discussed in our lessons, you have a system for conducting those stimuli to your brain." She gently touched his breathing gills. "Your olfactory organ is here. It receives and perceives smells. Do you smell me?" He did his best to sniff her aroma.

"Yes. You smell warm. I receive and perceive a pleasant chemical smell on your throat and on your arm that is not on your fingers. My olfactory organ transmits these smells to my cerebrum well and I am able to differentiate one smell from the other efficiently. The smell of the fingers of your hands and the chemical smell combine to produce a response that my cerebrum categorizes as not unpleasant and warm."

"Thank you," she said. I think. "But while your response is quite correct, it is more efficient to simply sum up that response. You could say 'Anne, you smell nice.'"

"Anne, you smell nice."

"Thank you, Ross. You smell nice, too."

"Thank you. Anne, your membranous organ is in your nasal cavity, too, is that correct?"

"Yes. Here." She pointed. "That's my nose, as you know." "These holes or openings are my nostrils."

"Do I have a nose like yours or Toby's?"

"Neither."

"What does my nose look like?" he asked. "Do I look like Dr. Douglas? Dr. Sheldon? My biological mother? The man who came to—"

"Stop, please, Ross. I can answer only one question at a time. You are different. Your appearance is unique, and unlike any of the other persons you have seen."

He seemed satisfied.

Alone in the room, Toby on an errand to the hospital laundry, the thing brooded silently.

Its mind was capable of things that transcended ordinary human understanding. The pulsating brain that sat encased on the upper left quadrant of the head, disgusting to most others in its bloody-jelly sac, so vulnerable and open on the malformed shelf of misshapen skullbone, was unique.

A suffusion of something inexplicable flowed through the thing's veins. Above him, glowing in the darkness of the silent room, figures moved on a screen. Two male adults, both burnt-color with birth-defect heads like his, played ball. One stood on a white thing not unlike a square hospital pillow. NEW YORK 1 ATLANTA 0 was superimposed. One of the dark brown males was named Braves, and below his name was a symbol that the Audionics system defined as "hatchet or short-handled ax."

Ross Edwards waited patiently until his caretaker returned. In the interim he considered what he had assimilated about hatchets or short-handled axes. The bright window box had supplied him with some knowledge of the implement's potential usage. Toby entered the room and Ross's eye fixed on the man.

If he was to manipulate Toby properly, it was conceivable that the man would take a hatchet or short-handled ax and smash the heads of the other young males housed within this place. Then their heads would resemble his, he reasoned. It was not an unpleasant thought. The tool could additionally be used to amputate their limbs. Toby could then poke out one of the eyes on the ugly, two-eyed faces, such as he had observed many times.

After a time he was able to gain his nurse's attention and he was moved into the wheelchair. He waited until Toby plugged him into the computer.

"Toby."

"Yes, Ross." Toby spoke carefully as Ross lip-read the man's words.

"Are there many others like myself here?"

"No."

"Are there other male children of my approximate age here?"

"I think so." Ross used words he did not comprehend. "Yes, Ross. Other children are here."

"What kind of children, Toby? Are there little babies here?"

"Yes," Toby said, anxious to please. "There are many little babies here."

"Where do they stay?" Ross asked.

"They stay here."

"No, Toby. I want to know where the little babies sleep."

"Sleep in their beds, Ross."

"Where are their beds kept?"

"Out there." Toby said, pointing. This was a difficult exchange and he wanted to watch the men play ball.

"Look!" he said. A group of fans held an incomprehensible sign bearing ballpark graffiti.

Ross concluded that males who produced printed signs for athletic activities did not always have a solid understanding of phonemes, syntax or idiogrammatical phrasemaking. Perhaps they also had severe birth impairment of some type.

"Where are the beds where the little babies sleep, Toby?"

"Out there, Ross. They sleep in their little beds out there. Little beds like you used to sleep in when you were a little baby and I took care of you just like I do now. Except you were hurt and slept in a little box."

"Yes."

"One side of your head was hurt real bad and I was not supposed to touch your head there and I—"

"Yes, Toby. How do the little babies breathe if they are in boxes?" That was too much for the man. He was stopped by that one.

Ross changed the subject. He told Toby, "Plug me in so I can use the telephone."

There was a simple phone jack for adapting the system to a telephone landline. The synthesizer and computer both were on-line with TeleCaption decoder and Superphone systems.

"Okay, Ross," Toby said. "Can I watch TV now?"

"Yes," Ross said, and, upon observing the audio element was disconnected, instructed the machine as to what he wanted.

"I wish to call the New York Public Library Science

Reference Department Hot Line," he said. Interactive software reached out for a company terminal. The new equipment had replaced the old TTD-Relay units, and he could contact them directly.

"My name is Toby Love." He gave New York Hospital's York Avenue address. Silently, machine to machine, the ten-year-old child conversed with a senior research librarian in the NYPL's Science Reference Department, their words locked inside the heart of Anne Sheldon's invention. The computer requested seven books:

Maladaptive Sociosexual Behavior by Sonnengen and Quarrels;

Socio-interpersonal Situational Psychology by A. L. Stern;

Early Metacognitive Abilities and Social Sexuality by N. Hockman;

Sexuality and the Physically Challenged by Shiffer and Kempe;

Function and Dysfunction by C. Crookshank;

Sexual Intimacy for the Physically Handicapped or Disabled by Gabler, Nilson and Grad;

Sex Therapy for Exceptional Children by C. J. Rushmont.

Unlike the tomes he'd requested on toxicology and related matters, one of which had been available on software accessible to the Audionics system, the books came to the hospital as hard copies and Hugh Douglas intercepted them.

"I think it's pretty clear what we have in our young patient," Douglas said to Anne Sheldon, who sat on the edge of one of the chairs opposite his desk. "We're looking at a brilliant mind inside the body of an anencephalic child who is cursed with sexual precocity. I've suspected it enough times, but—" He gestured toward the stack of books, which spoke for themselves.

"Poor little boy." Anne shook her head.

"Anne, you have to stop touching the child, I think. Giving him little kisses the way I've seen you do. For all we know, he's entering puberty. If he's as sexually precocious as this suggests, he may have misinterpreted your actions.''

"I'll have a talk with him."

"Would you rather I spoke with him first?" Douglas asked.

"No," Anne said, "I'll do it." She got up, picked one of the books at random, looked at the title and dropped it back on the stack. "I'll talk to you later." She turned and left Hugh's office, walking to Ross's room, her stride measurably less brisk than usual as she contemplated her options. She paused at the door. Inside, encased in orthotic carapace and helmet, was a pink/white worm-shaped human with open brain, nubs for hands and feet, and developed male genitalia. A ten-year-old genius, to make matters more complicated for both the child and those who now had to care for and direct it. She took a deep breath and entered.

Toby sat on the hospital bed, his eyes glued to the silent television screen on the shelf above. The boy sat in shadows, the protective helmet in place, the rest of his gear on, small prosthetics positioned to communicate.

"Hello, Anne," the metallic voice of the synthesizer said as she entered. It had turned the equipment on.

"Hello, Ross. Hi, Toby."

"Hello, Anne." Toby's gaze never left the TV.

"Dr. Hugh received some books from the library which you apparently requested. I wish you'd asked me. I might have been able to help you."

"I did not think you needed to be bothered," Ross said.

"It's my job to look out for your welfare, and to teach you, Ross. It's no bother. The books you wanted are not available on interactive software. Do you have particular questions about your development and behavior?"

"Yes, Anne. That is correct. I do. Toby, please wait outside in the hallway while I speak with Anne."

"Okay, Ross," Toby Love said, having learned that the child's was the superior voice of authority in his life. He got up, a sulky expression on his face. "How long do I stay in the hallway, about five minutes?"

"No, Toby. Stay out there until Anne tells you it is all right to come back in."

"Okay, Ross," he said, walking to the doorway, anxious to please. When he had closed the door, Anne spoke.

"Why was it necessary to ask Toby to leave, Ross?"

"Because, Anne, this is private."

"All right," she said, waiting. She noticed in his speech patterns the continuing advancement. The groups of echolalic phrases were gone. He was teaching himself.

"Anne, do you think I am pretty when my lower prosthetics are not attached?"

"Of course, dear," she said, tiptoeing through the minefield. "Why do you ask?"

"I think your limbs are beautiful. More so than the limbs of any other adult females of my species I have observed."

"Thank you, Ross. A more efficient statement would be—you have pretty legs. But such a statement is not appropriate when made by a ten-year-old child to an adult."

He activated the image keys he'd been waiting so anxiously to strike:

TOUCH
MY
P
P

"Please, Anne, touch it for me. It would feel good if you would touch it."

The pretty-legged female's words of rebuke stung him deeply. He was still seething from the things she'd said to him long after she'd left his quarters. He remained in his full wardrobe, plugged into the communications system. Toby was fascinated by a woman spinning a large wheel. "Toby," he said, speaking through the electrovoice, "am I heavy to carry?"

"No, Ross," the man said, turning his attention to the object in helmet and cagelike device. "You're not heavy."

"How far is it to Anne's quarters?"

"I don't know, Ross."

"How do you summon a taxicab, Toby?"

"Um . . . a cab? You call them on the phone, Ross, or you yell at them when they drive by in the street, and you wave, or you look the number of the taxicab up in the telephone book—"

"Yes. I understand. Who is on the night staff? How many persons are on night staff here, and what are their names?"

"I have a headache now, Ross. I have to go to the bathroom."

"You'll go to the bathroom when I tell you to, Toby, but not before. Now, here is what you will do. You will get me another blanket. You will get me a map of the city. You will find out where Anne Sheldon lives and give me the address of her living quarters. You will ask how many persons are on the night staff. Now you may go to the bathroom, but as soon as you have finished, you get me another blanket, get the map of the city and find out where Anne lives. Can you remember all of that?"

"Yes, Ross," the man said as he sulked out of the room.

When Toby had completed his first assignments, Ross made a mental note to ascertain the number and locations of the exits from the Pediatrics unit, and how they could reach one of them secretly.

He had suffered enough in his ten terrible years of life. Now it was *their* turn. The desire to strike back was as strong as the warm desire that seemed to flow through his urinary tract.

Anne was undressed and ready for bed when the doorman buzzed her from downstairs.

"Yes?" she said into the apartment intercom.

"Mizz Sheldon, there's a Mistah Love here, and he say he wan' to speak with you and it berry importan'."

"Who?"

"To-bee Luv," he carefully enunciated.

My God!

"Toby?"

"Ross down here with me." The man's voice spoke over the intercom. "Ross made me bring him. He's real upset, Anne. Can we come up? I don't know what to do."

"You've got Ross . . . you've brought Ross *here*?" Nothing was getting through.

"You wan' me to let them up?" the doorman asked.

"Yes, sure, of course," she said.

Toby rolled the collapsible wheelchair containing Ross Edwards toward the bank of elevators. Upstairs, Anne picked up the phone and dialed the hospital.

"May I speak to Dr. Douglas?" she asked. He'd left for the night. Quickly, she hung up and dialed his apartment number.

Below, they waited a second too long and the door closed on them while they tried to figure out how to manipulate the movable box, which frightened Toby, but Ross saw the instrument panel numbers corresponded to the Audionics system, and a small prosthetic finger carefully tapped the symbol for twelve. The moving room began its ascent. Soon the door opened again, and Ross motioned for Toby to wheel him off, and they started to find Anne's door.

"This way," she said when she saw them. She'd told Hugh what was happening and he'd instructed her to keep them there, in the hallway, until he could get there. She was completely nonplussed to see them in her apartment hallway, Ross outside, in his wheelchair, the synthesizer and keyboard waiting to be hooked up to an outlet.

Even as she started to question them, Toby moved into action. He had been fully programmed for this moment, and he lunged at her, as Ross had commanded him to do.

"*Stop!* Don't, *goddamn you, Toby*!" He was ripping her clothes, tearing her robe from her.

One moment she'd been about to speak to Toby, to chastise him for risking the child's safety, and now she was fighting for her life. Toby, who'd been little more than a piece of furniture, always in the background, was very strong. She'd never considered a physical confrontation between them. She shouted at him, but his awe of authority was limited to the greater authority, in this case the boy's commands.

She screamed again as Toby clumsily pushed her back into the apartment. The robe was off and he was tearing at the long sweatshirt she wore as a pajama top as he pinned her to the floor. *"Help!"* It was a chilling scream, but it was too late.

"Help me! Hel—" Toby backhanded her hard, and she almost blacked out for a second. As Anne's vision came back, she saw Ross trying to pull himself down out of the wheelchair. He'd never let on that he could manipulate his body so well. Neither she nor Douglas had any idea he could get in or out of the wheelchair without physical help.

Toby held her spread-eagled on the floor of her apartment, holding her arms in a death grip. Her long legs were loose. If that little bastard came close to her, she was going to kick him in the pee-pee so hard he'd *never* want to be touched there again. She screamed again as she saw the child drag itself up close to her head, moving closer, wormlike, dragging itself to her. Jesus! Oh, Jesus in heaven. He was going to *rub himself against the top of her head* where she couldn't even bite him.

She tried another scream. Toby had moved slightly, with most of his weight on her arms and upper chest, but he was having to move around so that Ross could position himself.

Somehow she managed to get a hand free as Toby fought to hold the woman in the way he'd been repeatedly instructed. They were on the floor near her small closet. The closet had a full-length mirror attached to the inside of the door. Her fingertips clawed for the closet door behind her, but she missed.

Slowly, nubs working diligently, doing what it had done only in secret for years, the thing was removing its prosthetics and orthotic carapace. The open-brained wormchild was backing up to rub its private parts against her.

She knew she had but one chance to save herself. Anne stretched her arm, wiggling her fingers, arching up, straining to make herself longer. She felt the tendons in her leg and her back muscles stretching.

Just as it touched her hair, although she was pinioned by Toby, she managed to angle herself slightly, and as a fear and revulsion that came near madness possessed her and gave her a jolt of surprising strength, she was able to catch the lip of the closet door. The mirror swung out into the small room, and for the first time in its life, *Ross Edwards saw what it was* under the mask and helmet.

It stopped.

Froze.

A wall clock in Anne's apartment ticked off a second that sounded as loud as a sledgehammer blow.

Although it had never spoken other than the expulsion of coughs and sneezes, and the synthetically produced speech of the computer, it opened its feeding orifice and let out a sound such as had never been heard on earth before.

At birth it had been a slug of breathtaking deformity and ugliness, but now—ten years later—it had grown, changed, *mutated*!

The brain . . . it had swelled, and wormy growths wriggled in a bloody-colored sac of disgusting grotesqueness. When it saw itself, the scream that came forth was the anguished reflection of a true vision straight from hell: a vomit-inducing, one-eyed, slimy thing crowned by something that appeared to have been sculpted from tainted meat and coughed up by the devil!

Hugh Douglas was totally out of breath, but at the sound of the excruciating scream from Anne's apartment, he found an inner reserve of strength and sprinted down the hall, bursting through the open door to be attacked by a confused Toby, who leapt at the intruder with a flurry of fists, kicks and madly clawing hands.

Toby was fighting to protect the boy—all he had ever cared about—and Hugh misjudged the powerful nurse's physical abilities. Toby had the doctor against the window and slammed his head into the thick glass, breaking it.

Anne, exhausted from her own struggles, paralyzed

with terror, had been backed into a corner as far as she could get from the raw slug.

Toby had Hugh's head out the window, and Hugh got a dizzying glimpse of the stalled clog of traffic a dozen floors down. Anne forced back her revulsion and grabbed the monstrous thing and hurled it in the direction of the window, which was now a gaping hole of jagged glass.

Toby's mandate was clear. Protect Ross.

He released Hugh, who dropped to the floor, and made a diving catch for the slug, grabbing for it as they both fell through the open window.

Hugh went to Anne, and they held each other, gasping for air, as the wail of sirens and blare of vehicle horns signaled the mess down below on East 64th Street.

FURIES IN BLACK LEATHER

Nancy A. Collins

Nancy A. Collins is the author of *Paint It Black* (1995),
Wild Blood (1993), *Walking Wolf* (1995), *In The Blood*
(1992), *Tempter* (1990) and *Sunglasses After Dark*
(1989). Her collected Sonja Blue Cycle, *Midnight Blue*,
was published by White Wolf in early 1995. She was the
writer for DC Comics' *Swamp Thing* series from 1991 to
1993. She won the Horror Writers of America's Bram
Stoker Award for First Novel and the British Fantasy Society's Icarus Award. She is currently working on the
comics adaptation of *Sunglasses After Dark* and the fourth
installment in the Sonja Blue Cycle, *A Dozen Black
Roses*. She was the coeditor of *Dark Love* (Penguin/Roc,
1995). She currently resides in New York City with her
husband, anti-artiste Joe Christ, and their dog, Scrapple.

Rolf sat in the back of the limo and fidgeted, waiting for the light to change. It was Friday night and he was late for his rendezvous with The Sisters. They weren't really related. At least not genetically. Then again, Rolf's name wasn't really Rolf, either.

Cissy, the youngest, was cute and perfect, the way china dolls are cute and perfect. Her hands and feet were tiny, complementing the doll analogy, although she sported an ice-cream-blond flattop. Meg, in contrast, was medium height and far from small—her breasts, hips and thighs perpetually threatened to push her over the brink of "Rubenesque." Her hair was curly and the color of spilled wine, hanging to the middle of her back in long, tangled tresses. Alexis, the oldest of the three, was tall and willowy, with cheekbones and attitude suitable for a high-fashion model, with sable hair that fell to her narrow butt.

Each of The Sisters had her own style—her own "shtick." Cissy played the teasing virgin, wide-eyed and innocent. Meg was the bawdy, foul-mouthed earth mother. And Alexis—Alexis was the cool and unattainable Ice Queen. Separately, they were three beautiful, sensuous women. But once together, they surpassed the sum of their individual natures. They were the very essence that is Woman. At least as far as Rolf was concerned, that was the case. And, to be honest, Rolf's interpretation of reality was the only one that mattered.

The light changed and the limo lurched into the intersection. Rolf checked his watch. Five minutes late. He was going to be five minutes late for his session. Mistress Alexis was going to be so displeased. Rolf writhed in anticipation of her anger.

The dungeon was located in the basement of an old three-story brownstone in the West Village. Rolf hurried down the dark stairs that led to the entrance under the front stoop. The shadows smelled of piss, which made Rolf's hands tremble even more as he punched his code into the security gate. There was a harsh, ear-jangling buzz and he eagerly yanked open the heavy metal door.

Cissy was lounging in the waiting room, dressed in her oversized pinafore and lollipop panties, demurely snacking on a pint of Ben & Jerry's Rum Raisin. Except for the heavy eye makeup and painted lips, she could have passed for a child of ten. Rolf felt himself begin to get hard.

"You're late," she said, not even bothering to look up from her Rum Raisin. "Alexis doesn't like it when you're late."

"Yes. Yes, I know—that was bad of me. Very, very bad—" Rolf was wheezing, but not because he was out of breath.

Cissy glanced up at him with those big, childlike eyes and licked her spoon with a flick of her little pink tongue. "Don't tell me—tell her."

"Of course. Of course." Rolf turned and headed down the narrow corridor that led from the waiting room into the bowels of the dungeon. In order to convert the basement into a proper S&M dungeon, the original walls had been knocked out and newer, smaller rooms installed. Each "fantasy suite" boasted a certain fetish motif. One was a "nursery" for bad little boys, another was a medieval torture chamber, yet another an enema clinic. There was even a special room for those who wished to reenact the Nazi concentration camp atrocities. But Rolf did not bother to check any of these rooms to see if Mistress Alexis was to be found in them. He knew exactly where she'd be.

The Room of Mirrors.

The cubicle was no larger than any of the others in the dungeon—possibly smaller—but the feeling Rolf always got whenever he stepped over the threshold was that the room went on forever. The reason for that, of course, was the collection of strategically located mirrors that lined every surface except for the floor. In the middle of the room a sturdy metal trapeze hung suspended from the ceiling, poised directly over a metal bar fastened to a heavy-duty ring set into the concrete floor.

The first things Rolf saw as he entered the Room of Mirrors were dozens upon dozens of frowning dominatrixes, their multiplied contempt enough to melt surgical

steel. And all of the dominatrixes wore Mistress Alexis's
face. She was dressed in a black leather Merry Widow
corset, the lacing pulled so tight at the waist it transformed
her figure into that of a queen wasp. Alexis's hips were
normally quite narrow, her breasts tiny little jiggly things
that looked like fleshy fruit cups. She was wearing black
stiletto-heel vinyl boots that nearly reached her crotch,
black leather tap panties and the black velvet opera gloves
that were her trademark. Rolf had never seen her without
her opera gloves or, come to think of it, the studded dog
collar that encircled her neck.

"You're late, worm."

"Yes, I know, mistress—I'm sorry. It's not my fault.
My driver got caught in cross-town traffic . . ."

"That's a reason, not an excuse," Alexis sniffed.
"Your session's already started, you know. You began
paying five minutes—no"—she consulted a diamond-
studded Cartier watch affixed to her left wrist—"seven
and a half minutes ago."

Rolf chafed at the billing, but said nothing. Alexis cost
five hundred a hour by herself. The Sisters, as a unit, ran
a cool thousand. But they were worth it—boy, were they
ever!

Rolf wasn't your usual punishment freak. At least that
was what he liked to think. He *needed* to be degraded by
beautiful women. He *needed* to be hurt, to be tortured—
to be made to pay for all that he had done in the past. He
was a sinner. He knew it. A dirty, wretched sinner who
deserved the harshest of treatment at the hands of punishing angels. He was weak and it was his due to be disciplined by those stronger than he was. He *needed* to have
his sins ripped from his flesh. His sins haunted his waking
hours, buzzing in the back of his brain like flies hovering
over ripe garbage. However, the problem was—Rolf
couldn't stand pain.

His sensory threshold was exceptionally low. If anyone
even pinched him, he screamed and writhed as if he'd
been stabbed. There was no way he could bring himself
to suffer the mortifications of the flesh, no matter how
much he wished to endure them. Over the years he had

drifted from mistress to mistress, dungeon to dungeon, in an attempt to find the woman capable of bringing his fantasies to life.

When he explained his predicament to Mistress Alexis, she suggested the use of what she called a "surrogate body"—a stand-in who would undergo the scouring that Rolf so badly desired. At first he was dubious and suspicous of the extra cost, but Alexis eventually talked him into it.

He never knew the name of the original surrogate, not that it mattered. No doubt some meaningless boho down on his luck and willing to rent his body out for a hundred bucks an hour. He wore a black leather fetish hood and nothing else, chained to the trapeze in the Room of Mirrors. At first the sight of another man's penis and testicles made Rolf uncomfortable, but as The Sisters began administering their peculiar brand of mercy to the surrogate, it was surprisingly easy for him to project his own face onto the black leather cowl. Whenever The Sisters would bruise or burn or whip the surrogate, Rolf found himself screaming bloody murder, as if it were his own flesh they were working on.

That was his first "interrogation" with The Sisters— and far from the last. Over the next six months Rolf began expanding on his fantasy, fleshing it out in greater detail as he became more and more confident. At first he'd been worried about blackmail, but relaxed once he realized he could always dismiss his weekly "interrogation" as an elaborate—albeit perverse—sex game. It was a fantasy, nothing more. Want to make something of it?

Rolf took off his clothes, watching himself in the multitude of mirrors. He was far from an impressive specimen with his balding pate and thickening middle. His penis looked naked and sad, hanging between his legs like a dead squid. But that would change the moment the surrogate began to writhe under Mistress Alexis's punishing hands.

"Did you get a good stand-in this time? I didn't like the one you picked last time. His dick wasn't nearly big enough to be mine."

Mistress Alexis's smile was like winter dawn on a frozen lake. "I think you'll find this week's body more to your tastes."

Meg and Cissy led the surrogate into the room. His head—like those of the ones before—was shrouded by a black leather fetish mask, the mouth zippered shut. Outside of the manacles fitted to his wrists and ankles, the surrogate was completely naked. There was no way to tell exactly how old he was, but Rolf suspected he was quite young. Possibly underage, judging by his height. Despite his apparent youth, the surrogate was far from buff. While hardly flabby, his muscles lacked tone. No doubt an incipient couch potato. Rolf was reminded how he, too, had been something of a "soft boy" in his youth.

The surrogate seemed unsteady on his feet as Meg unlocked his wrist restraints and fastened them to the far ends of the trapeze suspended over his head. Cissy busied herself with seeing that his ankles were secured to the bottom bar. No doubt the surrogate was strung out on something. Probably ex or junk.

Mistress Alexis left the room and reentered pushing a wheeled instrument tray, like those found in operating rooms. Arrayed across its gleaming surface was a collection of paddles, leather thongs, clothespins, carpet needles, brushes, dildos and candles. Rolf could already tell it was going to be a particularly memorable interrogation.

Mistress Alexis selected a broad paddle made from stiff leather and began circling the surrogate, lightly tapping the palm of her hand as she spoke.

"What is your name, worm?" she asked, her voice stern. Mistress Alexis was a woman used to being answered promptly and with respect. The surrogate said nothing. Not that he could, since the mouth of the fetish mask was securely zippered shut.

Rolf licked his lips, his eyes shifting from the flesh-and-blood participants to their mirror images and back again. It had begun. From here on, everything would go as it always did—following a script he himself had carefully prepared. Although Rolf allowed The Sisters a certain amount of latitude in the kinds of punishment they meted out and in what order they could do it—after all, he didn't want to become bored by predictability—every word was part of an elaborate call-and-response, as heavily laden with ritual and personal meaning as the holiest of religious observances.

"I *said*, what is your name, worm?!?" The leather paddle connected with the surrogate's naked left buttock, making a sound like a hand striking wet mud. The surrogate yelped and tried to get away, but was held in place by the manacles.

"Rolf! My name is Rolf!" Rolf barked in place of the surrogate's voice, sweat beading his upper lip. His eyes were fixed on the crimson welt on the surrogate's left asscheek.

"Your name is Rolf *what*?" Mistress Alexis snapped, bringing the paddle's broad surface down on the surrogate's other cheek. Again the surprised yelp and shaking of shackles.

"My name is Rolf, *mistress*!" he rasped. This part always made him excited because it was the only part of the confession that was a lie. His name really *wasn't* Rolf. It was something far more prosaic. And recognizable. The Sisters knew who he really was—after all, he paid for his "therapy" with his platinum Visa—but had never called him on it. For what he was paying, he could call himself whatever he liked.

Alexis snapped her fingers—a mean feat for a woman wearing opera gloves—and motioned for Cissy and Meg to assist her. Meg snatched up one of the leather thongs and looped it around the surrogate's flaccid dick, just behind the head, then yanked it forward with a sharp jerk, stretching it like taffy. Cissy chose a thin birch rod and presented it, hand over wrist, to Mistress Alexis, who made a few experimental cuts with the rod, smiling tightly to herself as it sliced the air.

"Did you ever serve as a counselor for a place called Camp Tippecanoe?"

Rolf watched the bitch cut a whistling arc through the air, licking his lips in anticipation of the blow he knew was sure to follow. The smell of sweat and excitement was already making the room feel hotter and closer than it had mere minutes ago.

"Answer me when I talk to you, worm!" shrieked Mistress Alexis, bringing the cane down on the length of the surrogate's penis.

The surrogate's scream was muffled by the mask, but Rolf helped him give vent to his pain by collapsing to the floor, rolling around and clutching his groin as if he had just taken the blow himself.

"Yes! Yes! Yes! I was a counselor there for a couple of summers, when I was nineteen, twenty years old!''

Mistress Alexis continued to strike the surrogate, moving her attention from his crotch to his thighs and lower abdomen, leaving wicked-looking welts in her wake. Rolf groaned and wailed and clawed at the floor as if it were his flesh taking the punishment, not that of a faceless, nameless stranger. The surrogate jerked and thrashed and shouted for help, but he was held fast by the manacles and by Meg's secure grasp on the thong looped around his dick.

Obviously this evening's surrogate had not realized what he was getting himself into. All the better. Rolf preferred it when his stand-ins were "normal." He disliked the ones who were into S&M, or the rent-boys who were used to weathering the worst degradations. He always had the sneaking suspicion the professionals were faking it. But this one—this boy honestly didn't appreciate what was being done to him. It made it a lot easier for Rolf to project his own face onto the black leather where the boy's should have been. The pressure in Rolf's cock grew, lifting its plump, mushroom-shaped head upward.

Mistress Alexis turned away from the struggling youth and handed the birch—now dripping blood—to Cissy, who carefully cleaned its length with a hand towel and placed it back on the tray. Cissy glanced at Rolf as he squatted on the floor, right hand frantically stroking his chubby erection, her baby-doll lips pulling into a rosebud of a smile. She picked up one of the larger dildos—it was made of black plastic and fixed with a handle at the cock-base that made it look like an obscene popsicle—and stroked its hard length. In her tiny hands the artificial phallus looked even bigger.

Meg let go of the thong circling the surrogate's dick and went over to the cart, choosing one of the beeswax candles and a cigarette lighter. Rolf nodded, approving her selection. Good. Very good. Beeswax melts at a higher temperature than regular candles, which made it perfect for coercing confessions.

Mistress Alexis took the riding crop from the tray. "While you were a counselor at Camp Tippecanoe—did you ever do anything . . . bad?"

Rolf licked his lips. "I don't understand. Wh-what do you mean by 'bad,' mistress?"

Meg struck the wheel on the lighter and a multitude of flame jumped into existence in the mirrors. Rolf gasped and trembled, his skin tightening in anticipation of the burning kiss of candle wax.

"Don't get coy with me, you worthless excuse for a man!" Mistress Alexis snapped, striking the surrogate across the ribs with the riding crop. As the surrogate once more tried to escape the blows raining down on him, Cissy, crouching between his spread-eagled legs, rammed the dildo upward, spearing the boy like a fish. The surrogate's scream was fairly loud, albeit muted by the leather mask.

"I confess! I confess!" Rolf blubbered, his body seized with spasms of shame and pleasure. "I did it! I did it!"

"Did *what*, little man?" sneered Mistress Alexis, pointing to the surrogate's abused genitals. Meg nodded her understanding and began dribbling melting wax onto his exposed groin. The surrogate shrieked like a girl and began thrashing about even more intensely than before, making the manacles rattle and jingle like sleigh bells. "What did you *do*?"

Rolf pressed his fevered brow against the smooth concrete floor, his breath coming in great wheezing gasps. His guilt burned between his legs, as if smeared with molten wax. The need to confess his sins, to speak the unspeakable, was reaching its zenith.

The surrogate continued to jerk and whimper and

twitch as Meg dribbled hot wax into his armpits and onto his nipples and Cissy punched at his bowels.

"What did you do, Rolf? Tell me—tell Mistress Alexis what you did!"

"I—I—" Rolf wiped at the sweat dribbling down his balding head into his eyes. This part was always the hardest—and the most delicious. Decades of having kept silent, of hiding the truth away from everyone, had created a natural reticence on his part. Only the ritual of the interrogation could bring him to breach the ingrained wall of self-preservation and allow him to speak the truth—to admit to his crimes—only then could he attain the release of forgiveness—the spasm that signaled absolution and erased his sins in a spurt of jism and blood.

"Tell me!" Rolf flinched as the riding crop smacked against the surrogate's trembling flank. *"Tell me!"*

"I did things to children!"

The words leapt from his lips like pus from a wound. He could almost see them hovering in front of him— black, vile things, given life and substance by the simple act of speaking them aloud. Now that the unspeakable had finally been spoken, Rolf could feel his past pressing itself against his teeth. He had to confess, spill his guts, purge himself of the evil secrets boiling away in his gut and his balls.

"I took them to the boathouse on the lake. Usually at night. Sometimes during the day, when I knew no one would be around. But that was dangerous. But sometimes I couldn't wait. I had to do things to them right then."

Alexis's eyes narrowed, but she didn't look surprised; she nodded her head, as if Rolf had confirmed all her suspicions. "Did you do things to all the children you were in charge of?"

"No. Not all of them. That would have been dangerous. Most of the kids who came to Camp Tippecanoe were the sons and daughters of wealthy, upper-middle-class types. Doctors. Lawyers. I could have gotten into real trouble if I tried anything with them—even though I wanted to."

"If you didn't do anything to the doctors' and lawyers' kids—whose children did you do things to?"

"A couple of weeks out of the summer Tippecanoe would host kids from some inner-city orphanages. It was some kind of charity write-off for the people who owned the camp. Most of the kids were niggers or spics. Their parents—if they had any—were junkies or whores or dead. I told them that I was their friend. I told them I was the only one who really cared about what happened to them. I'd give them candy and let them ride the ponies if they didn't cry and acted like they liked it."

"How many children did you do things to, Rolf?"

"I can't remember. Thirty, I think. Maybe more."

"Did you just rape little girls? Or did you rape little boys, too?"

Rolf frowned. That wasn't one of the questions she was supposed to ask. And she wasn't supposed to use the word "rape." That was too harsh. Too close to the reality behind his version of the truth. He was taken aback by the vehemence in Mistress Alexis's voice as well. For a brief second he saw genuine hate blazing in her heavily mascaraed eyes. This derivation from the ritual was bringing him down.

"Stick to the script. I'm not paying you to do improv." He tried to make himself sound like he was in his boardroom, but it came out sounding whiny. It was hard to come across as authoritative while groveling naked on the floor and jerking off.

Mistress Alexis nodded her understanding, her professional ice-princess mask sliding back into place.

The rest of the session went on as scripted, with Mistress Alexis continuing her interrogation while Meg and Cissy assisted her by using the surrogate as an ashtray, snapping wooden clothespins onto his scrotum and pricking him with needles. Each punishment meted out to the hapless surrogate prompted more screams, wails and futile attempts at escape, while Rolf confessed in detail to the molestation of dozens of equally nameless, faceless children.

Rolf was close to the edge. Sweat was pouring off his body, dripping from his balls like beads of pee. His arm ached from pumping his swollen dick. He looked away from the naked youth suspended in the middle of the room to stare at the reflections of his own penis cast by the mirrors. He was surrounded by hundreds of throbbing, swelling, twitching erections, all of them his. The very thought made him smile.

"I'm ready. It's coming," he rasped through gritted teeth, staggering to his feet. He stroked his pecker as if he were trying to yank it off his body.

Cissy put down the cigar she'd been singeing the surrogate's armpit hair with and picked up the knife. Or, as Rolf thought of it, The Knife. The Knife was an old-fashioned stiletto with an ornate golden hilt. Only Rolf was allowed to use The Knife in these sessions.

Mistress Alexis was suddenly by his side, her painted lips whispering in his ear. It was the closest she had ever come to touching him in the six months he'd known her. "Are you sorry, Rolf? Are you honestly and truly sorry for your wrongdoings?"

"Yes." It was almost impossible to speak because of the tightness in his throat. Tears welled up in Rolf's eyes as he let go of his dick and turned The Knife over in his trembling hands. His groin throbbed, keeping time with the pulse pounding away in his temples. The black leather mask of the surrogate seemed to twist and blur, taking on familiar features. He blinked to clear his vision, but all it did was make the tears run down his cheeks.

"You are a sinner, Rolf." Mistress Alexis's words were cold and sharp, like a breeze off Antarctica. "The world's biggest sinner. And the wages of sin are—"

"Death!" Rolf shrieked, plunging The Knife into the surrogate's heart as he simultaneously squirted his seed across the helpless youth's thighs. Just as he'd done every Friday for the past six months. The orgasm was so powerful it made him dizzy and he fell into a swoon, dropping to his knees.

When his head cleared, moments later, he realized something was horribly wrong. For one thing, there was blood on his hands and on The Knife. That was impossible. The Knife was a trick blade, like the ones used in magic acts. He prodded the blood-smeared point, only to flinch as it pricked his index finger. The surrogate was still trussed to the restraining trapeze, blood oozing from a large stab wound in his chest. Rolf looked at The Knife and back at the body, hanging as slack and lifeless as a side of beef, and cast the weapon away from him with a cry of disgust.

Rolf got to his feet, his eyes bugging out with fear. He instinctively wiped the blood on his hands onto his thighs, then cringed. His eyes sought the mirrors for answers to the questions he did not dare speak, but all he saw was the surrogate's corpse again. And again. And again. Into infinity.

"Wh-what's going on here? Alexis—? Meg? Cissy?"

Suddenly Alexis was there behind him, her velvet-gloved fingers digging deep into the flab at the base of his neck. Rolf was surprised—and frightened—by how strong she was. She pushed him against the blood-smeared body, gripping him so tightly there was no way to look away from the dead man's leather-bound head.

"I realize we're rather off-script here, Rolf," Alexis sneered, her voice buzzing in his captive ear like a wasp waiting to land a sting. "But I thought you might like to know who your stand-in for tonight was. After all, he *did* give his all for you, didn't he?" Alexis motioned for Meg to unlace the hood covering the dead man's head.

The sound that came out of Rolf when he saw the face underneath the mask was not unlike the sound that the children he took to the boathouse used to make, twenty years ago. When he could finally summon the wit to speak, all he could say was, "Oh—God—" over and over.

The surrogate had indeed been young. Sixteen, in fact. Rolf knew exactly how old the dead boy was, because he was his son.

"He was pathetically easy to catch. Cissy had been following him for the last month or so, to find out which bars in the Village he went to with his friends and his fake ID, and where he liked to score dope. All it took was a little free ex—the promise of some poontang—and a little smack and chloral hydrate, and he was ours: signed, sealed and delivered. Or should I say he was *yours*?''

Rolf tried to tear himself away from Alexis's grip, but he could not break free. "You crazy bitch!" he sobbed. "Brad—What the hell did you do this for? Why? Why?!?"

"Come on, Rolf," snorted Meg, shaking chloroform onto an used jockstrap. "You're not a *complete* idiot! Why do you think? You've only been going on about it all fuckin' night!"

Before Rolf could respond, Meg clamped the jockstrap over his nose and mouth and everything went away.

For a while.

When he came back to his senses, it was to find himself dangling in the place of his son, Bradley. The heir apparent lay stretched out on the bare concrete floor like a beef carcass, his father's jism slowly drying on his cooling thigh. Rolf wanted to weep for his murdered offspring, but he was too frightened by his predicament to do more than whimper.

"So—you're back." Alexis grabbed Rolf's thinning hair and yanked on it so that he was forced to look into her face.

"Why?" was the only word he could croak out. All the others he might have used seemed to have fled. "Why?"

Alexis stared at him for a heartbeat, then laughed—although she did not move to strike him, the laugh was enough to make Rolf flinch. "You really haven't a clue, do you? After confessing to us week after week, after all this time—you still don't know *why* we'd do such a thing?"

"It—it was all a fantasy. Not real. I never did things . . . to those children . . .''

"I don't think you're telling me the truth—are you, Skeeter?"

Something cold and hard uncoiled inside Rolf's gut. He

stared at Alexis's face—harder than he ever had before. He wasn't looking at her as a man appraises a beautiful woman—this time he was trying to find something familiar in the shape of her lips, the cast of her nose, the tilt of her eyes, but without success.

"How—how did you know that was my name as a camp counselor? I never mentioned that in the script . . ."

"Oh, there's quite a lot we know about you, Rolf. Or should I say Mr. O'Brien? You see, we recognized *you* even though you didn't recognize *us*."

"What—what are you getting at?"

"You see, the reason Meg and Cissy and I call ourselves The Sisters is because we're orphans. Meg's mother was a whore. Cissy's was a junkie. Mine was a lush. She started drinking hard-core after my father, a Greek sailor, shipped out to Athens without us. She ended up falling down a flight of stairs in a blind drunk and breaking her neck. I ended up in the care of some inner-city orphanage, where I made friends with the other kids. But they were more than friends. They were my new family, my new sisters. Of course, our names weren't Meg, Cissy and Alexis back then. We took those names later—after I'd graduated from Hunter College with a bachelor's degree, specializing in the classics. You can't get a job worth shit with a liberal arts degree, so I ended up in the sex business. We decided to go into it together—work as a team, y'know? So we picked new names to go with our new lives. And we called ourselves The Sisters, in honor of a far more ancient trio known for their ability to mete out punishment—Alecto, Tisiphone and Megaera. But I'm rambling, aren't I? You want to know what our old names were, don't you? They were Penny, Elizabeth and Alex."

"Alex?"

Alexis smiled then, stepping back, unhooking the dog collar that circled her throat. "Like I said—it was a long time ago. Twenty years. You were only nineteen years old. Cissy was seven. Meg was eight." Alexis took the collar and tossed it at Rolf's manacled feet. "I was just nine years old. And still a boy."

Rolf stared at the Adam's apple that bobbed up and down as Alexis spoke. He shook his head and made another trapped-animal sound.

"You had me going there for a few seconds. I thought you'd caught on to us when I asked if you raped little boys." Alexis's tone of voice was almost conversational as she stripped off her opera gloves, revealing hands far larger and wider than a natural-born woman's.

Alexis stepped out of her panties, kicking them across the room with a practiced flick of her boot. Rolf had always wondered what Alexis kept in her panties, and now that he had his chance to know, he was almost afraid to look. Her genitals seemed female enough, but he imagined he could make out the telltale signs of plastic surgery.

"I thought you looked familiar the first time you came to the dungeon, but I wasn't sure. Meg and Cissy couldn't tell if it was really you or not, either. After all, it *was* two decades ago. Not that time has had an effect on our memories. None of us forgot the things you did to us—and made us do—in that boathouse, Skeeter. To this day I can't smell suntan oil without fighting a panic attack!"

Meg took up the story, twirling the key ring to the manacles on one index finger. "None of us ever imagined that you'd show back up in our lives. And we certainly never dreamed you'd turn out to be Michael O'Brien, the president of O'Brien Furniture. Imagine! Our Skeeter—a Fortune 500 executive! I wonder what *The Wall Street Journal* would say if they found out you were a serial child molester with a taste for sexual torture!"

Cissy reentered the room, trundling a new instrument tray in front of her. She had changed out of her baby-doll outfit and was wearing a pair of battered jeans, Doc Martens and a Danzig T-shirt. "When you started talking about the camp, that's when we knew it was you. You used a made-up name—'Camp Tippecanoe'; gimme a break!" She snorted derisively and rolled her eyes. "But we recognized you, Skeeter. Your sins identified you as surely as fingerprints!"

"There's no reason for you to do this," Rolf blubbered. "I'm sorry if I hurt you. But that was a long time ago.

I'm sorry for everything I did—you know that—''

"Bullshit!" snapped Cissy, all pretense at being a living baby doll dropped. "You're not sorry and you fuckin' know it! Thinking about fucking little kids gets you hard! You'd still be out there stuffing your fist up bald twats if you thought you could get away with it! But you're chicken! You're not sorry about a goddamned thing—confessing your sins while some poor bastard takes the rap for you is just a way for you to get your rocks off and keep your ass outta trouble!"

"No—you don't understand. I really *do* regret all those things I did. I really *do* want to atone for my sins! It's just that I'm weak. I was scared—"

"I bet you're scared!" Meg laughed humorlessly. "You're afraid of what would happen if people found out! You'd lose your rich-bitch socialite wife and your country house in New Hampshire and your overpriced furniture racket!"

"Enough!" Alexis held up her hand and the others fell silent. "We are beyond recrimination and explanation! There is only expiation!"

"Y-you're not going to get away with this," Rolf stammered, his eyes never leaving Alexis's hands as she dipped into a box of safety matches and retrieved a single sulfur-coated stick.

"Maybe yes. Maybe no." Alexis sighed, motioning for Meg to hold Rolf's limp penis so she could wedge the match into its piss-slit. "Now, Mr. O'Brien—or should I call you Rolf? Or do you prefer Skeeter? My sisters and I would like to know the number of the Swiss bank account you've been using to hide certain funds from the IRS . . ."

It wasn't until the weekend was over that anyone realized something was wrong. Daphne O'Brien, wife of furniture magnate Michael O'Brien, called the police in New Hampshire to file a missing-persons report on her sixteen-year-old son, Brad. He'd gone into Manhattan last Thursday to spend some time with friends attending NYU and had never returned. She'd tried to contact the boy's father, who was also in the city for the weekend, but had been unable to locate him. Not that that in itself was unusual. The senior O'Brien was often hard to track down on the weekends.

However, by the middle of the week Brad had yet to resurface and his father had not bothered to check in with his office. Family and police began to grow concerned, as O'Brien was known to be a workaholic. An APB was issued for Michael O'Brien's limo. It was found—several days later—on one of the Park 'n' Fly lots at JFK. The limo's driver—one Nathaniel Underhill—was found locked in the trunk. Although he was in a rather advanced state of decomposition, it was clear that his throat had been slit from ear to ear. A subsequent autopsy revealed that his stomach contained a considerable amount of cognac mixed with tincture of opium.

The newspapers—the *Post* in particular—worked themselves into a hysterical frenzy extrapolating on what might or might not have happened to the millionaire and his son. The FBI was called in and the O'Brien home phone was bugged in hopes of recording the ransom demand everyone was sure would follow. The silence was, at first, baffling, then quickly became ominous.

It was two weeks before the bodies were found, and only then because of a power shortage. A freak summer storm knocked out a portion of the city's power grid, plunging the West Village into darkness. The electricity was restored within a matter of hours. However, the industrial-strength air conditioner in the ''dungeon'' blew a fuse during the power surge and failed to come back on when the electricity was restored. A few days later the residents of a three-story brownstone began complaining of a foul smell emanating from the basement apartments. The police were summoned. And the mystery of what had become of Michael and Bradley O'Brien was answered, if far from solved.

The *Post* called it ''The Kinky Downtown Dungeon of Death.'' The cops found two badly decomposed corpses—both male, both nude—in one of the abandoned cubicles. One body was that of an older man, the other that of a youth in his mid-to-late teens. The older man was found chained to a restraining device, while the younger one lay slumped in a corner, a large dildo still wedged in his rotting rectum. It wasn't until the coroner checked the dental files that the NYPD realized they had the missing O'Brien father-and-son team on the slabs. Both showed blatant evidence of sexual torture, but it seemed as if the killer (or killers) had saved the worst stuff for the father.

According to the coroner's report (combined with physical evidence gleaned from instruments left at the crime scene), Michael O'Brien had been beaten with a leather bullwhip with fishhooks braided into the lash, systematically burned on the genitals and inner mouth with a small propane torch, scourged with a wire currycomb, subjected to needles rammed under his fingernails, given an enema with boiling water, and—to top it all off—had his eyelids sewn open. That last bit seemed particularly grisly in light of the fact that the death chamber was lined with mirrors, and also seemed to precede the other tortures. Bradley O'Brien had died of a single stab wound to the aorta. Death was instantaneous. Michael O'Brien had died of a massive heart attack, although not before enduring the torments listed above.

The police recovered a stiletto that proved to be the murder weapon used on the younger O'Brien. However, what puzzled them was how the only fingerprints they could find on the handle belonged to the father. The same held true for the smear of semen crusted on the boy's thigh. Upon learning these particulars, the *Post* worked itself into a hysterical froth: MISSING MILLIONAIRE IN S&M AFFAIR WITH OWN SON!

The tenants of the brownstone were questioned regarding the basement's residents. They all agreed that there had been three women living down there. Some thought they were sisters, but weren't exactly certain. They all agreed that strange men came and went at all hours, but hadn't really thought much about it, since they all looked rather respectable and wore suits. One neighbor thought they were relatives of the girls living downstairs, since most looked old enough to be uncles or grandfathers.

According to the real estate records, the lease had been signed by one Alexander Poppas. The FBI ran a search, but all they could come up with was a few juvie arrests for male prostitution in the early eighties. Apparently Poppas—then in his late teens—was saving up for gender reassignment surgery.

The only other evidence the police had been able to turn up at the murder scene was a stack of travel brochures. There seemed to be a number featuring Greece as the ideal holiday spot. Interpol was alerted, but whatever trail there might have been was long cold. To this date, the torture-murders of Michael O'Brien and his son and the slaying of his chauffeur, Nathaniel Underhill, remain unsolved.

Such is fate.

YOU HEAR WHAT BUDDY AND RAY DID?

John Shirley

John Shirley is the author of the horror novel *Wetbones* (Zeising, 1992), to name his personal favorite. He is also a screenwriter, having adapted *The Crow* for the movies, and is currently working on the adaptation of Blake Nelson's *Girl*. One of the founding fathers of cyberpunk, Shirley has worked in every genre from men's adventure to erotica to suspense thrillers. His label-defying short fiction can be found in the collections *Heatseeker* (1989, Scream Press), *New Noir* (1993, Black Ice) and the upcoming *Exploded Heart* (Eyeball Books). Yes, John Shirley's one bad mother—shut yo' mouth! Hey, I'm just talkin' about John Shirley, man.

What Ray does, sometimes, he runs low, he goes to those jerk-off parlors, those adult bookstores with the booths got the sticky floors, and he hangs out in there, at the corner of the little maze of videopeeps, pretending to be reading those glossy cards on each booth with the pictures of people fucking; those cards show you what video channel for "Virtual Tight" or for, maybe, "Mama's Enema Party" . . . Ray stands there real casual but watching everyone, till he sees the kind of guy who's maybe got a gold watch, real well fed, crocodile shirt, say Coke-bottle glasses—some guy that doesn't get any ass. So then Ray catches his eye, snags him into a booth, pretends he's gonna suck the guy's dick, but he just sort of plays with it, the dude's pants are down and loose around his ankles and Ray's on his knees coming out with the Hot Talk, all the time his free hand getting into the guy's back pocket, snagging that wallet, says excuse me, I'll be right back, you're makin' me so hot, don't move! Then he cruises on with the wallet . . . some guys—straight guys, usually— are really expert at this, usually black hetero junkies and crackheads get into that shit . . . Ray actually learned this because it had been done on *him* when he was just eighteen. Some black guy in a booth started playing with Ray's dick, but he was into Ray's wallet—a big five bucks— and Ray caught on and he said, "You're not ripping me off, motherfucker." And he grabs the guy, but this is a big black junkie and he *grabs Ray's dick and balls*, I'm tellin' you, man! He starts *twisting*, saying, "You fuck with me, you lose 'em," but Ray pries the junkie's fingers off his parts and the junkie bolts out of the place and he yells, "You follow me, you white faggot motherfucker, an' I'll knock you out!" So Ray finds himself standing there between the booths staring after this guy and he realizes his pants are down around his ankles and his dick is hanging out . . . but he thinks, That could work for me sometime.

*   *   *

Ray's standing on a Larkin Street corner, thinking it's too fucking cold out tonight, maybe he'll try the adult bookstores again. Sometimes he scores that way; other times he maybe only gets five bucks, or nothing at all. Of course, he could let somebody suck his dick for a ten or a twenty, but he just *likes it better* when he rips them off. It's not that getting his dick sucked by some geek really bothers him; it's that ripping them off feels especially *good.* But you could waste hours standing around in those places and the Task Force has been busting hustlers in the booths lately . . .

"Hey, Butch," Buddy says, coming up to Ray on the corner.

"Don't call me that unless you mean it," Ray says, "and you don't." He's only a quarter Latino, but he's got the rolled-up headband around his head, trying to get the action that wants a Latin Lover.

Buddy's from Texas, long and muscular, tan starting to fade, tattoos, really tight buns; he dances sometimes at the Polk Street Theatre San Francisco's Finest All Male Dancers, but he gets fired every so often for picking up tricks there. He was in some porn, too. Ray keeps trying to get into some porn, but generally he smells a little too ripe; he likes to get loaded and tends to end up sleeping on floors and in places with no showers. "I got somethin' for us," Buddy says. "There's this guy that saw me in one of those Marines movies, I was fucking some real butch Marine guy, he thinks I'm totally tough, but he wants to watch me with somebody else . . . you know, him watching and shit . . ."

All of this is, maybe, twenty-four hours before I came on the scene.

Turns out this guy is some kind of computer nerd, into the black-market hacker stuff, too—and he's got a head iron . . . Buddy knows what a head iron is, because his cousin went ill behind one . . . but he always wanted to try one . . .

The dude's place is one of those real nice Noe Valley

flats, restored Victorian building, shiny hardwood floors, antiques, modern art paintings, expensive PC with one of those screen-saver things wiggling around in tastefully iridescent fractal dancing ... first editions of Oscar Wilde ...

Trick's name is Charlie; Buddy never could stand a Charlie ... anybody who went by Charlie when they could be Charles or even Chuck ... Trick's about sixty pounds overweight, hair real short in the arty, almost bald thing, walks kind of pigeon-toed, real nice clothes, good material, gold lambda earlobe ring ... WHOA, IS THAT A ROLEX WATCH? Yes, it is, and no, it's not counterfeit. This is looking like potential.

They drink red wine and Ray asks the guy if he's got any cocaine. Charlie sort of leers and says cocaine makes you impotent, don't want you impotent. And some quote from Shakespeare about swords being blunted.

"Take off your pants so I know you're not a cop," Ray says to Charlie.

Buddy gives Ray a look. Oh, yeah, sure, like this lisping, pigeon-footed, Noe Valley fag is a cop. You fucking bet.

But later Buddy figures out that Ray doesn't think the guy is a cop at all; he's just Taking Over. Telling the guy what to do. Laying it down.

The guy has dated some hustlers, knows the laws, knows that a cop is not allowed to take off his pants—so he doesn't argue; he takes off his pants to show he's not Vice, folding the trousers and the underwear neatly on the arm of the antique velvet sofa.

His little dick, hiding under his round white belly, looks like a snail under a boulder that got scared and it's going back into the scrotum, back into the shell.

Well. Maybe it'd be fun to fuck him in the ass.

Buddy asks for the money once the pants are off, and Charlie has it all ready, a hundred cash, more later if everything is good. Fine for starts.

Ray is loading up on the wine. Get what he can while he's here. Ray did some time in Vacaville, see. He's looking around a little too much at all the carefully dusted objecks-dee-art—there's a lot of carved jade stuff that looks like it might be worth money—and Buddy says, "So what're you into?"

First, Charlie suggests, just make yourselves at home. Perhaps you'd like to take a shower . . . together . . .

He makes it sound like it's part of the partying for them to take a shower and him to watch, which maybe it is, but probably it's mostly because they stink.

So they take a shower, soap each other's dicks and asses for Charlie to watch, Charlie's fat little fingers working that snail, coaxing it halfway out of its shell.

Ray and Buddy never did sex together before, they've been mostly, like, friends on the corner, but they're pros by now and Buddy doesn't let his embarrassment show. He kind of likes playing with Ray after a while. Takes him back to a circle jerk when he was eleven.

Half hour later, they're wearing only towels, still a little damp, Charlie's aftershave burning-cold in their pits. Charlie has opened a second bottle of this expensive wine. *C'est très cher, mai . . .* he says. Seriously: he said that.

Charlie looks expectant, so Ray and Buddy drop the towels and start full-on going at it. The scene is bothering Buddy a little, so he's not really keeping it up very well, his ropy dick is drooping a bit, but it's enough for Charlie, who's standing by the bed watching like a dog at a dinner table, grinning conspiratorially, really getting into the fantasy . . .

Buddy starts to think, We're this trick's video game. It's more than live porn, it's not Ray in control after all, it's Charlie, taking them through levels in one of those games where you go down and down into some cavern hole, and ol' Charlie's going to win when he spurts his little dinger . . . then they can get the fuck out of here, go to Mary's and get a burger or something and laugh at this fat fuck . . .

So then Charlie starts getting into the game himself, moving them around like dolls, reaching between them to personally guide Buddy's dick into Ray's ass, stroking their asses while they go at it, putting Ray's hand on his snail—that's when Ray says, "You like to do B&D, anything like that?"

Charlie's eyes shine, but he's a little nervous about letting Ray tie him up, but Ray says, "We'll tie you down to the bed and we'll fuck *on top of you* like you're the mattress . . ." And this gets Charlie so excited he's shaking, but he gets jumpy when Ray starts to tie his hands to the bedposts with the old silk neckties, so Ray says, "I'll just tie it with a butterfly loop, not really tied, and you can pull it off when you want, Charlie."

He does tie the guy's left hand just like that, and Charlie's not looking as close when Ray ties the right hand—Ray puts an extra knot in it—and Buddy does the ankles, and then Charlie says, "Go to my dresser drawer, there's an instrument behind the socks . . ."

Ray and Buddy figure the "instrument" is a vibrator or a whip, but it turns out to be the head iron. It looks just like an old-fashioned barber's electric razor, the kind they use to shave the nape of your neck, and it probably is the shell of one, but it was taken apart and they put, like, *gizmos* inside it, and it's got duct tape holding it together now, and a little glass cone at the shaving end instead of the cutting pieces.

"This goes on your head, right?" Ray asks. He plugs the head iron in and starts to try it on Charlie, but Charlie pulls back real quick, says:

"No, no, wait, it must go to a precise spot, or it can have very nasty side effects . . . one loses control of one's bowels"—for real, this is just the way the guy talks—"or one may have a seizure . . ."

So Charlie has Ray hold a hand mirror over his head. Then he has Ray put a piece of tape on a certain spot on his head, stuck in that short hair. That's the spot where the head iron goes. Then he tells Ray to go ahead . . . Charlie licking his lips, breathing shallow, kind of scared and kind of excited . . .

Ray puts the glass cone of the iron on the tape over the fat guy's spot—forty-five-degree angle—and pushes the *on* switch, and there's a little hum and then the guy's eyes instantly dilate and he moans and he goes rigid and then

limp and then rigid and then limp . . . his dick getting hard
and soft, hard and soft, like when somebody mainlines
cocaine . . .

Well, of course, naturally Ray has to try this. Ray, understand, is the kind of guy who used to be into glue and
huffing fumes and *just any fucking thing*.

"Now," Charlie is saying, "now, fuck on top of
me . . . fuck . . . fuck me and fuck on top of me and fuck
each other on me . . . I'm your mattress, do it, fuck on
top of me . . ."

But Ray is ignoring him; he's finding the spot on his
own head. A couple of near misses—one time he starts
choking for a second—and then, boom, he hits the spot.
He gets it. Big ecstasy.

Ray starts trying to fuck Buddy just because he *wants*
to.

Buddy pushes him off at first, but then Ray finds the
spot on Buddy's head—he gets just the right spot on the
first try and he pushes the button and it's like a big wet
explosion of GOOD, just plain GOOD pouring out of him.
Like you shot him in the head and what came out wasn't
blood, it was GOOD.

"Oh fuuuu-*uuuuuuuck*!"

And now it feels good when Ray shoves into him—in
this stoned-out place Buddy's in, it'd feel good if you
shoved a claw hammer up his butt, claw first. They go at
it and they're tripping, they're into some other place,
some place that's all penetration and skin-flavored pleasure and waves of maleness that metamorphose into fe-
maleness—

But then it starts to fall apart, kind of fizzing into decay,
like an Alka-Seltzer tablet in water; like a flare on the
street, bright and then going black . . .

Buddy starts to imagine what it would be like if his old
man could see him with this guy's dick up his butt. His
guts crinkle up . . .

Then Charlie starts yelling he wants another hit, he
wants them to do what they said, and Ray gets up off
Buddy and suddenly both Ray and Buddy are feeling all
wasted and hollow, like they might collapse into them-

selves, like a cigarette ash that's perfectly shaped till you touch it . . .

And Buddy feels a kind of icy, gushing rage he never felt before, and he looks at Ray and he can see the same thing in Ray's face. Ray's saying, "Buddy, all the stuff in this place could be our stuff . . ."

Charlie really starts yelling when he hears that, but he can't get free from that extra knot on his wrist and then Ray is standing over him, making it louder and worse. "You want another hit, here's anothermotherfuckin'hit!" And he starts whacking Charlie around the face with the head iron, making scallop-shaped wounds in him, Charlie screaming and Buddy saying something about the neighbors calling the cops, so Ray stuffs several pairs of dirty socks and underwear in Charlie's mouth—Ray's and Buddy's socks and underwear—and Charlie's screams are muffled and Ray gets up on the bed yelling, "You want us on top of you?!" And he starts jumping onto Charlie, coming down on him with his knees, so Buddy can actually hear Charlie's ribs cracking under Ray's knee-caps . . .

Buddy's been doing all this to Charlie in his mind same time as Ray does it, it's just like he's doing it when Ray does it, so his rage comes in that way and froths over and after a moment he can think a little and he says, "You kill him, we don't get his ATM number, bro . . ."

Charlie doesn't want to give up his ATM's PIN number, but of course Ray gets it out of him, also makes him write a bunch of checks and show Ray and Buddy his bankbook. Whoaaaaaaa! Twenty fuckin' grand! Strong! Maybe later they could get him to liquidate some of his stocks and property and shit.

Ray gets so distracted using the corkscrew on Charlie to get the ATM PIN that he almost forgets about the head iron, and Buddy puts some big willpower on the line and hides the thing. He really wants to wreck it, because it scares him, it scares him to feel that high and scares him even worse to feel that *down* afterward, but he can't quite get himself to wreck it. So he puts the head iron in a trapdoor into the attic.

The attic entrance is in the same closet they put Charlie in, in the living room. Charlie's still alive. They figure they're gonna need him. They make Charlie crap a few times in the bathroom first, set up a bicycler's sipping bottle he could suck some water out of and tie him into a corner of the closet, really tie him good so he can't bang on the wall to get attention. He looks like he's in the middle of a spiderweb afterward, with that soft white rope they found under the bed, tying him to the hinges and the clothes-hanger pole. Ray wants to pee on the guy, but Buddy won't let him, saying he doesn't want the smell.

Then Ray asks about the head iron, but Buddy puts him off, says let's wait on that till the drugs run out.

"What fuckin' drugs?"

"Let's go to the ATM. See what we can get. Charlie ain't doing shit, tied up like one of those guys in a cannibal pot."

"I got your back, man."

First Ray and Buddy do some of Charlie's expensive mail-order crystallized vitamins—they know about rushes and crashes and how to deal with that—and they eat a steak from Charlie's fridge, so they feel some better. The head-iron crash eases out.

And what do they find in Charlie's bedside table? Three guesses. Right, a piece! A .38 revolver that looks like it's never been fired. One box of shells. This is just getting better and better.

Ray stays with Charlie—watching MTV and drinking—while Buddy goes to a check-cashing place with a check from Charlie for a grand. The place calls up for confirmation, and Ray has the portable phone jammed up against one of Charlie's ears and the pistol up against the other. Charlie *approves* that fuckin' check, *pronto*.

Then Ray meets Buddy on the street, by the check-cash place. They divvy a thousand from the check and three hundred from the ATM, and they go on a mission. After

midnight, they can get another three hundred dollars from
the ATM, and it's almost midnight.

"I still feel kind of weird from that head-iron shit,"
Ray says. "But, man, that was a fuckin' rush!"

"That thing, I don't trust that shit, we gotta forget that,
at least for now, dude. Let's get some good rock, some
good ronnie, maybe some pussy . . ."

"Pussy, yeah, now the man's got an idea," Ray says,
but Buddy doesn't quite believe it.

About half an hour after midnight, Buddy and Ray
come to me. That's right, me.

All they could find was street hubba, it seems, which
is pretty much shit cocaine.

"You know Miss Dragon, right?" Ray says. "We got
the money. You could get us the good stuff."

I correct him. "That's Dragon Miss, they call her."

Me, I'm terrified of cocaine. Turns me into a hit-
sucking bug faster'n a vice cop takes a bag. Then I'm
gone for a couple of days on a run and I run the wheels
off that fucker and then I turn paranoid, which is maybe
how . . .

Well, it's one way people get killed.

So I stick to hashish—which I get from the Dragon
Miss—maybe sometimes opium, always some cognac or
Johnnie Walker Red. Speed if I need it. And so many
vitamins I smell like 'em.

Maybe what I most get off on is the second-story work.
One time I popped into this guy's apartment, he's sleeping
in the same room, snoring like a chain saw, and there's a
wallet on the nightstand, and I snag the wallet and flip it
open in the light by the window and see there's a *fucking
badge* in the wallet—the guy is a cop. I look over at him
and he's still sawing logs, but now I see on the other
nightstand there's a fucking .44 lying there like a chunk
of pure silver. *This is a cop's bedroom and he's got a
loaded .44 next to him and I've got his fucking wallet in
my hand!* Now, *that's* a rush!

I took the .44 and the wallet and I took a beer from his
fridge, too.

I used to be a writer, one time, plays and journalism. I even did a feature for *Esquire* once. I used to do those readings at coffeehouses that are so chic now, everybody playing beatnik. But then I got into the coke binges, and Louisa . . .

Well, they found her dead.

And after that, I had to live different. I don't know how to explain better than that. I couldn't go back to writing, but I couldn't be a basehead neither.

But I understand Buddy pretty well. I've known him a shitload of years. On Tenderloin time, anyway. Four years is a long time to know somebody in the Tenderloin.

So I get Buddy talking about what he and Ray did; he's like a free-association machine after he takes a hit on the shitty hubba. During the story Buddy's telling me, Ray is in the bathroom, jerking off by the sound of it. *Whuppawhuppawhuppa*. Some people when they do cocaine, they can't keep their hands off their dicks, which is funny because their dicks don't usually perform for them anymore.

Then Ray comes out of my bathroom looking uglies at Buddy, and Buddy takes the hint and shuts up, and to defuse the situation and just to follow this street and see where it comes out, I tell them, "Let's go see if the Dragon Miss wants your money."

Like I thought: turns out Dragon Miss wants to see this apartment full of antiques and art tchotchkes, and the guy tied up in the closet. "It sounds like just the *best* party, girls . . . if we can keep the Big Tummies out." She thinks it's cute to call the local cops Big Tummies.

"Neighbors are off on vacation or somethin', nobody gonna call the cops," Ray tells her. "What about the rock?"

She pauses in the doorway of her Japanese-decorated place, framed by the silk hangings, an ancient kendo sword mounted over her head. She's got a long face and eyes like a husky's, and cushy lips. Of course, she's got the big hands and the Adam's apple. One more thing about her eyes, they look startled all the time, like she's surprised by everything, even when she plans it down to dotting the *i*. She talks in that cute, surprised way while she puts a 9mm round in the back of your head.

Now she lets her green-and-gold dragon-figured kimono hang open so we can see both her big silicon tits and her surprisingly large dick. The joint effect, so to speak, always gives me a woodie.

She's got this rich Japanese Houseboy, president of a major airline corp by day, could hire five servants to do the housework—but when he gets out of that limo, his whole style changes on the flight up those carpeted stairs and he comes in with his eyes down and *begs* to be allowed to clean Dragon Missy's toilet. To lovingly arrange her shoes in her closet; to deliver her female hormone pills and cocaine on an antique ivory salver in the morning; to bring her the Xanax and Halcion at night. Waits on her hand and foot, and for his reward she beats his ass. One time I was visiting at the condo he gave her, and since he was going into the kitchen I asked him to take my glass for me and refill it and he said, big outrage, "What, you think I am homosexual?!"

Some phone calls and a cab and bang, we're over at this trick Charlie's house.

"My *goodness*," Dragon Miss says, hanging up her coat, "there's a *man* in the closet!" For a moment there's a flicker of hope in Charlie's eyes (and a flicker of feeling for him in me . . . just a flicker), but then Dragon Miss hangs up her coat in the same closet, well out of his reach, and, humming a show tune, closes the closet door.

Feet up under her as she sits on the couch like it's hers, Dragon Miss counts the money Ray and Buddy give her, lays out the fine cocaine on the glass-topped coffee table, the flaky chopped-from-rocks stuff that they only dream about on the street. Like a lady putting out the tea things, she sets up the little propane torch, the ether, the baking soda solution, the glass pipe for real freebasing, none of that piss-doorway rockhead bullshit. She puts on a CD of Mozart's *Requiem*. Maybe for Charlie, though he's still alive. Buddy and Ray would rather have the Pet Shop

Boys, but there's been a shift in polarity and Dragon Miss is in charge. Maybe I should mention that the Houseboy carries a gun. That's two guns now.

I distract myself from the cocaine prep by looking over the window locks, strategically unlocking a few, shutting off the alarms, mentally totting up the fence value of some of the smaller antiques and the old English silver.

We check on Charlie and his leg looks gangrenous. It's his right leg, maybe to do with the corkscrew wound, maybe it's the circulation being cut off, maybe both. He's feverish, squirming in his sweat and stink in the closet (Dragon Miss makes a come-out-of-the-closet joke); he's not quite there, but he mutters some stuff I hear when I'm squatting by him, and some of it makes me sick and some of it makes me flash on ideas.

I'm belting some Johnnie Walker and tripping on how this Charlie's dying and how I don't feel much about it, and how the Japanese houseboy does feel something but it's just fear, and how we're standing around the closet making fun—the others are sucking on the pipe—and it's like that Max Ernst painting of the demons chewing at St. Anthony, and now I'm one of the demons, and I don't remember becoming one. I'm tripping on it, but all the time I'm thinking what I can score on all this.

So then Dragon Miss's friends show up and one of them has royally fucked up: Berenson, this big black guy, has brought a bunch of whores with him, two black, two white, one maybe Filipino, and some stoned-out white asshole he met in a sex club who's got a lot of dope money on him. Berenson, funny thing is, gets actual money from the State of California to run a prostitutes' rehabilitation center—and of course he just keeps the money because the guy's a fuckin' pimp! He lays into those bitches with a belt, too. They seem to like it. I can't watch that shit.

I never once hit Louisa.

So all these animals are dancing in the living room, breaking the furniture, putting Charlie's smaller stuff in their purses and going through his medicine cabinets and

his liquor cabinets and his shoe rack, then checking out
his suits, some pretty expensive suits to sell, and they keep
coming back to suck on the glass pipes—there's four
pipes going now—and sometimes they go to the closet
and they kind of *fuck with* Charlie, just sort of . . . *fuck
with him*. He's EveryTrick to them, I guess, and they're
getting theirs now. Everybody debates about the best way
to drain Charlie's bank account without pulling down too
much attention. The air is in layers of smoke, it's got its
own ionospheres and tropospheres, and now somebody's
got the rap station on the stereo—so far Dragon Miss has
kept them from taking the stereo out, which is just common sense—and the Houseboy is looking *really pale and
nervous*. One of the whores is working on Berenson's
dick, licking his balls, too, and Berenson's willie is half
erect and it's going up, up, slowly, like it's being slowly
lifted on a crane, and another whore is on her knees in
front of a chair with her head under her girlfriend's skirt,
licking pussy, and Ray is kind of listlessly fucking a long,
skinny white girl with one pump on and the other skinny
silver-toenail foot bare and her underwear around an ankle, they're doing it on the rug in front of Charlie's closet,
Ray yelling at Charlie to look! look at this, Charlie, but
Charlie can't see outside his sick haze.

The doorbell rings and some transsexual prostitutes
who work for Dragon Miss come in, so shrill you can
hear them over the rap and the laughter, like the high-
pitched, whining noisemakers that cut through the bangs
and drums of a Chinese New Year's parade. They ooze
into the room like they're coming down the runway on
the lip-sync stage, invisible microphones in their hands,
three of them in pounds of makeup competing for attention. The glass pipes get most of the attention. But these
TV whores have got some ronnie with them, brown crystal heroin, and I manage to get a line of that. It puts my
head in order so I'm thinking priorities again.

Buddy is in the corner in a real nice chair, looking kind
of shrunken in on himself, maybe crashing from cocaine
and starting to see consequences in his mind's eye, look-

ing like he's going to panic. I give him the bottle of Johnnie Walker.

Ray is bringing out the head iron. "Y'all ever try this shit?"

I trip on the head-iron thing. It's got the heft of a small electric drill. It's like electronic brain drilling, I'm thinking. I'm tempted, but it still scares me. The smell of the vaporized cocaine in the air is tugging at me, and I know I'll never get to business if I get started with cocaine or head irons. I'm feeling rounded out and pleasantly heavy in the dick from the heroin and only a little nauseated. I wonder if Charlie's dead.

Buddy is trying to talk Ray into getting rid of the head iron, but it's too late, the TS whores are already squealing around it, practically spinning on their spike heels to try it . . . the whole feel of the scene is changing around this head iron . . . it's putting a weird off-buzz in the air that's like one of those freak waves you hear about that smashes boats . . . The Dragon Miss frowns at the head iron.

"I don't trust those things, I've heard stories, they are not sympatico with working girls . . ." she says.

But Ray has already done a head-iron hit and is reeling in waves of glory, and the paleness of his rage rises in him and he snarls something at her I can't hear, something about fake fag-bitches, and the Houseboy pulls his gun and Ray pulls *his* gun and Dragon Miss sees that and decides the polarity can shift for a while, and she pushes Houseboy's gun down, tells him to put it away and signals one of the girls. The girl's so fucked up she doesn't even seem to see Ray's gun and she starts playing with his dick, so he lowers the gun but doesn't put it away . . . The head iron starts to get passed around to everybody . . . Dragon Miss looks more startled than ever . . .

One of the queens is giggling on the phone. "You hear what Buddy and Ray did?" So now the thing's leaking at the seams.

I expect Dragon Miss is going to fuck Buddy or one of the younger guys here—I'm old enough to have damage from the New York Dolls—but she takes me by the hand and we go into the biggest bathroom, lock the door. The Houseboy sees this and writhes with jealousy, you can see it in his face. So much for fucking Oriental inscrutability. He doesn't do anything about it—me fucking his mistress right in the next room is more humiliation, which is what he's paying her for, so it all works out.

Till now, Dragon Miss's been watching everybody else's sex in a kind of preparation voyeurism. Now she's ready and probably figures I'm the one most likely to get a hard-on that'll stay, because I've been avoiding the C.

Bathroom's trashed because they've been in here going through it looking for drugs and anything salable. But we clear the junk from the floor and lay down some towels. She's been on the pipe for about an hour, plus did a line or two of the ronnie, so she's as wet as a pretend girl can get.

We do some things with the shower, both kinds. She jets out her ass, and she's a little apologetic when she asks me to pee on her in the tub. But she gets tired of being a dominatrix all the time for the Houseboy. Being a mistress is kind of fun, she says. But.

Then we get down to some serious business. I turn her facedown, I'm taking a drive through her ass, which could be mistaken for a female one, all right, maybe because of the hormone pills, and she's playing with her dick while I jam it to her, and twist one of her arms behind her back and whisper that she's a dirty slut; all of this by request, and it works for me, too. It's like when I fuck a she-male, two parts of me that are usually insulated flood together for a while and that feels good.

I'm careful with her tits, because they're silicon. I cup them gently and do a kind of suction with my palm on the nipple, and this gets her off. She can't come out of her dick, which only gets about two-thirds hard, but there's another kind of orgasm she-males can get, and about the time my knees are getting sore she flaps around in it, like a baby seal getting its head knocked in.

So I let go, and come, too.

Coming, I feel something in me loosen up, and I think about Louisa the night before they found her.

We were on the roof of her place, September evening, having a tar beach picnic, and I'm trying to zing the pigeons with pieces of a broken Mad Dog bottle somebody left, and she's telling me I should call my brother. I feel like her face is prettier and more real in that second because of what she wants me to do; it makes me feel like she maybe really does give a shit, because she wants me to call Dougie and tell him it's okay, that I forgive him for ripping me off, that's what junkies do and I understand that . . .

I can't do that, but I feel, for a moment, like maybe some of us are going to be all right . . . *"You got to be part of somebody or you nobody,"* she says. *"You not even real if you can't feel."*

It rhymes; she's pleased with that. "Stop throwing shit at the pigeons," she says. I kiss the back of her neck and cup her tits and she leans back against me . . .

But now Dragon Miss tells me to wash my dick and go out into the living room with her, it sounds like they're really going off out there, she's got to see how Houseboy's doing . . .

After we we go back out, the whole scene has changed again. The off-buzz saturates the place. The walls are screaming, there's a kind of peak to the noise and tension, two or three arguments going at once, and they're wrestling over the head iron. Two of them, no, shit, *three* of them now, actually fighting, hitting, scratching for the head iron.

Looking around now, I start to get seriously scared, because I can see everyone's been doing the head iron, *even the Houseboy.* And now there's three guns in view—Berenson's got his out, he's yelling at the Houseboy, and the Houseboy's Japanese skull's showing through the skin of his face with all his straining to control himself, but I can see he's going to lose it. The white asshole Berenson brought is out cold in the corner with his head in a puddle of blood. His wallet's lying next to him like a gutted fish.

Then I see a black whore in a skewed blond wig snag the head iron, because someone dropped it in the fight, and she's got the closet open and she's shoving the head iron against Charlie's head more or less at random, laughing, randomly stimming what's left of his brain, and he's foaming at the mouth and shitting himself and actually breaking some of the ropes with a really gone-off rage and she's laughing and slapping him with the iron, but she puts her hand too near his mouth and Charlie takes off three of her fingers, just as neat as a metal-shop tool, snipping them off with his teeth, and she screams and Berenson—nude, muscular but for that potbelly—Berenson, he sees what Charlie's done and he points the gun and really shakes with relief as he lets go: shoots Charlie four or five times, and the Houseboy gets mad because Berenson's fucking with one of Dragon Miss's assets and he starts shooting Berenson—

Buddy and I make eye contact and we both slide fast into the bedroom. The two other people in the bedroom are out cold, no, wait, one of them is out cold and the other one is dead, looks like a heart attack—and I shout at Buddy over the noise from the next room, the shooting and screaming; and we tip over an antique armoire so it jams the door shut and then we take care of our own business, but I hear the Dragon Miss stuck on the other side screaming for me to open the door, open it, they're going to, they're going to, but then bullet holes punch through the door behind the armoire and her blood comes through; along with her blood comes her scent, her perfume, right through the door . . .

It's the head iron, the glory and the insane rage and misery that come when you use it; with that thing it's like you get a lifetime of sin in one blast and then you go straight to Hell, do not pass Go, all in one minute.

And the head iron's stirring that room up like blender blades, we can hear it, screaming and laughing and crying in there, Ray thumping on the door now, Buddy crying because he wants to help Ray; he tries to move the armoire, but I won't let him, because they'll all come in with Ray then, and anyway, I've already made the phone call to 911. Meaning we got to *get out*.

So I have to half drag Buddy out the window to the fire escape and up to the roof, and as we go we get a diagonal glimpse through the window of the living room: there's Ray with Berenson and two whores, the three of them kicking Ray, who's probably already dead, but they're kicking him, kicking him, Berenson's dick wagging with every kick . . .

A little later we're driving a stolen car, just about a block away, when the sirens start wailing. I have to laugh. Buddy starts crying again.

What Charlie whispered when I almost felt something for him was what was in the false top of the armoire. It was a locked metal box. I guess Charlie was trying to make a deal . . .

The dead guy in the bedroom had a BMW key chain and there were only two Beamers on the street.

So next morning, really burned out, me and Buddy, we're at a rest stop halfway to Las Vegas, standing behind the maroon BMW, its trunk gaping, using a tire iron on the box. Takes us twenty minutes more to finally get the metal box open . . .

The box contains less than I hoped for but more than I expected. About thirty grand in cash total and about ten in loose diamonds. What about safe-deposit boxes, Charlie? Probably had one. But he was one of those guys who liked to keep some close.

Me and Buddy are doing okay. Cabo San Lucas has a full-on *scene*.

I'm trying to feel those other things again. It helps to think about Louisa. *You got to be part of somebody or you nobody.* I was just so loaded that night. I can't remember. I *can't remember*. I try, for her, but I can't remember: I don't know if I was the one who killed her or not.

PLAYING DOLLS

Melissa Mia Hall and Douglas E. Winter

Melissa Mia Hall's short fiction has appeared in such anthologies as *Whisper of Blood, Skin of the Soul, Dead End: City Limits* and *Masques 3*. She is a freelance journalist and photographer whose work has appeared in publications as diverse as *Disney Adventures, Crime Beat, The Bloomsbury Review* and *Amazing*. This is her second collaborative effort with Douglas Winter, the first being the 1989 short story "The Happy Family." A native of Fort Worth, Texas, Hall is decidedly single and is believed to use Colgate toothpaste and have a blind dog and a paranoid cat. She also states that she likes to pretend she's French.

Douglas E. Winter was born in 1950 in St. Louis, Missouri, and has since gone on to become a partner in the internationally based law firm of Bryan Cave and the author or editor of nine books, including *Stephen King: The Art of Darkness, Faces of Fear* and *Prime Evil*. He has published more than 200 articles and short stories in such diverse markets as *The Washington Post, The Cleveland Plain Dealer, The Book of the Dead, Harper's Bazaar, Cemetery Dance, Saturday Review, Gallery, Twilight Zone* and *Video Watchdog*. He is a winner of the World Fantasy Award and has been nominated for the Hugo and Stoker. A member of the National Book Critics Circle, his forthcoming projects include a critical biography of Clive Barker and an epic anthology of apocalyptic fiction entitled *Millennium*. Doug makes his home in the suburban splendor surrounding our nation's capital with his lovely wife, Lynne, and their differently abled Pekingese, Happy and Lucky. This is his second collaborative effort with Ms. Hall.

Laurie waits for the next word to hit, but the walls are thick around her. That's why she left her bedroom door open. So maybe she can hear them fight. Then they'd be normal, like other parents.

"Girl, your parents are so nice. I mean, they're like so nice they're from another planet. You know what I mean? Nice." That's what Mary Dawn Carlisle said the other night. Right after dinner. Cream of asparagus soup. Standing rib roast. Green bean casserole and twice-baked potatoes. Iced tea in crystal stemmed glasses. Linen napkins. It was Laurie's fifteenth birthday. She didn't want a party, just Mary Dawn over to spend the night, a compact disc player, gift certificates from Sound Warehouse, Neiman's and Saks. It didn't really matter, turning fifteen. Two years ago she had this incredible party, a boy-girl party, and everyone came. But it was awful. Being thirteen and not looking any different. Nothing had changed. Nothing changes. Or you don't see it happen. Like now. Like they are right down the hall and there's nothing happening, but there's something going to happen.

Laurie gets out of bed and tiptoes toward the door. There's still that stupid silence from the hallway. But she knows they're out there. Rob's probably dead asleep and can't hear a thing. And even if he could, he wouldn't care. She holds a breath and lets it out slowly. Her fingers circle the doorknob. It's cold. She opens the door a little bit more.

"You're drunk," Mother says in her know-it-all voice, silky-smooth and sensible.

"I had two martinis. Two." He answers in his let's-get-the-facts-straight voice.

Yell at her, Daddy. It'd be great if they were drunk, both of them. It's gotten almost fashionable to be a child of alcoholics. Laurie bites her tongue. Literally. It's nothing to joke about. It's wrong. She's wrong. When she sticks her tongue out all the way, she can see a tiny drop of blood on the tip. Fascinating.

"She drove the car to the mall, for Christ's sake. I'm supposed to be happy about that? You're her mother—"

"I didn't give her permission."

"What if she'd had a wreck?" Daddy's voice sounds a little less reasonable now.

"She won't do it again."

"She's been playing around with Chad too much," he says. "Chad." It's like there's something wrong with his voice.

"She's only fifteen, Walter. You can't have it both ways. Do you want her to grow up or not? Besides, you've always liked Chad. He's been good for her, you know that. He really has." Mom's voice is still silky-soft, but the sensible side is becoming a little strained. She sounds tired.

"She is fifteen, Rachel. That's the point."

"Are we talking sex here? Is that it? Is that really it?"

"Well, are we?"

"You tell me."

"Have you talked to her about it?"

"Have you?"

There is a gasp, the sound of the freezer exhaling cold breath into the kitchen. Ice cubes rattling into a glass.

"Look—" They've seen the open door to her bedroom. They know she's listening. They know. Laurie can't help smiling in wonder.

"She's your daughter."

"Right. You talk to her. I've tried. Do you think she listens to me?"

Silence. Then she can hear the gin. *Splish-splash.* Next it'll be the olives. Three of them. He likes lots of olives when he drinks.

"All the way to Lakeside Mall?"

The keys to the car were just there. Right there on the counter, where Mom always leaves them. Rob has his own car. And a license. Laurie doesn't. But she's a good driver. Rob taught her when she was ten. Everybody knows that. The keys to the car were just there and Mom had had one of those migraine headaches that send her to bed for hours. Laurie didn't think that she'd mind. If she ever found out. And anyway, she was home before dark, wasn't she?

It was fun.

Footsteps. Heavy ones.

Daddy.

Laurie jumps back into bed, draws the coverlet over her face. Bunny Bear's pink fur tickles her cheek. She looks almost like a child again. When he sees her like this, Daddy won't be mad. No way. Daddy's never really mad, anyway, not with her. But maybe, maybe, he could be. He might be.

"Laurie Lou!" He's calling her by the old name. The baby name. Suddenly Laurie wants to suck her thumb, to curl up in his lap. Instead she huddles under the covers, pretending to be asleep. "Honey? It's Daddy—I know you're awake. Get up a second, sweetheart, and talk to me. Okay? Hon?"

Daddy's sitting right next to her, on the edge of the bed. "C'mon, sweetie." Laurie throws herself into his arms.

" 'Night, Daddy."

"Laurie?" He smells like a Christmas tree. Those martinis are gross. "Is there something you ought to tell me?"

She has to say yes. She has to think fast. Daddy sounds scared. He brushes a lock of hair from her face and looks at her closely. He thinks there's something more. That there has to be something more. Laurie slips out of his arms. She picks up her foolish Bunny Bear, a fuzzy-wuzzy bear with bunny ears that she has had for so many years, and that she loves so much. She presses down on its black button eyes.

"Yes, Daddy." She looks up at him through eyes half closed, and he sucks in a judicial breath and readies himself.

Laurie can tell that he expects something really bad, something just . . . awful. It amazes her. She's been so good, forever and ever good. She makes almost straight A's, just a couple of B's and that one C in Earth Science, for goodness' sake. Compared with Rob, his horrendous report cards and his detentions, she's a saint. Terrific. And she never does anything bad. Really bad. One time she told Paula Smith that the whole fourth-grade class hated her. But she apologized the next day. One time she pulled the cat's tail so hard that it screamed out in pain. And maybe, once, she cheated on a math quiz and stole a lipstick from Eckerd's Drugstore.

"Well . . ." She holds Bunny Bear like a long-lost friend. "It's Chad and me."

Daddy's face is suddenly red. He leans forward. His hand is hot against her face.

Chad's her best friend in the whole wide world, next to Mary Dawn. But he's a boy. She's pushed the right button. That's what he wanted to hear. He's getting angry, she thinks. Very angry. Or . . . Laurie sends a mental prayer up to God or whoever's up there in the sky over the roof. Thanksgiving.

Daddy's fingers are against her lips. Shhh. Go slowly. She feels his breath upon her cheek.

"What, precious? What did you—"

What did I do? Laurie knows that she did not do anything. She's making a sacrifice. She's giving up Chad. For Daddy.

"I let him . . . You know, I let him—"

Daddy's hands cover his face, pull at his eyes. Laurie

loves his hands. His fingernails are clean, but they're not
sissy hands. They're good hands. Strong.

"I wanted to, Daddy. I mean, I'm old enough—"

A sigh. "Old enough for what?"

Laurie's lying. Chad's kissed her a couple of times,
done a little feeling and fooling around, but he's never
pressed for more. They're too scared. All that AIDS stuff.
Babies. They've even talked about it, talked about waiting
until they're eighteen to have sex, not just with each other,
but with anyone. It's too much trouble. They've both
agreed. And now she's lying. Betraying Chad. Laurie
can't believe her mouth. She can't believe the words that
are coming out of her.

"I . . . wanted it, Daddy. He wanted it, too. We made
love. I'm not a virgin anymore, Daddy." Was she crying?
Was she doing this right? Her mother had been a virgin
until she was twenty-one. Strange but true stories. So
maybe Mom's a liar, too.

Daddy keeps hiding his face. Laurie feels a sudden excitement. She's living in a movie, and she wrote the script.
She almost believes that she and Chad actually did it. Did
not. Did, too.

"Right here, in this bed. We didn't do it in the car or
anything. We smoke, too." That's pushing. Laurie hates
cigarettes. "And you know what? It was so . . . you know,
special. But don't worry, Daddy, he used a condom. We
know all about safe sex. From school. Don't worry."

Daddy's silent. But he's not mad. Laurie bites one of
Bunny Bear's ears.

He gets up and leaves. Without saying a word.

Laurie's green eyes are wilting. She can see them in
the mirror, shriveling into little slits. Tears spill over, but
she can't cry out loud. Not now. He's not angry, not surprised. Speechless. Tired. But not angry.

She has broken Daddy's heart.

She waits for about an hour, thinking that he'll come
back, or send Mother in. Something should happen, something monumental, dramatic.

Poor Chad. Everyone loves him, even Rob. He's so
nice, wild brown hair, sky-blue eyes, long basketball legs.

Laurie sighs and turns off her bedside lamp. "We're talking major disaster here," she whispers to Bunny Bear. "Earthquake. Typhoon. Tornado."

Then she hears the laughter. Her parents' laughter.

"Good morning."

"Hi." Laurie ducks her head and sits down in front of her place mat. Half of a ruby-red grapefruit is waiting. She eats the cherry perched in the middle and avoids her mother's eyes.

"So I heard that you and Dad had a talk last night." Mom empties a packet of Equal into her coffee and stirs it carefully. She smiles at Laurie, a sweet smile, but it's not sugar. Nutrasweet, maybe. An Equal smile. Bitch.

"Has he left already?" Of course he's left already. Lawyerman always leaves at the crack of dawn. He never eats breakfast. God forbid that Mr. G.Q. Esquire should ever gain a pound.

Rob breezes in to drink a half quart of milk and grab a bran muffin. "Hurry up, Red. I'm leaving in five minutes. El Pronto, babe—got it?—if you're riding with me—"

"Rob, she'll be ready," Mother says, tapping her long and manicured nails against the white coffee mug. "But right now—"

"I'll be ready," Laurie says. The script's going to have to be rewritten. She toys with her grapefruit, nibbles at a spoonful.

"Okay—" Rob disappears, leaving a trail of muffin crumbs in his wake.

The moment of silence. Then it begins.

"So, Lauren Louise. What about this story you fed Dad last night?"

"What about it?"

Laurie's blushing again and hates knowing how the pink bleeds into the red of her hair. She hates her mother's eyes watching her with such brittle amusement. Like at any moment she might start laughing. But it's not funny. Not at all.

"So—" Another moment of silence. "What do you think about it?"

"I don't have to think," Laurie says. "I don't have to do anything. Except die, I guess." Laurie puts her spoon down and looks around for her book bag. She stands up and presses her fingers flat against the cool oaken table. "So now you tell me what you think. I'm going to have to hear it sooner or later, right?"

"You don't expect us to believe that story. What you said about Chad."

"About Chad? What does that mean? You don't think he'd want to have sex with me?" She tries to control the shiver that stirs in her shoulders. "What's the matter, isn't he good enough for me? Or wait, no, I've got it . . . I'm not good enough for him, right?"

"Laurie, calm down." Her mother is standing. "This is ridiculous!"

"Ha! Yeah, you got it. You know what? You're warped, out there in orbit city if you think it didn't happen. It did happen, and you guys can laugh all you want . . . or just say no . . . but it won't change what happened." That's good; that's real good. "It happened." What a movie.

Laurie takes a shaky breath. Rob's standing at the doorway, gawking at both of them. That is what inspires her.

"And you know what else? I liked it. I did. We're going to do it again. And again. Maybe I'll get pregnant."

"Honey." Mother almost knocks her chair over. Wow. "That's not funny. Please calm down, okay? Let's get realistic. You and I both know what a good little girl you are. Why are you insisting on acting so . . . so childish? Isn't she acting childish, Robert?" Mom looks around for her son, but he's skipped out. In the car, no doubt, pretending to listen to the radio. She heaves a melancholy sigh and gives Laurie another smile. No Equal there. This time it's almost real.

"Tell you what. Let me take you to see Dr. Mossi. We'll get you some birth control pills. I've heard they do wonders for blemishes. But listen—"

Oh, my God, she was going to hug her.

"That doesn't mean that Daddy or I approve of you—"

Hauling her in like a puppy with those red fingernails and smokescreen of Le Must de Cartier. "It's not Chad. It's anyone. You're really too young, honey. It's just not—"

Then she holds her at arm's length. "But we are going to get you that learner's permit, and, when you're sixteen, a car. I told Walter this would happen. Sibling rivalry." The hand, smoothing her hair, petting the puppy. "You're just crying out for attention, honey. And I'm sorry that—"

She moves closer to Laurie. Laurie moves away.

"You don't believe me. You think I'm a liar."

"Oh, precious." Her mother pursues her, the long-nailed hands reaching, reaching for her.

"Get away from me. God, oh, God—" She slides her book bag from the counter. Closer to the door.

"Laurie!" Rob's voice, punctuated once, twice, by the beeping horn of the Volvo. For once, Laurie loves him more than anyone else in the world.

"I'm late," she says.

Her mother's hands, emptied, turn slowly in the air. "We'll talk about this later. Okay, sweetheart? Later."

"I'm out of here," Laurie answers, beneath her breath. Mom smiles at the air to the left of Laurie's ear. The smile wrinkles until the lines around her eyes are deep and dark.

Laurie's back hits the locker. The door handle jabs into her white Benetton sweater. Students grumble by, pushing and shoving their way to the next class. Rob's arm encircles her. He won't let go.

"Talk to me, dipshit. You've been avoiding me all day. What's going on?"

"Nothing."

"Stop pouting. I know I said you look like Molly Ringwald when you do that, but I'm sick of it, okay?"

"Can we talk about it tonight?"

"I was going to—"

"The game, I know, the basketball game. But—"
Couldn't he see? "It's about Chad. It's important. We
need to talk."

"We're talking now—"

"Hey, Laurie." Kent Leonard slaps Rob on the shoulder and grins at her. "How about going to the game with
me tonight?"

"Sorry, Kent, I've got—"

Rob looks at her. "A date?" He cants and eyebrow
and winks. Maybe he knows.

Maybe he knows, after all.

Kent just says, "Oh." He clears his throat. The bell
rings for fourth period. "So maybe I could call you sometime?"

"Sure, yeah. I guess I could manage it."

"So okay. Yeah. Maybe I'll see you at lunch."

Rob looks down at her. "A date?"

"Yeah," she says. "With Chad."

Laurie goes to her History class feeling buttery light,
all yellow and glowing. She's scared of what she's about
to do. But there's no choice now, is there? Mary Dawn
sits next to her. She knows that something's up. She
passes notes back and forth, right under Mr. Plimpton's
skinny nose. Mr. Plimpton's not very old, but his eyesight
is bad and he doesn't really care what happens in class
so long as everyone's quiet. He complains a lot about
sinus headaches and the Johnson Administration and the
plight of the American High School Teacher.

Laurie prints her reply to the first note in big block
letters. I'M IN LOVE WITH CHAD. She folds it over
once and casually slips it into Mary Dawn's notebook
while Mr. P. covers the blackboard with the seven major
factors contributing to the Great Depression. Too easy, as
always.

Mary Dawn reads the note and sends it flying back to
Laurie. "Tell me something I don't already know, fool,"
Laurie reads. So she scribbles on the same piece of paper:
WE'RE GOING TO DO "IT" TOMORROW NIGHT.

Mary Dawn's mouth makes an O when she reads Laurie's reply. She makes a funny sound and whispers,

"Oooh, child, are you asking for it or what?" She's a little too loud and Mr. P. turns around and frowns in their direction.

"I would appreciate silence, ladies. Please."

A couple of boys in the back of the room start snickering.

"That goes for you, too, guys, unless you'd like a refreshing few moments down in detention with our dear Counselor Thames."

Counselor Thames is also the football coach. The boys slink down in their chairs. Laurie laughs, covers up and looks over at Mary Dawn. But she's not smiling now. She wears a hurt little grimace that slides away quickly when she notices that Laurie is looking. When Mr. P. turns back to the blackboard, Mary Dawn throws the note back at her. Laurie opens it and reads: "Call me tonight."

Laurie nods, and decides she'd better start copying down what's been written on the blackboard.

Her bedroom is clean. Lina, their once-a-week maid, changed the sheets that morning. They smell like flowers. Laurie rearranges the pillows and hides Bunny Bear on the floor under the pink dust ruffle.

She checks out the room. It's not bad. The posters of Chris Isaak and Billy Idol can stay, but maybe she should stash Tom Cruise. He looks too paternal smiling down at her. She can't do a thing with him watching. So she rolls him up tidily and puts him in the closet with the other demoted poster guys, from Vanilla Ice to Bo Jackson. Then she checks out her bulletin board, full of snapshots of friends and family, and cutouts from magazines. A dancer she'd like to be. And Danielle Dax. Other things: her glee club medal. A valentine from Chad. There's a torn T-shirt that belonged to David Lee Roth, or at least Rob said it did. Rob and his ditzy girlfriend, CeCe, said they stole it from David Lee's dressing room. Maybe. Maybe not. But Laurie pretended to believe them. CeCe swore it belonged to him. Rob had winked, meaning . . . what?

There's a little bookcase, its top shelf full of Sweet Valley High books and some old Nancy Drews that be-

longed to Rachel, a dog-eared copy of *Jane Eyre* and one
of *Farewell to Arms* with tearstains on it. It's the only
book that has given her nightmares. Except for *The Shining*.

There must be something special she can do to her
room. She has an odd assortment of candles, but they're
not very romantic, a couple of old birthday shorties and
the rest in dumb shapes: a hamburger, unicorn and frog.
Juvenile. She could get some from the dining room, those
classy white tapers Mom uses for dinner parties.

And music. She needs the right music. Not David Lee,
that's for sure. Or Madonna. Wilson Phillips, maybe. Or
Rob's Kate Bush album, the one about the sensual world.
But she decides on Paul Young.

When she pops the CD into her new multidisc carousel,
she sees her Barbies, set out for display in the glass doll
cabinet Grandmom-mom gave her for Christmas last year.
She should put them out of sight. She's spent so much
time playing with them. They're like part of the family.
It wouldn't be too comfortable catching their painted
stare. But where could they go? Not under the bed with
Bunny Bear. There's the Barbie house way back in her
closet, beneath a pile of the clothes she's grown out of.
She could hide them in there.

Laurie opens the cabinet and lifts out the two oldest
Barbies, ones that had belonged originally to Rachel. A
Barbie and Ken. They're not looking so good. Old age
will do that to a person; dolls, too. Ken has fuzzy lemon-
colored hair that has rubbed off right on top, so he has a
bald spot. Barbie's ponytail is thinning, too. Her eyeliner
needs redoing, and her lips could use a touch-up as well.
Barbie's wearing her famous black-and-white swimsuit.
One hard boob peeks out. Laurie fixes that, and Barbie
looks like she could take a walk down Stewart Beach on
Galveston Island. But Ken's wearing trunks right out of
the sixties. He's so old-fashioned he's almost hot. Like
Mom says, you wait long enough, everything that goes
around comes around again. Like miniskirts. And Dem-
ocrats.

Finally Laurie takes the rest of the Barbies, one by one,

and piles them into a sweatshirt. God, she loved playing
dolls. Making up stories, little soap operas, playing all day
and all night, especially in the summertime. Sometimes
with Mary Dawn, even once or twice with Mom. But
usually alone.

She got her first Barbie when she was four, Ken the
following Christmas. She named her Barbie Sandy, because that was the color of her hair. Ken was named Tony,
like Tony the Tiger. Grrreat. But the Barbie she liked
best—and still does—is Star, a bendable twist 'n' turn
version, with thick crimson hair and a fuchsia leotard.
Somewhere around here there's a little Barbie gym, floor
mats and parallel bars and a jumping horse. Then there's
the Malibu Barbie, Misty, and her black friend, Joelle, and
Wedding Day Midge and the newer Ken doll, Josh. He
was a replacement for the one that disappeared, her favorite Ken doll. His name was Chad. Wasn't that interesting? Now the Barbies all lie in a heap at her feet,
forsaken. But not forgotten.

"Joshua." He stands in her right hand. "Star." She
reclines in her left hand, one arm raised in salute.

Laurie makes them kiss. Once soft, then again but hard,
twisting their plastic faces together, rubbing, rubbing. She
pushes him down on Star. They're having sex. She pushes
him again, harder. Star's legs bend wide.

"Give it to me, Star. I want you, Star."

"I love you, Josh. I love you."

"Don't talk, Star. Don't spoil it."

Star is on the floor and Josh is slamming into her, head
and groin and legs, hitting, then pressing, then hitting
again. "I . . . want . . ." Finally she smashes him down on
her. "You!"

Laurie looks up. Someone is at her door. But no one's
home. No one. Daddy's working and Mom's at her book
group and Rob's at the basketball game. She's alone until
ten. No. They're alone until ten. Laurie and Chad. Maybe
ten-thirty.

Just Laurie and Chad.

She drops the dolls back into the sweatshirt and ties its
arms together. She takes her bundle to the closet and

drops the Barbies through the open roof of the plastic Barbie house.

Now the doll cabinet looks terribly empty. Laurie re-arranges the other dolls left inside: the china baby doll that belonged to Grandmom-mom, Rachel's Tiny Tears and a few dolls Mom and Daddy have brought her from Europe. And the Madame Alexander dolls, Jo and Amy from the "Little Women" series. She can handle them watching. Just not the other ones.

The ones that are pretend adults.

It's seven-fifteen and he's still not there. Fashionably late. She thinks about giving him a call. But she can use the time. Maybe a little more makeup, just a touch of silver gray above the eyes. And she wants to brush her teeth again. Third time's a charm.

She wonders if she should give him a beer. Daddy always keeps some in the fridge; he'd never know that one or two were missing. Or maybe Chad would like gin. Tanqueray on ice. With three olives. No, that would be . . .

Wrong? What does that mean? Nothing could be wrong about this. Nothing at all. This was the right thing, this is the thing she wanted, this is the thing that was meant to be. Nothing was wrong. Nothing could be wrong.

Her Paul Young CD ends and she decides to play it again. She likes the way his voice sounds. So sad, but so true. She knows most singers are phonies, but when he sings she thinks he means it. What if the door opened and it was Paul, not Chad? Silly games. She wrinkles her nose at the mirror.

The telephone rings. But it's not him. It's Mary Dawn. Hi, how are you? And: Wasn't Mrs. Bowen a pain? Got to read fifty pages by Friday? And then: Girl, did you see Sandy Hillis's hair? And finally:

"Just what do you think you're doing?"

She sounds a little bit like Mom.

"Nothing."

"You were kidding me, right? That note you sent? About Chad?"

"What do you think?"

There's the doorbell. Laurie doesn't hear what Mary Dawn thinks, she just says, "Gotta go. See you tomorrow," and hangs up on the voice that's still talking on the other end. She runs into her parents' bedroom, squirts Mom's Obsession on the back of her neck, her wrists and then, just for fun, down the front of her sweater. Then she's down the stairs. The doorbell rings again. She stops running. Takes a deep breath. A deep, deep breath. Calm. All is calm, all is bright . . .

The door.

She opens it with a "Hi." The sun's almost down. Chad is sweaty and his hair is messed up. He should have combed it. He smells like he's been running. Like after PE. He's late and he knows it. Now she loves him even more.

"Hi." He's moving, but he's standing still. First on one foot, then on the other.

"So come in." She is so happy that she spins around, a dancer. Two circles. Her mini flares. She's wearing her white Adrienne Vittadini sweater and her short white mini and white tights. No panties. He'll find that out soon enough. Does he understand the white?

"Sorry I'm late. I—"

She's a little dizzy and she falls against him. Only a little on purpose.

"Chad."

Hands. Holding her. On her hips. Holding.

"Chad."

She kisses him. She's never done that before. It was always him first. Him kissing her. It's neat. Lips against his cheek.

"Chad."

Then on his mouth. And she tries, but can't. Her tongue doesn't want to work. She wants her tongue inside his mouth, but it won't go. So she kisses his lips, and then his ear, then back to his neck. Starts to break away.

"Let's go to my room."

"Okay."

But he kisses her right back. On the lips. He tastes like

catsup. Hands still on her hips. Her legs feel all woozy.
Then he lets go.

"So. What's up?" Now he looks around for the first
time. No Mom, no Dad. No Rob. "Aren't you finished
with that book report?" He's kidding, of course. "Told
you to read something short."

He follows her up the stairs. Her mini is what's short.
He can't be thinking about books. Anyway, she gave up
on Tolstoy. She decided to write her report on Henrik
Ibsen. *A Doll's House.* Now they're on the landing. She
can hear the music from her room. Paul Young starts to
sing about love. Love will tear us apart. Again.

"Chad." Going down the hall. "Rob's at the game."
Past the bathroom. "My parents won't be home till ten."
And the sewing room. "I thought maybe—"

They're inside her bedroom now. Billy Idol doesn't
blink. She smiles at him and falls back on her bed.
Doesn't care about her skirt as it zooms up her legs. Chad
looks funny. He can't take his eyes off her. But he doesn't
see. "Laurie—"

"Maybe we could." Serious eyes. She hopes that she
has serious eyes. "You know."

He looks at his watch. "If you wanted to go to the
game, why didn't you—"

"No game," she tells him. "Just you. And me." Her
arms open to him. "No game, Chad. I want—" He must
understand. He must understand now. "You. Hold me,
Chad. Me—"

Oh, my God, he doesn't know what to do. His eyes
roam the walls. The posters. The desk. The bulletin board.
The doll cabinet. It's like he's seeing her room for the
first time. Seeing her for the first time.

"Please?"

Now Paul Young has changed his tune, and suddenly
Chad is next to her, just like Daddy the night before. But
there's no Bunny Bear to hold on to. She wishes she could
pull on the sheets. Bring them up to her face.

But his hand is on her thigh, and it's burning hot.
"Don't—" Don't what? Too quick. He's going too quick.
"Laurie, I—"

"Shhh." Kissing him again. "Just hold me."

She looks at him like she knows what she is doing. When she reaches to the zipper of her skirt, she is looking at him. I am doing this for you. Only for you.

The skirt is gone. White sweater and white tights. His hand returns to the same spot on her thigh, and now it is flame. She feels nothing but that hand. Her leg must be melting.

A breath he can hear. Another kiss. Her tongue licks along his lips, but won't go inside. Can't.

She wants to see his chest. Fingers on buttons. No, snaps. So easy. One, two, three. His shirt is open. His chest is wonderful, amazing. So smooth, so hard. No hair. Just muscle. Solid. There are no nipples.

She kisses the center of his chest. Kisses there again. Feels his hand begin to move.

Now his shirt is off completely and she wants to hold him, hold him against her. Body to body. She starts to pull at her sweater, but his hands are there. So carefully. They surround her breasts. Feel her there, so small and hard and pointed. Then he lets go. The sweater passes over her head and onto the bed. She tosses it to the floor. She is wearing nothing underneath. He kisses the tips of her breasts. So hard. His kisses seem like pecks, not at all what she expected, his unopening lips pressed against her, then releasing. Dry. Cold.

"Now, Chad." She isn't going to cry. She isn't. "Want you now."

His hand is so very hot on her leg. Burning. She will blister. Melt. It explores along her thigh. Up and in. She can't even breathe. It's now or never.

She clutches at a belt loop of his jeans. Finds his belt buckle. A snap. No zipper. Laurie slides his jeans and underpants away. His long legs twine into hers. He is on top of her. Kissing at her face. His body is so sleek and sharp, yet light. So very light.

Her hands slide up then down his back, down into the cleft of his buttocks, and as she cups them she feels the openings between his buttocks and his legs. Her fingers slip inside, and when he arches up, they are pinched and caught and squeezed. Then free again.

Her hands reach to his shoulders, to the openings there where his arms rotate forward and back. Forward and back. His hands are at her sides, touching, not holding.

Now she reaches down, under, lower, across his stomach, that rigid abdomen, to squeeze at the air between his legs. She looks and sees the blank nub of his crotch. She closes her eyes, as if the magic of not seeing would work its wonders. Nothing doing. He pushes at her, nub against nub, their hard, bare, hairless mounds colliding.

"I love you, Chad. I love you."

She is slamming Chad into her, head and groin and legs, hitting, then pressing, then hitting again. "I . . . want . . ." Finally she pulls him down on her. "You!"

Now her knees do not bend, and her ankles are stiff, feet straight and steady. Her arms are locked, moving only at the shoulders. She cannot even look down; her neck will move from side to side, but her jaw and chin are set like a sculpture. She can twist and turn and that is all.

His forehead butts hard against hers; their lips do not meet, cannot meet, but slide against each other, solid and cold, the chill of painted plastic.

The doorbell rings: once, twice. Then a knock, soft but sure. Chad slides away and she lets him fall to the floor. When the doorbell rings again, she stands, takes her inevitable pose, the perky smile on an upraised chin, ponytail bouncy and taut, arms askew and hands raised in an empty gesture, her unbendable knees shining like marble balls.

She walks somehow. Along the plastic carpet. Past the plastic furniture, the plastic walls. Around her are scattered the bodies of her friends. She staggers past them and down the dollhouse stairs. To the front door, which she opens at last to the world outside. With a smile that is forever, and eyes that never close.

She sees everything.

FACETS OF SOLITAIRE

Christopher Golden

Christopher Golden is the author of *Of Saints and Shadows* (Jove, 1994), its sequel, *Angel Souls & Devil Hearts* (1995) and two YA thrillers, *Bikini* and *Beach Blanket Psycho* (both Bantam, 1995). He is currently working on *Daredevil: Predator's Smile*, based on the Marvel Comics character, for Berkely; the Harris Comics miniseries *Facelift* and a new novel entitled *The Justice Wheel*. His short fiction has appeared in *Stalkers 3* and *The Ultimate Spider-Man*. His extensive nonfiction credits include *Starlog, The Boston Herald, Disney Adventures, Billboard, Hero Illustrated*, and serving as editor on *Cut!: Horror Writers on Horror Film* (Dell, 1991) and *FLUX* magazine. A native of Massachusetts, he has escaped Manhattan for the land of his birth, taking his wife, Connie, and their young son, Nicholas, with him. Outside of comics, writing and his family, his other great loves are Cajun food and the Allman Brothers Band.

O n the way down . . .

It had been but a moment since Erika Raven jumped, or more accurately, simply stepped from the roof of her five-story brownstone. She plummeted, naked, toward the ground, her beautifully muscled, light brown flesh shining in the moonlight. Her dark red, almost auburn hair whipped past her face as she tumbled through the air and the wind stung her chocolate-brown eyes, bringing a rare tear.

Through those eyes, even as she fell, she watched the city. New York, the stinking pit she knew as home, was rotting on the vine of the world and it wouldn't be long until it crumbled to dust. In the distance she could see fires burning on the oil-slicked East River. It might as well have been the Styx. The city was corrupt, pustulent, and it was bad enough in the Bronx or around Times Square or the Village, where everyone was out for blood. At least there you knew the score. Here, where her Upper West Side brownstone stood, here survived that tiny percentage that still made up the middle class. The city was one cancerous body, she knew, and laced with the stuff, yet only parts of the skin showed the ravages of the sickness. In the city's center and in the outer boroughs lay the most putrid of tumors.

Erika Raven had been fool enough to believe she could make a difference. She had tried to take the burden of Atlas, and now she found that she didn't have the shoulders for it.

She was fast approaching the ground, yet she was perfectly calm. She had tried this before. If she got lucky, perhaps she would land on a drug dealer, killing him on impact. She would accomplish one final and completely insignificant act of vengeance on the infernal thing her city had become. And no one would weep. Not for the dealer and certainly not for her. Her family was dead or gone, her friends simply not, and as for lovers, the last one had died in her arms five years ago. She was empty, a shell, and completely resigned to the idea of that shell cracking into a million pieces as it hit the pavement.

As she hit the pavement.

On the way down . . .

Her tumble had brought her slowly, inexorably around to face the cracked tar as she neared impact. She did not close her eyes.

She hit pretty-face first with a thud not loud enough to rouse the neighbors. Amazing that a human body can fall so far and hit so hard and make so little noise.

At least that's what Erika was thinking as she stood up from the cracked and broken pavement and dusted her body off. She picked tar off her left nipple as she walked toward the front door of her building with her head hanging in despair.

She turned around to face the city just before she went inside, but there was no one on the street to see her. They were all cowering indoors, reasonably frightened of the night.

"This! Fucking! Sucks!" she screamed, and slammed the door. She had never been eloquent.

Morgan supplied the blue-boys of the 8th Precinct with all the crack they wanted. Just enough for them to have a little bit left over to sell back to him if he ran short. He didn't think of himself as one of the bad guys. Hell, with cops like these, you couldn't really call the sides good and bad anymore. Just us and them. No, he thought of himself as a guy who wanted to stay alive, a guy who saw an opportunity and took advantage of it. An entrepreneur, you might say. The Village was his territory, and he liked the power. He had taken the Kent Middle School trade away from the 9th Precinct cops and had the guys from the 8th to protect him. Funny, the way the cops worked nowadays, like gangs with their territories. These days, though, the gangs were more organized than the cops. 'Course, the cops had government funding.

Morgan's was a good life.

He'd never had any parents to speak of, just the street

people. But they'd taught him what he needed to know. How to read, how to write, how to steal, how to lie; it was all a part of his education. That and a little history. He was sick of hearing talk about the "good old days" when people like him could get farther north than 60th Street without getting shot, when there was a McDonald's on every fucking corner, when some of the movie theaters showed Hollywood's products instead of what came from the Manzetti Brothers' bedroom studios and the Village was home to the idle rich, or at least the arrogantly well-off. He hated it because when his older associates talked that way, they sounded like he knew parents would have.

Parents would have been a ball and chain. A couple of fogies whose backs he'd have to watch. His ass, that was all he worried about, and he liked it that way. If he had to move fast, there was nothing to leave behind. There were women everywhere.

"Wake up, asshole."

He'd been trying to sleep, to catch a few winks in what little downtime the modern-day drug dealer had available, but that fucker Malloy wouldn't let him be.

Morgan rolled over to stare up at the glaring lights and his eyes hurt, so he shut them tight. Not the reaction Malloy was looking for.

"I said wake up, you no-good, shit-for-brains, son of a . . ."

This pleasant stream of affectionate nicknames ran on for a minute or so before Morgan opened his eyes again. He sat up on the dingy cot in the back of the police station and rubbed his eyes. The room came into focus: disgusting, gray, paper-strewn, smelling like old coffee grinds and sweetly aromatic hashish. Anyone not used to it would probably have thrown up, but Morgan slept there a lot. That is, until Malloy decided it was time for a nap, and then it was out the door for a brother Irishman. Actually, that was an assumption. Morgan had no idea what his heritage was. Didn't much care, either.

The windows were dark, and he was surprised at how long he had slept. It turned out there was another reason for Malloy to wake him up. It was time for the evening pickup. He walked between two long rows of desks which were occupied by cops who might, if they felt like it, venture out onto the streets for an hour or so. It looked like a couple of them already had. Slikowski was haggling with a prostitute over how far she would have to take him to get out of spending a night in a cold cell, which would, if nothing else, cut into her profits. Walters, on the other hand, had nabbed a couple of dealers who were unfamiliar to Morgan.

"Good job, Wally. Keep the slime off my turf."

"It's our turf, kid; you just run the fucking concession stand."

Morgan smiled at the fat cop. One day he'd kill the big dick in his sleep, and then fuck his wife. Again.

He reached the door and opened the spyhole for a look at who might be waiting in ambush outside the door before opening it wide and stepping out. It closed quickly behind him, slamming, locking automatically. It was a nice night, if you enjoyed heat that made the pits of hell sound like exhilarating refreshment.

Morgan didn't. Never had.

He made his way past the houses with the boarded-up windows, past the only thing open at that time of night: Sal's All Night Beer & Grocery Mart. The only reason Sal was open was the money he paid the three guys with shotguns who stood guard in front of the beer chest. Sal waved to Morgan as the kid walked by; he was a regular customer.

He was about halfway to the pickup spot when he saw the woman. He could tell it was a woman by the way she walked. She was coming toward him on the road 'cause trash blocked the sidewalks all over the city. The summer swelter made it stink like death, and he was sure there was plenty of that adding to the stench. The air was hardly breathable from pollution, and the garbage smell made you not want it anyway. One of the newest things on the street trade was lab-filtered air. Clean air alone could get you high. The woman walked down the middle of the street, knowing as well as Morgan that there would be few cars. Only the cops and shooters drove cars at this time of night, and either one of them would be likely to gun you down for fun or money. If you heard an engine, you took cover.

The woman had come close enough so Morgan could see her pretty clearly. The moon was bright and the smog thinner than usual. She was pretty, not TV pretty, but that was all surgery anyway. No, but she was pretty enough for it to be rare. She wore a white tank top and denim jeans, white sneakers. Her breasts were fairly large and her nipples dark against the shirt. She was black, or, more likely, mulatto, because she was very light-skinned and her hair was red. Morgan wanted to beat the shit out of her, fuck her and take her money. Or at least take her money.

After all, it would be what she deserved for coming down into a neighborhood like this. Sure, it wasn't the worst neighborhood, far from it in fact. But then, it sure wasn't uptown. A woman like her should never come to the Village, even at midday. She would have had to cross through Times Square to get here, and that was a thousand times worse!

She was only a few feet away, and he changed his mind about wanting to beat the shit out of her. She was a big girl. Her arms were muscled and her shoulders wide and she was a hell of a lot bigger than Morgan. But what the hell, he was a businessman. What he couldn't take . . .

"Hey, baby, hot night. Need something to take your mind off the life you lead?"

"What'd you have in mind?" she said, eyes friendly.

"Two kinds of rock candy. The kind you smoke and the kind you choke."

"That sounds pretty tempting. What're you asking?"

"Cash or gash, what you got, I want." She smiled at him, and Morgan had a feeling she was going to go for it. This was too good to be true, but then, anything could happen in this city.

Her eyes seemed to go from smiling to furious, and then she seemed to, well, sad.

"Not tonight, baby. I'm not in the mood."

Shit!

She was starting to walk away.

"Come on, lady, you look lonely; let me take you away from this for a little while."

"Sorry, chum," she said, and she looked hard into his eyes. He saw something there, cold and dark.

"I'm looking for a big boy to play with tonight."

He grabbed her arm. That kind of put-down could not go unanswered. He wanted to prove to her what a big boy he was. He pushed her up against the wall, forgetting her muscles for a moment. He was delighted when she put up no resistance. He twisted a nipple with one hand while he held her face with the other. He kissed her hard, and after a moment's hesitation, she kissed back.

God! She's enjoying his, he thought. She got so lonely she came down here to get jumped. He reached for his fly. He watched her eyes, which were squinted shut with her want. Then her mouth stopped moving with his, her whole body stiff and rigid. Her eyes snapped open and stared hard into his with hate that scorched him. Before he had time to move away, she bit down hard on his tongue, severing the last eighth of an inch as it tried to escape her mouth.

His legs gave up on him and he fell down. On all fours, he screamed as blood dripped from his mouth. He sat back hard on his butt and covered his mouth with his hands, staring up at her in shock. She looked at him with what he thought was pity, and spit the piece of his tongue out into a pile of garbage. He wanted to cry, but he wanted to kill her even more. He reached for the knife in his boot.

And her foot came down hard on his hand, pinning it to the ground.

"You're an idiot," she said as she leaned over him. "Haven't you heard, hasn't anybody told you about me? I'm Raven, you dumb fuck. That knife wouldn't scratch me."

Jesus. He had heard, but figured it for a lot of talk. He knew guys who believed it, and he'd heard of women claiming to be Raven just so no one would jump them. But if there was such a person, then this bitch could be she. Not a good thing. Raven was said to disembowel drug dealers, and Morgan was kind of partial to what little guts he had.

Salvation arrived with the sound of a car engine. The headlights lit up the street, and Morgan hoped it was a police car, certain his buddies would bail him out of this thing. But it wasn't the cops, and the guns were already out the window. Moving as fast as he could, he dove into some fresh garbage, ignoring the smell. He looked up in time to see that Raven had moved only enough to turn and face the guns. They fired.

She moved back a little, an unconscious reaction, he guessed, because she knew she should be riddled full of holes, down and dying. But she stood there and itched where the bullets hit, as if she had mosquito bites.

Morgan just stared. He had a smile on his face and didn't know why. She was more than he'd ever heard. Then the car was turning around and the headlights fell on his hiding place, so he pushed himself deeper into the garbage. The car was coming back, the men inside probably very perturbed that their marksmanship was so poor.

Raven simply stood in their path. Morgan had no idea what she planned to do. Hell, she had no weapons but her hands. The accelerator roared and the car leapt forward. The impact sent Raven flying fifteen feet backward, where she landed hard on the street. Morgan did not know what to expect as the men got out of the car; then he noticed the damage. The front of the car looked as if they had wrapped it around a telephone pole, only there was no pole in sight. Only the men in back got out, and Morgan saw why. The driver's chest had been crushed by his impact with the steering wheel, the front-seat passenger's head lying half in, half out of the hole it had made in the windshield.

The backseat guys still had their guns and were moving toward the still figure in the road. Morgan didn't know what to expect as they bent over her body.

He should have known better.

Her hands came up at the throat of one, and he emptied his gun at her chest, point-blank. Morgan didn't see where the bullets went, but he thought that one of them might have ricocheted and hit its owner in the stomach. This all happened so fast that the last one, all in leather, had barely gotten a shot off when Raven lifted his partner over her head and swung him at the pavement so hard that Morgan heard his skull pop from thirty feet away. His brains were sloshing onto the street when Raven turned to the other one. He didn't bother firing at her. He ran.

Morgan figured him for the smart one. Problem was, Raven was fast. She covered the ground to him in a heartbeat, and lifted him up by his neck with her left hand. She carried him over to a brick building whose windows were boarded up, and she held him up against the wall. She cocked her right fist and drove it into his chest, through his rib cage, with a sickening noise, and then there was another sound. Blood splashed onto her white T-shirt, sticking it to her chest, and her nipples were pointed, erect. She dropped the corpse on the sidewalk with the rest of the garbage and Morgan could see in the light from a streetlamp that her fist had also left a hole in the brick side of the building.

Now he was definitely afraid.

She was walking around, eyeing the trash. In search of him, he was sure. The last thing in the world he wanted was for her to find him, and he stayed as still as he could, not breathing. He had no idea how keen her senses were if everything else worked so well.

She's not fucking human, he thought.

He watched her as she made her way to the middle of the street, stopped and looked around. She seemed completely alert, looking, smelling, listening. He realized that the chumps in the car might have saved his life. Her eyes settled on his hiding place and his heart was beating so loud and hard he thought it would explode.

God, he didn't want to die! He felt like he was going to piss his pants.

Her gaze shifted to another pile of trash farther down the street. And then, suddenly, she relaxed. It seemed like all the air went out of her. She turned and began to walk back the way she had come, giving up, at precisely the moment that Morgan's bladder released.

The piss against his pants was nearly silent, and in all this trash, he couldn't smell it. He didn't know whether she heard it or whiffed it, but it didn't matter. She turned around and looked right at him, groveling there in the trash. He froze.

From across the street, she called to him.

"What's your name?"

He saw no point in lying.

"Morgan."

"See you again, Morgan," she said. "Soon."

And walked away.

Erika was tired. Not sleepy-tired, just tired of everything. It had been a stimulating night, taking out those scumbags and scaring the hell out of poor . . . Morgan, yes, that was it. But what it all came down to was shit. The city was a big toilet; you could flush a load of shit down the pipes, but there was always more where that came from. It was exhilarating while she was doing it, but the high, the arousal, was gone the moment it was over.

And God (whoever the hell was using that title these days) didn't give a fuck.

She was lonely. Like a bitch in heat, she scolded herself. She was into it when Morgan was heating her up, and then she wanted to kill him for it. Upon reconsideration, she thought she would let him live a while longer and get nice and paranoid about her return. That way when she did show up, he'd probably have a fucking heart attack.

It was past the point of obsession and she knew that the absence of a lover in her life had driven her over the edge. She had given up hope for herself and for the city at the same time, and had been trying to do herself in since that day. Only it just wasn't happening.

There had never been a time when she appreciated her abilities. The mutations which had taken place within her genetic makeup had shown themselves at a very inopportune moment. It was a Friday night, and Mikhail had made them a beautiful dinner at his place. She was nineteen, he twenty-four, and every moment they had together was spent talking, laughing and fucking. Sometimes all three at the same time. That night was nothing special. Or at least, no more special than the other nights she spent with Mikhail. She could close her eyes and imagine the tight fit of his cock inside her, but that usually did nothing except prompt another suicide attempt.

"Oh, God," he'd moaned. "I love you."

"And I. Love. You. Oh, I'm coming!" she'd screamed back. Her nails dug into his back as she hugged him tight, ripping his flesh from his bones as her orgasm ripped through her, unable to halt her convulsive limbs in time to stop them from crushing his bones, collapsing his rib cage so that white spikes appeared through his back.

And then the screaming started, his cock still inside her. She recognized the screaming right away as her own, but could do nothing to stop it.

Erika had never understood why her mutations had chosen that moment to manifest themselves, or why they'd shown up at all. As far as she knew at the time, she was unique. Maybe her mother had been exposed to radiation while pregnant, but then, these days, who wasn't? It could have been any number of things: common street drugs taken by millions every day in New York alone, top-secret government supergerms, radiation, pollution (probably the damn pollution!), natural fucking selection, all of the above or some combination of elements. She could be the next step in the evolutionary chain. Who knew? And in the end, did it matter? She was what she was now, and if there was one thing she knew, it was a one-way process. And once they got wind of it, the government would want a piece of her, she was sure of that. But for the moment, it had happened to *her*, and that was all that was important.

After.

She had to be in constant control around innocent people, so she tried not to spend too much time with them. It wasn't very difficult. She ate infrequently and rarely went out during the day. It was much better to be able to tear out the hearts of the city's maggots. She found that the blood turned her on. It was a sick fascination with the way Mikhail had died, but she wouldn't do that again. She had to satisfy herself by masturbating, and most of the time she just used her hands. Dildos, vibrators, broom handles all tended to break at the end, and just weren't worth the hassle since she could barely feel them. She had a steel bar she used once in a while, heated in the oven. That she could feel.

The first time she'd ever used that bar she was disgusted with herself. She had looked at herself in the mirror, sweating, coming down from the climax.

"That's pretty fucking lonely." She'd laughed, derisively, at herself.

She had actually found one other person with a similar mutation; he thought himself something of a hero. Just her luck he turned out to be gay. It was a cruel joke. Like that "If you were the last man on earth" line. Well, for her, he pretty much was, and he wasn't interested. She spoke to him only once. After that she considered trying women. It wouldn't have been the first time, but she thought it would be just as dangerous for them as for a male lover.

So where did that leave her?

Tired.

Leaning against the kitchen counter, she finished her coffee and rinsed out the cup. In only her robe, she wandered about her small, Spartan apartment. Whitewashed walls and wall-to-wall carpet were barren of decoration, of things that might represent an interest, or even a passion for something, anything. It hadn't always been that way.

Her robe fell to the ground, and Erika's hands wandered over her body of their own volition as she found her way into the bedroom.

She couldn't stop thinking about the feeling of Morgan's hand on her breast, his tongue in her mouth . . .

Enough!

Stripped naked, she punched in the phone number, and then her credit number after the command. As she heard the line connect, she picked up the bar, hot from the oven. It burned her hand but did no damage. It hurt good. She turned the phone away from her mouth so she could listen but would not be heard.

"You there, baby?" a man's voice said softly.

"Oh, yeah, I'm here," came the reply. A very young girl, Erika could tell from the sound of her voice. Probably a teenager who shouldn't be on the line at all. But it gave Erika an extra jolt.

"What's your name?" he asked.

"Monica."

"I'm Lance." And that was his real name? Erika wanted to laugh, but she was too busy trying not to moan.

"What are you doing right now, Monica?"

"Well, I woke up in the middle of the night from one of those good dreams, you know? The kind where you wish someone was next to you to act them out? Well, there was no one there, so I'm lying here in bed, naked."

"Are you touching yourself?"

"Oh, yeah," she answered breathily.

"I wish you were here," Lance said.

"Me, too. What would you do to me if you were?" she asked, and that started it.

They detailed to each other what they would love to do if they were not however many hundreds of miles apart and total strangers at that. Lance wanted her in the ass, and that just got Monica hotter. She wanted him in public, to suck him in front of a crowd. It didn't take long before it broke down into a series of grunts and groans and "fucking you"'s, and Erika came right along with them, bucking and biting her lip not to moan. It was all she could do not to crush the phone in her hand, but she wanted to hear the end.

And she wasn't glad she did.

Click.

"Lance?"

The slime, Erika thought.

"Lance?" Again Monica said it, plaintive but knowing.

"Thank you," she said, and Erika could hear the loneliness, like her own, which had been abated for just a moment, only to come crashing back. She wanted to reach out to the girl, but what, after all, would she say?

She heard Monica hang up, and then another line clicked on.

"Hello?" she heard a male voice say. "Any wet babes out there?"

She dropped the phone into its cradle, and it wasn't long before she slept.

Tomorrow she would have to find a taller building, maybe tie some weights to her legs. More than likely, tomorrow night she would murder some more babyfucking killers, and then come back to her home and her bed and her hand.

God, she loved a routine.

"A woman?" Walters laughed in disbelief as Malloy finished crudely stitching Morgan's tongue. The kid was in pain and humiliated to boot, and the big cop was loving it.

"I'm thelling you the tooth!" Morgan insisted. "God, how 'ong my going thu thalk 'ike this?"

"Could be weeks," Malloy said, all seriousness, and got the reaction he wanted from Morgan. The kid's eyes bulged.

"I'm just kidding. In a couple of hours, if you speak slow, you should be able to talk pretty normal."

Relief washed over Morgan. He hadn't been getting as much lately. It was still plenty; after all, he had the drugs. But he hadn't been looking much. The sluts just bored him.

But that bitch who bit his tongue . . . His pants became uncomfortable in the crotch as he thought of her nipple hard at his fingertips. He wanted a piece of that. She'd said she would be back, but he had an unfortunate feeling that her only interest in his cock might be in shoving it down his throat. That was not on Morgan's agenda. He'd have to be on constant alert. And the cops were no help. If they would stop laughing for a moment, they might realize what a threat she was to their life-style, and do something about it. But they wouldn't take it seriously. Morgan had a feeling it would come back to haunt them.

* * *

This time she kept her eyes shut tight as she fell. She did not want to see the disgusting city as it flew by her with the wind. Naked, her red mane flying behind her, she stretched her arms out, gliding on the wind. The building was a couple of blocks from her own, much taller this time, and even though she knew it probably wouldn't help, she was looking forward to the impact. It was early evening, and the smell, whipping past her nostrils, was repulsive. She wondered for a moment why she always did this naked, but the answer was obvious. She liked it, plain and simple.

She was spread-eagled as she struck the pavement, and she lay there for a while in the imprint of her body. It reminded her of making snow angels as a little girl when the winter blizzards would subside for a few hours. Now the weather sucked, one way or another, year round, but at least it was predictable.

All of this nostalgia was her way of avoiding the fact that she was still alive, but it could not be dodged for much longer, so she stood up. And a wonderful thing happened.

It hurt! How glorious was that feeling? Granted, it was only slightly, but damn if her back didn't hurt. She was giddy, and when she realized how insane it was, she laughed out loud.

When she had retrieved her clothes and was dressing, she thought about which neighborhood she should tear apart for the evening, although she found it increasingly difficult to keep the slimeball Morgan from her thoughts.

The air that moved through the police station was poorly filtered and barely cooled by the ventilation system. All in all, it was slightly more comfortable than hell, but with hell right outside the door, and the only other option, it didn't completely suck either. Morgan's general opinion of the precinct house was something he rarely repeated to any of the officers; it wouldn't be healthy. That was what he had been thinking about when he drifted off to sleep. That and the hope that he would snore loud enough so that nobody else in there could doze off.

And snoring he was, sawing away an irregular beat, interrupted by short bursts of that combination cough/ choke brought on by any air even slightly cleaner than the stuff outside. He was dreaming nice thoughts, though, and didn't allow himself to be coughed awake. Nice thoughts of hard love, red hair and green eyes and . . .

She was there. Even in his sleep he knew it, and the feeling shook him awake after a second. No, she was definitely there, standing in front of him. Not conjured up by his hard-on either, but right there, watching him sleep, now watching him wake.

"You know what I hate?" she asked him, but he was still groggy, and it took a moment for him to register it.

"I hate drugs," she continued, spreading her arms wide to indicate the massive supplies of drugs which filled the room.

"But you know what I hate even more than drugs?" she asked, offering up a smile that was both cruel and seductive.

"Drug dealers?" the wise guy croaked with his tired voice.

"Yes, big-mouthed asshole. I hate drug dealers. I'm so glad the cops finally caught you and threw you in here. You deserve it."

His jaw dropped. He couldn't believe it. She'd actually bought the whole . . .

"Just kidding," she said. "Do you think I'm stupid enough not to understand how this whole thing is put together? There's nothing worse than cops dealing drugs, and I'll tell you, that's not going to happen here anymore."

"Oh, and what's going to happen instead?" came a voice, and Morgan saw Malloy and Walters behind her. "Are you Morgan's girlfriend? The one who kicked his ass the other day? So, baby, what can we do for you?"

Malloy smirked as he said it.

"Or better yet," Walters added, grabbing his crotch, "what can you do for us?"

Erika only smiled.

"Now, that depends," she purred.

"On . . . ?" they asked in unison.

"On what it is you want," she told them as if they should have known the answer all along.

"Well," Walters blustered, sucking in his gut, "how 'bout a blow job for starters?"

He didn't quite know what to expect, but it wasn't . . .

"Not a problem."

She licked her lips as she said it, and gave a sidelong glance at Morgan as she moved toward the two cops. There was a light in her eyes that he remembered so clearly. He knew he should say something, but with her looking right at him—Lord, she was beautiful!

But she looked away.

"Jesus, Walters, Malloy. Don't do it, man. She's . . ." He was dumbfounded. She was looking at him again. And then she was crossing the room, leaving the two cops clutching their balls.

"Shhh. Shush now, Morgan. You'll get yours, eventually."

Her green eyes were ice, her burning tresses falling over chocolate-brown features and full bloodred lips . . . lips that came oh-so-close now and brushed lightly across his forehead. His breath came ragged. For a moment he'd forgotten how to breathe.

"Raven, I . . ." he began in a whisper.

"Shhh," she said again, her long fingers lightly tracing his face, his eyes, down his body, over his crotch. A chill ran up his spine—cold, terrified, yearning.

"Hey, bitch. Over here first," Malloy shouted at her as he pulled out his thick, stubby penis.

Raven looked at him one more time before turning away, and the room's light seemed to dim except where she stood, moving slowly. Morgan was enchanted, he knew, but there was nothing magical about it.

Erika took turns with the two cops, using her mouth and hands. Malloy's was a stub compared with Walters's monstrous penis, but she paid them equal attention. Soon she was working them both, Walters in her left hand and Malloy in her right, and then she looked over at Morgan, who watched the whole scene with abject terror and a painful erection.

Her face clouded over and her eyes squinted. There was thunder there, and Morgan wanted to close his own eyes, but could not. She licked her lips, looked back up at the men with blue around their ankles and effortlessly ripped their cocks off. She tossed their lifeless flesh in the corner, trailing bloody roots, and the cops screamed and flailed on the ground. She looked back at Morgan, destruction in her eyes. It turned her on.

"Go. Now. Or I'll tear you apart with this building."

The choice was easy, and he watched from outside as she slaughtered every cop who fought her. The ones who ran, she didn't chase; they had at least the brains to be afraid. And then she brought the building down on top of them. When she emerged from the rubble, he was gone.

She didn't want to pick up the phone—not after what Lance had done to Monica the night before.

But if she called, then she might not be thinking about Morgan, his erection and his awe of her. He was a drug dealer! She didn't know why she hadn't ripped the fucker's guts out. Or did she?

Wasn't it because she wanted him? Wasn't it because he knew what she was, what she did, was terrified of her and still wanted her? What she saw in his eyes was perverse, obscene. It wasn't love and that's why she liked it. It was more like worship. He would do anything to be inside her, but did that include dying? Should she bother giving him a choice? Was she becoming Morgan's goddess?

Shut. Up.

Ego-tripping, messianic loony bitch, she told herself. You read all that in his eyes and his pants? Be serious. He'd probably wet himself. Again.

She picked up the phone and dialed. She listened, but her mind flipped back and forth between The Lance & Monica Show last night and Morgan's fervent stare, and she couldn't get off. She fell asleep with the phone cradled in her ear. In the morning she would be glad the connection lasted only thirty minutes, otherwise her credit card would have been maxed out. Not that she would need it. She planned to swan-dive off the city's tallest landmark in the afternoon. Her credit cards would long outlive her.

Twilight.

Okay, so it wasn't the city's tallest landmark, but the Eastwood Tower didn't have guards by the entrance to the roof who would be slightly apprehensive about a naked woman hurling herself from its peak. Still, she had tried to be inconspicuous as she made her way up there. All the answers could be scraped up off the ground.

And she was pretty sure it would work this time. Yesterday her back had hurt, and this building was a full twenty-seven stories higher than that one. It had been almost a game before. Her nocturnal adventures were useless. One person could not make the difference in Sodom; Lot had proved that millennia ago. Everyone she'd ever cared for was dead or gone, and to top it all off, she was pretty sure she was incapable of making love without committing murder at the same time. And so now she was . . .

Falling. Slower than before, or so it seemed. She had much more time to think. She was only a third of the way down when she decided she couldn't watch anymore. Before, it had been different. This time, she was fairly certain it would work. She closed her eyes tight and tucked her body in, stretching out again with her face aimed at the pavement. Her eyes were still closed.

Her life didn't flash before her eyes, though there seemed plenty of time. Interminable, unendurable time. There was no one who loved her, who might miss her, and she could not show her love in any case.

The wind whistled past her face, ripping the second tear she had shed in quite a time from her eye. It had become nearly impossible to breathe, and she held what little breath remained in her.

Her speed seemed to triple. She knew, could sense, that she was almost there. She could practically smell the asphalt freshly baked from another sweltering day. She tried to smile but could not. Finally, she stopped falling.

Simply stopped. The wind was no longer rushing past her face; the sensation of falling was gone. Her eyes were still closed as she realized that she had somehow suspended her fall, effectively postponing her death. Something snapped inside her and she felt happy. Giddy. The hell with it, she thought, and started to laugh.

And, laughing, she nodded her head slightly toward her chest . . . and bumped it on the tar.

She opened her eyes and laughed even harder when she saw the surface of the street barely two inches away. She glanced around. Erika still didn't know how she was holding herself in midair, but she sure as hell knew why. She had things to do! Suicide? What a stupid idea. The jig was up. Game over, man. This was not, had never been, the answer, just a way to expunge those feelings of guilt over Mikhail.

She had read something once about that self-styled superhero who spurned her for a boy wonder. She'd read that he could fly. At the time, she had ignored it as nothing but hype. Science-wise, she could almost understand the mutations that their bodies had gone through. They seemed possible enough, especially when her own flesh was indisputable evidence. But flight, that was fantasy, pure and simple. Or so she'd thought.

Now she was starting to think that whatever process had accelerated her DNA to deal with a different set of environmental rules had also worked on her brain, expanding far beyond the tiny percentage of the gray cells that are normally utilized. Perhaps there was something to the physical power of the psyche, to telekinesis and all that. What was happening to her certainly seemed like levitation or something. And if that was so, why couldn't she simply float back to the roof of the building, where she could retrieve her clothes? After all, she chided herself, it simply wouldn't do for a tremendously sexy, full-bodied woman to be seen hanging suspended in midair wearing nothing. Nudity was, as always, out of fashion.

Morgan was special, but not that special. She would

give him what he wanted, and what she wanted as well. And afterward, no matter what happened, she would keep icing dealers by night, but maybe she would have a life during the day as well. And whatever men came after Morgan . . . so be it. There would be men who would give anything to possess her just once, and once would be all they could manage.

Morgan was good at hiding. He had to be. His protectors had been killed by Raven, and even now, in the wee hours of the morning, the rest of the cops would be after him. Some for justice, to pay him back for his role in their comrades' demise; others for fun, to make him regret his arrogance in the past. Not to mention the other drug dealers who would be busy muscling in on the territory that was his only a day earlier. But what the hell, he was as good as dead. Not because the whole city wanted him dead, but because he knew that she would be looking for him as well. And unlike the rest of the city, she would find him. He knew that.

He prayed alternately for her to stay away and for her to come and take his misery from him. If he was to give up his life, better it be in her hands, the hands of a goddess on earth. He hardly deserved that, though. Hell, he was slime and did not deny that to himself or to anyone else. He had never wanted to deal drugs, to be a common criminal, but oh, was he good at it. The money was great and the women were attentive.

Women!

He crouched there in the shadows of the old warehouse, trying desperately not to think of women. Of one particular woman who was more than a woman.

Yes, Morgan was good at hiding. But he wanted to be found. Knew beyond a shadow of a doubt that he would be found, by her. And so it did not surprise him to see her in the open door of the old warehouse, silhouetted in the moonlight that streamed in from outside. Ah, moonlight, he thought. What a rare commodity. He could almost remember when it was common. When a clear sky was the norm.

She was really there!

Tired as he was, it took him a moment to focus on her, and on the reality of her presence. She had not said a word, simply stood there looking at him. Her red hair was set aflame by the moon, her chocolate skin in shadow. He could not see her eyes, but he knew they were watching him. He was entranced by the soft folds of her sleeveless emerald-green cotton dress as it clung tightly to her. The muscles on her arms bulged, and he remembered . . .

He fell to his knees before her.

"What—?" she began to ask, but he interrupted.

"I've seen what you can do, and I know why you're here. Just do me and get it over with."

"Morgan," she said, as if chiding an infant.

"Please, just do it. I can't deal with the waiting." He wondered how long it had taken her to find him, just how easy he had made it for her.

"Morgan," she said again, trying to get his attention. And it worked, for a moment. He looked up at her face, and then back down at the floor.

"You're the most beautiful and terrifying thing I've ever seen," he said before he could stop himself.

"Thank you," she said, and he could hear the amusement in her voice, which was not quite sarcasm. She didn't seem to be moving in for an attack.

"Do you like my dress?" she asked, and the incongruity of the question brought his head up.

"Uh. Yes, it's . . . uh. Beautiful."

"I bought it today. For you."

He didn't know what to say. She smiled at him as he stared in awe at her. She was his goddess now, and he had been resigned to death at her hands. Now he might have given his life gladly had she asked. He didn't know what magic she was performing on him, but it created a pure desire that bordered on obsession. He belonged to her now, had forfeited to her his life, to do with what she would.

And now she did.

She lifted Morgan in her strong arms and carried him to the back of the warehouse. A large pile of foam packing there made a dusty but comfortable mattress. She undressed him slowly and carefully, like a child with a doll. She caressed him slowly, teasing. Then she stood, stepped out of her shoes, pulled the dress from her shoulders and let it drop to the floor. She wore nothing underneath. For the first time in his life, Morgan was speechless.

She pushed him back onto the foam and straddled him. She leaned over and kissed him, and he slid easily into her. He finally moved for himself, and began to lightly trace his fingers across her breasts. She broke their kiss and sat up, riding him slowly. Her hands went to her own breasts and she began to knead them. She looked down on him and he thought he saw a sadness in her eyes. She increased the pace until her breath came in short, hitching gasps, and her eyes were shut tight. In a moment tears came, but the look on her face told him they were tears of joy. Morgan had made his goddess happy. He was worthy.

Morgan couldn't hold back any longer, and his orgasm exploded inside Erika. His goddess began to shudder, and let out a loud moan as she began her own climax.

It was the last and greatest moment of Morgan's life. Spattered inside and out by his love, Erika thought what a wonderful thing it was to be so desired and worshipped. She longed for the feeling to continue, and was determined to make sure it would. There would be others to worship her, to knowingly, willingly sacrifice all that they were for her love.

Erika promised herself that her loneliness was at an end, then stretched and rose to her feet. For the moment, at least, her emptiness was filled.

THE PICTURE OF JONATHAN COLLINS

Karl Edward Wagner

Karl Edward Wagner graduated from the University of
North Carolina School of Medicine, practicing psychiatry
briefly before becoming a full-time writer. He has written
or edited over forty-five books, including fifteen of *The
Year's Best Horror Stories*, six books in the Kane series
and two collections of contemporary horror fiction. Karl
died of heart failure on October 13, 1994. "The Picture
of Jonathan Collins" was one of his last stories written.

The advert had promised "Psychic Consultations" and
listed an address in Chelsea.

Jonathan Collins stood before the door of this address,
still considering. He was a slightly built man, apparently
just nearing thirty. He was clean-shaven, had neat but
longish black hair, bright brown eyes, very good features

and wore a dark blue pin-striped suit—de rigueur for a middle management position at the largish London hotel where he worked. He had on tight black leather shoes, neatly laced. At a glance, he was a handsome young man on the way up.

He sucked in his breath and rang the bell.

The door opened.

"Yes?"

"Miss Starlight?"

"Yes?"

"I'm Jonathan Collins. I arranged for a consultation."

"Please, do come in."

Victoria Starlight appeared to be somewhat older than Collins. Her hair was a mass of brown elflocks bound with a tangerine scarf. She wore a shapeless black smock, many necklaces, bracelets and rings, and gold-framed granny glasses straight from the late sixties. Her flat was cluttered with books and objets d'art, but meticulously dusted. She had four cats that were visible.

She ushered Collins to a small table. The table was set with a deck of Tarot cards and a crystal ball. Collins felt like a fool.

"Fancy some jasmine tea? I've just put the kettle to boil."

"Not just yet."

"I read tea leaves as well."

"My nerves can't manage tea just now."

The kettle was at a boil. Victoria saw to it and returned with her cup of tea. She sat across from Collins, waiting for him to speak.

Collins sighed and decided to get on with it. "Miss Starlight, I collect pornography."

"What?" She seemed poised to throw the teacup.

"Not modern smut," Collins said hastily. "My interest is only in material from the turn of the century—antique French postcards, art studies, that sort of thing. Somehow I seem to identify myself with that period. I hope this doesn't offend you."

"That you have an affinity for the *fin de siècle* does not. Pornography does. Why are you here?"

"It's these." Collins reached into his suit-coat pocket and produced two aging photographs. "I obtained these at an estate auction as part of a collection. I should warn you that they are explicit."

Victoria examined them with distaste. They appeared to be late-Victorian photographs.

The first was of two young men. One was wearing a garland, woman's black stockings and white silk knickers with lace and ruching, open at front and back. He was crouching upon a hassock. The other young man was standing, wearing black stockings with ribboned garters and a petticoat, which he was holding high above his waist as he thrust his cock deep into the other man's ass. The crouching man was looking back to watch the action.

The second photograph was similar, with the same two men, but shot against a different backdrop. One young man was standing bent over, holding his knees. He wore a garland and a lacy dress and black stockings with garters; the dress and petticoats were pulled above his hips. The other young man was wearing black stockings with ribboned garters and a black corset. He stood behind his partner, his cock thrusting into the other's ass. Their faces were cherubic with pleasure.

"Why show me this trash?" Victoria threw the photographs back to Collins.

Collins spread them out on the table. "Look closely. That's Oscar Wilde. I've verified that from other photographs."

"So sell it to *The Sun*. I'd always heard that Wilde was dead butch."

"And the man wearing the garland looks all too much like me."

Startled, Victoria reexamined the photographs, studying Collins's face. "He *does* look like you. A relative? Or coincidence? Or is this a hoax?"

"Not a hoax. As to the rest, I was hoping you might be able to tell me."

"Perhaps you may have had a gay ancestor. Perhaps he did have a fling with Oscar Wilde or someone who resembled him. Does this make you uncomfortable?"

Collins peered at the photographs. "I think that may be *me* wearing the garland. See? Even the same mole over the left cheekbone."

Victoria sipped her tea. She was not actually a psychic, but she had a smattering knowledge of the occult. The loonies who consulted her kept her off the dole. This man was a megaloony.

"Right, then. Are you telling me that you are over a century of age, and that you were photographed being buggered by Oscar Wilde in drag?"

"I don't know what to think. Not for certain." Collins pocketed the photographs. "I was in London during the Blitz. All of my records were destroyed in the course. Evidently I was buried in the rubble when my house took a direct hit. I lay in a coma for more than a week. No one could say how I survived. After, I had no memories. I had to learn to walk and speak all over again. But there were no scars."

Victoria reached for a cigarette. She was trying to quit, but . . . "So you're going on sixty-something. You're certainly keeping fit."

"I put it to good diet and regular exercise," said Collins. "But after I discovered these photographs, strange memories of a life before the War began to haunt me."

"Memories of a previous life?"

"Of this same life."

Victoria glanced at her mantel clock. She usually booked sessions for one hour, but this time she must find a way to cut it short.

Collins went on: "You've read Oscar Wilde's *The Picture of Dorian Gray*?"

"I have," she said carefully.

Collins withdrew the photographs and looked at them again. "I believe that the premise of the story is true. And I believe that Wilde based the character Dorian Gray on me."

"I'm sorry." Victoria was pouring herself more tea. "You believe that you are Dorian Gray?"

"No. Just the model for his character. I was young and pretty. Wilde used me like a woman. I think one of his set *did* paint a portrait of me—a portrait that aged through the years, whilst I've remained the same."

"And why have you just now come upon this conclusion?" Victoria had two Tarot readings scheduled for the afternoon, then an evening crystal gazing.

"I told you: these photographs," said Collins, still fumbling with them. "Memories came back. Began to distill."

Likely distilled single malt whiskey, Victoria thought. "What is it you wish me to do?"

Collins seemed desperate. "If this is true, then I have to find my portrait so that I can protect it."

"Didn't it go up with that bomb?"

"No. Of course not. Otherwise I wouldn't be here."

Victoria composed herself. Loonies paid. "What you need to do, Mr. Collins, is to channel your thoughts back to the last century. By doing so, you may follow the path of your portrait and rediscover your lost years. I have some gems and crystals that will assist you—aquamarine, black tourmaline and rose quartz. They are pendant to a silver chain which you must wear as you meditate upon these thoughts. You may need to reenact past experiences of profound emotional energy to help the crystals lead you back."

And she took him for fifty quid, mainly for the baubles, and after Collins left, she made doubly certain of the bolts.

Victoria Starlight then picked up her favorite cat, a monstrously obese gray tabby, and cradled her. "Oxfam, that was bloody well the craziest git we've ever let into our flat."

Jonathan Collins actually had held a number of positions since the War. He was very good at middle management, but shifted positions frequently—banks, hotels, brokerage firms—before he actually reached boardroom level. He was generally well liked by his fellow workers, who gossiped that he dyed his hair, lied about his age and worked out regularly. The latter two were correct. He was a quiet, polite man, something of a womanizer, seldom drank, but would stand a round or two. When the subject of conversation turned to Collins, it was agreed that he was one of the last of the old school, born out of his age. Only a few associates, mainly female, had ever seen his collection of *fin de siècle* pornography.

To the best of his knowledge, Jonathan Collins had never had or considered having a homosexual experience of any sort. Then he discovered the photographs. Strange and disturbing memories began to overwhelm his dreams. Why could he remember the taste of Oscar Wilde's come when he awoke?

Collins tried to meditate with the stones. He only grew bored, then fell asleep. After several such failures, he decided that either he didn't know how to meditate or the woman was no more than a well-paid fake. Nonetheless, she had advised him that he might need to reenact past experiences of profound emotional energy in order to channel.

Collins waited another week, then explored the phone boxes. His dreams had become disremembered fantasies, leaving him with only a sleepless haze of uncertainty. His fellow workers at the hotel expressed concern about his health. Collins explained it all as a bout of flu. It was going around.

The phone boxes in the West End were festooned with daily supplies of cards advertising sexual favors of any sort and including a phone number. Some were nicely illustrated. Collins passed over the spanking, schoolgirls in uniform, water sports and the usual. After three or four boxes, he selected one which read: "Stern TV Wardrobe Mistress Seeks Submissive Slaves for Training."

After three or four days, he phoned the number.

Collins was given an address near Baker Street. Desperate by now, he presented himself at the door of the flat promptly as scheduled. He was certain that at any minute his hair might be thinning and that his teeth probably were loosening in their gums. His nails seemed to be pulling away from the quick, and his digestion was not good. He had to find the painting.

A tall blonde in a tight, long velvet dress answered the

bell. Her features were quite feminine, heavily made-up and very stern.

Collins almost stuttered. "Good evening. I'm Mr. Collins. I believe I have an appointment."

"Get inside." She practically dragged him past the doorway. "I am Mistress Gwen. You will always address me as Mistress Gwen. You will answer only to Miss Joan. And why are you wearing those ridiculous clothes, Miss Joan?"

"I . . ."

Her riding crop smacked his backside. "No excuses! Show me your forty quid, and I'll soon see that you are properly attired for a young lady."

Collins pulled out the two photographs from his suit-coat pocket, along with his wallet. "This is what I want."

Mistress Gwen looked at the pictures, then looked shrewdly at Collins. No, not from the police. Some twisted Yuppie out for a night's thrills. She didn't usually perform sex—most clients just liked to dress up and be dominated, then wank off. But . . .

"That's another forty quid."

Collins paid her and was led into a large bedroom.

Mistress Gwen smacked her riding crop. "Out of those clothes. All of them. Right now."

Collins hesitated over his boxer briefs, but a smack from the riding crop made him drop them with the rest of his clothes.

"Good," said Mistress Gwen. "You please me when you obey. If you're a good little Miss Joan, perhaps I won't have to cane you. Now, then, put on this condom. I won't have you soiling my wardrobe."

Mistress Gwen unzipped her dress. Beneath it she was wearing a black leather corselet with six suspenders attached to black seamed hose, and black, six-inch stiletto pumps. The corselet showed some cleavage, but the bulge in her black knickers revealed that she was a he. Mistress Gwen began choosing things from her chest of drawers.

"These should fit you, Miss Joan."

Mistress Gwen helped Miss Joan put on a black bra

with foam rubber falsies, then a pair of black tap pants over a black suspender belt and black seamed hose. After that came a black corset, laced tight, and a pair of ankle-strap stiletto shoes. She made Miss Joan sit at the dressing table whilst she applied makeup to her face and lips, then fitted her with a curling black wig.

Miss Joan minced around the room, getting lessons in deportment and frequent whacks from the riding crop.

"Now it's time for the rest of your training," said Mistress Gwen. "Get on your knees on the bed. Now!"

Miss Joan did as she was told. Mistress Gwen had pulled down her knickers, revealing a formidable erection. She rolled on a lubricated condom, then yanked down Miss Joan's knickers and climbed up behind her on the bed.

Miss Joan gasped for breath as Mistress Gwen's cock pressed into her. She pushed her face and padded breasts into the bed pillows, stifling a moan as the head pierced her and the rigid length slid in behind. Mistress Gwen began to thrust quickly, lovelessly. Her hand reached around for Miss Joan's cock and stroked it.

Mistress Gwen was deliberately brutal as she fucked her. She stroked Miss Joan's cock as if she were trying to pull it off. Mercifully soon, Miss Joan felt Mistress Gwen's cock pulse and strain inside her ass; then came her own orgasm.

Miss Joan passed out upon the pillows . . .

Collins was crouched upon a hassock. He was wearing lacy open knickers and black stockings. Oscar Wilde, clad in black stockings, his petticoat upraised, was buggering him soundly.

"Hold that!" someone called out.

Wilde paused, his cock partially withdrawn. There was a bright flash, then a plume of burned powder. Collins turned his head. The photographer was removing the glass plate, inserting a new one.

Wilde resumed sodomizing him, thrusting slowly. "We'll have these to show to select friends to see how pretty you are now," Wilde said. "You'll treasure these photographs when you are old and decaying."

Collins glanced up at the windows, shuttered from outside. Lettering there read: "J. MacVane. Photographic Studio."

Wilde surged deeply into him, coming in violent spurts. There was another flash of light . . .

Miss Joan was lying across a bed, and someone was shaking her. She opened her eyes and found that she was in drag with a filled condom on her drooping cock and a sore ass. She groaned and sat up.

Mistress Gwen was watching her with concern. All she needed was a dead John on her premises. "You feel all right? You were passed out for a minute or so there. You got a condition of some sort?"

"I just was carried away," said Miss Joan.

"Yes. Well, you gave me a fair start. Now, change your clothes and be off. I have another client in an hour." Mistress Gwen considered telling Miss Joan not to come here again, but eighty knicker was eighty knicker, and she was a good fuck. Responsive. Perhaps too responsive.

Collins tried the directories, on the chance in a million that the firm of J. MacVane might still be doing business. It wasn't. Not under that name, at least. Countless wasted phone calls told him nothing. He realized that he was only assuming that the studio had been in London.

He phoned the auction house whence he had obtained the photographs. They furnished no useful information. The lot of photographs was merely an item from an estate: the deceased was not to be named.

After a week of blind ends and disturbing dreams, Collins made another appointment with Mistress Gwen.

Mistress Gwen received Collins with mixed feelings. She knew he wasn't police, and a regular at eighty quid was too good to turn away. That fainting spell: if it happened again, she might have to reconsider.

The session went much as before. This time Mistress Gwen was dressed mainly in black latex and leather gear. She soon had Miss Joan wigged and corseted, with red latex spanking knickers, open at the back, and matching latex shoulder-length gloves and stockings. She added a slave collar with a lead, then instructed Miss Joan sternly, often using her riding crop on Miss Joan's exposed bottom.

Having put Miss Joan through her paces, Mistress Gwen ordered her to stand before the white bedroom wall. She took out a Polaroid camera from a drawer, demanding that Miss Joan pose for her.

Miss Joan protested. "You could use these for blackmail."

Mistress Gwen worked the camera. "These are Polaroids. No negatives. Yours for a keepsake. Something to remember how pretty you are, Miss Joan, and where to come to be pretty again at any time. Besides, I think you rather enjoy being photographed. You really do like to pose."

Mistress Gwen took ten shots of Miss Joan in various poses, set the photographs aside, then said, "These will be another ten quid."

Watching her clock, Mistress Gwen next commanded Miss Joan to kneel upon the bed, then undid the zip of her leather knickers. She rolled on a lubricated condom, gave Miss Joan's bottom a few more whacks to improve her own erection, then mounted her. She pressed her cock into Miss Joan's rectum as quickly as she could force it, anxious to complete the session, and began to move her hips furiously. She had let an aging queen in maid's costume give her a blow job earlier that day, and this second ejaculation would take time. Time was money.

Miss Joan was rocking from the ceaseless drilling she was getting. She moved her hand back to her cock, hard and throbbing beneath the latex spanking knickers. She was about to come . . .

Collins was standing beside a plaster mock-up of a Greek column. Behind him was a backdrop of a Doric temple. Collins wore a garland in his hair and nothing else. The studio was quite warm.

"Just a moment, Jack."

Oscar Wilde rose from his chair. He was also naked, and Collins remembered being sodomized by him only minutes ago. Wilde stroked his cock, bringing Collins to full erection.

"Much better, Jonathan. Take the photograph, Jack."

Again a flash and a puff of smoke. Collins blinked.

"That was a beautiful pose, dear boy," said Wilde. "Your body perfect, your lovely penis saluting the flag and your face aglow from a good buggering. I think I shall have this one mounted and framed."

"I wish I could stay like this forever, if it pleases you."

Wilde smiled. "Go on and toss yourself off. I want to see it."

Collins began to jerk his rigid cock. He hadn't come during his buggering, and he was close to ejaculation. "I would give my soul to remain forever young as in that photograph."

His come spurted from him as Wilde watched thoughtfully. There was another flash . . .

"Wake up!" Mistress Gwen slapped Miss Joan's bottom with her crop and shook her roughly.

Miss Joan opened her eyes, trying to recognize her surroundings. Her latex knickers were sticky with come; the condom had either slipped or burst.

"Good. Do you make it a habit of passing out when you reach your orgasm?"

"Perhaps this corset is too tightly laced."

"Well, then, let's just unlace you. Then clean yourself and get into your clothes. And don't forget your photographs."

Mistress Gwen again considered telling Miss Joan to stay away, but she reckoned she might hit her for a hundred quid next session. Perhaps add some bondage, a good spanking, a gym slip instead of a corset, a pair of schoolgirl's knickers she must wear home. Miss Joan had all the marks of a regular and profitable client.

Besides, the man was clueless.

Collins asked for a week's holiday from the hotel. Despite short notice, it was readily granted. The staff had commented for some weeks that Mr. Collins appeared to be under some stress. A holiday was well overdue.

He had previously obtained a pass to the library at the British Museum, and he spent the first days researching any material regarding the life and times of Oscar Wilde. Wilde's notorious affairs were discussed with varying degrees of discretion. Nowhere was there mention of anyone named Jonathan Collins or a photographer named Jack MacVane. But then, such matters as these had been strictly clandestine in that era.

Collins phoned Victoria Starlight for an appointment. He told her that he had twice been able to channel. She told him to keep at it and hung up. He left several messages on her answering machine, but none were returned.

Collins phoned Mistress Gwen, who did pick up her phone for him. "I want to do some shopping," he said resolutely, "and I shall need your assistance. I wish to acquire a woman's costume of approximately 1890— original, if possible."

Mistress Gwen was already consulting her filofax. A dead Thursday until ten. "Is this for you to wear?"

"Yes. Of course, I'll pay you for your time and expertise—and as before."

"Won't come cheap." Mistress Gwen left that openended. "I do know all the shops, and I suppose I can cancel a few sessions. Come round with a taxi as quick as you can, and we'll shop for your wardrobe." And mine as well, she thought as she hung up the phone. It wasn't going to be a dull Thursday after all.

Mistress Gwen was modestly dressed in black tights and minidress, stilettos and a chained and studded motorcycle jacket when Collins came to her door. They got into the taxi, and Mistress Gwen gave an address near Portobello Road. As the day progressed, Mistress Gwen would give many addresses.

They found several petticoats, some open knickers with lots of lace, a chemise and a camisole, and two corsets— Collins insisted that Mistress Gwen must have the black one—at the vintage clothing shops. Mistress Gwen insisted upon high-buttoned shoes with five-inch heels, and a shop that catered to transvestites supplied these for them both, along with black silk stockings and ribboned garters. The dress took some doing, but after a search, a shop in Camden Passage had a lovely ball gown which Mistress Gwen judged would fit Miss Joan once she was tightly laced. She picked out a pair of twenties vintage silk camiknickers for herself and included them with the sale. Collins stopped at a florist's and, after some doing, managed a floral garland.

Well laden, they arrived back at Mistress Gwen's flat by midafternoon. Mistress Gwen had also had an excellent luncheon at Collins's expense; she saw prospects of yet more knicker and was in the very best of spirits. The man must be made of money. She poured two glasses of sherry.

"Now, then, Miss Joan. Shall I help you try on your new wardrobe? You should be very pretty."

Collins reached into his suit coat and withdrew one of the photographs. It was the one of the young man in drag, skirts thrown up, standing bent over as the other man in a black corset and stockings sodomized him.

"I want it just like this."

Mistress Gwen dealt with clients obsessed with their fetishes every day. She returned the photograph. "Then let's get dressed properly."

"I want it just like this," Collins repeated. "No wigs, no makeup, no falsies, no condoms. Just like the picture." He handed the photograph back to Mistress Gwen. "Does your camera include a timer?"

"It does."

"I want a photograph of the two of us, just like that."

"This will all cost a little more, of course," said Mistress Gwen.

She set up her camera on a tripod as Collins undressed. She did get frequent requests from clients for photographs of the two of them together. She removed her wig and makeup, brushed up her short black hair, then got out of her clothes. Miss Joan was struggling into her new garments and required assistance. They laced each other into the corsets, and Mistress Gwen finally settled Miss Joan into her dress. It was a good fit.

Miss Joan bent over, pulling her skirts over her hips. "Is this like in the photograph?"

Mistress Gwen checked her camera for frame and took a shot. "Very much so. You even look like the boy you're dressed up as. Let's try another."

Mistress Gwen was wearing just the corset, stockings and garters, and her new shoes. She applied lubricant to her cock, set the timer, then stood behind Miss Joan. She guided her cock just past the head into Miss Joan's ass as the camera flashed. Withdrawing, she collected the photograph and showed it to Miss Joan, along with the Victorian picture. "It's a very close match."

"Take another to be sure." Miss Joan was tottering on her five-inch heels. Her hands were braced on her knees.

Mistress Gwen reset the timer, then moved behind Miss Joan, reinserting her cock a short way. "Are you all right?"

"Yes. It feels good. Now smile for the camera."

The flash went off, and Mistress Gwen plunged her cock all the way into Miss Joan's ass, grasping her hips to keep her from falling. "Just try not to faint on me this time. I don't want you dangling from my dick." She began to work her hips slowly back and forth against Miss Joan's lace-encircled ass. Mistress Gwen was enjoying herself; no need to rush a good fuck. Many of Miss Joan's fifty-quid notes would be hers soon enough . . .

Collins was sitting on the edge of a bed, his dress soiled and his face running with tears. Oscar Wilde had finished getting dressed and was laying five pounds upon the dressing table.

"Please, let's not have further histrionics. You surely must have known that you were only a passing infatuation."

"You used me like a girl," Collins sobbed. "Now you're paying me as if I were a prostitute."

"I'm certain that you will find other men," said Wilde, moving toward the door. "By the by, if you pop round to Soho, Jack should have some photographs for you. Keep them and remember your beautiful youth."

"I never want to see them!"

"That's not what you said short days ago. And what's said is said." Wilde adjusted his hat and left the room . . .

"It's not a painting. It's a photograph," Miss Joan murmured.

"Of course," panted Mistress Gwen. "I just took them." Miss Joan was about to fall over, but Mistress Gwen held her hips tightly and made several more deep, quick thrusts as her orgasm jetted into Miss Joan. It was one of the best, and a pity she had to charge for such pleasure. Miss Joan had been silent during most of her screwing; there was semen running down her stockings, so Mistress Gwen assumed she had been quietly tossing herself off beneath her heaped petticoats. At least she hadn't fainted. Mistress Gwen let her spent cock slip out of Miss Joan's ass, pulled down Miss Joan's skirts and helped her to sit down on the bed.

"It's a photograph!" Miss Joan did seem a bit scattered.

"Yes?" Mistress Gwen collected the last photograph she had shot. Very good, indeed. A close reenactment of the Victorian original, and Miss Joan's resemblance to the buggered boy in the dress was uncanny.

"That bastard!" Miss Joan pointed to the original. "He fucked me for a few weeks, paid me off as if I were a whore, then wrote a book about me!"

"I think a glass of sherry will do you good," said Mistress Gwen. "Settle you down a bit."

Collectors know other collectors, whether they collect coins, stamps, books, old cars, whatever. They make acquaintances and sometimes friends with those of similar interests.

Having exhausted all other avenues, Collins thought of phoning fellow collectors of vintage pornography. Secretive by nature and necessity, only a few others were well enough known to him personally to phone for assistance: any information on one Jack MacVane, photographer with studio in Soho, circa 1890.

On his fourth call, Collins got lucky. The call was to

an acquaintance, Herbert Musgrave, an established dealer in antiquarian and esoteric books. His tastes in other matters were also esoteric.

"Yes, dear boy. J. MacVane. Yes, I have a number of pieces of his work. Bit of a decadent by all accounts. Yes, I heard about your luck at that estate auction recently. Look, why not pop by here this evening, say about sixish? You show me yours, and I'll show you mine. Excellent. Cheers!"

Herbert Musgrave had a semidetached house in Crouch End and a small bookshop in Kensington which specialized in deluxe bindings, antiquarian books and other sorts, if you asked properly. He was a short man, putting on flesh, somewhere past fifty, with graying hair and beard, and bifocals. He and Collins often met at book fairs, exchanging pleasantries over a glass of wine and sometimes exchanging wrapped parcels.

Collins arrived at half-past six, owing to traffic. Musgrave greeted him enthusiastically. He was wearing a smoking jacket, and he had set out sherry, cheese and biscuits.

Once settled: "Well, give us a look at your find." He examined the two photographs with keen interest. "Oh, yes. These are the work of J. MacVane. That's his studio. Quite rare. Excellent find! I have a few others from these sets, but not these two. Would you consider selling them?"

"Sets?"

"Yes. For the elaborate staging as seen here, photographers often took a dozen or more plates, selling the best in packets of six to ten sequential photographs. Here, let me show you."

Musgrave had already set out a photo album. He quickly turned through it. "Yes, here they are. Some others in the sets."

There were six photographs. Of the first pair, one was of the young man in the dress, assisting the other with his corset; the next portrayed him giving the other man a blow job. The next four were from the other set. The first showed the two men dressing each other; next, the man in the petticoat smiling as he guided his cock into the other's mouth as he crouched upon a hassock; another, with his cock completely engulfed in his bent-over ass; the last, with the man in open knickers lying on his back on the hassock, legs high in the air, while the other man stood between his legs, fucking him as if he were a woman.

"MacVane's work is rather scarce," said Musgrave, reaching for the sherry. "I can offer you a good price."

"What do you know of the man?"

"Very little. He had a studio in Soho for a short time; took very good photographic portraits. He mingled with the most decadent of the artists and writers, that sort of thing. Said to have been intimate with Aleister Crowley and that lot. Most of his work was done on private commission—largely just nude studies of all ages and gender, but he also did a good bit of what you see here. Again, mostly on private commission. However, some prints got into circulation, and a scandal resulted. MacVane left London a jump ahead of the police and set up shop again in Paris. After photographing some memorable postcards, he was found dead in his studio. Talk was that he was poisoned, but the inquest ruled natural causes—he was a notorious drunkard—and so the matter and MacVane were soon forgotten."

"I think that's Oscar Wilde in these photographs."

Musgrave adjusted his glasses and peered closely. "No, no, no, dear boy. Of course not. Some resemblance, certainly, but if you'll pardon my saying so, the other man looks far more like you than does his lover resemble Oscar Wilde."

Musgrave sipped his sherry, for which he had a weakness, and studied Collins's handsome face, for which he also had a weakness. Thinking about it, he decided there really *was* an astonishing resemblance to the young man in the photograph. Musgrave wondered if Collins might have had a gay ancestor. Might it run in the family . . . ?

"I have a few of his nude studies over here." Musgrave pulled down a larger album. "Got them as part of a larger lot of Victorian photography at Sotheby's some years back. It was an unsorted jumble, so I had it quite cheaply.''

Collins paged through the album. There was a buxom woman, another buxom woman, a girl of about ten, a boy of about the same age, another buxom woman, a boy in his teens, a muscular man of about twenty-five, another buxom woman, a girl of perhaps five, two buxom women embracing.

"This next is my favorite," said Musgrave, sliding closer.

Collins stared at the photograph of himself, standing nude beside a plaster Doric column, against a Grecian backdrop. His mouth felt dry, and he reached for his sherry.

"The same dear boy as in those other photographs. And he *does* look very much like you, Jonathan. At least the face does."

"I really must have this," Collins said.

"There's another pose on the next page that shows him wanking off."

"I'll trade you my two photographs."

Musgrave shook his head.

"And add to that one hundred pounds."

Musgrave considered. The offer was really a very good one. But Collins seemed *very* interested in this one photograph. The sherry had gone to Musgrave's head and made him reckless. Besides, he hadn't known that Collins was interested in male pornography. Still waters.

He looked again at Collins's two photographs. "Acts like this. Between two men. I mean, have you ever . . . ?"

The next morning Collins phoned for a taxi. Musgrave saw him out, still in his dressing robe, and invited Collins to come again soon. Collins left without his two photographs, short by a hundred pounds, with Musgrave's come due to meet somewhere between his stomach and his rectum. But he had *the* photograph wrapped securely and in his hands.

As he got into the taxi, Collins wondered if he hadn't played the fool all along. The man in the picture should have aged whilst *he* stayed young. Neither of them had aged. Perhaps there actually had been a painting. Perhaps the aging portrait was only Wilde's embellishment. Musgrave had been all over him throughout the night. He was too wrung out to want to think of his next possible move. Perhaps another session with Mistress Gwen.

After kissing Collins good-bye, Musgrave lit a cigarette and poured a glass of sherry. An enchanting but exhausting night; he was pleased that today was Saturday, so that his young assistant would be there to open shop. A shame to have taken such advantage of young Jonathan, but experienced collectors must learn never to permit their eagerness to acquire an object to reach the attention of its owner.

Besides, Musgrave had also purchased the glass negatives as part of the auction lot. He would have a new print made straightaway. Collins could still boast of having the original.

Climbing to his attic, Musgrave rummaged around and found the box of glass negatives, barely glanced at after the auction. Yes, it should be here. He carefully sorted through the plates. All of these were promised to be of the prints in his album. Here was the young man tossing off by the Greek column. Perhaps Collins would come back for that one.

The last plate was of a hideous, bloated old man, bald and toothless, sagging belly, covered with scars and blotches.

"Bloody hell! What was MacVane thinking when he took this!" Musgrave complained. "On one of his binges when he had this creature pose!"

He set the plate aside with a shudder. Two careful searches through the glass negatives did not reveal the plate he wanted.

"Cheated again!" Musgrave said angrily. In vexation he snatched up the offending glass negative, carried it downstairs all the way to the back, then hurled it into the dustbin at the back wall.

The glass negative shattered impressively. Musgrave felt somewhat better.

The taxi driver heard the scream from the backseat, turned his head to look, screamed himself. He went over the curb and struck a lamppost. He was still screaming when passersby pulled him out, head bloody and smashed against the steering wheel.

There was no point in pulling out his passenger, if that was what it was.

It was still clutching in one rotting hand a parcel which was found to contain an old photograph of a nude young man. As the police pulled the parcel away, the crumbling hand, still clutching, broke away.

The driver had a concussion and no memory of the morning.

The body had crumbled into broken bits and dust.

The police suggested some bizarre prank. The inquest reluctantly concurred. There simply could be no other explanation.

The picture disappeared into police archives.

Jonathan Collins was never found.

HAPPY COUPLE

Danielle Willis

Danielle Willis was kicked out of Barnard in 1986 and has since worked as a nanny, poodle groomer, stripper and dominatrix. Her play, *The Methedrine Dollhouse*, was produced at Exit Theatre in 1989. Her books include the poetry volumes *Corpse Delectable* and *Dogs In Lingerie*. Her poetry and fiction have appeared in such markets as *Taste of Latex*, *Tantrum*, *Screw* and *On Our Backs*. She currently makes her home in San Francisco's Mission district.

I wake to the squeaking of the exercise wheel in the rat cage and Miranda lying on her back staring blankly up at the ceiling, a big greenbottle fly crawling across her left eyeball. I shoo it away and it buzzes maddeningly around the room, refusing to light. The clock on the nightstand says three-thirty and cars thumping Prince and mariachi music parade sluggishly beneath the window, the drivers occasionally honking their horns or yelling at each other in Spanish.

I brush my hand down over Miranda's eyelids the way they do in movies to close dead people's eyes, but they keep opening back up. Pressing her eyelids shut with my fingers doesn't work either, so finally I just lie back down and pull the sheet over both of our heads.

Miranda's body is cool as tile in the August heat and I feel along her sharply articulated rib cage, down to the hollow of her stomach and between her legs. She mumbles something and pushes my hand away, her claws prickling against my skin. It's the first movement she's made in over twenty-four hours.

"Miranda?"

No answer, so I give her a shove with my foot. She moans and twists over onto her belly, hands scrabbling for cover under the bloodstained pillow. I shove her again. It's fun, kind of like watching an amoeba react to being stuck with a pin.

"What do you *want*, Elizabeth?" she asks into the mattress, her voice choked and rusty with sleep.

"I want you to wake up and talk to me."

"What time is it?"

"Three-thirty."

"Afternoon or morning?"

"Afternoon, I think." It's hard to tell in this apartment because the shades are always drawn and the windows themselves are blacked out with tinfoil, old rock posters and construction paper. The only light from outside is whatever seeps in through the rips—dusty, filtered beams that crisscross each other in the dim closeness.

"Then let me sleep until seven at least. It's still daylight."

"It's not daylight in here. Can't you at least sit up in bed and watch a video with me? I rented *Salo*."

"Oh, God, that's so slow. Especially when that fat old blond bitch is telling her twenty-minute shit-eating stories."

"I didn't know you'd seen it." I always feel so stupid around her.

"Some trick took me to see it in the theater when it came out. The whole audience was either vomiting or walking out in disgust. I thought it was kind of funny, but I couldn't sit through it again. Just please let me sleep."

"You've been sleeping for a day now."

"I know. Sometimes I sleep for two days or even a week. I've been known to sleep for months."

"It's a wonder your eyes haven't been eaten out by maggots, then."

"What are you talking about?"

"There was a fucking *fly* crawling around on your eyeball when I woke up. If you're going to sleep with your eyes open, you should at least pull the covers over your head or wear one of those satin beauty masks or something. It's not sanitary."

Miranda sits up and clutches my wrist. Her eyes are blazing yellow and there is a slight grayish cast to her skin. It's unnerving how quickly she can move sometimes.

"Did it lay eggs? How long was it on my eye?" There is that edge of panic in her voice that usually precedes one of her fits of hypochondria.

"I don't know. It was there when I woke up."

"Oh, God. Can you see anything?" She pulls her bottom lids down and rolls her eyes up into her head.

"No, Miranda. I'm sure you're fine. I just told you that so you'd—"

"You don't *understand*!" she shrieks. "I could be *dying*!" Then she scrambles out of bed and runs down the narrow hallway into the bathroom. I hear the door slam and the faucets turn on full blast. Looking down, I see tiny droplets of blood welling up on my wrist. I lick them off and go after Miranda, sincerely hoping this isn't going to take all afternoon.

Miranda is crouched over the sink, rubbing handfuls of this really nasty antimicrobial soap she gets from the funeral home into her eyes and then rinsing them out with scalding hot water. A large puddle is forming on the mildewed linoleum at her feet and the mirror is clouded with steam. Hearing me come in, she looks up, eyes running

with pinkish suds, and tells me to go get the formaldehyde.

"It's under the sink in the kitchen," she says.

"You'll blind yourself."

"Just a dropperful in each eye won't do any harm. I've
done it before."

I'm sure you have, I think. "Miranda, if there *was* anything in your eye, it's gone now."

"It's not. I can feel them itching." She sounds like
she's on the verge of tears. Why did I have to make that
comment? I should know by now that anything having to
do with rotting meat sets her off. Oh, well, at least she's
awake. I go up behind her and put my arms around her
waist.

"Sweetie, they're itching because you've got a ton of
soap in them. Why don't you just rinse them out and we
can take a bath together, okay?"

Her muscles stiffen. "I shouldn't sit in a bathtub—it'll
accelerate the process. I'll just take a quick shower and
dry off." She says this in a rapid mutter, more like she's
giving herself laboratory instructions than actually talking
to me.

"There's no process to accelerate, Miranda. You're
fine. You don't have The Rot. I don't even think there is
such a disease."

"What do *you* know? Can you even imagine what it's
like to live with the knowledge that someday your body
is going to figure out that it's supposed to be dead and
just start decaying with you in it?"

"Miranda, I'm sorry, I just—"

"It is *not* something I made up to be neurotic about for
fun, Elizabeth. I've seen people die of it, horribly, over
the period of weeks or even months. It can start out as a
tiny patch of mold on your fingertip and next thing you
know, your stomach's so swollen with tissue gas it bursts
open and there's Rot going up your spinal cord into your
brain and your face gets all green and distorted and—"

"It's not happening to you, I promise. You've got to
calm down. *Please.*"

"HOW CAN I CALM DOWN WHEN WORMS ARE

GOING TO START HATCHING OUT OF MY EYES ANY DAY NOW?'' she screams, writhing out of my grasp and curling up in a sobbing ball underneath the sink. This is good—once she starts crying, the worst of her fit has most likely passed. I kneel down beside her and stroke her hair, which is brittle with Aquanet and the stench of her last trick's cigarettes. I would never say anything, but I think her hairstyle's really funny—long, parted on the side and feathered back like some hooker's on a rerun of "Vega$." Judging from the photo albums I've seen, she's always been consistently ten or twenty years behind the current trends in fashion.

"You're going to be okay, Miranda. I'll go get you the formaldehyde if you want me to."

I start to get up and she grabs my arm.

"No. Stay here," she sniffles. Her eyes are still full of soap, the whites beginning to turn red from irritation. I pull her onto my lap and listen to her whine about her impending putrefaction for about ten minutes before she finally goes limp with resignation and allows me to coax her into the shower.

Exhausted, I wander into the kitchen to see if there is anything at all in the way of food. Miranda's kitchen is a very scary place, the tiny wastebasket overflowing with dried-out rats, piss-soaked newspapers and cedar shavings, bloody rigs and empty bottles of hummingbird food. The sink is full of blackened spoons and small porcelain dishes from which all but the most minute traces of heroin have been scraped with an Exacto knife. Miranda saves these dishes until she's accumulated ten or twelve, then soaks the dregs of the heroin off them with a little bit of water. She can usually get one or two very weak shots that way.

On the counter next to the sink is one of her disgustingly neglected rat cages, in which at least twenty half-starved albino rats clamber over each other in a frenzy of hunger and boredom. Two of the females have litters of naked pink babies, some of which have been partially eaten. Miranda has this fucked-up theory that if she breeds her own rats she won't have to go to the pet store as often.

She once told me her paranoid fantasy that the Mexicans who run the pet store are into Santeria and that they'll figure out she's a vampire if she goes there too much and get the whole neighborhood roused against her. I made some joke about torch-bearing villagers and she snarled that it wasn't funny.

"They used to cut our hearts out and nail them to their doors, you know."

The cabinets are empty except for a few cobwebs and faded boxes of Hartz Rat Pellets, and the only item in the refrigerator is a bottle of hummingbird food, which Miranda rationalizes as being nutritionally viable on the grounds that "blood is mostly just sugar and water anyway." This is irritating, because I remember buying milk and cereal a few days ago, and while it's conceivable that the milk might have gone bad in Miranda's shitty refrigerator, which isn't even cold most of the time, I bet anything she fed my Honeycombs to her fucking rats because she's too high and lazy to go to Woolworth's and buy them real food. I decide that I will go buy them some food myself. I need some fresh air and breakfast anyway.

I fish through the piles of rancid clothing on the floor of the bedroom until I find a pair of not-too-crotchy-smelling jeans and a wrinkled T-shirt with the Rolling Stones mouth logo across the front. The concert date on the back says Madison Square Garden 1973. My sock prospects are all too dismal, so I just put my shoes on with bare feet. On my way out I stick my head into the bathroom and yell to Miranda that I'm going to the store and that I'll be right back. I don't wait to hear her reply.

Outside, the sunlight is a shock, almost physically painful after being in the apartment so long. I'm not sure if it's been a couple days or a week. There are no clouds and the air is literally rippling in the heat, the mingled smells of exhaust, fish and garbage cooking to a nasty pungency. Mexican girls in pastel stretch pants walk by pushing baby carriages, orangey makeup glistening. It must be Sunday, because there are all these families out with their overdressed and irritated little children, boys in miniature three-piece suits, girls in frothy pink, white or yellow dresses; elaborately ringleted hair done up in ribbons and plastic butterfly barrettes, tiny crucifixes dangling from thin gold chains around their necks. As I close the steel gate behind me a large woman in a dark floral print skirt and matching blazer yanks her two daughters out of my path, muttering something about "*that house.*" I can see why Miranda gets paranoid living in this neighborhood—people still believe in the Devil here. Walking down the street, I'm aware that every third store sells plaster icons and glossy framed pictures of the Virgin Mary. Even the psychotic Vietnamese gift shops with windows full of light-up ballerina fountains, cable-car snow domes and ceramic Buddha pencil holders have one or two mirrorized Last Supper clocks prominently displayed.

None of the fluorescently lit, orange-tiled cafeterias with their vats of mysteriously bubbling food and sparse patronage of old men with urine stains on their inner pant legs seem particularly appealing, so I grab a couple of stale cookies with rainbow-colored sprinkles on them at the Dragon City Cafe and eat them on my way to Woolworth's, where I spend about ten minutes staring at an enormous cage full of blue and green parakeets before finally selecting an appropriate box of rat pellets.

When I get back to the apartment, Miranda is sitting cross-legged on the bed in her maroon velour bathrobe cooking up a shot, wet hair hanging in reddish, dripping tendrils down her back. Devoid of makeup, her features are especially drawn and vulpine, yellow eyes recessed deep in their hollow sockets. I wonder when the last time she actually fed was, on something other than hummingbird food, that is.

"There's enough for you if you'd like some," she says, never raising her eyes from the spoon. I seem to remember a study where monkeys were given a choice between two buttons, one which dispensed food and one which dispensed drugs—cocaine, I think—and they all starved to death.

"I don't know, maybe later on." My stomach's still upset from the stuff I did yesterday, and the smell of it in the air triggers an instant nausea response.

"I think you'll like this batch," she continues as if I hadn't said anything at all. "I've been going to this guy since the fifties; you can't get stuff like this from anyone else. He's not going to be around much longer either, just got home from the hospital. It's the second stroke he's had this year . . ." Her voice tapers off as she sets the spoon down on the nightstand and drops a piece of cotton into the dark brown liquid. Then she draws it all up into the needle, taps out any air bubbles and digs around in the back of her left hand until she gets a register. Her eyelids flutter slightly and a look of dull pleasure washes over her features. After a moment she sticks the needle into the God-knows-how-old glass of water she keeps beside the vomit bowl on the nightstand, draws up some water and shoots the faintly bloody solution into her mouth. It occurs to me that I might be able to come into contact with her blood if I don't clean the needle properly. I can't believe how stupid I've been not to think of it earlier.

"Just cook me up a little shot," I tell her. "I don't want to be throwing up for hours. Make it look more like iced tea than Coke, okay?"

"Anything you want, dearest," she drones, fangs glittering in the half-light, "but I don't think this batch will make you sick. It's only been cut with milk sugar, nothing nasty."

"Still, I don't have your capacity. I'm practically a virgin, remember?"

"Oh, well, more for me. Why don't you clean that rig while I'm getting your shot ready—the bleach is on the floor next to the bed somewhere."

It takes me a minute or two to locate the half-evaporated bottle amid the general detritus, after which I sit with my back to Miranda, pantomiming the motions of sterilizing the needle. When it comes time to rinse the bleach out with water, I take the needle into the kitchen with me, supposedly to get a fresh glass. Holding it up to the light, I see all that is left of Miranda's blood is a pinkish tinge in the very bottom of the chamber. Certainly not enough to infect me with vampirism, but a start none-theless. I think about getting one of the bloodier works out of the garbage but decide against it because a) she'd almost certainly notice, and b) whatever traces of the virus were present are probably long dead. The subject of viruses in general brings to mind the possibility that Miranda might be carrying a few of the more common mortal ones, such as HIV or hepatitis, but I figure the risk is worth it and besides, I'm already fucking her. I fill a glass with water to create an alibi if necessary, leave it on the counter and go back to the bedroom.

Fortunately, Miranda is too high to notice anything amiss and ties me off and shoots me up without comment. Watching needles go into my veins usually makes me queasy because of the anticipation of having to throw up, but this time it turns me on, and after she pulls it out of my arm I push her down on the bed and start kissing her, deliberately cutting my tongue on her teeth. She tolerates my caresses until they reach her crotch, then pushes my hand away and mumbles, "No . . . let me do you. I'm too numb," and slides her way down the length of my body, pressing her cold mouth against my skin.

She eats me out with detached professionalism, occasionally glancing up to utter such lines as "Are you gonna come now, baby?" and other stale endearments that sound like outtakes from a bad porn video. It's obvious she just wants to get me off so I'll leave her alone. Ordinarily when she's like this I get embarrassed and fake a squirming orgasm within minutes, but right now, with the smack coursing through my body, I'm really enjoying the pure sensation of cunnilingus and decide to let her work at it until I really do get off, which, considering the effect of opiates on female sexual response, could very easily be never.

Never is interrupted about ten minutes later by a sudden twisting in my stomach and my mouth filling up with metallic-tasting saliva, the thirty-second precursor to a bout of uncontrollable vomiting. I make it to the bathroom just in time to fill the toilet bowl with rainbow sprinkle bile, then kneel on the damp floor dry-heaving while in the bedroom Miranda puts a scratchy Deep Purple record on the turntable. She probably thinks they're still together.

When I finally stumble back to the bedroom, Miranda has her hideous robe back on, the sash tied in a tight bow around her waist, an obvious Don't Touch Me maneuver. She's propped up against the wall with her eyes half shut, hands limp at her sides. Her claws are painted a neutral brownish red with tiny crescent moon decals on them so that people will mistake them for acrylic nails.

"I guess that was stronger than I thought," she says, her voice a narcotic drawl. "Sorry . . . it's nice, though, isn't it?"

I lie down beside her and put my head in her lap. "I'll be okay," I mutter, beginning to sink into a depressive stupor. After the initial rush is over, heroin makes me feel slow and stupid, the way I used to feel when I was on Mellaril at my parents' house and I'd sit on the sofa in the den and watch five or six videos back-to-back, take a nap and watch some more. It's a dense, impenetrable loginess, like trying to swim through heavy syrup. I picture myself getting old, slumped in a wheelchair, in a puddle of my own urine, in the day room of some retirement home, Miranda coming to visit me, her face full of boredom and contempt, some new girl on her arm. If she even still knew where I was, since she'd probably have left me years before I ever got to that state. There's been dozens before me and there'll be dozens after me, mostly thin, pale girls in their late teens and early twenties with long, wavy blond or light reddish-brown hair, the occasional effeminate boy thrown in for good measure.

She keeps their pictures in a cardboard box shoved under the bed, some with names scrawled on the back, others blank, all jumbled together in no particular order, yellowed black-and-whites and crumbling sketches in the same pile as color Polaroids of girls in white satin blouses with crimped hair and frosted lipstick, variations of the same face repeated year after year; sleepy, heavy-lidded eyes, mouths that curve slightly downward at the edges. I wonder who the original was. The oldest picture in the box is a tiny faded watercolor of a girl named Darla wearing a blue hat with a feather in it, dated 1893, but I know she couldn't have been the first.

I begin tasting salt in the back of my throat and soon tears are leaking out of the corners of my eyes. I stay quiet, not wanting Miranda to know I am crying. She runs her hand absently through my hair, lifting strands of it up and letting them slip through her fingers. Gradually everything dulls and I just drift.

MYSTERIOUS ELISIONS, RIOTOUS THRUSTS

Kathe Koja and Barry N. Malzberg

Kathe Koja and **Barry N. Malzberg's** collaborative work appears in a variety of anthologies and magazines. Barry has written over eighty novels, including *Beyond Apollo* and *Galaxies*, and numerous short stories. Kathe's novels include *Cipher, Bad Brains, Skin* and *Strange Angels*; her short fiction appears in many anthologies as well.

So: squat and dark as a stone: but soft, wet vegetable effluence slick as seaweed against her shoe and she scraped at it, exhausted, impatient, dragging her heel against the front stoop—for fuck's sake, what now?—and finally got it off, fat black lump like a piece of meat. It smelled, too, like something left past rotting, something that had rotted in the dark. The heat. Long summer of wet days and sullen humidity, the porch light was broken, the air conditioner was broken, that prick Gerald was late with the alimony again and if she called her lawyer, well, what would he do? Call Gerald's lawyer? A five-minute phone call stylized as a mating dance, as a ritual duel billed at rates higher than her own consulting fees. She was working her ass off just to afford her own spite and what good was that? None. None at all.

So again: what? Take the car into the shop; call the repairman for the porch light and the central air, sit in the dark and the heat and sweat. And drink scotch, Gerald's scotch; hate the taste but drink it anyway because it cost him plenty, he left it in the house and now he can't have it back: it says so in the papers, all the pages and pages initialed by them both like some important treaty, borderlands and disarmament, wife versus husband, the decent versus the inhumane. The newly celibate versus the professional cunt-strummer—oh, boy, but she had known that from the first, hadn't she? Soft eyes, and mouth like a child's seeking at her breasts, at the warm, dark places of her body, and hadn't she known that in the restaurant, that very first night? Heat like an oven, her shaking hands on the cup of coffee—you don't need to spend eight years in Vienna to figure that one out. Maybe to figure out what happened next, yes; but not that night or all the nights afterward: rushed and hurried, hot together against a door, mouths and hands, up and down and in and out and in six months she was out of the first marriage and the rent-controlled town house, she was fucking him on his own dining room table, she was going down on him as he lay like a pasha, some antique king, talking and breathing on the phone as she swallowed his load, oh boy. She had not known to whom he was talking, but that came later, didn't it? Along with the phone bills, the itemized calls. Why pay an investigator when you could just flip through that list yourself, call one or two of the numbers for good measure, for verification: for laughs? For a name to scream at him, one name and two names, and no one, she told herself, standing mute and bitter before the judge, no one knows this better than you; you have no one to blame but yourself.

Legs uncrossed, splayed, tired; an extra long day today and tomorrow would be worse. The smell, she found, was still on her shoe, half meat, half shit, half something else, she could not name it; she was without imagination these days, because it cost to have imagination, cost to think, to imagine him with his new girlfriend, that stupid little smooth-haired bitch with her yes and no and whatever you think, gaze down and I know what you're thinking, she wanted to say, I know just what you're thinking, but guess what? It isn't worth it. Six months, a year of great sex and you're out on your ass; at least he married me first. Maybe he'll marry you, too. I want to take *care* of you, her unfocused sneer in the dark, dreamy scotch fumes in her face as if the ghost of her folly breathed the breath of life upon her, the reanimating air of her own hatreds; I want you to be *happy*. I'll be happy when you're dead, that's what she should have said. I'll be happy when I can for once be sure I know exactly where you are.

Expensive suit, meat smell, shit smell, scotch on her lips and she was drunk again, a little and more than a little. After the first few swallows, the scotch was not so bad and she found she had drunk quite a lot of it, quite a lot there in the chair in the dark smelling shit and meat; and a little sound, a very little sound, came to her, slumped in the chair: a sound like scratching, nervous scratching, the sound an itch might make. *Scratch scratch scratch* against what? The floor? The door? The front door, some animal or kids or something: and on and on, whatever else they were, they were persistent and at last she rose to scare it, them, all of them away. She was more than capable of producing fear, and very quietly she crept almost without weaving to the door, slung it open—
Hey!—

—on something squat, and dark, and wet. Lying like meat on the stoop.

Grinning up at her.

Doppelganger; troll; elf's child; Rumpelstiltskin. Spin flax to gold, turn blood to water, tell me my name and I'll give you three wishes. Meat smell, strong now, and breathing, there in the dark. It was certainly alive, oh, yes, staring up with those tiny zeyes as if there were already some pact between them, as if it had come in response to her darkest wish.

What are you? there on the parquet floor, but she did not say it aloud, was afraid to make a sound, make a move, touch it as it lay there as if it already knew everything she might say and was neither impressed nor dissuaded from its original purpose: which was what? Meat and shit, what do you want? Animal, vegetable, ethereal, creature of blood, creature of dream, creature of spite come to her in response not to what she wished for but for what she feared to want: to need aloud: hunger's child come creeping and grinning, dragging the richness of its body, the thick wet thump of its flesh against the door, the floor, against her feet; oh, God, it had moved, moved, it was touching her now. Touching her.

Warm.

It was very warm.

She did not move, trembling and sick with the scotch and the fear, the fear of flesh for dream, did not move as it rolled itself against her, vague humanoid hands on her ankles, on her expensive leather pumps, breathing like a wolf against her skin; stumpy little hands, on her ankles, on her calves. Moving up her legs.

Absolutely still, still and it was crawling now, hauling itself up her legs like ladders, up and warm and oh, God, it was under her skirt now, burrowing, rubbing, her body held perfect and still in the excess of her terror and it was pushing against her, oh, *God*

and it was warm

and its fingers were very small and hot and its *smile*, oh, its smile against the folds and secrets of her flesh;

with that smile it told her its own secrets, told her what she wanted most to hear: told her in the language of heat and meat and absolutes and: head back, legs bent in the thrust and grind, push and pull, totem and god, the dark, squat, compact body up and down between her legs, engine, appliance, nameless hot necessity to scrape ecstatic the tender human flesh of her straining thighs, scrape it till it ran black with blood and her own wet effluence, till the penultimate sweep of orgasm left her bucking and stunned on the floor, stinking and bruised and shivering, to watch it drag itself away, determined humping motions like a body sheared limbless and left to fend for itself: move, or die. Die in the heat and the darkness, die like a piece of meat, and then it was gone, passed from her vision, the stunned-ox stare and the smell, all over her, oh, God, it was all over her.

Sex-smell: the smell of meat. Cooking.

Too much scotch, and heat, and the swim of memory and anger; it could happen to anyone, some kind of hallucination, but that was all bullshit, she knew it was bullshit, she remembered the way it had felt. Heat: and that smile: the stink and the burrowing, the tiny hands. Scars on her thighs, thin pink glyphs; tell me my name and I'll give you three wishes, I'll make them for you, I'll give you what you really want. What do you want? I'll tell you your true name, the name you want to hear, the name you're afraid to say even to yourself in the secret dark of your room when your fingers walk the planes and hollows of your flesh. I'll give you the name you give yourself when you make yourself come. I'll tell you what you really want: do you want to know?

Do you?

Did she?

There were no marks of any kind against the door, the floor; the smell had gone, washed away by the hours, by the sluggish rain, the flap of the newspaper against the stoop; the mailman's step, the sound her own shoes made (different shoes, new pumps: she had thrown the others away). Three messages on her answering machine, one from her lawyer, and in his voice a new hesitancy, a shrinking: what was so bad that he could not say it, could not leave its spoor on the tape? Call me, he said. We need to talk. About what? Some new perfidy of Gerald's, some fresh gray swinishness to fit jigsaw with his other evils and denials? Fuck him, she said to herself, to the message, to her lawyer's hesitant voice; fuck him fuck him *fuck* him. She was trembling, her jacket half off in the deep brisk refrigeration. The repairman had come and fixed the thermostat; everything in here was cold. Cold hands against the phone, her lawyer's number and then: no: calling another number, a man she knew, knew and vaguely disliked, but tonight, now, that did not matter, she did not particularly care: two rings, three rings, she would not leave a message. Four rings. Pink scars on her thighs.

"Hello?" he said.

Fuck him. "Hello," she said.

Long dinner, light drinks, he did everything right: rubbed her, touched her, kissed her, wore a condom; it did not matter, it was not enough. Gone before midnight, trundling taillights down the street like myopic and lecherous eyes, it was raining again, raining with a smell as stale as semen, a smell ungiving and unfecund, it was the female principle that gave life, wasn't it now? Wasn't it just. The female principle in a camisole and panty hose, in T-shirt and panties, the female principle throwing her purse against the wall. The female principle in heat and anger, in water and blood, pouring and spilling the scotch all over her: hands and wrists, unguent and oblation, and this time she heard it almost before it happened, heard it because she wanted to hear it, because she must. Heat and rain and scotch and blood, pink scars, her hands shaking as she opened the door.

Scratch scratch scratch: but only a formality.

This time she picked it up so it would not have to crawl. Who's come knocking at my door? who was that thing when the lights went out? she crooned without hearing, molding it with her fingers, struggling to grasp it between her elbows, stumbling to the bedroom in careful and racheting tread and oh, *oh,* thin—

—thin the blood she could feel moving within the veins and tendrils of the thing, the reaching and riotous blood, the riotous little thrusts within the ganglia and the stalks, and she put it on the bedroom's bare floor with a sigh, one *uh* of release and delight as the slick, vapid thing tore from her hands and she watched it scuttle on the floor. Oh, baby, she said, oh, baby, I know what you want and I have what you want. Impatient, she struggled with her panties, the thin carapace of her being, feeling the rush and rumble of her own blood as if from a great distance; yanked off the panties, then reached to take off the T-shirt she had put on in the man's casual departure, in the scuttle of the man to leave the blot of damp on the sheet and the vessel into which it had so inaccurately spilled. Cunt, she thought, cunt, that's what we are for them, isn't that the truth. Don't eat where you shit, don't shit where you eat, leave the shit behind and go on to another place, the next place, leave the damp and dangerous cunt. But that isn't you, that isn't you, baby, is it? she said to the troll, mooning and crooning through her little cracked lips, the lips of her pudenda flexing in their own dialogue, and she stood, heaved, yanked, felt its little suction feet come free of the floor as she deposited it beside her on the bed, her magical humping machine, the thunder and riot, effluvia and damp pools of its little body trembling squat and dark beside her. Oh, go, she said, *go,* and

leaning back, missionary position, opened deep, opened wide and the thing went into her like a dog taking point on a high hill. She could feel the vicious tumble of its impact and then it had flung itself inside her, the high, feathery, maddening net of its ganglia penetrating like a drug in water, like a dissolving poison pill. The first time with Gerald—remember the restaurant parking lot, the first few hours alone? Unable even to get to the car before, in squirming and desperate necessity, they had stumbled against a wall, brick in her back, and once, some college date had fucked her on top of a manhole in back of the

snow sculpture, ice-cold swans, and the steam from the
manhole seeming to steam from her orifice, come straight
from the heat between her legs . . . but nothing even ap-
proximating what the thing between those legs was doing
now, snaffling and snuggling, the deep ridges of its little
claws penetrating, and she thought, I'm cunt, it's turned me
into cunt, I'm a hole surrounded by a scream, I am a vacuum immersed in my own desire; and it went, it went at her
with a desperate and subterranean eagerness as if long de-
nied, pent up by generations of some unknown mythology
to get inside her but good, and she felt it tearing in and out
of her, a solidity, a consanguinity of the blood she had
never before apprehended. She was coming; she had come;
she would be coming again, the come was tearing her inside and out and she felt the thing spend and spend and,
screaming, she spent back, taking thrust for thrust, dirt for
dirt, knife for knife until at last, as she felt herself torn open
and at the rim of a first real fear—would it kill her through
overuse, this humping machine?—the thing fell away,
opening a vast and spendthrift space between them, and
rolled on the sheets, rolled bloody, she could see from the
periphery of sight, the red-and-green streaks of its own
blood smearing the sheets, and then it hit with a thud on the
floor. Her own fluids seemed to mix and congeal, their
blood was running together and she wanted to slide back,
slide into a long, slick, thunderous passage of light and
shadow, but something, some amalgam of instinct and
fright from within told her that she had best not do this, that
this would be a terrible mistake, and so she forced herself to
track the thing off the bed, watching it twist on the floor
and, still bleeding, eventually hunker in place like a hound
seeking its own spoor, finding its own damp; the thing sank
in the juices on the floor as she watched it with a sudden
and grave concern, an excess of sobriety and observation
which settled upon her like a blanket, like a lover's coat
wrapped around her: and from that stance she stared upon
the thing.

Its round, blind face peered at her, the implacable blank
surface not a mask but somehow a persona, a thing of
metal and pulp and blood, and she reached toward it,

stroked the thing, feeling the dark pools of its respiration against her detecting touch. Thinking, then, thinking: the sudden glassy vulnerability of the thing, its expenditure and bleak dark, the humping machine ungeared, and as she looked into that metallic surface, that blunt expunged refraction of a face, something fluttered on it, across it; the features began to move, to drift like gelatin, to gelatinously reconvene in a different and terrible aspect, and she found herself staring at a sudden and brutalized version of Gerald's face.

Gerald's face, Gerald's face staring back at her from the floor, the little nostrils exuding breath, flaring against her hand as she jerked that hand away, as she felt herself moving back, back against the bed. The face, that face, Gerald's face in the sum of all darkness, regarded her in that swoon with a perfect fixity of attention. Unable to fall back farther, she froze in that convulsion and stared, stared as it stared back, the cool and luminescent eyes now Gerald's as they had regarded her in that restaurant, that beginning, measuring. Measuring, hoping, taunting, her own mountain king waddling from the depths first in the parking lot, later in fifty hotels, then in the marital bed and now, dark meat of the sun, still expelling within her. I am a dead thing, a voice whispered to her from the center of the creature's reassembled face, a dead and driven thing. I come to show you the destiny of the night, all the nights, your nights. Dead and driven and gone since last Friday and that's my calling card, the thing said, twitching and squirming on the floor, then gathering itself to leap and mount once again: she screamed, it leapt, she swatted and bellowed, it exploded, the clambering chunks of meat falling like rocks on the stunned surfaces of her body. Dead, Gerald fell in chunks and expulsions like rain upon her, the rain that falls like iron from the sky. She lay on a field of steel, her vulva torn, her thighs on fire, her emptiness poisoned and yearning, waiting for that damp posthumous clutch as earth, rain and fire gathered them in.

There Paolo; here my lovely Francesca. Falling and falling as a dead body falls.

STATIONS
OF THE CROSS

David Aaron Clark

David Aaron Clark is the author of the novels *The Wet Forever, Sister Radiance* and the recent *Juliette: Vengeance on the Lord*, which he describes as "a modern-day S & M gothic sequel" to the Marquis de Sade classic. His band, False Virgins, released two albums at the turn of the decade, and he is known for his infamous and extreme performance art, which involves live mortification worthy of the early saints, some of which are collected on the video "Bleeding Heart." He was the senior editor of *Screw* magazine for several years and recently migrated from the mean streets of New York City to San Francisco's far gentler climes, where he lives with his performance partner, Joanne, and three cats, including the green-eyed Jesus Terror, "who needs to have his balls cut off real soon."

The repetition was numbing, except to her arm, which was becoming sore. Sweat stung her eyes and made her fear for her eyeliner, all thanks to the faulty air-conditioning. The big, outdated machine blurted industrial wheeze from the corner where it lurked, alternating jets of sickly warm air with shudder-inducing blasts of muddy ice-cold.

Mistress Medusa stared fixedly at the wispy black hair coiled on the nape of the man she was beating, sought some abstract satori that would carry her through another session. Ah, money, the root of it all. Or the love of money, was the exact quote.

I would do anything for love, but I won't do that, a blandly tortured AOR singer softly bleated from the boom box on top of the air conditioner, the lyric jumping out at her in sharp relief. Medusa, known off duty to friends, lovers and the telephone company as Mary Ellen Masters, rolled her eyes and thought about her empty apartment.

It didn't have to be empty. Her slave was due to pick her up at the end of the shift—Billy, who was so handsome in an unlined boy-next-door sort of way, but, unfortunately, owned the cognitive abilities—and aptitude at pouting—of an eleven-year-old. But then, who else would come pick her up at 1 A.M. on Christmas Eve?

Even though Medusa was only five years older than Billy—not yet thirty herself—sometimes she felt like a horny, corrupting old witch, next to his childish, muscular simplicity. He reminded her of Lenny from *Of Mice and Men*. When she'd tie him down to her bedroom floor and tease him with her naked ass, swaying it inches from his gaping mouth, the meat of it pulled apart by her sunken-in red nails to reveal the brown wink of her asshole. When she'd step on his hard cock with her stiletto heel, grinding into the main vein in sharp half circles until tears came to his eyes. But hey, if it wasn't her, it would end up being somebody who might really fuck him over.

She noticed that her client was shivering, and it wasn't from the rain of blows she was delivering. She dreaded the inevitable complaint about the climate inside the dungeon. What was she supposed to do? The Manager was in the back, snorting cocaine with a bunch of rock 'n' roll transvestites and other drug-hungry hangers-on, the whole brood kept watch over by Stubby, the burly black bodyguard in muscle T-shirt and cowboy hat who popped up to lend immoral support whenever The Manager was feeling particularly paranoid.

"Can't we do something about the air-conditioning?" the client whined. She winced at the chalky slide of her teeth gritting. She absolutely hated it when clients whined. As if she didn't have enough fucking problems in the world.

She didn't disagree, though.

"Now, you know I told you I'd do what I could last time, but how much trouble do you want to put your mistress through? Isn't it a slave's place to suffer?"

"Only the way he wants to, when he's paying."

You fucking asshole. She strode up behind him, grabbed a handful of hair and pulled his head back so he could see the white-hot chill in her narrowed eyes, the exaggerated flare of nostrils made so artificially elegant by a plastic surgeon's hand.

"I'll see what I can do."

She shut the dungeon door behind her, leaning back on it for a moment, shoulders slumped, exhaling. Sasha, the other mistress on duty, looked up from her copy of a French fashion magazine. She had violet eyes, narrow and heavily lashed, with heavy eyeliner that ended on either side of her face in vaguely Egyptian squiggles.

"Tough one? Old Eddie acting up?"

"It's the fucking air-conditioning. What's it doing on in December, anyway?"

Sasha winced, squinching up her nose. She laid the magazine down on her naked stomach, a flat, pale expanse that ran from the bottom of her chain-mail bra all the way to the waist of her black leather skirt.

"That room's stuffy all year round. I hate it."

"It doesn't bother me."

"The haunted room."

"Yeah, right, I heard about that. Pair of feet, right?"

"Yeah. Jennie, The Manager's girlfriend, said she saw them at three-thirty in the morning when she stayed over alone one night."

"Whatever. I've got to deal with this."

The Manager was sprawled on a black leather divan, his Air Force flight suit complemented by a sad, haunted look around the hollows of his sunken-in eyes, and by the two-day stubble gristled against his cheeks. Medusa noted the open magazine on the coffee table, spine up. In the shadow between page and highly polished Formica glinted the signature glass straw he used in the ongoing demolition work he was perpetrating against his nasal cavity.

"My client's complaining about the air-conditioning again."

The Manager shifted uncomfortably on his ass, favoring the leg that bulged through the jumpsuit at the thigh, where there was dressing wrapped over a recent bullet wound. She hated it when he was in shorts and she had to stand there and wait for him to process a credit card number, with nothing to stare at except the quarter-sized yellow stain marking the slowly healing wound.

"Tell him it's a slave's place to suffer."

"He didn't buy it."

The roomful of hangers-on looked around uncomfortably, not wanting to be drawn into the controversy, or to be reminded what it was like to work for The Manager, rather than just hang out and do his drugs. Stubby gingerly picked up The Manager's ferret and drew him close to his face, making a project of attempting to stare the beady-eyed creature down. She couldn't decide which beast looked less clever.

"Well, Jesus, *mistress*"—The Manager punched the word with sarcastic emphasis—"I don't *know*. Handle it. It's your session. I called the repairman twice, but he never showed. And here I am, trying to have an important business conference with my associates about some new creative projects that might bring us all, including you, more money, and you're bothering me because you can't deal with some pathetic slave of a client bitching at you?"

Stomping by Sasha on the way back in, Medusa met

the other girl's inquiring eyes with a vicious shrug and the usual prayer: "I hope to God that fuckhead OD's!"

When she got back to the dungeon, the client was seated on the rough wooden bench, lacing up his shoes. His pants were already back on. His white shirt lay unbuttoned and sagging open, displaying the smooth paunch of his belly. Slouched down to reach his shoestrings like that, he almost looked pregnant.

"Look, I'm really sorry. I did what I could," she apologized, feeling exceedingly stupid standing there in the middle of the room in her leather corset and thigh-highs, all dressed up with no place to land her blows.

"It's okay. Keep the money. I'll just have to ask when I call next time to see if the air-conditioning's working right. Or else just go somewhere else."

Do that, bastard. In a way, she was almost relieved to end the session early, even if it meant possibly losing a regular. This regular was predictably arrogant and unpleasant, always demanding and complaining, hardly the soul of a submissive. Always wanting to see her tits, and trying to get her to let him lick them, too.

He buttoned his shirt and stood up to stuff it into his pants. Looking at his weak chin, his petulant eyes, she smiled. He'd be back, anyway. She had his number. She had all the clients' numbers. They shared, after all, the same exchange.

Sasha's shift ended at midnight; when Medusa left an hour later, the dungeon would actually close down for twenty-four hours, as The Manager drank and snorted his way into an even thicker stupor than he usually inhabited.

Sasha waved good-bye, making a quiet escape in order to thwart the keen hearing of The Manager, who would have insisted she come to the back of a holiday line of blow. Medusa was sucking at the bottom of a waxy cup of iced coffee, her third of the evening. She'd hoped the caffeine would keep her awake, but somehow she was still nodding off, only with her teeth grinding against themselves even as her chin headed for the pillow-white expanse of her chest.

As she slipped between states, her gaze focused and

unfocused on the set of weird ceremonial masks on the wall, another of The Manager's psycho art touches. Their fierce multicolored stares, empty eyeholes full of nothing but shadow and maybe that doorway to the plane of unreason where restless spirits and malevolent angels flew in circles, seeking a pathway into reality, where they could commit the sort of chaos and atrocity that was their food.

Something on the wall moved. With a start, she threw her head back and woke up.

What a place to spend Christmas Eve.

But with rent nearly due and her credit card balance still suffering from that last extravagant trip to Wicked Pleasures—the iridescent violet latex sheath dress and matching riding crop—here she sat, G-string digging into the crack of her ass. And an old, smelly G-string to boot—Alex, the Rolex-wearing shit freak with the receding hairline, had called to schedule for today, and he always tipped her $100 for the juiciest, most stained underthings she could supply. Of course, he hadn't shown up.

The phone was ringing sporadically, the usual crew of phone freaks reduced in strength somewhat by an actual alternative activity, be it busing home to the folks out on the island or drowning their loneliness in front of a beer tap. Bill the Floor called to tell her he was spending Christmas Eve rolled up in a cast-off rug by the main entrance to Macy's, where all the shoppers would be forced to tread on him on their way in and out. He asked her if she would bail him out if he were arrested. She laughed and hung up on him.

Slave Milton called, too, wanting to reminisce about the time she'd had him dress in his best garters and stockings and suck her boyfriend's cock while she sodomized him. Nostalgia did not run high for her; that boyfriend had been an asshole; she'd found him in the filthy bathroom of an East Village bar with some mascara-poisoned goth bitch attached to his dick by her gaping mouth. When she'd flung open the door, he'd gazed at her stupidly, as if to say. "*I* don't know how she got here!"

When the phone rang at quarter to twelve, she thought it would be one of them again. Instead it was an unknown male voice, anonymous under a sheen of street noise and static. Calling from a phone booth.

"Hello, I was hoping to make a last-minute appointment."

"Have you been here before?"

There was a hesitation that made her sigh: another creep.

"No, not actually, but I'm familiar with the place, and with you, Mistress Medusa. I saw your ad in *Domina Directory*, and everybody says you're the best mistress in New York City."

Oh, please. The shameless lines they fed you. Still, *Domina Directory* was a specialty magazine, the sort you had to go to a particular kind of store to find, and it was not cheap.

"Well, it is late, you know. We were about to close."

"Oh, please, mistress. I promise to make it worth your while. I'll bring you a gift."

She ticked off the possibilities: bad cocaine, half-dead flowers from the Korean bodega, some piece of St. Mark's junk jewelry. Still, the rent, the rent. No sessions tonight. Cat food. Okay. The Manager wouldn't even realize how late it was until she brought him back his cut after it was all over but the screaming.

"All right. You have five minutes to be at the door. Any later and I'm not answering. Do you know where you're going? Where are you?"

"I know where to come."

She went back and informed The Manager there was a last client on his way in. Just to be contrary, he complained about having to operate on Christmas Day, though she knew he was more greedy for the money than she was. She gave him a what-can-you-do look and went to reapply her makeup in the tiny bathroom. Since it hadn't been cleaned by a house slave since the night before, she was economical about brushing any exposed skin against its surfaces.

When the buzzer went off, she bumped her knee against

one of the skinny silver legs holding up the orange-stained sink, and cursed, even though the leather of her boot muffled any real sting.

He was actually pretty handsome.

She thought for sure that only a troll would come creeping in at such a ridiculous moment, in the fleeting moments before the day of Christ's birth. But what the fuck, nice hair he had, long and smooth, brown and blond like in a shampoo commercial, sort of like a well-groomed rock star's, just on the verge of tumbling too far over into pretty boy, but not quite.

The goatee was trendy and appropriate, too, emphasizing the angularity of his cheeks, the long thinness of his nose. His blue eyes wove spells of gentle fascination in the air as he gazed forthrightly into her own brown eyes. She felt like she was looking into a three-dimensional greeting card, a Midwestern Protestant version of Jesus. *Jesus, have you come to save me?* she thought, transforming her amusement into a smile of greeting.

"Hello," he said warmly and without embarrassment.

"This way to the dungeon," Medusa said, and smiled as she stood aside to let him pass, straightening her back so her breasts stood higher on her rib cage.

Once in the room, she instructed him to strip while he told her his scene. This was the part she sometimes dreaded, when the gross, angry things that went beyond the mere animal and into the black hopelessness of addictive depravity reared their reptilian heads and hissed thick crèmes of poisoned hormone and past trauma at her. It was a new episode—several times a day if her bank account was lucky—of "Welcome to My Fetish": *Hi there*, could you tell I was a piss freak, a toe sucker, a navel licker, an asshole sniffer, a shit eater, an aspiring transvestite, a mommy's boy who wants daddy to sodomize him, a nigger slave in need of a good and bloody beating from the mistress of the house, a guilt-eaten Jew begging to be fucked in the mouth and ass with the stiletto heel of a black-raincoated SS officer?

"I think a scourging is in order, mistress," Jesus said, a sad smile drawing his upper lip underneath the soft-looking hair decorating it. Without being asked, he handed her two still-crisp hundred-dollar bills, which she tucked into the top of her boot. She wondered if he was a good fuck.

"I think you'd better face the wall, then, slave," she replied without even having to consider, stepping as she spoke toward the equipment rack. Wrinkling her nose at being reminded of The Manager, she used a bobby pin she kept stuck in her bra to spring the tumblers on the small gold lock installed on her favorite rubber whip's handle.

It was late; she would start with the rubber. Billy would be here soon, and though she usually took pleasure in keeping him waiting as long as possible, tonight she just wanted to get out of this constricting place and . . . where? Home? To have to watch Billy jerk off on his knees at her feet before she pushed him whining out the door? To a bar, where everyone could see she had no steady boyfriend, no family or friends she cared enough for to be with?

The rubber lash arced and snapped down so perfectly, it barely made a whisper before stopping short with a loud, sharp snap against the client's shoulder blades.

He quivered once, and stood his ground. This was sick, on Christmas Eve. But she was going to enjoy it.

After five minutes of working him over, she had driven his knees not quite to the Burmese carpet, but nearly. The battle between their forces of will made her aware of her pussy in a very itchy, insistent way. She felt the seam of her red plastic G-string slide against her crotch, catching against the outer folds of her vulva, freshly shaven that morning.

"So you're a tough little slave, huh. I'll bet you're always begging to be beaten, crawling around on your hands and knees looking for a beautiful woman to wail the shit out of you."

"I am here because I should be."

"You're so right, you—" She stopped, distracted by a warm breeze brushing her back, abrupt but welcome in the dungeon's refrigerated chill. Thinking The Manager

or one of his stupid, coked-up flunkies had barged in, she
spun around, angry invective already boiling on her
tongue.

The blue door was still secure, but wriggling there in
front of it was a baby in a pink diaper. A delicate web of
black follicles glossed the egg-shaped head. When the
spit-glittered slash of a mouth began to curl open, Medusa
found herself torn between a deep instinct to rush forward
in maternal concern or coil back in primal terror.

An oversized tongue slowly curled from within the
foundling's mouth, a black, scaly phallus split at the end
into a pair of greasy pink antennae, like you'd find on a
slug.

In the shadows beneath its cheeks, she detected a row
of wormy white legs sprouted a few centimeters out of
the flesh imbuing the face with a subtle animation, a soft
blur.

She averted her gaze, head snapping away as if she'd
been slapped. A weightless terror rippled up swiftly from
her feet, disappearing into a tight cubbyhole somewhere
inside her head. She looked back and was confronted by
a bare spot on the floor, bland and sure of its own innocence.

The client was still facing the wall, the muscles embracing his slim skeleton insinuatingly evident under his
thin, nearly golden skin. She buried her shock in an avalanche of resentment for his beauty, and shoved his face
forward until it rebounded from the wall against her
gloved palm. She brushed his hair aside with her nose so
she could crunch her teeth nearly together through the
brittle lobe of his ear.

"You know you're keeping the mistress from important
matters with your petty need to be punished," she whispered to him. That was it. Concentrate on the script, play
the scene, live the part and don't worry if you're suddenly
prone to acid flashbacks. It's not like it's *Jacob's Ladder*
time or something. Next stanza.

"But that's what you want to do, isn't it? Make me
angry so I'll hurt you even more. You're all so predictable, I'm afraid. You're just like the rest. Pigs."

She dragged him over to the large wooden cross set against the south wall, varnished oak that gleamed with ten thousand moments of hired pain, a thousand different men's fetish-wrapped passion plays. In moments of boredom when there were no clients, and no other mistresses around, she would bend down and lightly kiss it, imagining she could taste the dark vibrations.

Quickly binding his wrists and ankles with the leather restraints chained to the cross, Medusa then squatted down before his cock and wrapped it neatly with a leather cord procured from her belt. When she was done, a series of black coils squeezed it so tightly that the head was of twice greater diameter than the shaft. On the other end, the testicles were separated by a harsh set of loops that promoted a whisper of blue across a surface tension so overripe it was painful just to witness.

Then she stood back and laid into him with the red cat-o'-nine-tails. Intent that he get his money's worth of suffering.

The slap of each blow was so sharp that its report was an affront unto itself, a brittle bark to set your teeth on edge. Each tongue of leather drummed against the flesh, and red welts eagerly dashed up to greet them. Ready to be transformed, ready to fuck with, ready to fuck, down to the atom.

Gentle moans spilled out of him, sexual in their careless intimacy, rising and falling in response to each lash. Infected by his passion, Medusa luxuriated in the bristling static traveling the circuit between them.

When she struck him harder, the cries grew in intensity but not volume. Pleasant. His features were drawn taut, an elegant mask begging to be shattered. Harder.

The first dash of blood was unexpected, a brief smear across his ribs that was dispersed with the next blow. Then two more appeared, and soon it looked like red paint across his torso. She had rarely beaten somebody this badly, and certainly never without discussion beforehand. What drove her now?

As soon as she questioned it, the compulsion dissipated, and she found herself rubbing her sore shoulder. The urge to apologize gripped her, until she saw that the client was smiling at her in a loving but mocking manner, presuming empathy with a stranger. What egos these bastards had!

"Slave. Nothing to say for yourself? Shall I whip you some more?"

"Do what you will." A politely delivered challenge.

She stalked forward and forced open his mouth. Turning her face as if to kiss him, she instead filled his mouth with an eruption of foamy spittle.

She stepped back to strike him again, but paused to watch her saliva pour back out over his lip, riding a wave of some amber liquid wallowing up from his throat, a greasy-looking resin that slopped down over his chest. It sizzled where it met bare flesh, and flared like sugar over a gas flame where there were blood and open wounds.

Blinded by the sudden, furious constellation, Medusa saw another vision.

A goat, coat matted with burrs and spiked with dirty spit curls. Its horns were ancient, so cracked they seemed as if they must be petrified, dry as dust except for a gelid smear at their center. Its cock was forked.

"Shame the devil," the client whispered encouragingly. She snapped out of it to see him hanging there by his wrists, limp and weary, his chest a red mess. She slapped him so hard her fingers stung, even inside her glove, and she felt her nails pushed back where his skin had caught against them and yielded up some of its own.

"Piss on the devil. And piss on you, you weird little fucking worm," she hissed, playing now not at all, excited in a way she had never been during a session.

"It's time to take Mistress Medusa's fucking communion. My Christmas gift to you," she told him, twisting a nipple so greasy with blood it nearly slipped from between her fingers.

Unbuckling him from the cross, she didn't even bother to massage his wrists to restore circulation. Instead she pushed him flat down on the carpet, and shinnied her G-string down across the swell of her hips and thighs, catching it briefly on the tops of her boots before slipping

completely free of it. The crotch of her fishnet tights was
already torn out; these were her work clothes.

She stood over him, legs apart, eyes squeezed shut. She
concentrated on the warmth above her hips as her kidneys
spasmed and released a hot, filling spray that came jetting
out from between the lips of her vulva, cooling a few
degrees in the open air before spattering in golden explo-
sions all over her client's angular face, clear beads collecting in his beard and mustache. *They gave him vinegar
to drink, mixed with gall.* The words came into her head—
were they from the Bible?

When she looked down she screamed without sound,
no air in her lungs to expel. There was a black funnel
between her legs, wet and spinning, pulsing like the inside
mouth of a snake. The glittering twist of her urine was
quickly lost in its whirring hunger. When the funnel
bumped its hot edge against her thighs, she felt faint for
a moment, everything lost in a gray, hazy buzz.

When her vision cleared and thought returned, she saw
that what was bumping her thighs was the client's ears,
and that his all-too-human face was placidly braced
against her cunt, only the slightest gurgling betraying the
efficient drain of piss down his throat. In a gesture just
short of inadvertent, her gloved hand brushed across her
belly, PVC fingertip grazing the most upward jut of her
clitoris. The preorgasmic wave that resulted was strangely
welcome. She clamped her thighs tightly, smothering the
client, the tension of the contracted muscles trailing a
warm finger up her spine.

Then the world dropped away again and she was in a
dark circus, surrounded by a listless, jabbering crowd pep-
pered with leering clowns. She was small and holding a
big man's hand, rounded dry tips rasping against her soft
little-girl palm, wishing he would pay attention, wishing
he would stop talking to the lady with him, her, and her
big white boom-booms all spilling out of that purple
dress. The worst part was always afterward, when he'd
hold her tight on the subway ride home and whisper to
her, his breath sour and unpleasant with the hint of some

unimaginable bad thing, that this was just between them, right, their little secret, don't tell Mom, how about a soda pop, sweetie?

One of the clowns shuffled close and started making a fuss over her, patting her head and waving a pink balloon in front of her face. Dry fingers slipped from her hand and she lurched off-balance, a warm resistance covering her limbs as she fell into the clown's arms, but they weren't arms, they were huge snakes of some sort, long white organs with pulsing veins that rose and fell across the wattled surface as if their entire widths were each a huge lung, or one vein throbbing with a mountain's stream of blood.

Hot to the touch against her face, the snakes contracted for a moment before growing even larger, even as she felt more of them curling around her legs, spreading them apart, around her waist, bracing it firmly, around her arms, binding them.

She looked down at the floor, the leather harness limp around her high heels, waiting to be pulled up so it could hoist the large, realistic dildo resting loosely within its ring tight against her crotch. White angels danced over the shiny black surface of her boots.

Not only another hallucination, but now she was losing real time as well, during which her body could evidently act upon its own. Shit, this had to stop! Was it time to take a cab to Bellevue and check herself in?

Finish the session, just finish the fucking session. Make the asshole come and let him wipe his dick and put his clothes on and get the fuck out. No, don't even let him wipe his dick. And then a sedative. There were a couple of Darvons in her purse.

The harness fit snugly up the crack of her ass, and when the last buckle was secure she threw her shoulders back, adjusting to the extra weight with a flourish, happy to adopt an exaggerated male swagger from where she could feel safe and in control. Open up your asshole, asshole.

"Time to really get down to business, worm. Time to turn you into my little bitch; you're such a pretty little

thing, you'll like that, won't you? I bet it won't be the
first time for a slut like you.''

The client looked at her with his peculiar eyes, and
sighed.

''No, I suppose it won't,'' he agreed. His mouth turned
down a bit, making him look something like a pouty rock
star, soft hair coyly masking one cheek.

She bent him over the bondage table, his bloody chest
pressed down against the burnished ebony surface. Leaning against him, rubbing the shaft of the cock between his
haunches, she removed her elbow-length gloves. Then she
drew her nails sharply down from his shoulders to his
haunches, leaving trails so deep that irregular beads of
blood dotted the path. The client moaned in pain, agony
more musical than ever.

She laid open his cheeks and fit the grease-smeared
cock in the depression there. She considered the mercy of
gently working it in. Decided otherwise.

His head reared back howling when she penetrated him
as abruptly and deeply as she could. The butt of the dildo
pressed against her pubic mound, eliciting a jolt of pleasure. She drew her hips back so that the dildo eased nearly
free, so that the flare of the corona popped out, and would
have to be jammed back in.

Then she started to really fuck him.

She liked to count strokes. It was an idiosyncracy of
hers, a macho little thing. She lost count somewhere
around a hundred.

Now she could feel the resistance ebbing and flowing
as his sphincter spasmed open and shut, an involuntary
reaction in no way dictated by his own pleasure. His
cheek was pressed against the ebony table, his one visible
eye gleaming from within twisted folds of skin, a geog-
raphy of pain and humiliation distilled into the base language of the flesh.

She reached her arms out to rake his back, her nails
just freshly manicured that day digging their honed tips
into the flesh again, digging and rending until more blood
began to well up around them, a near match to her shade

of enamel. His back and chest were now uniformly ravaged.

Mistress Medusa shuddered under the pressure of the gold ring she wore in her clitoral hood as it was pushed back by the dildo at the apex of its thrust.

As her orgasm approached—an orgasm with a client? she dimly thought in some far compartment of her mind— the body beneath her began to transmute, turning thicker, saggier, the long brown meadow locks going brittle and pale, the top of the head emerging as the hair receded, an eclipse reversed.

The slim, hungry hips she had clutched disappeared in folds of loose skin, the golden caste changing to liver-spotted brown and white-pink, like exposed meat. The writhing muscles in the back disappeared in waves of rolling fat. Her slashes, however, remained, now looking so much crueler, so much more merciless, against the texture of this ugly, vulnerable skin.

Though she couldn't see the face, head hunched down between collapsed shoulders, her belly jumped with fear and the first faint whisper of hysteria. She recognized this man, by his body, his posture, his scent. At the exact same moment she knew by the proof of her senses that it was him, her mind rebelled and told her why it could not be:

He had been dead for three years.

In fury, in desperation, trying to drive out this incarnation of the demon she was trapped in the room with, she fucked him harder, driving the rubber prong as deeply between his flabby haunches as her hips could shove it. So hard her thighs ached, standing as she was in these heels, and her head swam, and her belly ached as the moment of climax drew even nearer.

Just as the first rolls of white pleasure crashed over the vines of her nervous system, he, to her horror, spoke. Spoke in that voice that had read her ''The Cat in the Hat,'' had scolded her for bad report cards, had whispered soothing sweetnesses to her in the middle of the night so she wouldn't scream and wake anybody up.

''Sweetie? I know it hurts. I'm sorry, it's my fault. You

weren't a bad little girl. I loved you, but I did something wrong.''

Her orgasm broke in full force, a universe of ash congealing into gray jelly that burned and cleansed with the force of twenty-two years of bad dreams and abusive boyfriends and bulimia and cocaine-fueled orgies where somebody always came out bloody and a nervous laugh that could never be called happy and a granite death wish that weighed down the very pit of her heart, that rushed forward only in moments of extreme drunkenness or depression, but someday would surely have its way.

She squeezed her eyes until they ached, trying to stave off the river of tears that forked down either side her nose, meeting and pooling on the quivering ridge of her full upper lip. The sobs racked her entire torso, wrenching and rippling against the equally strong twitches of her singing clitoris.

She howled his name in two long syllables that seemed to turn her lungs inside out, a wail of anger and despair refining itself into a contralto of forgiveness and regret. She felt an incredibly perfect love, born in the warmth far underneath the flesh, in the faint electric charge bearing the particular flicker of one soul, that her life's entire experience seemed compressed into one beautiful, terrible, ultimately predestined moment of empty peace. She thought she had died.

Her eyes were still shut when she felt the pressure of his ass against her thighs vanish. The nimbus of blue flame that caressed her limbs and thickened into a crown around her head began to slowly wane.

Her spirit rattled in her bones, and the ride came to a stop. Opening her eyes, she surveyed the empty room before her. The air conditioner wheezed in the most stupid of ways.

Under its mechanical rhythm a whisper rose from the nothingness to teeter just on the edge of audibility, a voice without gender or inflection: ''This gift I give to thee, that thy sleep might be easier.''

She knew she should be screaming, or praying, or banging her head against the wall until all memories of this vision retreated into an understandable reality. Instead she squatted there, rocked back on her compressed haunches, the oily black dildo dangling in its impotent greasy innocence like a child's sticky toy.

She began to hum to herself, to smile, when the warm wetness called her attention to the palms of her hands, from which blood had begun to weep. Somebody was banging on the door; dimly she heard Stubby's voice, and Billy's, too, frightened for her, confused.

She brought her palms close to her face and inhaled deeply, hoping for a smooth copper high that would head off hysteria.